The Not So Common Sense

The Not So Common Sense

Differences in How People Judge Social and Political Life

Shawn W. Rosenberg

Yale University Press

New Haven and London

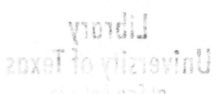

Published with assistance from the Mary Cady Tew Memorial Fund.

Set in Adobe Garamond type by The Composing Room of Michigan, Inc.,
Grand Rapids, Michigan.
Printed in the United States of America.

ISBN: 0-300-08427-7

A catalogue record for this book is available from the Library of Congress and the
British Library.

∞ The paper in this book meets the guidelines for permanence
and durability of the Committee on Production Guidelines
for Book Longevity of the Council on Library Resources.

10 9 8 7 6 5 4 3 2 1

To my mother and father, Florence and Harry,
who taught me how to receive
and
to my children, Angele and Phillip,
who are teaching me how to give

Contents

Acknowledgments

I would like to thank my graduate students Scott Winterstein, Mark Sellick, Molly Patterson, Chris Hanks, and Joe Braunwarth for countless hours of stimulating discussion and for their help in bringing this book to fruition. I owe them a special debt. I would also like to thank David Easton, Catarina Kinnvall, Ann Crigler, Janusz Reykowski, and Kristie Monroe for their willingness to read early versions of the manuscript and for being so generous with their comments.

Chapter One Postmodernity, Not Learning, and the Not So Common Sense

In this book I explore the sense people make of the world around them, from the private world of their personal lives to the broader arena of social and political affairs. I provide theoretical argument and empirical evidence that there is an underlying structure to the disparate understandings and judgments that a given individual constructs. Whether one is trying to explain why a friend is unable to find a job or why unemployment is high in Germany, or whether one is trying to judge the desirability of a potential lover or the appropriateness of American military intervention in Bosnia, one is engaged in an activity, in thinking. In each case, there is a personal attempt to make sense of the particular event or choice. In the process, these concerns are given a subjectively reconstructed meaning and value. While the substance of the ensuing understandings and evaluations may vary with the question considered, they will all be structured in a way that reflects the distinctive qualities of the individual's own way of thinking.

By claiming that cognition is structured, I am clearly departing from psychological theory and research that adopt more piecemeal and noninterpretative approaches to the analysis of cognitive functioning. This is not necessarily to deny the findings of this work, but to suggest that its results must be reconsidered. My aim here is to offer an overarching framework for explicating the findings of several of psychology's diverse research traditions. In particular I reexamine several strands of social psychological research on cognition and their relationship to developmental psychological research on the same topic.

The approach I adopt in this book also differs from interpretative sociologies, both classical and postmodern, that offer some reified notion of society and imply or directly assert that individuals are simply cultural products. These sociological views suggest that there is a material or intersubjectively defined social reality that structures interaction and discourse. The individuals that are incorporated in this scripted drama simply learn the actions, beliefs, and values required to play their parts. In this view, a person is her roles and her social identities. Contrary to such views of society and socialization, I am suggesting that the qualities of individuals' action are not so simply determined. In their attempt to make sense of their experience, individuals operate on the social demands placed upon them and the cultural messages to which they are exposed and reconstruct them in their own subjectively structured terms. This is not to suggest that this activity of reconstruction is necessarily or even commonly self-conscious. Nonetheless it is ever present and its effect is pervasive.

At the same time, I do not adopt an idealist position wherein objective and social realities dissolve into subjective constructions, nor do I adopt a psychological structuralism that suggests a universal cognition with no social or historical relativity. I avoid both by conceiving of thinking as an activity and viewing the formal structure of understanding and evaluation as its outcome. In this vein, I argue that thinking is pragmatically related to an external, primarily social environment. Consequently, the individual's attempt to define objects and establish relations among them is realized in interaction or discourse with others. This introduces an external and potentially transforming influence into the activity of thinking. At the same time that it is subjectively directed, thinking is also regulated and thereby reconstructed according to the terms of the interaction or discourse in which the individual is engaged.

Cast in these terms, my focus on subjectivity clearly does not exclude social and political considerations. To the contrary, I regard these concerns to be central, indeed analytically inseparable from more psychological ones. On one hand, social structure and culture are critically implicated in subjectivity as the setting in which reasoning is realized. As such, they stimulate or inhibit cognitive development and provide a basis for understanding individual differences in reasoning. On the other hand, subjectivity is critical to the understanding of social structure and culture. As a mediator between social regulation and individual action, subjectivity contributes to the determination of the organization and definition of collective life. Ultimately, it is in the interplay, both interactive and discursive, between subjects that social life is realized and created. In the latter regard the analysis of subjectivity is seen as a point of entry for considering matters of social structure and culture. The intellectual strategy adopted here is that, armed with a more adequate understanding of subjectivity, one can then better analyze the nature and dynamic of collective life.

To introduce this approach and to provide an illustration of its potential contribution to social inquiry, let us consider two puzzling social phenomena. The first revolves around the failure of people to learn what is required of them even when the benefits of learning are high and the information required is readily available. The second pertains to the apparently stark differences between individuals in their capacity to learn and thereby to adapt to the demands of their immediate social environment. In both instances, discussion opens with some anecdotal evidence of the phenomenon in question. The fact that the relevant behavior is not readily understood becomes a basis for questioning the theoretical frameworks typically used to make sense of social and political life. The limits of these theories are then drawn upon to indicate the direction that should be taken to construct a more adequate framework for social and political inquiry.

A FIRST PUZZLE: THE FAILURE TO LEARN

Everyday social life is replete with examples of people's failure to learn what is required of them. Although occasionally acknowledged, this is rarely accorded much attention in social and political theory. Instead, it is the presumption of successful learning, or at least reasonably successful learning, that is often incorporated as a foundational claim in contemporary theorizing. In this context, failures to learn are simply ignored. When they are addressed, they are regarded as anomalous and are explained away. To ground a reconsideration of this issue, I offer several examples of failures to learn. The first addresses a general phenomenon, the apparent failure of most people to adapt to the demands of modern life. The remaining examples are much narrower in scope.

The Crisis of Postmodernity

There is a growing sense that the twentieth century has been a period of great, pervasive, and rapid change. Not simply a circumstantial matter of advanced technologies, political institutions, and mass migrations, the changes that have taken place have permeated the social fabric and overturned whole ways of life. As the witnesses and subjects, we have seen these changes reflected in how we conceive of ourselves and others, how we have families, how we work, how we communicate, and how we collectively regulate our lives. In a world awash with the relativism of individualism, multiculturalism, globalization, and rapid social change, nothing seems particularly stable, bounded, or clear. Once stable patterns of social interaction have become increasingly uncertain and ill defined. As these regularities have evaporated, so have the sense and legitimacy of the social norms that are intended to reflect and govern them. In complementary fashion, the assumptions underlying everyday discourse are increasingly subject to questioning and doubt. Moreover, just as these common foundations are disintegrating, the previously accepted means for negotiating disagreement seem to be losing their authority.

To many of us, this changing social landscape appears complex and bewildering, an arena in which one is readily lost. We are aware that transformations are taking place, but we generally do not understand what they now involve or where they will lead. The present lack of concrete rules and clear answers breeds a disorienting and occasionally frightening sense of uncertainty, meaninglessness, and lack of direction. At moments, this condition is eulogized in popular culture, for example, in the violent nihilism of such contemporary films as the American *Pulp Fiction* or the British *Trainspotting*. It is also reflected in the amorality of African-American rap music and the skepticism of the lyrics such as those of the Canadian Alanis Morisette and the Irish Sinead O'Connor. It is also evident in the fragmented, ill-defined selves of such characters as the hero of E. L. Doctorow's *City of God* (2000).

For the most part, however, this confrontation with postmodernity has led to various attempts to escape the vicissitudes of contemporary life and to recapture some familiar, more concrete form of certainty and guidance. This is reflected in a proliferation of everything from self-help books like *I'm Okay, You're Okay* (Harris, 1967) and *Men are from Mars and Women are from Venus* (Gray, 1992) to new spiritualist and neotraditionalist religious movements. As refuge, each of these solutions provides a confirming, sympathetic acknowledgment of the paralyzing confusion of postmodern life. This is accompanied by denial of the complexities of the postmodern circumstance and a relatively simple statement of what a person concretely can and should be doing. Alternatively people have sought the desired certainty and direction in ritual and routine. The relief offered by these routines, be they of the church, the workplace, or the gymnasium, is evident in the energy verging on desperation with which they are sustained.[1] Still others can see no solution and thus attempt to disengage from the postmodern world. They seek refuge in a variety of rejections: in nature, in regressive social movements, and in simple emotional isolation. This then is the crisis of postmodernity—one in which people are asked to inhabit a world that they cannot understand, cannot feel comfortable with, and cannot do what is required of them. It is a crisis that grows as the realities of postmodernity reach out to colonize and transform ever more of the residual nooks and crannies of everyday interaction which bear the mark of premodern modes of exchange.

Cast in these terms, the crisis is, at its core, the result of a failure to learn and adapt. At a collective level, the quality of cultural definition and social regulation is changing. Traditional and hierarchical organization with its clear center, its authoritatively determined definitions of social circumstances, and its concrete directions for action is giving way to a new order. This change is being propelled by several forces: the personal independence and critical attitude fostered by a democratization of politics, the fragmentation of cultural authority produced by multiculturalism and globalization, and the veneration of novelty and efficiency nurtured by capitalism and science. Of course, much of life is still traditional, but the purview of tradition is diminishing and even in those settings where its authority has been strongest, for example, the family or the religious community, fundamental changes are occurring.

In the new emergent regime, there is an increasing demand that, in the various locales of daily interaction, people actively negotiate and thereby create the meaning and the conditions of their exchange. From the workplace to the sports venue to the home, traditional cognitive strategies involving the knowledge and application of authoritative definition and "common sense" is proving less effective. To deal with the relative uncertainties of postmodern exchange, individuals are now being asked to develop new cognitive orientations. The aim is to be able to engage in a cooperative effort with others to create, sustain, and, when necessary, reconstruct the definitions, values, and rules that govern their interaction. To do this effectively, individuals must learn to critically assess current practice and belief, imaginatively consider possible alternatives, and do so with regard to the present and potential understandings and interests of both themselves and the others with whom they are engaged.

Viewed in these terms, the cognitive requirements of contemporary life increasingly demand a level of abstraction, integration, and hypothetical thinking beyond what is required to satisfactorily meet the demands of traditional life. To facilitate the development of these skills, the culture is replete with the necessary definitions and exemplars. These are displayed in film, books, and television through both fictionalized and documentary accounts. Similarly, the social structure offers a number of settings in which to learn and practice what is necessary. These include such diverse sites as schools, psychotherapy, and management training. In this way, individuals are provided information and direction they need to self-reflect, self-direct, and if necessary self-reconstruct, while at the same time developing the capacity for critique, generating alternatives, and cooperatively engaging others.

The problem is that most people are not meeting these demands. They are not learning what they need to do and who they need to be. This is the case despite the fact that the requisite direction and the opportunities to learn are provided. It is important to keep in mind that this failure to learn occurs even though the costs of such a failure are high. The individual is left to confront a world that she does not understand. In its incomprehensibility, this world becomes one that is unpredictable, bereft of meaning and value, and populated by strangers. The result is personal disorientation, isolation, and anxiety. At the same time, this failure undermines the social life that individuals share in common. Insofar as individuals are unable to coordinate their exchange under these new conditions, this shared arena becomes increasingly disintegrated, uncertain, and potentially dangerous.[2]

Appalachian Reform, Chad Health Aid, and University Instruction

The key question raised here is why people fail to learn the skills and orientations required when the necessary information is widely available and the rewards are great enough to motivate the requisite learning. To complement our consideration of broad social changes, let us consider several specific examples of the failure to learn where the rewards are high and the information is readily available. One such example is provided by the experience of a friend, John, who was a community organizer in Appalachia. His experience parallels that of many reform-minded activists who attempt to have an impact on local communities. Although he came to the mountains with the general aim of political empowerment, this was often realized in a more specific effort to teach miners how to utilize the local government services available to them. Typically John spent six months in a small mining town gaining the confidence of the local people and giving them civic instruction. An exemplary case was his instruction on the use of a petition to request the installation of a traffic light at an unregulated street corner where a number of school children had been injured. John told the local people that the town government would respond to such a request. He also showed them how to get the necessary forms, fill them out, and gather support from parents and then how to submit the request. At each step, the local people did the required activity themselves, but John was there to instruct and support. Shortly after the request was submitted, the town bureaucracy responded positively and several months later a traffic light was installed. Approximately a year later John returned to the town only to discover that virtually none of the skills he had taught had been employed in his absence. This result was puzzling. Why did the people not seem to learn from the instruction they had been given? The presentation of information was clear, the opportunity to practice the skills in question was taken, and the rewards for performance were tangible and significant. Yet no further changes had been instigated. No enduring learning was evident.

Another illustrative example is offered by the experience of a friend's brother, David, who was working for the Peace Corps in Chad. David stayed in one region of Chad for more than a year. A friendly and sensitive man, David was well liked by most of the people with whom he dealt. One serious problem David encountered in this region was water contamination. The water was infested with microscopic larvae. When imbibed, the larvae lodged in various parts of the body. With time the larvae grew into worms which could reach several inches in length. These worms then slowly ate their way out of the body. Reaching the skin, they would break through and slowly exit. The native population had learned that if they simply pulled at the worms, they would break and life-threatening infection would follow. They did not, however, recognize that the worms came from the water.

David's aim was to teach the local people that the water should be chemically treated or boiled before drinking. He would explain that the eggs were too tiny to see, they entered the body when someone drank untreated water and later grew into the quite visible worms. His explanation was typically greeted with some combination of amusement and friendly dismissal. It was obvious that no worms could be seen in the supposedly contaminated water. If they could not be seen, how could one assume that they were there? A resourceful man, David developed what he assumed would be a persuasive response. He brought along a small bowl of finely ground cayenne pepper. He instructed the person or people he was talking to dip their forefinger in the pepper and then asked them blow the pepper off. Once this was done, he asked them if they saw any pepper. They responded that they did not. He then asked each individual to put his or her own finger in her own eye. They refused. When he asked why, they responded that there was pepper on their finger and it would sting. David then made his point: the pepper was there and able to sting even if they could not see it. It was the same with the worms. This reasoning by analogy had no impact on the audience. In a dozen or more attempts, almost no one was convinced. Even more interesting, it became clear to David that the relevance of his pepper experiment was not recognized at all. It was simply regarded as some sort of humorous aside.

David's experience is puzzling. He was addressing an issue—the worms—that was of substantial interest to his audience; their lives were potentially at stake. Moreover the people clearly had no adequate way of combating the problem. Still they did not learn from the information David gave them nor did they follow the instructions for decontamination. Perhaps it is easier to account for why David's direct information regarding the genesis of the worms was not utilized. As an outsider, he may have lacked the requisite credibility to be believed. Alternatively his instructions may somehow have inadvertently contradicted those of tribal authorities. What is more difficult to understand is why the argument by analogy with the pepper was deemed so uninformative that it did not evoke any agreement and so wholly irrelevant it did not even necessitate any real counter. It is as if the audience simply could not draw the requisite inference from one set to another set of circumstances in which the substantive elements involved differed.

One final example draws more directly on an experience many readers of this book share, that is, the experience of the classroom. In the course of the eight, ten, or fourteen weeks of a term, we offer students lecture and reading regarding a particular subject matter. As part of the materials presented, students are provided both specific facts and general theoretical frameworks with which to interpret those facts. For the most part, the latter is emphasized over the former. We are often explicit about the importance of theory as the context in which available facts are rendered meaningful and potential implications may be drawn. The books we use tend to emphasize this point as well. On occasion the role of theory may be graphically illustrated by juxtaposing frameworks and indicating that not only do they lead to conflicting claims, but the concerns deemed central in one theoretical context may not even be addressed in another.

The common result of these pedagogical efforts is evident in extended conversations, term papers, or essay examinations where it is clear that some students seem to appreciate the issues raised. They self-consciously attempt to use theories to order the disparate facts and ideas presented to them. But often the majority of students are unable to do this. Despite the classroom focus on interpretative frameworks or theoretical positions, the students seem simply unable to assimilate or use the information given. We know this is not simply a matter of some being motivated to learn and others not. When we get the chance to know our students, it is often clear that those who do understand in the manner required do so relatively effortlessly. More important, many of those who do not understand are clearly motivated and hard working. Their effort is evident in the large number of specific facts they have accumulated. Their failure is apparent in their inability to present these facts in an integrative, self-consciously interpretive fashion.

The foregoing examples are intended to supplement the more general case of the failure to develop the cognitive skills required to adapt to postmodern life. The Appalachian miners, the Chad natives, and the university students are all presented with data about problems that are important to them. Learning opens up the possibility of improving the everyday conditions of the miners, the possibility of combating dangerous and painful infestation of the natives, and the possibility of succeeding in university and gaining the social approval and advancement which follows. Yet like the members of postmodern society, most of the individuals in these specific cases do not learn.

THEORETICAL UNDERPINNINGS
OF THE PUZZLE

For many of us as social scientists, this failure to learn is puzzling. This is because the implicit understanding or framework we typically utilize to make sense of the problem does not allow us to readily comprehend what is going on. To the contrary, it leads us to expect that where the information is presented and the motivation to assimilate it is there, people will learn what they need to know. This is especially true when the concerns are the practical ones of everyday life. In this regard, the foregoing examples and the crisis of postmodernity itself are not only enigmatic, they constitute potentially disconfirming instances of the theories that orient our social understanding. To illustrate, let us consider two basic perspectives that orient most current social scientific thinking about social and political life.

The Liberal Institutional Perspective

The perspective that orients most Anglo-American analysis of social and political life is a liberal institutional one. With its roots in the liberal tradition from

John Locke through John Stuart Mill and Jeremy Bentham, this perspective underlies most contemporary analysis of governmental institutions and public policy. It is perhaps most elegantly reflected in neoclassical economics, especially in its application to social and political issues.[3]

This liberal institutional perspective is based on certain core assumptions regarding human nature and social life. A first assumption is that, for the most part, individuals accurately perceive the elements of the essentially objective world around them. Like the physical world, social interaction has an objective quality to it. As a result, because individuals do perceive accurately, the basic components of social life are transparent to those who engage in it. In a manner consistent with this basic claim, it is also recognized that perception may be subject to interference. One problem that may arise is that of the availability of information. This becomes an issue when social interactions are embedded in larger contexts where relevant factors may be remote or otherwise obscure. Another problem that may arise is one of motivation. The issue here is whether individuals are sufficiently motivated to attend to and make use of the information that is available. While these problems of information availability and motivation are recognized, they are regarded as secondary concerns. Except where these problems are particularly evident, it is assumed that all people can recognize the basic elements of the social environment in which they act.

A second core assumption underlying the liberal institutional perspective assumption is that individuals have the capacity to reason. In this context, this means that individuals can integrate the pieces of information they accumulate in a manner which reflects the actual relationships among the various elements of social exchange being considered. In the process, causal and categorical inferences can be drawn. The result is a working understanding of the social environment. This is then drawn upon to determine the probable effects of the various courses of action that the individual may adopt.

A third and final core assumption is that individuals have preferences. These preferences consist of the things that people want or seek to avoid. So defined, these preferences are objective. They are subjectively held, but they are defined and differentiated from one another in terms of the particular external objects (e.g., money, food, and others' approval) to which they refer. Drawing on the reasoned understanding of a situation, these preferences guide the individual's choices and motivate their behavior. The result is calculated, goal-oriented action initiated by individuals with the aim of maximizing personal satisfaction in light of the limits and possibilities inherent in existing circumstances.

Together these three assumptions define the nature of individuals. This then provides a basis for deducing the nature and dynamic of the social arena in which individuals interact. In simplified form, individuals engage one another in the attempt to satisfy their interests. When unregulated, this interaction becomes unpredictable and potentially dissatisfying or dangerous for all parties involved. To minimize these costs, individuals enter into agreements, tacit or explicit, for regulating their exchange.[4] These regulations and the manner in which they are enforced constitute the institutions that govern everyday life. In essence, these institutions achieve their effects by determining the costs and benefits associated with the various action alternatives available in the exchange being regulated. By virtue of their capacity to perceive and reason, individuals understand how this institutional regulation affects the manner in which their interests may be best satisfied. Guided by this calculus, they behave accordingly. This may include an attempt to renegotiate the regulations that govern them.

This constitutes the skeletal core of the liberal institutionalist perspective. It has spawned a family of social and political theories. Central to all these analyses is the interplay between individuals and institutions. On one hand, the focus is on the effect of individuals on institutions. It is here where significant differences among the various perspectives initially emerge. At issue is the solution to the practical problem of how to best facilitate the process of translating individual preferences and goals into collectively agreed upon regulatory policy. On the other hand, the various theories also deal with the reciprocal part of the social dynamic, the effect of institutions on individuals. Here, however, there is basic agreement. This is not so much a matter of explicit analysis as tacit assumption. In a matter consistent with the liberal view of human nature, it is assumed that individuals have the requisite perceptual and reasoning capacities to learn how their environment is structured. Put in other terms, individuals learn. When the information is available and sufficiently consequential, people will learn how to behave in the manner required to maximize their satisfactions and to minimize their pain. This may take some time (a matter of months or a few years), particularly if there are newly institutionalized arrangements that significantly conflict with previously adopted beliefs and practices. However, people will learn the new structure of reward and punishment and their attitudes and behavior will change in the manner required.[5]

This assumption of learning is one of the cornerstones of the liberal institutional understanding of social life. The problem, of course, is that our analysis of postmodernity and the examples of the Appalachian miners, the Chad natives, and the university students suggest that this assumption is not completely correct. In the general case and the three more specific ones, the information is available, the incentives are great, and the motivation is manifestly there. There also has been time to experience, observe, and understand. For the Chad natives, this was a matter of several hours or days. For the miners, it was six months. For the students, the learning session could be viewed as extending for the length of a term or the three or four years of their university education. In the case of postmodernity, the opportunity to learn is not a matter of months or years, but lifetimes and generations. Still most people did not learn and do not seem capable of learning what is necessary.

In sum, the liberal institutional perspective offers an understanding of social life and a framework for analysis that is predicated in part on certain psychological assumptions which suggest people learn to behave in a way required by the changing conditions of everyday life. In these terms, the failure of people to adapt to the demands of social exchange constitutes not only a puzzle, but also a challenge to the very core of the liberal institutional understanding. An attempt can be made to explain the phenomena away. Failing this, some basic theoretical reconstruction is demanded. Rather than rendering the failure to learn as anomalous, new theory must redefine human nature and social life such that this phenomenon is comprehensible, even ordinary.

The Sociological Alternative

A second approach commonly adopted is sociological. In part, this approach stands in opposition to that of the liberal institutionalist. It has its roots in the conservative[6] and romantic[7] rejections of liberalism that emerged in the late eighteenth and early nineteenth century. These critics focused on the social troubles of the time ranging from urban poverty and prostitution to increasing crime rates and violent political revolution. They understood these phenomena to be an outgrowth of cultural developments and public policy based on liberalism's misconception of society and social life. In particular, both conservatives and romantics viewed liberal claims regarding rationality and self-direction with extreme skepticism. In their view, people are not particularly rational or self-directing. To the degree to which individuals are able to comprehend something or direct their action appropriately, this is not a matter of reason, rationality, and reflection but rather is the product of faith, intuition, or feeling. The latter serve to connect individuals to something higher or more general than their particular selves. Existing beyond individuals, this transcendent community is typically ascribed an essentially mystical quality. Although it therefore may not be fully known, it is nonetheless a real social force. It can shape social exchange and is thereby capable of directing and even transforming the individual. Thus the community, be it spiritual, natural, or social, becomes key. It is viewed as the true source of meaning, value, and proper direction.

In this light, it is argued that the liberal reliance on the individual as the foundation for political and moral analysis is mistaken. Viewed from this conservative perspective, it is apparent that the collectivity, not the individual, is the appropriate point for departure for any understanding or evaluation of social life. In a manner consistent with the epistemological skepticism of this view, the vehicle for this journey is not reason. Given the tremendous complexity or depth of what is to be known and the individual's limited cognitive abilities, reason cannot be expected to take one very far. Rather, it is on faith or insight that people must rely. Even proceeding on this basis, the transcendent nature of community demands a humble recognition of the limited understanding that any one individual embarking on this journey can acquire.

In the mid and late nineteenth century, this mystical recognition of the centrality of the community gave way to a more scientific and reasoned attempt to understand the inherent nature of society. The earlier extraindividual focus and the anchoring of knowledge and value in the community were retained. The spiritualism, however, was rejected. Instead, attempts were made to understand the collectivity. This was fueled by a somewhat liberal faith, albeit one necessarily dampened by a recognition of the structuring influence of history and culture, in the technical and emancipatory potential of reasoning and reflection. Karl Marx's work was particularly seminal in this regard. The result was the emergence of the sociological point of view.[8]

Contrary to liberal institutional formulation, most classical sociological analyses regard individuals as a secondary or derivative concern. Individuals—that is, their thoughts, preferences, and actions—are conceived of as a social outcome rather than a social cause. In his *Rules of Sociological Method,* Emile Durkheim explicitly cautions against any sociological analysis that builds on assumptions regarding human nature or choice.[9] In an essay written some seventy years later, Louis Althusser takes the position even further and argues that the very ideas of individuality, self, and purposive behavior were themselves socially structured, ideological outcomes.[10] Instead of beginning with the individual, sociological analyses focus on the inherent structure of the collectivity. Description and explanation are cast in terms of society itself. Consequently, any elements of the analysis, the social objects described, or the social forces identified are understood to be internally differentiated aspects of the collectivity (e.g., classes or discourses). In this context, the activities of individual members of a society are assumed to be collectively caused and culturally signified. The claim here is that social action (be it a behavior or verbal statement) is organized and therefore determined and defined at an interpersonal, interactive, or discursive level. As a result, even a direct consideration of individuals returns us back to extraindividual and essentially social concerns.

In spite of this self-conscious attempt to avoid basing social analysis on any psychological claims, foundational psychological claims nevertheless are made, if only implicitly. Moreover, they are quite central to the sense of the sociological approach. Most sociologists clearly reject any cognitive claims that individuals are inherently logical, fully self-reflective reasoning beings. That said, they cannot avoid making alternative cognitive claims of their own.[11] Allowing that individuals are not born aware of all the meanings and regulations of social life, it is clear that they must have the basic capacities to learn them. In this regard, even the most militantly antipsychological sociologist is forced to base her analysis on certain inescapably psychological assumptions. First, it must be assumed that an individual is capable of perceiving both general cultural messages and direct behavioral feedback in a reasonably accurate way. This assumption is quite similar to that made by the liberal institutional analyst. Second, it must also be assumed that an individual can integrate what she perceives at least to the point of constructing chunks of learning, each of which is sufficiently elaborated such that it can be used to identify relevant social situations and guide the individual's action in them. The cognitive claims regarding reasoning made here certainly attribute more limited capacity to individuals than do most liberal analyses of rationality. Nonetheless, there is a claim regarding reasoning, one quite consistent with the orientation adopted in contemporary social psychological research on schemas.[12] Third, it must be assumed that an individual will in fact utilize these perceptual and cognitive capacities when sufficiently motivated to do so. Together these three assumptions define the sociological conception of the psychology of learning. Typically this process of learning is referred to as socialization. Because the psychological side, the actual learning, is assumed, sociological analyses of socialization focus on the social and political processes that determine the content of the "lesson."

Although the capacity of individuals to learn what socialization demands of them is largely a matter of assumption, the claim is a critical one. Although society may be its own immanent cause and thus be self-structuring, this immanence and structuration is virtual. It is realized only in the concrete and specific ways in which people act toward or converse with one another. That said, this dependence on individuals and their action for the realization of society is not seen as either problematic or complicating. There are two reasons for this: (1) the only structuring or organizing force operating is that of the collectivity and (2) individuals have the capacity and the motivation to perceive social influences and learn from them. Therefore, the manner in which social structure is expressed in the concrete behavior of interacting individuals is not a particular problem for the sociological perspective. For the most part, one can assume it simply happens. People can learn and therefore are socialized to behave in the manner required. With this issue safely dealt with as a matter of presupposition, one can then turn to the more central business of understanding the quality, trajectory, and conditions of change of those transcendent, virtual social forces. Where there is an apparent failure of socialization, one simply assumes that society is internally contradictory (the Marxist solution) or fragmented (the postmodernist solution). In this light, the issue is not a failure of socialization. It is not that people are not learning. Rather the problem stems from a mistaken conception of the forces that constitute the socializing influences to which the individual is exposed.

The foregoing theoretical presuppositions regarding socialization, particularly its psychological dimension, are challenged by the present circumstances of postmodernity. Despite a social environment replete with direct messages, substantial reinforcements, and practical opportunities, individuals do not seem to develop the understanding and emotional orientation that their socialization demands. Like the liberal institutional perspective it rejects, the sociological approach cannot make sense of this failure to adapt. Sociologists may try to explain it away by referring to the countervailing, if waning, influence of the traditional culture being eclipsed. Thus they may suggest that people will adapt, but more time is required. Alternatively, they may argue that the very fragmentation of postmodern culture limits the degree to which postmodernity can penetrate the whole of a postmodern society. These accounts have some merit, but traditional forms of exchange have been largely eclipsed. Older forms, for example, the institution of marriage, persist in name but have taken on a distinctly postmodern quality. In addition, the reach of postmodernity may vary across the various subpopulations of a society, but its effect is widely felt nonetheless. The contemporary realities of mass communication, the global integration of previously local or national markets, the demands of "bottom line" capitalist economics, and the advancement of the politics of individual rights and cultural equality suggest that even those who may be affected less are still importantly affected. To be brief, I do not find this sociological finesse of the problem of the failure to adapt—which is essentially to suggest that the reason most people are not postmodern is because postmodernity has not yet reached them—particularly persuasive.

In sum, the two basic perspectives that inform most contemporary social and political analysis assume a view of learning and socialization which leaves little conceptual space for understanding the difficulty individuals are having adapting to the conditions of postmodern life. Nor do they provide much leverage for understanding why the Appalachian miners, Chad natives, and university students fail to learn. (The sociological view may lend itself to explaining away the cases of the miners and natives with reference to cross-cutting social influences, but the case of the university students, who see the requisite learning as clearly to their advantage, is less easily dealt with.) To better address the phenomena, the analysis of the effect of institutions or society on individuals must be expanded in two related respects: (1) the nature of learning must be reconceptualized and (2) the distinction between the individual and society must be more clearly recognized and sustained. I will consider each of these two suggestions in turn.

An Inadequate Conception of Learning

An implicit assumption that orients both liberal institutional and sociological analyses is that all social and political learning is of the same basic type or qualitative nature. Arguably this is not the case. Some learning tasks seem manifestly more difficult than others. They demand something qualitatively different from the learner. For example, the requirements of learning algebra are clearly greater than the requirements of learning addition. For the most part, addition requires a simple recognition of numbers and a memorization of tables of sums. Algebra is not so dependent on memorization. More central is the assimilation of the logic of algebraic formulation and problem solving. Similarly, the task of learning another's point of view is inherently more complex than that of learning certain basic civilities. In the case of civilities, one need learn only specific behaviors (e.g., how to respond to another's greeting or how to eat with a knife and fork) and the particular situations in which to apply them. Like addition, this is a matter of recognition and memory. In the case of making sense of another's point of view, the task is more complicated. Beyond the simple recognition of specific claims the other person makes, it requires inference and inductive reconstruction regarding the presuppositions and linkages that underlie her way of making sense of things. Like algebra, this is a matter of understanding the general logic of how associations are made.

While analysts adopting either a liberal institutional or sociological approach would probably acknowledge these differences, neither approach incorporates a recognition of these differences as a significant, much less a central, element of the theoretical understanding it offers. And yet I would argue that the conceptualization of these differences and their implications must be central to any social theory that can address the failures as well as the successes of socialization and adaptation. Indeed, the difference between the learning of addition and civilities, on one hand, and the learning of algebra and how another person thinks, on the other hand, suggests the kind of distinction that may be critical in understanding the defining requirements of postmodern life and the difficulty individuals may have in adapting to them. In a sense, the accommodation to the demands of traditionally regulated social environments has much the same quality as learning addition or specific civilities. Traditional life is a matter of specific authoritative dictates regarding what specifically to do and when. The requisite behaviors along with the circumstances of their enactment must be recognized and remembered. Similarly, the accommodation to postmodern social life seems to make cognitive demands similar to those of learning algebra or making sense of another's way of thinking. In both instances, learning requires integration, abstraction, and interpretative reconstruction.

Regardless of any specific theoretical claims regarding how the relevant distinctions should be drawn, the key point here is that an understanding of the crisis of postmodernity (understood as a failure of adaptation) requires a framing of the issue in which distinctions among different types of learning must be made. This must include a specification of the different cognitive demands that different types of learning require. The net result would be a cognitively differentiated typology of forms of social action and discourse. This could be utilized to differentiate among types of social environments and the demands and difficulties associated with the change from one type to another. Developed in this manner, such a typology could then provide a basis for a social psychological analysis of the transition from traditional to postmodern life or of the more specific instances of the learning required of the Appalachian miners, Chad natives, or university students.

Social and Psychological Reductionism

Another limit of liberal institutional and sociological theorizing is that, at least for analytical purposes, they effectively reduce society to its constituent individuals or vice versa. Viewed from the perspective of the liberal institutionalist, social life is only what individuals create. Because of the limits of what people know, their actions may lead to unintended consequences. However, institutional and cultural realities are nonetheless defined relative to the action strategies and beliefs of the individuals involved. From the sociologist's perspective, conceptual priorities are reversed. Social life is an irreducibly collective creation. This creation may be fragmented and internally contradictory, but it is still an extraindividual phenomenon. Who individuals are, what they believe and do, is thus publicly constituted and defined. Thus in both frames of reference, the difference between the individual and the society is eliminated or minimized. Along with an undifferentiated concept of learning, this reductionism constitutes the frame of reference that supports liberal institutionalist and sociological assumptions of successful learning and social adaptation.

The problem is that the case of the failure of individuals to adapt to postmodern life contravenes these reductionist premises. In a contrary manner, it suggests a basic disjuncture between culturally dictated meanings and socially structured interaction on one hand and subjectively reconstructed understanding and personally directed action on the other. Indeed, the whole issue of adaptation is premised on the existence of this disjuncture. It is because individuals do not have a subjective orientation that corresponds to how their social environment is organized and defined that adaptation is necessary. Further and even more significantly, the failure of adaptation indicates that this lack of correspondence between the collective and the individual persists despite considerable social and psychological pressure to bring them into agreement. This suggests that the disjuncture of the collective and the individual is not merely a passing phase of development, but rather a central feature of social life.

Consequently, any attempt to understand the failure of individuals to adapt to the conditions of postmodern life must move beyond the reductionism of the liberal institutionalism or sociology orienting most contemporary theorizing. New theory must be premised on a recognition that the individual and society are fundamentally distinct forces driving social interaction and discourse. This is not simply a matter of distinguishing levels of analysis, each with its own separate domain of concerns. The problem of adaptation suggests that the individual and society operate on the common terrain of what people do and say to one another. Two consequences follow. First, insofar as individual and collective meaning and action are structured differently, they may offer conflicting direction to social exchange. The manner in which this exchange actually unfolds is therefore rendered intrinsically somewhat uncertain. It could be personally or socially dictated. Second, through this uncertain but common terrain, the individual and society are intertwined and each exerts a potentially restructuring or transformative influence on the other. Development, be it collective or individual, must be understood accordingly.

To summarize, the failure of individuals to adapt to the demands of postmodern social life cannot be comprehended from the two perspectives, liberal institutional and sociological, which orient most social analysis and public policy. The problem is that both perspectives assume that learning or socialization will occur. This assumption is supported by other allied assumptions regarding the basic similarity of all social learning and a de facto reduction of either the individual or society to the analytical terms of the other. The crisis of adaptation thus demands moving beyond these two analytical perspectives. Such a theoretical move must be predicated on a recognition that (1) there are qualitatively different kinds of learning tasks which different social formations may set, (2) both the individual and society each constitutes a structuring force which orchestrates thought and action, and (3) these two structuring forces may define and organize social life in distinctive and more or less incompatible ways. Only within such a frame of reference may the current crisis of postmodernity be fruitfully comprehended.

A SECOND BASIC PUZZLE:
NONCOMMON MEANING

Thus far we have focused on the problem posed by what people don't learn and what they seem unable to understand. Here we introduce a second issue, that of differences between people in what they are able to learn and understand. This raises another set of critical concerns regarding the more standard approaches to social analysis and provides further direction for the construction of a better alternative.

In the discussion of postmodernity, emphasis was placed on the pervasive failure of people to adapt to the emerging conditions of interaction and discourse. This failure to learn was underscored in the examples of the Appalachian miners, Chad natives, and university students. What was obscured in the discussion of each case was the otherwise obvious fact that whereas many or most do not learn, some do. There are many people who do seem capable of accommodating to the conditions of postmodern life. They succeed in constructing a more autonomous self and are able to forge a more cooperative and constructive connection with certain other people and their community. Similarly, in the case of the specific examples mentioned, there were natives who did come to understand the genesis of the worms, miners who did learn how to manipulate the local government, and students who do learn the logic as well as the rhetoric of the theories to which they are exposed.

When considering these differences in what people are able to learn, it is important to keep in mind that in all cases the incentives to learn are substantial and consequently the motivation to learn is commensurately high. Therefore differences in learning suggests, at least in part, that there are basic differences in cognitive capacity. The way in which people reason may differ and as a result so will the quality of what they perceive and the kind of understanding they can make of those perceptions. These differences are reflected in the distinctions they can learn to make and the connections they can learn to draw. It is important to emphasize that the individual differences in cognition being referred to here are not simply a matter of specific knowledge or training. To reiterate the mantra of pragmatists and linguists in the Wittgensteinian tradition, the key issue here is not what people know, but how they know. This shifts the focus from the particular facts that people have learned to the subjective system of meaning into which those facts are assimilated. In this context, it is recognized that different people may understand the same statements or behaviors in fundamentally different ways. This will be evident in their differing capacities to learn and thus in the different kinds of behavioral or discursive strategies people are able to pursue.

Before going further, let me acknowledge that the issue of individual differences in cognition may be an explosive one. The political ramifications are potentially serious and noxious. Following a conservative tradition, some might argue that an individual's political opportunity and power should be commensurate with her intellectual ability. Those people who reason less well should be given less responsibility over themselves and others. Given the structural pragmatic view of reasoning that I present in chapter 2, such a view makes no theoretical sense. As I have argued in earlier work, the development of reasoning depends on having the power and opportunity to act. Environments that present individuals with greater challenges and the opportunity to respond are likely to facilitate intellectual development. In complementary fashion, environments that are more restrictive and repressive are likely to obstruct this development.[13] Nonetheless, several well-meaning colleagues have argued that the claims I make regarding individual differences in reasoning are readily extracted from the general theoretical framework. As such these claims may be easily misused with noxious political implications and therefore should not be made at all. I disagree. I do not believe that the reality of differences—one that is as apparent to the casual observer as to the trained investigator—should be ignored in a presumably polite or politic fashion. In my view, the attempt to construct a social or political understanding which contradicts people's everyday experience is self-undermining and itself potentially dangerous. Significant differences in how people reason and therefore in what they are capable of understanding are manifest and omnipresent facts that must be addressed by any adequate social, political, or indeed moral theory. Only then can social and political realities be persuasively comprehended and public policy be effectively influenced.

The nature of these differences in how people reason is a central concern of this book. To give the reader a preliminary sense of the kinds of distinctions made, let us consider several examples. The first is anecdotal. When I first began teaching, my classes were relatively small and I was able to have direct contact with students. One result was that my office hours were often used by students not only as a supplement to class time but as an opportunity for a mix of secular confession and casual therapy. In one such case, a pair of Iranian students, a heterosexual couple, visited my office regularly for a term. On several occasions the discussion wandered in the direction of their current relationship and impending marriage. The woman was somewhat dissatisfied with the relationship and her lover could not really understand why. He argued that the two of them shared all that was necessary for a successful relationship. They had similar backgrounds; they were both Iranians raised in California. They shared friends in common. They liked to do the same things and enjoyed the same kinds of entertainment. Finally, they enjoyed a satisfying sex life. On this basis, he concluded that all was well and he could not understand the woman's dissatisfaction. In her turn, the woman acknowledged the truth of what the man had said. However, she indicated there was something else of concern. In the course of her four years at university, she had been exposed to a number of new ideas. Her way of thinking about the world was beginning to change. She had begun to reflect on her beliefs and values. She wondered about how they emerged, how they were related to one another, and if they were correct. It worried her that her lover did not appreciate her inquiry nor was he apparently willing or able to participate in it. In this light, she did not feel understood or properly connected to the man. Responding to her comments, he admitted not understanding the meaning of what she was talking about, but he was also not particularly concerned. Indeed, he argued that the whole issue was not significant. After all, her concerns did not affect the day to day of what they did together, their friendships, or the other factors he had identified as central to a good relationship.

From my perspective, the failed communication between these two lovers was not a matter of specific knowledge or preferences. Rather it reflected a basic, structural difference in how they conceptualized people and relationships. In the man's case, a person was conceived of as the collection of specific behaviors she performed and the preferences she voiced. A relationship between individuals was based on common membership in a group and in the commonalties of what they did, believed, and preferred. From the woman's perspective, the foregoing was relevant but not complete or even central. In her view, a person was the ideas she had and how she made sense of them. The issue was not the specific content of the ideas but how those ideas were integrated and understood. Similarly, the relationship between people involved a process of coming to an understanding, and thus a true recognition, of one another. This did not depend so much on shared features, but rather on an appreciation and respect for differences. Whereas the man's social reasoning was somewhat fragmented, categorical, and oriented to concrete specifics, the woman's reasoning was more integrative, abstract, and general in orientation. As a result, the realities of the social relationship differed for the two partners. Each conceived the substance and value of what they ostensibly shared in very different terms.

The following excerpts from two in-depth interviews provide a second example of qualitative differences in reasoning. These excerpts offer the reader an opportunity for a direct comparison of differences. The interview involved a discussion of a significant other. The interviewee was free to choose whom he or she wanted to discuss. Typically people chose to discuss a close friend, spouse, or lover. Once chosen, the interviewee was asked to describe the person and the relationship they shared. A semistructured interview, the interviewee's comments were followed by probing questions intended to clarify the meaning of what was being said.

The first set of excerpts is from an interview with Linda, a thirty-three-year-old resident of New Haven, Connecticut. Linda is first asked to describe another person whom she knows well.

INTRV.: I'd like you talk about someone you know well. It can be anybody, a man, a woman anybody. Just keep one person in mind. Okay? What I would like you to do is describe this person to me. Tell me what they are like.

LINDA: Well I know millions of people, but I guess the closest friend to me is my sister. I mean we're close in age. I have a lot of sisters, but I have one particular sister I'm close to. She's stout, extremely kind, and conscientious. I'm not sure what you want. She works, has a husband and two children, lives in a big ranch in Hamden . . .

INTRV.: Okay you said that she's kind and conscientious. What do you mean she's kind?

LINDA: She would do anything that she can to help anyone. She's religious too, but not fanatically religious. She's the kind of person you can call in the middle of the night and she'll . . . If you say that you need her, she'll come. She's always conscious of others' feelings. Like I might blurt something out, but she would stop and think about it first, if it's going to hurt someone she would rephrase it or not say it at all.

INTRV.: You also said she was conscientious. What did you mean by that?

LINDA: She's always conscious of others, of her surroundings. She stops and thinks before she speaks, that's the difference . . . because I blurt things out.

Linda is then asked to explain her sister's character.

INTRV.: Okay. Why do you think . . . you say she's conscientious. Why do you think she is that way?

LINDA: She's always been that way. I guess it's just her nature or whatever. She's always been that way, even as a child.

INTRV.: Okay. You said that you have a tendency to like blurt things out where she has a tendency to think about them.

LINDA: She thinks about it, is it going to . . . how is it going to come out. Before it comes out. I just say it. Then after it's said, if it's not too nice, when it's done then, then I think about, "Oh, I shouldn't have said that, because that hurt Jody's feelings or whatever."

INTRV.: How come she thinks about it first?

LINDA: Well, maybe because she's a couple of years older than I am. Maybe she's just more mature, I don't know.

Finally Linda is asked to characterize her relationship with her sister.

INTRV.: Can you tell me something about how the two of you get along?

LINDA: Oh we get along fine. If I call her and I want to talk to her for three hours, she'll talk, but if she calls me, I would do the same thing. You know, we go a lot of places together. As a matter of fact, we went to Nassau last December. We do a lot of things. We talk about the kids. We talk about our husbands, our houses. We talk about our jobs. We talk about other people. If . . . she's financially better off than I am, so I usually do the needing, but if I need money or something I can always get it, you know, but if I had it she could get it. I don't know. Anything that I need, she's always there with it.

INTRV.: What's the most important thing, do you think, that you do together?

LINDA: I think, well, we discuss our children, if there are any problems with them, how we can solve them. What we should do about it and if there are other problems. I think that's the most important thing. We have confidence in each other. Which is a very strong kind of bond.

The second interview is with Dick, a thirty-year-old New Yorker about to move to Los Angeles. Dick is also asked to describe someone who is close to him. After initially fighting the interviewer, he finally does offer a characterization of his lover.

INTRV.: What I'd like you to do is describe this person to me. What is this person like?

DICK: She's female. You want a whole bunch of categories now? Does it make a difference to you whether you rate them in terms of what's most important?

INTRV.: Tell me about her.

DICK: She's a female. She's white, twenty-eight years of age, lower-middle-class family, currently a doctor, third year of residency training program. She went to medical school at Yale. I've known her for about three and a half years—lived with her for maybe a year.

INTRV.: Okay. What kind of person is she?

DICK: She's a nice person. Warm.

INTRV.: Can you tell me anything more about her? You said she is nice, warm.

DICK: Well I mean what layer of the onion do you want to be at?

INTRV.: The layer you consider relevant.

DICK: But I am starting at layer one, but then you work your way down. You know someone for three years. You want me to tell you about her secret fears or her unrealized ambitions or her internal torment or her relationship with her family?

INTRV.: Tell me what you think it would be useful for me to know to have a sense of her.

DICK: Well that would take about five or six hours.

INTRV.: Tell me a little bit.

DICK: Well Nancy is kind of an educated woman. She's had four years of medical training and three years of undergraduate and yet she's strikingly uneducated at the same time. She doesn't think very systematically about herself. She is capable of real introspection and great insight, but she has a difficult time generalizing that into the day-to-day world. She's . . . (pause)

INTRV.: She's capable?

DICK: No, she's not very capable of generalizing things.

INTRV.: But she is capable of introspection?

DICK: Yeah, sure, most individuals are. Everybody I know who is not very introspective is practically comatose, okay, or lives in Los Angeles. She's kind of basically bourgeois in her values, materialistic. She finds her salvation, I think, in things. To a lesser extent, in people. She is ambitious, relatively self-sufficient, is beset with a bunch of internal difficulties—her relations with men, I think, generally are a bit difficult for her. Her father was a kind of weak figure in her life and a source of much resentment and hostility and is the kind of ultimate male model, male role model. She has a lot of difficulties in her relationships with men.

INTRV.: Difficulties in what sense?

DICK: She's reticent and self-contained and finds it difficult to be extremely giving of herself. Feels that she's going to be disappointed. A pattern which I may say has some justification. That's about it, I can go on.

Dick goes on to suggest that Nancy is both ambitious and reclusive. He is asked to explain why she is this way.

INTRV.: How do you explain the desire for acclaim on the one hand and the reclusiveness on the other hand?

DICK: Well, there's a lot of different. . . . I mean individuals are little cauldrons of desires and they don't all rationalize in some perfectly coherent sense. It makes them kind of interesting, you know? Show me a linear-oriented personality where every little piece fits together and you come out with a real kind of solid constellation, and I'll guarantee you you'll be bored to death. She's got a lot of conflicting impulses. Her relations with men—on the one hand, she wants them to be strong, but if they're strong, they compromise her independence. And on the other hand, if they're weak, they remind her of her father, who she hates, and there are fundamental tensions there. And there are fundamental tensions in her career path and her kind of life preferences. There no question at all about that, but that's unremarkable.

Dick also claims that Nancy bullies and humiliates others. He is asked to explain this.

INTRV.: Okay a further question. Why is it do you think that Nancy relies on tactics of fear, humiliation rather than tactics of a more positive sort?

DICK: That's a very difficult question. I think some of it is situational. She's in a profession which tends to maintain discipline by the use of those instruments. It's all fear of failure or fear of negative review . . . and part of it is personality. Over a period of dealing with human beings, she developed certain proclivities towards manipulating them. I mean I hate to sound Machiavellian about the whole thing, but you find that certain people respond in certain ways. Certain things work with them and she's been used to dealing with people in those modes. I mean she's capable of other ways of manipulation too.

Here we have examples of two people who subjectively reconstruct what they observe in very different ways. As a result, each creates a very different kind of understanding of the people and events around them. Linda and Dick are both speaking of people they know very well, and yet it is clear that there are stark differences in the quality as well as the substance of the inferences they make. For Linda, her sister is a collage of the specific, concrete things she does and says. The concrete, fragmented quality of her description of her sister is reflected in her explanations as well. To explain is to find a single specific causal force, internal or external, which is linked to the effect observed. Dick reconstructs Nancy in a very different way. For Dick, Nancy is understood in more general terms. He focuses in part on how it is Nancy thinks, how she makes sense of the world around her. This then provides a framework for interpreting the meaning of the particular activities in which she typically engages. At the same time, Dick considers different aspects of Nancy (her family history, her relationships, her attitudes toward work, etc.) and places them in relation to one another in an attempt to understand the coherence and inherent conflicts of her personality. In sum, Dick and Linda appear to have two very different ways of conceiving of another person, a difference which parallels that between the two Iranians discussed earlier. As a result, Dick and Linda are likely to learn very different things about another person to whom they are exposed and are similarly likely to engage that person in quite different ways.

In this light, it is worth reconsidering the earlier examples of the miners, natives, and students. In the initial presentation, each example was considered as an illustrative case of a failure to learn. Here we may regard them as examples of individual differences in reasoning. In each instance, there is a clear difference between the nature of the understanding of the person serving as teacher and the understanding of the audience. Thus, the Peace Corps worker example may be reconsidered as a case where the structure of worker's reasoning differed from that of the Chad natives. Similarly the Appalachian case can be viewed as an instance where the structure of the political activist's reasoning differed from that of the miners. Finally, the university example may be viewed as a case where the structure of the professor's understanding differed from that of the students. Indeed, the difficulties associated with the learning task in each case can readily be understood in terms of the structural differences between how the task was conceived and thus set by the teacher on one hand and how it was defined by the potential learners on the other.[14]

As with the failure to adapt, this phenomenon of underlying or structural differences in reasoning cannot be comprehended from the perspectives of liberal institutionalism or sociology. Again the problem is that the phenomenon observed contradicts foundational assumptions upon which those perspectives are based. Although their claims about human capacities differ, the two perspectives share the same foundational claim that all people think in basically the same way. Some may be quicker, some more knowledgeable, but all people share the same basic capacity to perceive and make sense of phenomena in their environment. In liberal institutional analysis it is assumed we all share a common rationality, that is, a basic capacity to integrate information and deduce appropriate courses of action in what is loosely referred to as a logical or rational manner. In some more recent theorizing, the assumption of rationality has been weakened and the claim is only of a "bounded rationality."[15] In either case, however, it is assumed that individuals calculate in order to choose and the nature or structure of this calculation is fundamentally the same for all people. In sociological analyses, it is assumed that our capacity for thought is more limited. Rather than engaging in rational calculation, we are oriented by specific schemas, definitions, and action scenarios that are provided to us by the regularities of daily life we directly experience and the cultural messages or themes to which we are exposed. In this view, the suggestion is that we rely less on reason and more on perception and memory. Even though our capacities are thus diminished in the sociological view, they are still universally shared. Thus both sociological and liberal institutional theories assume all individuals (at least all "normal" individuals) cognize in the same way and have the same basic capacity for learning.

This assumption of common reasoning or cognitive functioning is by no means trivial. It underlies the presumed unidimensional quality of both institutions and culture. It is because both are understood by all in roughly comparable ways that an institution or culture is realized similarly across the host of interactions it is intended to regulate and define. Let us consider one restricted, but exemplary, case: the realization of the institution of marriage in the case of a specific couple. From liberal institutional or sociological perspectives, it is assumed that the institution exists as a set of regulations of behaviors and attitudes that are commonly perceived by the husband and wife. Their specific role requirements may vary, but each understands what is required of himself or herself and by the other partner. In this sense, the institution has a singular realization. It is perceived and responded to by both individuals in the same or a complementary manner. We can therefore speak of *the* marriage, as a singular phenomenon. For the institutionalist, *the* marriage exists as a commonly apprehended set of alternative courses of action, each with its associated rewards and punishments. For the sociologist, *the* marriage exists more as a set of commonly understood roles and scenarios that determine what should be done and when. In either approach, further analysis regarding the place of the marriage in the larger environment or the consequences of specific changes in practice or belief may then be conducted on this basis.

Problems for this conception of institutions and culture arise when those individuals who are affected do not reason in the same way. The presumed basic singularity or unidimensional quality of social institutions and cultures disintegrates into multiple realizations that may more or less overlap. To illustrate, let us speculate about a marriage between the Iranian couple just described. Clearly the two are likely to understand and operate within the institution of marriage in rather different ways. The man will tend to see marriage in terms of specific conventional prescriptions for how he should behave, what he should believe, and what he should anticipate from his spouse. For the most part, these prescriptions will be conceived in rather concrete and rigidly defined terms. In a similar vein, the man's understanding will also include conventional notions of what the alternative courses of action are in any given situation and of the costs and benefits that are likely to follow from each. What he actually does will be affected accordingly. Given the different quality of her reasoning, the woman is likely to see their marriage quite differently. She may tend to view the institution of marriage as a conventional societal construction. As such, she may regard it to be less a matter of clear value and worthwhile direction and more as an inflexible, potentially oppressive form of social regulation. In this light, she may demand a more open, questioning, and constructive orientation to marriage. This may require that she and her partner determine how they as individuals can best be with one another. This constitutes a very different basic understanding of the condition of marriage and leads to a commensurately different set of standards for judging the value of different action alternatives.

The question then arises, what is the nature of *the* marriage between two people who understand and value the substance of that marriage in qualitatively different terms and therefore orient their action in two very different ways? Clearly such a marriage is complex, a partial integration of distinctive realizations of its cultural meaning and institutional regulation. Cast in these terms, the presumed unidimensional marriage with its relatively coherent meaning and integrated regulations is thus reconceived as a multidimensional collage of somewhat related meanings and sometimes overlapping behavioral imperatives. To comprehend such a marriage, analysis must focus on the interplay between differences in subjective understanding and the qualities of the somewhat common ground of interaction upon which these different subjects meet. These concerns go well beyond what either conventional institutional or sociological analyses are able to address.

Implications for Theory and Empirical Research

Evidence of individual differences in reasoning contradicts the assumptions of liberal institutionalist and sociological theorizing and therefore cannot be understood in these terms. Moreover, this evidence denies a basic tenet of these two standard approaches and therefore constitutes a challenge to the general way in which they represent social life. Evidence of differences in reasoning among the individual members of a society or group suggests that cultural dictates may be perceived, understood, and responded to differently by different people. Similarly it suggests that institutions, as regulators of interaction, will also be conceived and responded to variously. Thus, institutions ranging from marriage to the laws of contract to a popular election might be understood in qualitatively different ways by different people leading to different kinds of response to the same institutional regulation.

The net result is that the integrated and unidimensional conception of the institution in liberal analysis or of the culture or social structure in sociological analysis is exploded. What remains is an array of fragments, a set of coexisting but different layers of meaning and different modes of discourse and interactive engagement. In this context, new theoretical questions must be addressed. What is the nature of the social and psychological dynamic whereby these fragments are constructed, sustained, and transformed? What is the nature of their coherence, even if it is only a "loose" coherence? The latter question may be addressed at several interrelated levels, that of the integration of the collective, that of the integration of the self, and perhaps most fundamentally, that of the relationship between these two loci of integration. These questions define some of the key parameters that must guide the development of new theory.

In addition to theoretical revision, the issue of differences in reasoning demands a reconsideration of research methods. Both institutionalist and sociological empirical work adopt designs that assume that all individuals, including the researcher (at least when they are socialized in the same sociocultural environment), share a common understanding of the specific attitudes, themes, or behaviors being investigated. As a result, data collection can proceed assuming no need to interpret the understandings constructed by the researcher or by the various members of her research population. In this vein, such standard methods as the experimental design with controls over stimulus presentation and such standard tools as the survey questionnaire make good sense. With the introduction of a claim of qualitative differences in reasoning, the sense of these methods and tools is now subject to doubt. The "objective" or "intersubjective" and therefore shared meaning (and hence implication) of social stimuli and responses can no longer be assumed. Constructed in part by individuals who may reason differently, social actions and events that are ostensibly the same may be differently constituted and directed. Consequently the comparability of meaning, or the lack thereof, must be explored empirically. This requires a research design that not only allows for individual differences, but also actively explores them. This in turn requires open-ended, interpretative techniques that can elicit and probe the subjective meaning of the specific connections that a given individual makes when speaking of or pursuing an action strategy. Only then will the extent and nature of individual differences be apparent. In a self-confirming manner, close-ended, noninterpretative research can only conceal these differences behind the veil of the assumed common meaning of response alternatives.

CONCLUSION

We have considered several examples of how some people successfully meet the challenges of new social learning and how others do not, even when the requisite information is available and the cost of failing to learn is significant. Our analysis suggests that these cases highlight those aspects of everyday life that contradict the foundations of much contemporary social and political theory. Apart from revealing the inherent limits of current theorizing, our analysis suggests the direction that new theoretical efforts should take. First, such an effort must recognize that there may be fundamental differences between individuals in how they structure their understandings and their action. Similarly there may be differences between societies in how the culture or social order is structured. An attempt must be made to specify the nature of these differences. Second, new theory must avoid sociological or psychological reductionism. Both the individual and society must be viewed as structuring forces that contribute to the definition and dynamic of social life. While interrelated, it is possible and even likely that these two forces will also be at odds with one another. Attention should focus on the consequent uncertainties and tensions that are inherent in everyday life and the role these conditions play in societal and individual development. Finally the relation between social and psychological structures must be considered in light of the foregoing claims of how structures of each type may vary. On one hand, differently structured cultures and social organizations may set qualitatively different kinds of learning tasks for the individuals to be socialized. The impact of these differences on the development of the affected populations must be considered. On the other hand, different individuals think differently and therefore may be more or less able to learn in the manner demanded by the conditions of their social interaction. The constraints these differences impose on how institutions are realized and how readily social change is accomplished must also be considered.

This theoretical effort must be complemented by appropriately designed empirical research. To begin, this is a matter of adopting the appropriate focus. The theoretical concerns voiced here require an examination of the coherence and differences among structures of individual reasoning and structures of social discourse and interaction. After this has been established, an investigation of the interplay between these interpenetrating psychological and social structures may be conducted. In particular, this would entail an exploration of the social and psychological conditions that facilitate individual development and adaptation on one hand and societal transformation and development on the other. In addition to determining a substantive focus, the theoretical direction suggested here also has implications for research methodology. In particular it demands that systematic observation be supplemented by research designs that facilitate the recognition and interpretation of differences in the underlying structure of action and speech.

The arguments in the remainder of the book are developed with these concerns in mind. In chapter 2, an attempt is made to sketch a theoretical perspective that captures the complex, essentially social psychological dynamic of social life. In the next three chapters, the psychological implications of this vision are developed. In chapters 3, 4, and 5, three modes of thinking are described. In each case, this includes a characterization of the structure of thought that is produced and a depiction of the kinds of understandings and evaluations of social and political life that are constructed. In chapter 6, methodological concerns are addressed. This includes a discussion of general questions regarding appropriate methods as well as a description of the specific instruments and procedures used in the research. In chapter 7, the results of the empirical research are presented. They provide strong support for the theoretical claims regarding differences in individual reasoning. The presentation of results is supplemented by the inclusion of three annotated interviews. They provide examples of the three forms of reasoning discussed in chapters 3 to 5. In the concluding chapter, the implications of this research for social and political analysis are considered. There we return to the larger issues of social psychological theory and the consideration of the interplay between the individual actor and cognition on one hand and social organization and culture on the other.

Chapter Two A Structural
Pragmatic Social Psychology

The theory that underlies the concepts and research presented in this book is developed in this chapter, beginning with a brief sketch of the philosophical foundation upon which that theory builds. The approach I have employed focuses on how people understand their personal lives and the larger social and political world around them. This is understood in terms of the interplay between subjective and intersubjective constructions of meaning. The theory offered here is in part an attempt to offer a more adequate point of departure for making sense of the failure to learn and noncommon meaning, discussed in chapter 1. More broadly, my intent is to provide a theoretical basis for a social or political psychology.

THE STRUCTURAL PRAGMATIC
APPROACH

Structural pragmatics is a term I use to describe the epistemological and social theoretical approach adopted in the book.[1] The name reflects the two traditions, pragmatist and structuralist, upon which I draw. My discussion of structural pragmatics begins a reconsideration of these two original perspectives. A social psychology is then constructed on this basis, one which takes the dually structured quality of social life as its point of departure. In this context, such concepts as the duality of structuration and structured uncertainty are introduced. These concepts provide the basis for an analysis of the dynamics of social life, which then leads to a discussion of the transformation of structures, both social and individual. The explication of structural pragmatics here is rather brief. My aim is not to offer a fully elaborated theoretical vision, but to give the reader a sense of the broader theoretical vision that frames both the concerns addressed in the book and the methods used to explore them.

The Pragmatist Dimension

A largely American philosophical enterprise, pragmatism was developed in the work of Charles Sanders Pierce and William James at Harvard, George Herbert Mead at Chicago, and John Dewey at Columbia.[2] Their aim was to develop an alternative to epistemologies that view thought in terms of representation and define it in largely static terms. For the pragmatists, "thought" is viewed as "thinking," and the latter is regarded more as an operational activity than a representational one. It is a matter of "knowing how" rather than "knowing that." In these terms, thinking is purposive, active, and action-oriented. It is an operative response to external conditions, one that initiates action (intellectual or physical) in order to achieve some end. In the course of this operation, meaning is constructed. Objects and actions are placed in relation to one another as they are deployed in the attempt either to act on objects in the physical environment or to interact with others in the social environment. These pragmatic relations extend beyond the response to include aspects of the initial stimulus.[3] In this manner, these constitutive objects and actions of the stimulus and response are subjectively reconstructed as elements of the individual's purposive activity, and each is defined by the particular role it plays.

To illustrate this pragmatic concept of meaning, consider the game of chess. Any particular piece has a specific identity determined by its distinctive appearance and more fundamentally by the specific manner in which it may be moved. In these terms, we can objectively differentiate a bishop from a knight or pawn, and so on. Despite these objective constraints, the pragmatic meaning of the pieces is defined (and redefined) by how they are used relative to one another in the course of the game. Thus in one situation, the way in which a bishop is moved may be a support in an attack, a deceptive maneuver in a feint, or a buttress in a defense. Thus the pragmatic meaning of the move depends on the larger purposive activity of which it is a part. Of note, this activity also defines the stimulus to which the move is a response. Thus, if the move were a defensive buttress, the pragmatic context would also constitute the other player's prior move(s) as an attack.

Another example is provided by speech. Statements that people make have some referential meaning—that is their meaningfulness derives from their agreed upon connection to some external objects. Thus the statement, "It is cold in the room," depends in part on its connection to some physiological sensation of uncomfortably low temperature and to a walled-in space in a building. However, neither the social or subjective meaning is thus delimited. The meaning of the statement depends on how it is utilized in conversation. Thus if two friends are joking with one another on a summer day, the statement "It is cold in the room" constitutes a sarcastic speech act. As such, it will be understood not as a reference to the cold but rather to the heat of the day. Alternatively, if the statement is made by guests in the course of polite dinner conversation, the statement may constitute an indirect request to turn on the heat or close an open window. In this light, pragmatists have argued that meaning is most importantly a matter of use.[4]

This conception of thinking as a purposive activity and meaning as constructed by use has a number of important ramifications. One is the continuity of the subjective qualities of thought and the objective or intersubjective qualities of action. As a purposive activity, thinking infuses action with subjective meaning. In a manner suggested by the preceding examples, the meanings of actions and objects are tools that are subjectively defined by the individual's pursuit of the task at hand. At the same time, however, thinking also opens up meaning-making to the extrasubjective qualities of action. As an activity oriented to operating on phenomena external to it, thought is necessarily intimately related to the objective and intersubjective conditions of action in which this activity is carried through. As the circumstance and the medium of the action to which thinking is oriented, these external conditions contribute to how actions and objects may in practice be interrelated. They thereby help determine how purposive strategies may be formulated and thus the kinds of subjective connections that thinking may forge.

To illustrate this latter point regarding the impact of objective and social conditions on thinking, consider again the examples of chess and speech. In the chess game, one's ability to use (and thereby define) a bishop as feint depends in part on the specific objective possibility (as governed by chess rules) of the bishop to move in the particular manner required. At the same time and as important, the intended use and meaning of the move also depends on one's opponent viewing the bishop as part of a developing attack. Similarly in the conversation, one's ability to be sarcastic or to make an indirect request requires that the listeners recognize and accept the manner in which the statement is being used. In this sense, one's thinking—the purposive strategies one constructs—is delimited by the extrasubjective context in which that thinking is taking place.

This pragmatic conception of thinking also has important implications for how both the individual and society should be conceived. Oriented by a liberal epistemology, most social inquiry presumes a static separation of subject and object. Linkages between these two separate entities are then forged through sensation, representation, and reference. Sensation allows the individual subject to apprehend objective experience. These sensations are then "re-presented" or encoded as mental images or ideas. The latter are considered meaningful (or its equivalent, correct) by virtue of their correspondence to the elements of the objective reality to which they refer. Anchored by sensation and reference in an extrasubjective reality, subjective representations are objectively defined. At this point another layer is introduced, that of logical reflection. It operates on representations through creative recombination, categorization, and causal linkage. Like the representations themselves, the sense of this reflection depends on the correspondence of its product with some external reality.

There are several important consequences of this view for the contemporary psychology of thinking. First, the object of such a psychology, thought, consists fundamentally of representations. These are static entities. They are conceived as snapshots of an external world. Second and related to the first, each representation may be understood on its own terms. It is not defined relative to other representations, but rather with regard to the specific aspect of the external world to which it refers. Third, these representations have a universal or common meaning. They reflect and refer to an objective reality to which all human beings, given the requisite exposure to the particular phenomenon in question, have comparable access by virtue of our shared sensory capacities. Fourth, these representations are learned through immediate or socially mediated experience. They are therefore explained as a direct result of the objective or social circumstances to which the individual subject is exposed. Fifth, apart from issues of content that are objectively determined, the means whereby objects are cognitively apprehended, represented, and referenced are assumed to be attributes of mind. As such, the means of thinking (e.g., modes of perception, categorization, or inference) are assumed to exist independently of specific sociohistorical conditions and are thus universal. An artifact of mind, thinking is regarded to be the exclusive preserve of psychology. Only a concern with the substance of individuals' representations shifts the ground to more sociological and historical considerations of differences in what these individuals have experienced.

The pragmatic view adopted here suggests a very different approach to the study of thinking. Rather than representations that are significant by virtue of the objects to which they refer, the focus shifts to the overarching purpose or strategy of the individual subject. Thus the straightforward empirical analysis of representations predicated on a notion of reference gives way to a self-consciously interpretative account, which considers the subjective meaning of the moves an individual makes. Moreover, this subjective meaning is now understood as something actively constructed rather than passively assimilated. In the language of liberal epistemology, representations are not simply learned and thus objectively determined in a commonly apprehended way. Rather they are subjectively constructed through the use a specific individual makes of objects and actions. As a result, pragmatism confers a more profound agency on individuals than its liberal counterpart. Apart from choosing goals and deciding on courses of action, the individual is also assumed to be engaged in the active and ongoing (if not necessarily self-conscious) construction of the sense or meaning of the objects and people upon whom she acts.

At the same time, the pragmatic approach does not suggest that the individual constructs meaning in an unfettered manner. The moment her strategies for action are realized in practice, the individual opens her way of thinking to conditions of action that are materially and socially conditioned. In attempting to move from one place to another, an individual may operate as though walls were permeable, but actual practice will quickly negate this subjective definition. Similarly, an individual may assume that her desire is sufficient to motivate another's action. But here again practice quickly deconstructs the subjective meaning she is attempting to establish.

It should be emphasized that not only do these extrasubjective circumstances negate the meanings individuals construct, they also are positively and intimately implicated in the construction of that meaning. In pragmatic terms, the subjective construction of meaning involves the deployment of actions and objects in the context of attempting to get something done. This is not only a matter of a mental or internal coordination of represented action schemes, but also, and as importantly, it consists of what is practically worked through in one's exchange with the environment. The latter depends on the social and material conditions of the person's interaction with her physical surroundings and

with other people. Insofar as those conditions vary, so will the connections individuals can make and therefore the kinds of meaning they can construct. A
good example of this is provided by Benedict Anderson's analysis of the growth
of nationalism (1991). He argues that the unusual material or geographic situation of the European colonists in the Americas rendered their social identity
problematic. Forced to conceive of themselves both by association with and in
distinction to their home country, they developed an unusually acute sense of
collective self-consciousness. The latter provided fertile ground for the genesis
of a nationalist conception of one's group. As suggested by this example, thinking and the meanings it creates are sociohistorical products. Thus the pragmatic point of view suggests that the analysis of thinking must incorporate sociological considerations in the core of its theorizing. In other words, cognitive
psychology must be an essentially social psychological inquiry.

A pragmatic perspective also yields a different, more dynamic conception of
society. First the focus shifts from static patterns or rules of interaction and established beliefs to the ways in which individuals engage one another in interaction and discourse. This interpersonal exchange is then reconceived.
Rather than being considered as a reflection of the rules regarding what each
person does or should do in a particular situation, the interplay between individuals is regarded as a creative exercise in which virtual rules and actual
practice determine each other. Considered from the perspective of the individual participant, her own action constitutes a response to the other's action
and an initiative oriented to the other's forthcoming response. In the process,
each participant subjectively defines the others' initiatives and responses and
thus what those other people are doing and who they are in the interaction. To
interact, the participants must coordinate their action trajectories and associated definitions relative to one another. One result is that the effective meaning
of individual action and the nature of individual selves are thereby interactively
negotiated in the course of exchange. Additionally, regularities of interaction
and the effective intersubjective significance of the moves people make are established. These results of interaction then become resources that are drawn
upon in subsequent interaction and the consequent possible renegotiation of
meaning. In this light, rules of interaction and discourse are understood both
to regulate exchange and to be reconstructed as part of the ongoing negotiation
of how concrete individuals will in fact deal with one another.[5]

Viewed from this perspective, institutions and culture consist of the ways in
which specific interactions and specific discursive practices are regulated. Because these interactions and discourses involve individual subjects, social regu-

lation is imbued with their creative energy. It is dynamic and potentially self-transforming. At the same time, a pragmatic social analysis recognizes that this subjective constructing force is conditioned by the objective and intersubjective circumstances of any interpersonal exchange. By delimiting the way in which the social or material environment can be engaged, these conditions guide the subjective construction of meaningful trajectories of action and hence the manner in which intersubjective negotiation occurs. Consequently, different material and social conditions of exchange will produce different kinds of subjects, different kinds of intersubjective negotiation, and therefore different kinds of cultural meanings and interactive regulations.[6]

As the foregoing discussion suggests, although the individual or psychological implications of a pragmatic approach may be distinguished from its social or sociological ones, these two dimensions of the analysis are radically integrated. On one hand, the pragmatic orientation suggests that the social arena is populated by individuals who are purposive thinking actors. They are subjects, each of whom organizes and directs her own action and thereby defines the meaning of what she does. Individuals enter into interaction with one another in this manner. Their subjectively constructed strategies guide both the overtures and responses each individual makes to the other. Consequently, the interaction between individuals will unfold in a manner that reflects the nature of the connections made by each of the individuals involved. Similarly the way in which conversations occur will reflect the pragmatic intent and thus the subjective meaning of the individual participants. As a result, the discourses and the interactions that make up social life are necessarily infused with connections and meanings that individuals are constructing. On the other hand, the pragmatic understanding of meaning also suggests that these individually constructed strategies and aims will be shaped by the socially regulated and defined conditions of action. The latter delimits what action can be taken, what consequences will follow, and what ends might possibly be pursued. Consequently, the individual's subjective organization of her own action will necessarily incorporate both the substance and the organization of the regularities of social exchange. Considered in its entirety, each particular interaction between individuals is at once a social and a psychological accomplishment. The result is thus a profoundly social psychological view of social life.

The Structuralist Dimension

In addition to American pragmatism, the perspective adopted here also draws on a European structuralist tradition. The latter was initiated by the linguistic structuralism of Ferdinand de Saussure and further developed in the philosophical writings of Maurice Merleau-Ponty and the anthropological writings of Claude Lévi-Strauss.[7] Analysis here focuses on the formal structures that underlie the apparent organization of mind, language, or social life. This leads social inquiry beyond the typical pragmatic consideration of particular subjective strategies, discourses, or social regulations. From a structuralist perspective, these more narrow and substantive pragmatic concerns are regarded as epiphenomenal, the manifest expression of some more essential form or underlying structure. This structure delimits the logic and quality of the kinds of connections among actions that may be manifest and, by derivation, the quality of the individual actions and actors that are thus connected. Particular action and interactions, even specific subjective strategies and social regulations, cannot be explicated in their own terms. Rather they must be interpreted and explained with reference to their underlying structure.

To illustrate the concept of a structure and its analytical implications, let us consider two examples intended to parallel one another: the analysis of a hologram and the analysis of society. Most readers are, I assume, familiar with holograms, perhaps having seen one in a science museum. For those who are not, holograms are three-dimensional images created by the intersection of beams of laser light. The lasers used to project the light are carefully positioned relative to one another to produce the desired effect. Each laser projects a different two-dimensional image. At the point of intersection, these images combine to create the three-dimensional image. For present purposes, let us assume that the image created is that of an automobile.

As an object of analysis, the holographic image of the automobile can be conceived and consequently described and explained in a variety of ways. From a more atomistic perspective, one begins with the specific concrete entities involved in the production of the image. These individual objects are assumed to constitute the essential qualities of the observed phenomenon. Thus description focuses on the laser projectors and their characteristics, for example, the nature of the specific image each projects and how the lasers are positioned relative to one another. At its most elaborated, this yields an account of a system—in this case as a set of lasers, each with its own projection, which stand in particular relation to one another.[8] Explanation follows accordingly. Focus is again on the individual constituent elements of the observed phenomena, the particular lasers. Singly and in combination, they are understood to be causal forces. In this context, the image of the automobile is relegated to the status of an effect and thus ascribed secondary or epiphenomenal status.

A structuralist account of the same phenomena begins rather differently. The essence of the situation is sought through a consideration of its coherence, in the fit among the aspects of what is manifestly observed. This coherence, however, does not itself constitute the essence of the situation. In this view, it is only a manifestation, the result of an "immanent cause" or a virtual or underlying structure. In this vein, the analytical focus shifts from the individual lasers to the holographic image. Description and explanation are offered accordingly. Description centers on the qualities of the image. Thus the account offered revolves around the idea of an automobile and how it is elaborated in the differentiation and juxtaposition of the specific elements of the image in question. Thus the description focuses not on the lasers and their contents, but on the parts of the automobile, the tires, steering wheel, hood, and so on, and how their interrelationship expresses the idea of a car. Explanation is cast similarly. The essential cause is the idea of the automobile. It becomes manifest in the creation of the holographic image. This then determines that lasers will be used, what image each laser will project, and how the various lasers will be positioned relative to one another. Reversing the conceptual prioritization of the atomistic approach, it is the virtual dimension of the event that is considered essential and the concrete elements of its expression that are regarded as epiphenomenal.

This contrast of atomistic and structuralist analysis may be readily extended to the task of making sense of society. Adopting an atomistic approach, analysis focuses on the individual, concrete observable elements of society, that is, the particular actors involved and what they do to one another. In this light, the description of a society or group becomes a matter of describing the members of the group. The focus is on their nature, especially their attitudes, capacities, and proclivities to act, as they relate to how those individuals behave toward and react to one another. Society is then characterized both as the aggregate of these individual level characteristics and with reference to the evident patterns of specific action and reaction. Such collective notions as institutions and culture are conceived and described accordingly. Individuals and their characteristics are again the point of departure for explanation. The causal force in social life is the individual. It is she, as the author of her own action, who in interaction with others produces the social life they share. Cast in these terms, social analysis becomes most fundamentally a microsociological or psychological inquiry. Good examples of this are provided by Almond and Verba's classic study of civic culture (1963) or Inglehart's more contemporary analysis of postmaterial values (1990).

Again the structuralist approach suggests a completely different analytical strategy. Concrete social behavior and the nature of individual actors are understood to be epiphenomenal, the expression of some integrative, determining reality. This reality does not inhere in the specific behaviors or actors that may be directly observed. It can only be inferred from the relationships that exist (or cannot exist) among those behaviors and actors. Thus explanation focuses on the virtual structure of society. It is assumed that this structure constitutes an organizing, defining force that produces and orchestrates the patterns of concrete social exchange. As a result, individual actors and the way in which they engage one another are regarded not as the causes of social life, but as its outcome. So oriented, structuralist description eschews psychological considerations of such individual-level phenomena as the attitudes people hold or the particular action they initiate and avoids constructing any empirical generalizations based upon them. In this view, these atomistic concrete "facts" are by nature partial, fragmentary expressions of the sense and organization of the underlying structure. Instead, structuralist description focuses on the qualities of collective life itself and the manner in which it is internally differentiated. Consequently, description is cast in the language of class, gender, hierarchy, and so on. The latter are regarded as the constructed elements of social life. As structured outcomes, these elements of collective life are not understood in their own terms, but with reference the general underlying structure of interaction, discourse, or power, which differentiate these elements from one another and determine the shape which each takes. Foucault's description of types of punishment (1979) and Habermas' discussion of types of discourse (1987) provide good examples of this structuralist approach.

This focus on underlying structure in the analysis of social phenomena poses a difficulty. Unlike specific courses of personal action or particular social exchanges, structures cannot be directly observed. Their nature must be inferred from the ways in which the observed phenomena cohere. The problem is that the nature of the phenomena themselves, that is, their elemental nature and the kinds of relationships that are being manifest, can only be properly apprehended with reference to their underlying structure. For example, we cannot know whether the meaning and quality of the assertion "$2 \times 2 + 6 = 10$" until we determine whether it is an expression of an arithmetic combination of specific relationships or a specific example of a more general algebraic formula. Of course, the interpretative tool we need, the underlying structure, is the target of the inquiry and at the outset is itself unknown. The methodological result is that structuralist analysis is something of a bootstrapping exercise. Beginning with an observed system of intertwined relationships, one must seek to discover some common form. This provides a first conception of the underlying structure. The utility of this initial conception is then assessed by examining the degree to which it captures not only the few observations from which it was derived, but if other particular relationships may also be accounted for in these terms. If they can, then something of the validity and power of the concept of the structure advanced is demonstrated. If additional relationships cannot be accounted for, then the conception of the underlying structure must be reworked to encompass the new observations.

Although he antedates the structuralist movement, Freud's analysis of the unconscious provides an excellent example of this process. The problem for him was to discover the coherence in the odd sets of behaviors initiated by his patients and in the collage of events depicted in their dreams. At the outset, he assumed such a coherence existed even if it was not apparent. In so doing he suggested that the underlying form or structure of neuroses or dreams was different than that of rational or conscious thought. It was a product of the unconscious. Thus Freud concluded that the observed incoherence of the neurotic syndromes or dream content was a result of improper interpretation rather than intrinsic lack of meaningful integration. Pursuing this course, Freud made a series of attempts to characterize the nature of the unconscious. In each instance, he adopted the same basic strategy. An underlying structure was inferred. This structure was then drawn upon to interpret the essential meaning of what appeared to be organized, but not in any comprehensible fashion. The adequacy of this structural interpretation was then tested through application to the analysis of his patients or in reflections on himself and on culture. Where elements of the observed situation did not appear to cohere in the manner expected, an attempt was made to reconstruct the orienting conception of the underlying structure so that they might be meaningfully incorporated. In this manner, Freud offered a number of solutions, from his early analysis of the structure of dreams (1955) to the consideration of the interplay of Eros and Thanatos (1930).

A Pragmatic Structuralism

In most structuralist writings, particularly those that follow in the tradition of de Saussure and Lévi-Strauss, structure is conceived in rather static terms. It is a form of relationship that is then variously expressed in the particular relationships one may directly observe. In this view, the formal qualities of a structure are conceived quite independently of the nature of the specific content upon which it operates. To the degree to which there is a connection between the two, it is unidirectional. Structure determines content. Like a deity, it gives form to an otherwise amorphous substantive reality. The content has no reverberating effect on the structure.

Consistent with my more pragmatist leanings, I draw more heavily on a conception of structure that is cast in more active and dynamic terms. In so doing, I draw on structural Marxism, such as that of Louis Althusser, and more especially on the genetic structuralism of Jean Piaget. From this perspective, a structure is a formal system that is itself an elaboration of a process of structuration. Thus structure is itself understood as an outcome of a particular mode of praxis or operation, depending on the theoretical tradition being adopted. The structuration process occurs as the structuring mode of operation is realized in the particular things that are done. For Piaget this transpires in the course of actually attempting to operate on things in a personally directed way. For the structural Marxists this occurs in the course of actually regulating social interaction in a manner determined by the mode of production. In either case, the mode of operation or regulation is realized in concrete social exchange. The result is the construction of relationships that are substantively different but share a common formal quality. In the process, the otherwise indeterminate flow of action is constituted as a structured activity.

To illustrate this structuration process, let us consider both a psychological and a sociological example. Consider first the psychological case of a structure of thinking. The assumption here is that the various relationships an individual infers share qualities that reflect the manner in which she forges connections. This mode of thinking delimits the structure of her thought. For example, one mode of thinking entails abstracting actions from the flow of events and then reconnecting them in an atemporal, somewhat decontextualized frame of reference. This involves beginning with one of the actions, using it as a kind of conceptual anchor, and then placing other actions in relationship to it. This mode of thinking constitutes the individual's general capacity to engage and thereby make sense of her environment. In the course of the concrete experiences the individual has, this capacity gets elaborated as a set of specific understandings of what the world consists of and how it works. For example, the individual may be confronted with the problem of making sense of another person.[9] In the structured terms of her reasoning, the attempt to understand a person consists of using that individual as the cognitive anchor and then collecting all the actions that are linked to her. This will include the set of things the person does and has done to her by other people or by circumstances. The result is the discrete category of that person. This particular cognitive construction has two aspects. It entails the construction of a substantively grounded definition of a particular person, and it constitutes an instance of the elaboration of a general type of categorical relationship. In the latter regard, other attempts to make sense of other people or other social objects (such as a social group or nation-state) will yield categorical constructions that are constituted in the same way and evidence the same basic underlying structural form.

Another problem that typically arises when an individual thinks in the aforementioned manner is one of explaining why an observed action occurs. The mode of thinking is the same; it begins with the focal action as an anchor and seeks to establish its observable connection to other concrete actions. The problem is solved when the anchor is connected to an antecedent action or series of actions. The latter is defined relative to the former as its cause. The result is a particular causal explanation of specific action now understood as an effect. In the process, not only is a specific understanding reached but another formal relationship, that of linear causality, is constructed. Like the categorical relationship already discussed, this causal relationship constitutes part of the structure of the understanding that this form of thinking produces. It will be evident in the various particular causal relationships stipulated in the course of explaining whatever other actions become objects of attention and thought. More generally, the two kinds of relationships, categorical and causal, are understood to share common qualities, for example, the reliance on a concrete conceptual anchor. This commonality is explained in terms of the single process of structuration that produces both types of conceptual relationships.

The foregoing example is psychological, but the same basic structure may be elaborated at a social or collective level. Consider the case of the social regulation of exchange. This would involve a form of praxis in which specific actions are abstracted from the flow of events and then the connections among them are specified in concrete and specific ways. Here again this may be accomplished by the selection of an orienting concrete anchor to which other abstracted concrete actions are connected in an atemporal frame of reference. This basic mode of social regulation, when realized in the coordination of particular exchanges, yields various types of relationships which share a common structure. For example, one such relationship involves the definition and distribution of power. In the present instance, power is defined and power relationships are constructed in the course of social regulation that involves a focus on one action and connecting others to it. In this context, power is construed as a force that has a linear causal structure. It inheres in a prime actor or action that then causes other actors and action. The power inheres in the capacity to produce an effect. This effect may in turn produce other effects, that is it may lead to the direction of other actors and action. Several iterations of this relationship yield the classic chain of command. Such a chain of command or hierarchalization of power constitutes the basic form of institutional relationship in such a structured society. As such, this type of power relationship should be evident across the various specific sites of social organization (e.g., the family, the workplace, or the government).

In the governance of day-to-day life, another function that is performed involves the distribution of specific behaviors among individuals. For a society that is formed through the concrete, anchored form of regulation described immediately above, this distribution is accomplished through the definition of specified roles. Each role consists of an anchor, a particular place in a given situation. An example might be that of adult male in a nuclear family. The role is then constructed as a set of specific behaviors that should be performed by the role holder as well as a set of specific behaviors that should be directed toward him. The structuralist claim here is that the several kinds of relationships that combine to determine the coherence of social interaction and discourse in a given society are commonly structured and therefore share a common form. Thus the relationship among actions and actors designated by the regulations of role is presumed to be structurally isomorphic to the relationship among actors and actions designated by the regulations of power.

To reiterate in light of the foregoing psychological and sociological examples, the structured quality of personal and social life requires that social observation be conducted in a self-consciously interpretative manner. For example, Angele may be observed to tell Phillip to perform a specific behavior and then Phillip may be observed to respond as instructed. The question then arises regarding what exactly has been observed. Assuming that the interaction is structured according to the foregoing examples, one might view the matter from a social perspective and reasonably infer that the interaction consists of an elementary exercise of power within a hierarchically ordered relationship. Assuming the same structure is operative at a psychological level, one might consider the point of view of the superior, Angele, and reasonably infer that her command is understood by her to be a simple cause to which Phillip's behavior is the effect. The key point is that the interpretation depends on assumptions regarding underlying structure.

If other modes of structuration are operative, the social and psychological dimensions of the interaction would have to be conceived quite differently. For example, it might very well be that the observed interaction was a consciously exploratory moment in an ongoing negotiation between Angele and Phillip over the rules whereby the relationship between them will be governed. Similarly at a more psychological level, it might be that Angele regards her initiative and Phillip's response as a complexly determined phenomenon, that is, one which is defined and determined by the interplay of several factors, such as her way of understanding their exchange, his way of doing the same, and the cultural norms prevalent in the larger social environment the two of them share. In this second context, the concrete interaction between Phillip and Angele is constituted quite differently from the first one mentioned. It suggests a different underlying structure, one in which structuration involves constructing an overarching frame of reference within which the concrete particulars of the situation are actively interpreted relative to the relationship assumed to exist between them. The outcome of a different mode of social regulation or cognitive construction, the interaction has a qualitatively different meaning, will be produced under different sorts of circumstances and lead to different sorts of effects. In other words, the very social and psychological reality of the interaction varies with the manner of its structuration.

Structures, Structuration, and History

This focus on a mode of structuration rather than on structure per se has several important conceptual implications. Most significant for our purposes, it opens up form to content and gives structures a history. In a more static structuralism, the formal structure is an inert abstract entity. It is an immanent force that exercises a determining, transforming, and constituting force on manifest social realities. In this regard, the structure is a first cause: it produces effects but is itself unaffected. Therefore structures do not have history, they exist beneath history and are expressed through it. In this light, Lévi-Strauss can conclude that social inquiry may begin with a concrete historical analysis, but this is only a first step that must be transcended.[10]

Structuration constitutes the means whereby aspects of a structure are initially produced and then maintained over time. The activity of making connections yields not only a specific substantive relationship that is structured in a particular manner, it also produces and reproduces the general form of relationship of which the particular case is an example or single manifestation. In this latter regard, the quality and persistence of structures are dependent on the ongoing manner of their realization in the actual making of connections and coordination of action. Thus in the constructive activity of structuration, the formal and the general qualities of the structure of discourse and social interaction are immediately related to the concrete nature of what actually occurs in specific instances. As the former conditions the qualities of the latter, so the latter conditions the qualities of the former. In the second half of this reciprocal relationship, the possibility of conceiving a history of structures is introduced. In a static structuralism, structures simply determine. Conceived in this manner, they cannot be subject to influence outside of themselves. In a more dynamic pragmatic structuralism, the quality of structured relationships depends on the specific manner in which they are realized. Consequently, the formal structure may itself be transformed by the concrete, particular conditions of how it is realized in the coordination of specific social exchanges. This introduces the possibility of the transformation of structures and thus a history of these transformations.[11]

Such a historical analysis distinguishes Marxist and Piagetian structuralists from the mainstream of structuralist work. Theorists of these two types speak of stages of structural development in societies or individuals. Before going further I would like to note that I view this history differently than adherents of either of these two streams of dynamic structuralist analysis. Both social and psychological structuralists tend to view the consequences of structural transformation in totalizing terms. When a structure is transformed, the entirety of personal meaning-making or social regulation is restructured accordingly. Whereas I sympathize with this aim and understand it as following from the logic of a structuralist analysis, I suggest that social and psychological realities are a bit more complicated than this.

Consider the case of subjectivity. In their psychological theorizing, Piagetians offer a totally transforming conception of structural change. With the development of cognition, the manner in which an individual reasons is transformed. Not only is all subsequent experienced constructed in these newly structured terms, but prior experience, once brought to mind, will be reconstructed in this manner. I believe this view misunderstands the nature of memory and its relationship to personality formation. The Piagetian account of the stages of an individual's cognitive development from childhood to mid-adolescence suggests that the child's understanding of her experience is structured very differently than her later adult understanding. In the case of the child, reasoning is tied to the flow of present events. Immediate experience tends to fill the cognitive field, encompassing the child's considerations at the time. As a result, the import of a current event looms large and its effect is likely to be more emotionally overwhelming. In addition, the child's conception of experience is global. Elements of the events are crudely distinguished and the line between these elements, the various objects and actors involved, tends to be readily transgressed. The adult's thought is more abstract, differentiated, and integrative. As a result the adult tends to place experience in the context of other experience and thus mitigate the immediacy of its effect. In addition, the elements of events are more readily distinguished from and then self-consciously related to one another. Thus the permeability of boundaries characteristic of childhood thought is largely eliminated.[12]

In Piaget's view, when an adult reflects on a childhood experience or is directly exposed to similar experience as an adult, she naturally reconstructs and thus redefines the childish understanding in adult terms. As suggested by the brief distinctions made above, the adult contextualizes the child's experience thereby reducing its emotional impact. Similarly, inappropriate associations are rejected and replaced with relationships constructed in an adult manner. In my view, this is often not what in fact happens. Instead, earlier experiences are encoded in memory in their structurally distinctive manner. Depending on the circumstances, when these memories are evoked later, they are represented as they were structured in childhood. This "past" structure may then not only continue to define the experience as it was understood by the child, it may also determine how the circumstances of its current evocation are understood and responded to by the adult. In metaphorical terms, the view of cognition I am suggesting is one of a sedimentation of structures. Thinking consists of structurally differentiated layers of understanding, each of which was elaborated during a particular period of the individual's development. These structures are not wholly alien to one another. Through self-reflection, the concerns of earlier or lower ones may be translated into the terms of later or higher ones. This translation, however, does not constitute an authentic understanding (this can only be articulated according to the structure of the initial experience), nor is it necessarily a source of self-transformation.

Here I only present this sedimentary view of the individual as a largely unsubstantiated claim. As such it merely constitutes a direction for further conceptual development and empirical investigation. For now, I offer suggestive illustration. The sedimentation of structures of understanding within a single individual may be evident in the relative difficulty one has in translating the sense of childhood memories into adult language. For example, one may remember the texture of the feelings that followed the sudden death of a parent when one was young or the punishment administered by a loved authority figure. At the same time, one may have a clear feeling of the inadequacy of one's attempts "to put into words" the sense of that remembered experience. In that feeling of inadequate representation, we find evidence of the coexistence of past and present forms of understanding, that of the remembered experience and that of the current words or frame of reference in which we are trying to place it. At the same time, in our inability to express our sense of childhood experience adequately in present terms, we find evidence of the relative incommensurability of meanings constructed through the two modes of reasoning.

This example may be taken a step further when we consider the susceptibility of childish understandings to later efforts to reconstruct them in a manner consistent with the structure of adult thought. In a sense, this is precisely the task of most psychotherapeutic discourse. For the child who suffers the sudden death of a parent, adulthood may be plagued by a fear of intimacy and by attempts, often counterproductive, to maneuver relationships to protect against abandonment. Whether in formal psychotherapy or just in friendly conversation, the adult may engage in a self-reflective attempt to address the childhood understanding and to recognize its current effect on the adult's visceral response to intimate relationships. The common and frustrating discovery adults make is how manifestly resistant those earlier understandings are to attempts at reconstruction and change. The ability to talk about and "come to a mature understanding" of the childhood roots of one's behavior often does not produce the desired redirection of feeling or behavior. This suggests the structural nature of the difference between these understandings and the consequent relative inaccessibility of one sediment/era of understanding to another. In addition, this also suggests something of the consequences of the sedimentation of understandings for personality formation.

As in the case of psychological structures, I also believe that social structures are more complexly constituted than structural theorists commonly suggest. Here of course the issue is not one of memory. Following the lead of such post-structural theorists as Michel Foucault, I believe that collectivities are less coherent and uniform than structuralist theorizing would suggest. Rather than a structured whole, a society is a complex of locales of social organization that may be structured differently.[13] These differences may be related to the history of social transformation. Some sectors of social life may be more central to the newly emergent structure and be transformed according to new forms of regulation more quickly than more peripheral sectors. The latter are simply less relevant to the new form of organization and hence less subject to pressures for change. An example of this is the relatively slow transformation of the family as compared to that of the marketplace during the emergence of the modern, capitalist form of life. The result is that different forms of regulation coexist in the same society at the same time.

Apart from structural centrality or relevance, an additional issue that must be considered here is that of power. Different groups in a society have more access to resources that confer power. Insofar as the status of these groups is a product of a particular social structure, they will tend to actively resist structural transformation, even after it has begun to regulate social exchange. Depending on their resources, this resistance may prove effective in at least delaying social changes that directly impinge on their internal functioning. Thus given its relatively great resources, an institution like the Catholic Church can continue to sustain its hierarchical structure and authoritative ideology against the onslaught of capitalism, democracy, and multiculturalism with their demands for autonomy, critique, and creative exchange even as other hierarchical institutions are swept away or transformed. Similarly, the resilience of advantaged groups that are differentiated on the basis of now-contested categories of gender and nationality can be understood in these terms.

Finally I would like to note in passing that social fragmentation may be induced and sustained at a local level by variation in the needs and capacities of the individuals involved. Anticipating the discussion of the duality of structuration that follows, I suggest that social organization is in part a product of the purposive attempts of individuals to engage one another. It therefore necessarily reflects something of their capacity to direct their own action and respond to that of another. Insofar as the structural qualities of reasoning vary across individuals, we may expect that individuals may be more or less able to meet the demands of social regulation. Insofar as individuals of different abilities congregate at different social sites or locales, we may expect variation across sites in how social interaction and discourse are structured. Thus whereas there may be a relatively dominant or prevalent structure in a given society, psychological factors may contribute to the creation of various sites of exchange that are structured differently. Of course this claim and the others regarding power and structural relevance are stated in such a way as to merely sketch my concerns in this area. As such, they are not elaborated theoretical statements, but rather are markers that point to a direction for further theoretical elaboration and empirical investigation.

Duality of Structuration

As developed thus far, the conception of structural change is linked to the pragmatic embeddedness of structuration in the substance of what is being structured. This calls for an account of the bases of any substantive resistance to the force of structuration and the kinds of coordination that structuration yields. This sets the stage for the discussion of the idea of the duality of structuration that is the keystone of my view of social life. As reflected in the several examples given in the preceding pages, I suggest that social action is structured at two levels, that of subjective reasoning and that of intersubjective or collective regulation. In these terms, both the individual and the collective are forces for structuration. This very general and essentially social psychological claim has a number of specific theoretical implications.

Consider first the implications that follow from the claim that social action is dually determined. As a purposive actor, the individual coordinates her own action in order to operate on the environment and achieve certain ends. Although elaborated in particular ways in specific contexts, this pragmatic coordinating activity has a general quality that is its mode of structuration. This is evident in the formal nature of the connections among actions that are forged. Proceeding in this manner, the individual constructs a subjective definition of the environment she engages and acts upon it accordingly. For example, consider a player who reasons such that she makes sense of the game of chess through identifying pieces by their appearance and then understanding those pieces in terms of the particular ways each can be moved. Such a player is likely to play the game by considering only a single move and its particular consequence. She is unlikely to consider combinations of moves involving herself and her opponent, nor is she likely to think through the multiple possible consequences of any particular move. The key point here is that this way of understanding chess and actually making particular moves in specific game situations is operative despite the fact that chess is socially constructed as a complex game of recursive strategy recognition and formation. Indeed, the individual's mode of playing generally proves quite resistant to pedagogical efforts designed to make it more consistent with the game's inherent structure. In structural terms, the player is destructuring the socially constituted definition of the game and is restructuring it in her own terms.

There are of course more socially relevant examples of this. A case in point is how lovers relate to one another in Britain at the turn of millennium. As nicely discussed by Anthony Giddens in his *The Transformation of Intimacy* (1992), the social structuring of modern love relationships demands that lovers come to an understanding of their own personality, the other's personality, and the sense that each of them is makes of the relationship they share. With this in mind, lovers must then engage one another in an open, trusting, and continuing attempt to craft the terms of their relationship. Giddens refers to this as the "pure" relationship. I believe his description captures much of the current structuring effect of modernity on the regulation of intimate relationships. Here, however, the key issue is that, despite these social demands, many individuals tend to subjectively reconstruct the requisites of relationship according to the structure of their own reasoning. In this vein, the demand to understand a person's way of thinking and personality is often subjectively transformed into a matter of identifying that person's specific wants. Similarly the demand for creative engagement is reconstructed as the need to compromise some of one's own demands in the face of the other's needs. Moreover, the resulting compromise is understood as an enduring rule, a regulation to be followed rather than a tentative agreement that may be legitimately reinterpreted, renegotiated, and revised. In this manner, the individual, through the structural pragmatic nature of her thought, destructs the culturally regulated quality of an intimate social relationship and reconstructs it in her own subjectively structured terms.

In spite of this psychological restructuring, social action is also intersubjectively or collectively structured. Thus an individual may play the game of chess in the concrete, piecemeal manner suggested above, but the game proceeds according to its own social regulations. It remains the interplay of strategies and unfolds accordingly. This is the case even if the individual players do not understand the game in these terms or direct their action accordingly. In such an instance, the individual players will not understand the socially structured meaning of any particular move. They therefore will be frequently surprised and confounded by the short- and long-term consequences that follow from it. Similarly, an individual lover may understand an intimate relationship as the venue for the satisfaction of a set of her own and another's needs according to specific prescriptions for action. Nonetheless, the social structuration of intimacy insures that intimate relationships are a matter of negotiation of the rules of relationship on the basis of mutual understanding and trust. As a result, as with the players in chess, lovers will find the consequences of their initiatives often difficult to predict and their relationships to be unstable, confusing, and often uncomfortable. As suggested by the foregoing examples, a social or intersubjective context structures interpersonal exchange somewhat independently of the purposes pursued by the individual participants in the exchange. In so doing, the social regulation of interaction destructures the subjective intentions and understandings orienting individuals' action and restructures this action in intersubjective or social terms.

This social restructuring of the subjective direction of action is particularly well illustrated by an early experiment of the Swiss social psychologist Willem Doise and his colleagues (Doise et al., 1975; Doise, 1986). Operating within the Piagetian framework, Doise was interested in examining the role that social environments play in facilitating personal cognitive development. Here I use his data to a different end. In my view, the work provides one of the few clear empirical demonstrations of the distinctiveness and power of the social structuring of action. In the first part of the experiment, subjects—children—were tested for their level of cognitive development. Only those subjects who reasoned in a "preoperational" manner were included in the experiment. These children were then asked to perform an initial task. They were presented with a pencil supported so that it stood perpendicular to a flat surface. The support for the pencil was attached to three strings. Together the strings could be pulled or loosened in order to move the pencil. On the surface was a simple drawing. The task was to move the pencil in such a way that it followed the lines in the drawing. This required coordinating the tension placed on the strings. In accordance with the preoperational quality of their thinking, the children were unable to coordinate their pulling and loosening of the strings to guide the pencil adequately.

On a second occasion, the children were given a variation of the task. They were asked to perform in pairs. This second task demanded that two people pull on the strings at the same time in order to maneuver the pencil. As in the initial task, the movement of the pencil was the interactive result of the use of all the strings. Consequently, the second task created an interdependent relationship between the partners in each pair of children. The fascinating result of this second experiment was that together the children successfully performed the task. They were able to guide the pencil so that it traced the lines of the drawing. This suggests that whereas neither child alone could subjectively coordinate the movement of the strings, the two children together could. In the terms of our present discussion, the intersubjective context produced a structured form of coordination that the individual subjects could not produce or even reproduce on their own.

Overall the foregoing examples suggest that social action and discourse are structured both by the individuals involved and by the overarching social context of their interaction. Moreover, the examples make clear that the psychological and social structuration of action may be clearly different from one another. Because the modes of personal and social structuration may differ, there may be formal differences between the structure of subjective understanding and purposive action on one hand and the structure of intersubjective discourse and social interaction on the other. Despite these differences, these two sources of structuration are intimately interrelated because they both operate on the common ground of specific, concrete, interpersonal exchanges. *Consequently, the meaning and regulation of specific action is always dually constituted, both by the individual subject and by the intersubjective or social context.* Referring to the foregoing examples, the chess player's move will always be defined in the context of her subjective understanding and be directed according to her strategies. At the same time, however, the game between the players will be intersubjectively defined and the exchanges socially structured. Similarly, the individual lover may act to satisfy wants and presume the enduring quality of the specific regulations of her intimate relationships. At the same time, her overtures may be regulated according to the structured regulations of Giddens' pure relationships complete with their demand for mutual understanding and creative engagement.

The theoretical claim that social action is dually constituted has a number of important implications for the conception of everyday social exchange. To begin, it suggests that the meaning and direction of a particular action at a given moment will be intrinsically uncertain. Insofar as the action is dually structured, the quality of its connection to other action and its own intrinsic definition is neither a simple product of the individual or of the social context. In any specific instance, both sources of structuration are attempting to operate on the concrete ground of what is occurring and coordinate it in their specific terms. The result is a *structured uncertainty,* an uncertainty bounded by the determinations of both the reasoning subject and the regulating social context. At any given moment of a particular social interaction, the flow of events may be more or less determined by one or the other source of regulation.

To illustrate, imagine the animated discussion between two students, two politically interested undergraduates, dressed in the requisite black, who are considering Foucault's rather abstract analysis of the circulation of power. Let us assume that the conversation is being structured at two levels. (Readers with teaching experience should find quite familiar the following division of the theoretical meaning of statements from the subjective understanding of the student uttering them.) On one hand, the discourse is structured by the intersubjective conception of Foucault's meaning (provided by lecture and classroom discussion), which is manifest in the theoretical rhetoric that the students are using to communicate with one another. This rhetoric carries its own definitions and makes its own connections. At any moment in the conversation, this may lead either individual student from one specific statement to the next. On the other hand, the conversation is being structured by the individual students' subjective reconstruction of the classroom rhetoric regarding Foucault's claims according to the structure of their own way of understanding. This subjective structuration is likely to be quite different from that underlying the rhetoric. As such, it will establish different kinds of connections and therefore lead the student to follow a specific statement with a different one than might be suggested by the classroom discourse. Consequently in the students' conversation, the significance of any statement made is thus intrinsically uncertain. Its meaning and regulation is structured in two different ways at the same time, and therefore what particular statements will follow is rendered indeterminate.

This illustration suggests another dimension of this bounded or structured uncertainty. The dual structuration of action not only results in an inherent uncertainty, but also a tension. Sharing the same ground of operation, the two different structuring forces of subjective reasoning and social determination contravene one another and compete for substantive realization. Each struggles with the other in order to operate accordingly to its own logic. The integrity of either structure is thus placed at risk by the other. In this vein, the individual may move to undermine the power of social regulation by regarding it as nonsensical, inhumane, or simply irrelevant. In complementary fashion, the collective may move to delegitimate the individual's understanding by defining it as silly, stupid, or degenerate. Whereas both moves are extreme, they are suggestive of the range of what regularly occurs. They also indicate something of the occasionally palpable, but always potentially manifest, tension of social interaction and discourse.

The Transformation of Structures:
The Social Psychology of Development

Although potentially different from one another, social and personal structures operate on the same concrete ground of action. Thus far, we have considered the consequences of this for the character of social exchange, that is, its inherent uncertainty and tension. Beyond this immediate effect, there are also more profound structural consequences. In our earlier discussion of the nature of structuration, we noted that the specific manner in which a particular action or discourse unfolds has a reverberating impact on the structures that operate upon it. In the context of a theory of dual structuration, this effect of concrete outcomes on structural determination becomes the avenue whereby collective and individual structures can affect one another.

Where they differ, social and individual structures are continually engaged in an attempt to restructure each other's definition and coordination of specific social interactions. As a result, each level of structuration is regularly confronted with the concrete effects of a systematic effort to coordinate interaction in a structurally different manner from its own. Initially, the result is potentially destabilizing. As the individual's personal structuration of action is regularly compromised, self-doubt ensues. Similarly as collective or intersubjective efforts to coordinate the interaction between individuals fail, they are questioned and delegitimated. This structural destabilization opens up the possibility of a second effect, that of a structural transformation of one level of coordination to meet the manifest pressure exercised by the other level. This reciprocal pressure to restructure that constitutes the developmental dynamic of social life.

The social psychology of individual development. Consider first the social pressure for the structural transformation of the individual. Imagine the circumstance of an individual entering a world of social exchange that is structured differently than her understanding of that world. Oriented by the structure of her subjective understanding, she engages others. She pursues specific strategies and anticipates specific consequences. Problems arise because the social exchange is structured differently than her plans and expectations. As a result, the meaning and trajectory of her action are transformed by the terms of their social regulation. These concrete expressions of her personal reasoning are thereby deconstructed and then reconstructed in a socially structured fashion. Similarly, the reactions or responses that follow are intersubjectively determined in a manner that is inconsistent with her subjective definition. From the perspective of the individual, the immediate consequence is that events often do not unfold as expected and conversations frequently seem not to be understood in the manner intended.

Apart from the immediate surprise and confusion, this social restructuring has a potentially more profound and enduring psychological effect. Where there is a structural difference between the social orchestration of interpersonal exchange and the personal conception of that exchange, we may expect that the disjuncture between the two will be evident across a variety of specific encounters. The individual will regularly be confronted with unexpected consequences and miscommunication. A first effect of this will be a destabilizing of the subjective structuration of action. Confronted by a recurring failure to direct action or affect discourse, the person will develop a pervasive sense of not knowing how to act effectively or communicate meaningfully. The resulting self-doubt may direct the subject inward, to a focus on how she knows rather than on what she knows. She may begin to take the terms of her own under-standing as object. In this manner, she is led to a potentially constructive self-reflection. This process of doubt leading to an objectification of one's ways of understanding is identified by Piaget as central to cognitive development. He refers to this process as one of "reflexive abstraction" (e.g., Piaget, 1970a).

Whereas Piaget assumes in somewhat sanguine fashion that doubt generally will lead to such a constructive outcome, I do not. In my view, self-doubt is typically emotionally costly and therefore will often not lead to productive reflection. In everyday life, a person is generally engaged in the business of defining and getting what she needs. Although often a matter of micromanaging the minutiae of interpersonal exchange, the business is a serious one. The personal cost of misunderstanding and acting inappropriately is potentially quite high. In the immediate context, it is a matter of the failure to achieve one's specific purpose and thus satisfy a particular need. Across situations and over time, the effect is the recurring frustration of one's aims. It may also lead to denigration or outright rejection by one's friends and acquaintances. Thus, the personal experience of the disjuncture between personal understanding and social organization may evoke anxiety and fear. The individual's likely response will be to reject the social circumstances that challenge her ways of acting and understanding. If the individual has the resources, this may entail a denial of social regulation through a forceful and, if necessary, violent reconstruction of the interaction on her own terms. In general, however, an individual lacks such power and her rejection is likely to take the more passive form of withdrawal. Thus she may simply disengage from exchanges that unfold in confusing or unexpected ways. In either case, the individual does not use the challenge posed by the environment as an opportunity for creative exploration and personal development.[14] This personal inclination to reject or withdraw may also receive collective expression. The failure to adapt to the demands of postmodernity and the emergence of regressive social movements discussed in chapter 1 may be understood in this light.

For self-doubt to lead to constructive self-reflection, the environment must be relatively safe and supportive. The cost of making mistakes must not be too great. This requires that other people be patient, sensitive, and responsive. Even when the individual is acting and conversing inappropriately, her purposes must, in part, be recognized and satisfied. In this manner, the consequences of her failure will be diminished. This may then provide the security the individual needs to creatively play with her own understanding of social interaction. She may feel freer to suspend her typical assumptions and modes of reasoning and be more willing to try to create new ways of making sense of events and to experiment with alternative ways of engaging other people.

Social structuration does not only destabilize personal structuration indirectly through its effect on the discursive and interactive results of subjectively defined and directed initiatives. Through explicit cultural messages and the efforts of various agents of socialization (e.g. parents, teachers, employers, etc.), social structuration also operates on personal understandings and strategies at the point at which they are being formulated by the individual. It is thus a socializing force that penetrates individuals' modes of reasoning directly. Here social structuration takes an expressly pedagogical form. This is evident in the various ways in which individuals are offered explicit guidance, in terms they can understand, as to the specific actions and reactions that should be taken in particular settings. This may be a matter of offering specific examples of what to do in a specific situation. Alternatively it may involve highlighting certain elements of the complex flow of social events to which the individual is exposed and indicating how these elements affect one another. Whereas the specifics of any particular example or illustration are cast in the subjective terms of the individual's understanding, the connections among these examples reflect a social level of construction. These connections and the socially structured relationships they reflect are further supported by the introduction of a rhetoric that gives those relationships linguistic incarnation. In the terms of the Russian developmental psychologist L. S. Vygotsky, this overall effort consists of an attempt to establish "a zone of proximal learning."[15] The aim is to create bridges that are anchored in the individual's way of understanding but lead beyond it toward the mode of structuration underlying the social definition of meaning. Here again, the success of any transformative effort depends on providing a supportive environment—that is one that rewards effort and minimizes the cost of failure.[16]

To illustrate this process of socially induced personal transformation, let us return to the example of a traditional lover confronted with the modern regulation of intimacy. In that example, a clear structural disjuncture was posited between the understandings crafted by the lover and the qualities of the interaction defined by the social context. Whereas the former consisted of somewhat isolated rules for specific action, the latter emphasized more general regulations for engaging in a jointly negotiated process of rule construction and change. Here we are interested in the potential for psychological transformation inherent in such a situation.

To begin, the individual's engagement in love relationships is likely to be personally destabilizing. In accord with her way of understanding, the individual assumes that a love relationship is a static connection between two specific people. Each is supposed to act toward the other according to particular rules (e.g., one has sexual intercourse with and only with one's partner, lovers cohabitate, lovers help each other, etc.). As they are understood, these rules imply specific behaviors and are assumed to be natural and enduring. Armed with this vision, the individual then engages others. She plans her action, argues her sense of what is necessary and correct, and anticipates the responses of the other accordingly. The problem is that regularly, if not always, the individual's initiatives lead to unexpected consequences. If this were simply the matter of a breakdown in relationship, this would be understandable. Confusion arises when the other person claims to be in love and appears to often behave in such a manner, yet continues to regularly violate the expectation. The problem is exacerbated by the argument that follows. Here the individual is confronted with a situation in which claims that she believes to be indisputable are challenged and the other person's counterclaims seem vague and somewhat incomprehensible. On top of this, the manner in which the troubled lover argues her position may also be challenged. For her, the correct claim need only be asserted and, if necessary, supported by reference to common cultural practice or authoritative cultural dictate. Yet in discussion, claims made in this way do not have the expected persuasive effect. Indeed, the general argumentative strategy may be discounted. The net result is that specific interactions and conversations do not unfold as expected. She is left with a strong sense of confusion and misunderstanding. As a result, she begins to doubt her way of understanding love and love relationships.

What happens next is very much a matter of circumstance. On one hand, if the individual feels threatened or somehow seriously at risk, it is unlikely that she will productively engage the other. Depending on the situation, two possibilities open up here. One is a forceful restructuring of the interaction. If the lover has control of resources which others, particularly her lover, require, she may be able to force the other person to interact and converse with her on her terms. Alternatively, if the lover does not have this power, she may simply attempt to withdraw. This may include not only leaving the relationship, but also avoiding similar relationships in the future. If, on the other hand, the individual feels secure and supported by her environment (including her lover), her sense of self-doubt may open up the possibility of a restructuring of her mode of engagement. This is facilitated in two complementary ways. The first is very much self-initiated. Confronted with her strategic and communicative failure, the individual may attempt to reflect on her own way of understanding. Rather than relying on her sense of rules of action to guide her assessment of particular situations, she may consider the rules themselves. This in turn requires the creation of a frame of reference for considering these rules. Until this point, a given rule has been considered in isolation and in terms of the particular actions to which each refers. Now the rules must be considered relative to one another. In addressing these issues, a new way of thinking, one involving a more encompassing and integrative mode of constructing relationships, emerges to handle this new cognitive demand. The individual thus begins to understand relationships and act in a manner more consistent with the structure of the social environment in which she is operating.

A second way of facilitating the personal restructuring of an individual's way of understanding is more a matter of direct social intervention. At the same time the individual is engaged in constructive self-reflection, her social environment may provide instructive opportunities designed to assist the individual in seeing how relationships are socially structured. In the case of our lover, other people or mass-mediated stories may highlight the variability of how individual lovers engage one another and provide focused examples of the manner in which they negotiate the specific ways in which they will relate to one another. To supplement these references to specific experience, a new language of relationship, one that provides a vocabulary for representing means of creative engagement, self-realization, cooperation, and the rest may be provided. Together these examples and the associated discourse may stimulate, facilitate, and guide the process of constructive self-reflection. In this manner, the individual may be led to develop a way of thinking more consonant with the structure of the environment in which she lives. She may therefore be able to understand more adequately the particular situations she confronts and to act more effectively in them.

In sum, the social structuration of interpersonal exchange may lead to a transformation in the structure of an individual's understanding and action. This is accomplished in two ways: by blocking the realization of subjective modes of structuration in a manner that leads to reflexive abstraction and by creating a zone of proximal learning that promotes the personal assimilation of socially constructed relationships. The resulting change is not a matter of specific knowledge or practice. Rather the change is deeper and more general. It consists of a transformation of the way in which the individual reasons and coordinates her action. In pragmatic terms, it is a transformation of how the individual knows and then, by implication, a transformation of the quality of what she can know and do.

The social psychology of social change. The dynamic of structural change operates in two directions. Complementing the social impact on individuals is the
pressure for structural transformation that individuals exert on their social environments. It is a pressure that is exerted both on the rules of discourse and on
the norms of social interaction.

The social structuration of exchange consists of the coordination of the
myriad of everyday interactions and conversations that occur among the individual members of a community. This social coordination of exchange does
not require that individual participants direct their own action and orient to
one another in precisely these socially structured terms. Indeed it is probably
more effective when they do not. Rather, social coordination only requires that
the individuals operate as actors in the manner required by specific interactions. For example, in a given society there may be a hierarchical distribution of
power. This reflects a social structuration of exchange that involves a specific
mode of defining roles and role holders and placing them in relation to one another. But the effective regulation of social interaction does not require that the
individuals who populate the hierarchy understand the underlying logic of this
form of social integration. Instead, it only requires that individuals are able to
perceive and respond to its effects—that is, the specific roles that are thus constituted and their implications for specific action in particular situations. Individuals who are capable of understanding this and only this are most effectively
regulated. They can learn what is required, that is, how to specifically behave
when in what circumstance. This is sufficient to insure their active integration
into the larger society. Moreover, insofar as they do not understand the underlying mode whereby this power configuration and its associated cultural
"truths" are constructed, they are likely to understand these social products not
as products, but as in some sense natural or real. This increases the probability
that they will view the demands placed on their behavior as necessary and legitimate and therefore that they will be more likely to comply.

Problems arise when individuals are unable to recognize or adequately understand even the more specific demands placed on their action. In such an instance, these individuals will be largely unable to learn what is required of them
and therefore their interactions cannot be effectively regulated. In structural
pragmatic terms, because the psychologically structured reconstruction of action does not meet the minimal demands of the social structuration of interaction, the latter will fail. Returning to the example of the socially structured hierarchical distribution of power, imagine what will transpire if the individuals
to be regulated reason in a manner that is embedded in the immediate and the

sensory and follows the flow of unfolding events. Thinking in this manner, these individuals focus on what is emergent in the immediate situation. As such, they may be unable to understand the significance of social categories or rules of conduct that begin with definitions and then impose those definitions on events. As a result, they will be unable to learn the distinctions and regulations that the hierarchical distribution of power requires of them. Moreover, what specific behaviors they do learn are unlikely to be reliably sustained over time. Under these conditions, such a social structuring of interaction is unlikely to be realized.[17]

An obvious example of such a psychological undermining of a socially structured coordination of action is one in which children are asked to interact with one another in an adult manner. In essence this consists of an attempt to coordinate their interaction according to a structure of exchange that demands a form of understanding which is largely beyond their capacities at the time. The result is the imposed mode of social coordination is not realized—they typically do not interact in an adult manner. This example raises two points of more general theoretical significance. First, increasing the rewards and punishments that are significant to the children will not produce the desired form of compliance. The key issue is not one of motivation but one of capacity. This makes the management of this situation in the desired socially structured terms largely impossible. Second, in naturally occurring situations of this kind, there is nonetheless an effective institutional response. Typically coordinating entities create degenerate or simplified terms of coordination to produce social results that at least approximate what is desired. This does provide a solution, albeit less than a perfect one, to the social coordination problem created when individuals cannot direct their action in the manner required. Thus in any complex group, we may assume that a variety of modes of social coordination, each of which is functioning at different levels of inclusion, abstraction, and flexibility, are likely to be operative.[18]

In the above circumstances, the pressure placed on the terms of social interaction may be viewed as regressive. Individuals are engaged in a reconstruction of social demands according to their own narrower and concretely specified terms. When individuals' mode of structuration equals or exceeds the level of integration of their collective coordination, however, the pressure for social transformation is exerted in the direction of greater integration and diversity. The immediate effect is also undermining of the social order, but in a different way. In such a case, the social regulation of interaction and discourse may be readily viewed as arbitrary at best and simplistic or silly at worst. In either case, the demands of the social order may be understood, but they are likely to be rejected as illegitimate and even unnatural. There is little sense or internal motivation to comply.

To illustrate this kind of psychological pressure for progressive social transformation, consider the somewhat self-serving example of the faculty of the contemporary university. This institution is basically structured in linear terms. The result is a set of regulations that are authoritatively defined and relatively specific in the behaviors they require. This is elaborated in part as a set of prescribed roles. Each role is defined in terms of the behaviors expected to be performed (e.g., a certain number of classes to be taught in a rather limited way on a limited range of subjects). Control is centralized and power is hierarchical. Both flow from the chancellor or president at the top through to deans and the department chairs and within departments from senior to junior faculty. Giving them the benefit of the doubt, we may assume that faculty reason in a more integrative and flexible manner. As a result, they understand that conventions of practice and definitions of role are the product of a particular mode of coordinating social interaction. In this context, they may regard the regulation of instruction, interfaculty contact, and faculty-student relations to be the somewhat arbitrary product of a certain place and time. Moreover, given their way of understanding social interaction, they may view this arbitrary result and the associated way of defining roles and distributing power to be primitively conceived and fundamentally illegitimate. Therefore, in their everyday behavior, individual faculty may orient their behavior and discourse in ways that reflect a more integrative, flexible, and egalitarian vision of educational practice that they have subjectively constructed. In so doing, they may interact in ways that subvert the conventions of university life and thus create an internal pressure for its transformation.

Here the dynamics of social control are somewhat different than in the preceding case. On one hand, there is no effective institutional or organizational response to the destabilizing effect of this type of individual-level undermining of social institutions. The only satisfactory result is a social transformation that leads to a new level of social construction, one able to offer forms of regulation that in their greater integration and flexibility will be viewed as sensible and legitimate. While the structure of a social system or culture is thus more vulnerable to this kind of transformative influence, it may nonetheless control interaction and sustain itself. In a case such as this, individuals may dismiss the social structuring of exchange, but they nonetheless can understand it sufficiently to act as required if they were inclined to do so. The issue is thus one of motivation rather than capacity. Where the control over resources supports existing social institutions, individual compliance may be compelled. Again this result is a less than perfect one. Compliance without legitimacy requires monitoring and the latter can never be complete. Still where the power arrangements are reinforcing, the social structure can be sustained, even if somewhat imperfectly. This is clearly evident in our example of the university. After all, its basic mode of coordinating exchange has remained unchanged at least for the whole of this century, if not the last two centuries. In the process, errant faculty are regularly returned to the fold through the use of the carrot and the stick or, failing this, they are simply dismissed.

The trajectory of development. While complexities are introduced by the various ways in which the tensions fostered by the dual structuration of action may be resolved, there is a basic developmental logic to the transformative impact that individual and social structuration may have on one another. Consider first the individual. In her efforts to plan action and meaningfully communicate, the individual is always confronted with the twin manifestations of social structure. On one hand, it is evident in the way in which her overtures are reconstructed and thus realized in often surprising and ill-understood ways. On the other hand, it is evident in her exposure to stylized experiences and guiding rhetoric, which are intended to facilitate her recognition of socially structured regulations of interaction and discourse. In the attempt to adapt to the demands of the social context, the individual transforms the nature of her reasoning. This process of adaptation entails a series of structural transformations. At each step, the individual goes through a cycle of active construction, discovery of limits, self-doubt, and reconstruction.

The individual's social adaptation is directed both by the push of constructive self-reflection and the pull of the assimilation of socially structured regulations of interaction and discursive meaning. Together, these two forces define the trajectory of psychological development. The self-reflective aspect is a relatively internal phenomenon. It consists of an individual building on and beyond the terms of her present mode of reasoning. As suggested by Piaget, this begins with the mode of reasoning characteristic of the neurophysiologically determined responses of infancy and proceeds through a series of self-objectifications. At each step in this process, self-objectification consists of the reflective act of taking one's way of thinking as the object and thereby engendering a necessarily higher order of thinking. The result is a developmental progress. It is marked by the emergence of reasoning of greater integration and flexibility. Beginning at the same point, the responses of infancy, and proceeding in the same fashion, through the objectification of the existent mode of reasoning, this self-reflective aspect of structural transformation suggests that all individuals should follow a similar development path. Three successive steps along this path—sequential, linear, and systematic reasoning—are discussed in chapters 3, 4, and 5.

The claim of the universality of the trajectory of psychological development is tempered by a consideration of the socializing aspect of structural transformation. Personal development is stimulated by the destabilizing effect and pedagogical manifestations of the social structure in which the individual is embedded. Insofar as the mode of social structuration varies across or within societies, there will be differences in the nature of the social demands and guidance to which individuals will be exposed. These social influences motivate and facilitate the transformation of the individual's mode of reasoning. This suggests that the extent to which an individual develops will depend on the quality of the social structuration of action that dominates her environment. Where demands are minimal, for example in an environment where social interaction is largely face-to-face and the regulations of exchange tend to remain the same over time, the individual will not have to develop very far in order to operate in a satisfactory manner. But where demands are greater, for example in a context where social interaction tends to involve absent participants and social regulations are actively being constructed, the individual's mode of reasoning will have to develop further. Thus, whereas the trajectory of development is cognitively delimited and universal, the extent of development is socially determined and thus relative.

The development of a society complements that of the individual. Existing modes of social structuration are destabilized by the success of their impact on the individual actors whose action is to be regulated. As these actors are socialized, not only does their mode of reasoning become more socially appropriate, it also becomes more cognitively developed. In the latter regard, individuals become more capable of integrating information, understanding underlying factors affecting action, and critically evaluating the constraints being imposed upon them. One result is that individuals may become increasingly able to understand and thereby manipulate social regulations to their own advantage. Thus the process of socialization, complemented by constructive self-reflection, may produce individual initiatives that are no longer readily coordinated by existing social regulations. In another language, we have a subjectively generated dereification of social norms and definitions. A new level of regulation is then required, one that can operate upon and coordinate the existent regulations, which no longer govern exchange but are self-consciously deployed by actors to their own individually defined ends.

As in the case of psychological development, social development is a matter of building upon and beyond an existing structuration of action. Here the motor is the intersubjective construction of meaning. At any point in a group's history when its members are self-consciously orchestrating existing social regulations rather than being unself-consciously orchestrated by them, the individual members of that group are left to their own devices to try and coordinate their exchange with one another. Prior convention or appeal to some form of social authority no longer suffices. In their attempt to come to some agreed-upon way of interacting, a new basis of regulation will emerge. In making this claim, I do not suggest that the individuals involved intend to create what emerges between them or adequately understand it once it has been established. I expressly wish to avoid such a form of psychological reductionism. New forms of social structuration are not subjectively produced. They are intersubjective products. They operate and can only be understood at that level.

This said, the basic logic of development remains the same. New forms of social regulation, to be most effective, must take the existing and now inadequate form of regulation as their explicit object. This inadequate regulation, now understood and deployed by individuals to direct their personal action, must be intersubjectively addressed. In the process a new mode of engagement must arise to coordinate the form of exchange that has emerged in the attempt to address this new object of social concern. The result is an intersubjectively constituted social-objectification in which the existent forms of social regulation become the object and thus the point of departure for the construction of new forms of social structuration.

This formulation may seem strange because it implies that reasoning and the reflective reconstruction of reasoning are attributes of both individuals and the terms of their social exchange. But this is precisely the point. The aim here has been to argue that social life is structured—that is, it is actively defined and organized. Moreover, this definition and organization is dually constituted by individuals and the social environment that encompasses them. Thus both are sources of social structuration—that is, both are constructive, meaning-making, and directing forces which operate on everyday social interaction. Viewed in the context of the transformative social psychological dynamic that this creates, this suggests that each of these two sources of structuration has the capacity to constructively restructure. This self-transcendence is an ever-present potential both in subjectively directed thinking and intersubjectively directed discourse. The social psychological logic of structural development in either individuals or societies is understood accordingly.

Contingencies. Above I have described the basic trajectory of social and psychological transformation. Again it must be emphasized that this a description of a general transformative potential. While it provides an analytical framework for historical investigation and suggests the possible directions which change may take, the analysis of any particular individual or social group must be grounded in the consideration of the specific circumstances of each case. *Whereas considerations of the interplay of individual and social modes of structuration of action may suggest certain possibilities for either personal or social transformation, the concrete conditions affecting either the individual or the group in question will determine which of those possibilities, if any, are in fact realized.*

In the analysis of an individual's psychological development, it is necessary to consider the dual structuration of that individual's action and the dynamic potential this yields. In this vein, empirical investigation is necessary to determine how an individual is reasoning now, and how and to what extent her social environment is restructuring her social initiatives. Drawing on structural pragmatic theory, an analysis could then be made regarding how the individual would reason if a structural transformation were to occur. It is then necessary to consider the specific factors that will have a decisive affect on what change, if any, actually does occur. Thus the analysis must also focus on such potentially relevant factors as the individual's subjective sense of security, the power and resources that individual has at her disposal, and the possibilities open to her for withdrawal and escape from personally destabilizing social demands. Specific factors such as these will determine the actual trajectory of the individual's development—that is, whether change will occur and whether it will be progressive or regressive.

Similarly mixed concerns must be addressed in the analysis of society. Again the analysis of the dual structuration of social interaction and communication will suggest what transformative potential, if any exists, in the case at hand. This requires an empirical investigation of how social interaction and communication is currently structured. This must include an examination of how and to what extent individuals are restructuring these social and cultural regulations. Drawing on structural pragmatic theory, a determination could be made regarding how interaction and discourse would be socially coordinated if a structural transformation were to occur. To determine what social change, if any, will actually occur, a number of additional factors, particular to the situation at hand, must be considered. This would include a consideration of the extent to which the society in question is fragmented, the way in which relevant resources and hence power are distributed among groups affected by potential change, and the capacity of institutions to absorb individual-level demands without engaging in any fundamental reorganization.

It is important to keep in mind that the nature of the specific factors and their impact on the potential for either psychological or social transformation will vary with the character of the structure currently operative. For example, in the case of the individual, the sense of personal security is relative to the quality of the person's reasoning. Thus in one case, it may be that security consists of the assurance that physical punishment or frustration is not forthcoming. In a second case, it may be that security requires a sense that one is not violating rules in a significant fashion or that how one is viewed in the eyes of others is not at risk. Finally, in a third case, it may be that personal security is understood in such a manner that it depends on a sense that one's action does not threaten the integrity or coherence of one's self. As these three constructions of security are quite different from one another, so are the social conditions that must be met to give the individual a sense of security. Thus whereas the freedom from a threat of physical punishment may be enough to facilitate the transformation of one individual, it may be insufficient for another.

A parallel example for the case of a group could readily be made for what will constitute "resources" in settings that are socially structured in different ways. Where social interaction is structured in such a way that the focus is action and its causes and effects, resources or power will clearly revolve around the ability of particular actors or categories of actors to cause action and produce specific concrete effects. Where social interaction is structured in a way that revolves around principles of exchange and systems of interrelationship, however, resources and power are constituted in systemic terms and will inhere in social regulation itself. Individuals are thus the vehicles of power rather than its source. As resources are defined differently, so they may be deployed in different ways. Clearly, considerations of the conditions of affecting the transformation of these two kinds of social structures must take these differences into account.

Summary. In sum, social life is marked by structured uncertainty, inherent tension, and a transformative potential. All this is realized in the concrete reality of the unfolding events of everyday life. It is on this field of social interaction that both the individual and social structuring forces are operative, each one engaged in an attempt to coordinate the same action according to its own logic. Confronted with each other's contravening efforts, this leads to an attempt to restructure the other's definition and coordination of specific instances of social interaction. Which structural force will succeed in any given instance is uncertain, a complex result of the distribution of the psychological and social resources being deployed at the time. Over time, there is always a possibility for transformational change. Confronted by the limits of their own ability to act or to communicate and guided by the culturally prevalent pedagogy, the individual members of a group are always in the position of potentially reaching beyond their current way of thinking. At the same time, confronted by this development and its consequent delegitimation of existing social regulation, the social structure and culture of a society is always in the position of potentially transcending its present mode of social coordination. Overall, the dynamic of social life creates the potential for social psychological development, a development in which individuals attempt to transcend themselves in order to accommodate to a social formation that, in its effort to coordinate their exchange, attempts to reconstruct itself in order to transcend what individuals are becoming.

When structural transformation does occur, it is qualitative and general. In the case of the individual, it is not a matter of changing particular values, beliefs, or patterns of behavior. Instead it constitutes a basic change in the way the individual reasons about the world. This will be reflected in the qualitatively different way in which the individual reaches conclusions or makes judgments. This in turn will affect the type of objects that are considered and the kinds of concerns that are valued. Similarly in the case of the collective, transformative change is not a matter of changing particular rituals of behavior or culturally prevalent beliefs and values. Again the change is in the underlying manner in which social interactions are coordinated and discourse is regulated. This is reflected in the quality of the interaction and communication that become possible. In the process, rules, institutions, groups, and individuals come to be constituted in a qualitatively different manner.

Having thus stipulated the qualitative and general nature of individual or social structural transformation, it should be remembered that there are limits to the generality of this change. In the case of the individual, a key limiting factor is memory. Memory somewhat circumvents structural transformation leaving the individual with a repertoire of modes of structuring her experience. While this complicates the results of structural changes in reasoning, it nonetheless is the case that the more recent transformation will have broad effects and structure the vast majority of the individual's current action and speech. In the case of a society, the totality of structural transformation is limited by the fragmenta-

tion of society and the exercise of power. Typically, societies are not tightly integrated wholes. Locales of social exchange may operate somewhat independently.
Some may be less central to social interaction as it is being reconstituted and
thus the effect on them may be delayed for long periods of time. Other locales
may be insulated from social change when earlier forms of the locale's constitutive relationships have been invested with resources and power that may resist
changes being imposed. As in the case of the individual, these factors limit the
totality of structural transformation, but the effect remains quite general.

TYPES OF THINKING:
A PRELIMINARY OVERVIEW

This structural pragmatic conception of social life provides the broader frame
of reference within which the particular psychological concerns addressed in
the book are conceptualized. The focus is on thinking. Consistent with the
view explicated here, thinking is assumed to be structured. Consequently, the
various understandings and judgments an individual constructs are assumed to
share formal qualities despite great variation in the substance of what is addressed. At the same time, there is a recognition that thinking is in part a sociohistorical outcome and therefore different individuals may think in qualitatively different ways.

The explication of the three types of thinking presented in the following
chapters is somewhat lengthy and complex. To provide the reader with an
overview of the terrain to be covered, a short description of each type of thinking is offered here. This affords the reader the advantage of a preliminary sense
of the three types of thinking and how they differ from one another. It should
be kept in mind, however, that this sense is very much preliminary and is as
likely to be as distorting as it is illuminating. An adequate understanding will
depend on a reading of the theoretical accounts offered in chapters 3, 4, and 5
and the exemplary interview texts presented in chapter 7.

Sequential Thinking

Sequential reasoning involves the tracking of events as they transpire. The focus is on the immediate and present events observed and the memories of earlier ones evoked. These events are connected to one another by overlaps, in
time as they unfold in a sequence, in space as they exist along side one another,
and in memory as they share aspects of similar appearance or feeling. In all
three cases, each event flows into and becomes the next. As such, any one event

is viewed in a global, largely undifferentiated, and context-specific way. Operating in this manner, sequential reasoning consists of the reenactment of the sequence primarily through actual participation in the repetition of concrete events or by a talking through of the story. Particular events are not abstracted from the sequence and then analyzed in an atemporal fashion to establish cause and effect or category membership.

Sequential reasoning leads to the construction of an understanding of the social world that consists of currently observed and remembered sequences of events. The time of social life is thus limited to a passing present. There is little consideration of events that occur either before or after the sequence in question. Consequently there is little sense of history as a linear progression. Instead there are remembered sequences (personal or collective) that are evoked again and again in a time of observed cycles of repetition. Social space is immediate. The present may evoke memories of absent events, but the other time and place of those remembered events tends to flow into the immediacy of the here and now. In this context, it is difficult for sequential reasoning to construct a sense of the social arena beyond the boundaries of what is currently or recently seen. People are not natural objects of thought, abstracted from the flow of events and then defined as categorical entities. They are understood relative to their participation in a particular sequence, not as an entity across sequences. Similarly, categories of people or social groups, such as classes, ethnic groups, or nation states, are not spontaneously constructed or readily comprehended.

Political concerns are not a natural product of sequential reasoning. It can generate little sense of the importance of nonpresent actors, the dimension of states, the structure of political hierarchies, or the consistent application of laws. Cognizance of the political domain depends on direct exposure through immediate personal experience or mediated contact through television. The focus here will be on the concrete sequence of events observed as isolated vignettes. Although the sequential thinker does not normally think about politics, groups, or hierarchies, they may be present in the environment and communicated through language. Where this is the case, they will either be ignored or reconstructed in sequential terms. Thus, groups and states may be defined with reference to particular representative individuals, national leaders, or symbols (such as their flag). Hierarchies are reduced to the ability of one person to tell another what to do, suggesting very immediate contact between a leader and specific followers.

Sequential evaluation consists of feeling and needing. Embedded in present experience or cued by memory, this evaluation depends on sensory experience (e.g., pain and pleasure). These sensed emotions or reactions are understood as an aspect of the personally experienced sequence of events in which they are evoked. In this regard, subjective and objective dimensions of experience are not well distinguished. The objective dimension is infused with subjective feeling and that feeling is identified with the objective condition under which it is elicited. Sequential evaluations are thus inextricably linked to concrete events and thus to the entire sequence in which those events are embedded. At times, events in a single sequence may elicit different feelings. These simply coexist in the context of the sequence. Because they follow from experience more than define it, sequential evaluations and the internal dispositions they create are very changeable. Based on the individual's direct experience of feelings, sequential evaluations are quite egocentric.

Sequential thinking is not well suited to the activity of verbally negotiating with others. Talk is very much a secondary exercise. It is relevant only as it is implicated directly in events. Even then it is more an accompaniment of action than a domain of its own that is independent of events and can then be applied to those events. When utilized for practical purposes, talk is a learned step toward expediting the unfolding of a desired sequence. With experience of relatively simple and recurring patterns of verbal exchange, sequential reasoning can enable an individual to be very adept at making the verbal moves required to produce the wanted chain of events. In this context, argument is merely a means to achieve satisfaction or avoid undesirable scenarios. A claim here consists simply of a demand or a request for the desired trajectory of events. There is no offer and little understanding of justification. Counterargument (this is understood as a refusal) engenders two comparable responses: a simple reassertion of the initial claim or an attempt to move matters along with physical coercion.

Linear Thinking

Linear thinking involves the analysis of sequences of action that are directly observed or have been recounted by other people. This entails the abstraction of the elemental actions and placing them in atemporal relation to one another. In any particular case, the focus is on a specific action that is then placed in relation to the others. The relationship constructed is imbalanced. One action serves as a conceptual anchor and the others are defined relative to it. Operating in this manner, linear reasoning leads to the construction of understandings that are anchored in the immediate present, but at the same time extend beyond this. Through causal analysis, it can go beyond the present to the past or future to consider an absent cause or effect. Through categorical considerations, it can import general knowledge of the type of action or actor in question and apply it to the present case. Through a match to a learned standard of normal or conventional behavior, absent criterion of what is at once correct and true can also be introduced. Despite the considerable power of linear thought, it remains grounded in present experience—thinking begins there and builds outward. Thus thought is oriented by present conditions or the specific information other people introduce.

The social world constructed through linear reasoning consists of concrete actions—potentially if not actually observed. These actions are extensive; an action is always understood in relation to another action. This may be done in several ways. First, an action may be viewed as a cause or an effect of another action. Strung together in a chain of causation, a linear history of social events may be constructed. People are defined relative to action—they are essentially actors (the causes of action). Second, several actions may also be linked to a common action or actor creating a category of actions. Thus a person may be conceived as the category of the various things she does. Social roles and groups are understood in similar terms. Finally, an action may also be viewed as a step in a standard sequence of actions (e.g., a common practice, ritual, or law). Its meaning and necessity are understood accordingly. In this latter regard, linear thinking is deeply conventional. In these various constructions, the social action in question is generally defined in light of a single linear relationship. Linear reasoning lacks the structure to consider multiple relationships simultaneously. As a result, the understanding of the social world is fragmented, a collage of categorical definitions, causal analyses, and determinations of what is correct.

Politics is viewed as a particular category of social life. It consists of actions and actors that are conventionally labeled as political (e.g., voting) or are associated with government. Like the social world, politics is concrete and active— a fragmented set of stages inhabited by single individuals and groups who perform as actors, each pushing in its own direction with more or less power to affect the behavior of others. Each stage is structured. It is partitioned by alliances (based on common identity and direction) and their associated opponents (defined by different identity and opposed direction). Each stage is also infused by currents of power that are organized into simple hierarchical structures. Connections among political practices or claims are not established except where they are experienced to be in direct association with one another. Consequently, there is little understanding of the general structure of the collectivity or the intersubjective quality of political life.

Evaluating circumstances in a linear manner, a person decides what she specifically wants to do, what concrete others or objects she likes and what sequences of activity are appropriate. Linear evaluation consists of constructing a unidirectional link between an actor or action to be evaluated and another anchoring action or actor that already has a value attached to it. The value of the anchor tends to flow to those actions or actors to which it is related. This evaluative relationship may be causal. For example, if an action is positively valued, actors who initiate such an action or have that action done to them may be positively valued. The relationship may also be categorical. An actor who is positively valued will tend to transfer her positive value to all the elements, actions, beliefs, preferences, and so on that constitute the actor. Similarly, if a group is positively valued, then all members and activities of the group will tend to be positively valued. The result is definition and evaluation often imply each other in linear thought—common concrete identity or categorization produces common evaluation. Alternatively, common evaluation produces common categorization. Finally, the relationship may involve placing a sequence of actions relative to prevailing social conventions or with regard to what normally occurs. Prior personal judgments, social conventions, and cultural dictates are generally the bases, not the object, of evaluation. As a result, values and conventions are typically reified.

Linear thinking produces a discursive style which, while crude, is nonetheless suited to the requirements of rudimentary argument. The purpose of conversation is to produce action that is desired, good, or normal. This is achieved through an attempt to persuade by giving reasons. This consists of linking the object of contested value to other objects (actions, actors, or social conventions) that have established value. These reasons are themselves not evaluated or justified. When confronted with counterclaims, the linear response is to simply reassert the initial justification and when necessary, perhaps add another concrete evaluative link (e.g., this is good because it makes Tom happy and, in addition, it is normal behavior). Within the context of linear thought, argument consists of a clash of assertions of fact or value. The conflict is practical—both cannot be true or right in a particular case. Resolution requires that one of the participants surrender to the authoritative force of the winning claim. Failure to agree tends to lead to mutual withdrawal, dislike, and possibly physical conflict.

Systematic Thinking

Systematic thinking is an essentially interpretative activity. It involves making sense of events by juxtaposing the concrete relationships among interactions and propositions. In this manner, a number of observed actions and assertions of fact or preference may be considered simultaneously. Always juxtaposing, there is an overarching inclination toward interpretation, toward understanding the specifics of what is considered in a context. There tends to be a synthesis of the narrow and the particular into the broad and the abstract, and a complementary analysis of the general into its particulars, which facilitates the induction and deduction characteristic of systematic thought. On one hand, this leads to the construction of systems with the attendant concerns of integration and coherence. On the other hand, it leads to the construction of principles with the related considerations of lawfulness and levels of generality. The resulting conceptual frameworks provide a basis for a consideration of the possible and the hypothetical in conjunction with the here and now. They also provide a basis for a reflection on the activity of reasoning itself with reference to its embeddedness, coherence, and logic.

The systematic view of social life focuses on the social interactions and discourses that occur in communities and on the purposive actions and subjective claims of individuals. At the level of either individuals or collective entities, these substantive interactions and specific propositions are understood either to be integrated into systems of interaction or meaning or to be examples of classes of interaction that are regulated by underlying principles of relationship. The description of events is therefore regarded as a necessarily interpretative act and explanation necessarily invokes some underlying hypothesis and broader theory. Analysis is conducted at two quite distinct and sometimes incompatible levels, that of the individual and that of collectivity. In the systematic view, an individual is both a subject who constructs and is oriented by her own understandings and a personality wherein her beliefs, actions, and needs are integrated. The statements a person makes and her interaction with others must be understood in one of these two systemic contexts. A social group consists of a weave of interactions and cultural claims. Thus it is defined with reference to its organization (of interaction) and its culture (of meaning). In this frame of reference, groups are not conceived with regard to qualities of the individuals involved. Instead individuals are conceived as abstract placeholders who only gain particular definition as they are implicated in specific interactions.

Systematic reasoning generates a relatively powerful and integrative conception of political life. The focus is on specific political interactions, but these are always understood in a context—either that of a broader system of interactions or an overarching principle of relationship. These contexts are regulative and definitive; they determine the dynamic of the relationship among interactions and the meaning of any one interaction. Consequently, the analysis of a political event always requires interpretation. This often leads to a two-tiered understanding of political phenomena, such as in the case of the exercise of power. On one level it consists of the apparent control one person has over another. At a more fundamental level, it consists of a societal force that both distributes control across individuals and delimits the ways in which that control may be used.

Politics is understood from both a systemic and a principled perspective. Approached from a systemic perspective, politics is viewed as a subsystem, one that is differentiated by the function it performs in maintaining the integrity of the larger social system. Where social integration breaks down, chaos and conflict ensue, and governmental intervention is required to restore coherence. This may involve the creation of law and subsequent enforcement or an attempt to manipulate existing cultural beliefs or to introduce new ones. Approached from a principled perspective, the notion of a sociocultural system recedes into the background. In the fore is politics. Here it consists of the interplay between the regulation imposed via the rule of law and the creation of that regulation through the participation of the individual interactors subject to it. Both regulation and participation are conceived relative to general principles of interpersonal exchange. As in the systemic view, politics deals with conflict. Here, however, the aim is not to eliminate conflict. Rather conflict is assumed, and the aim is to contain and direct it so that it may be utilized to productive political ends. This principled approach tends to yield a concept of political and social life based on universals of social exchange and discourse.

Systematic evaluation is a matter of interpretation and judgment. The focus is on specific interactions, social conventions, cultural norms, expressed preferences, categorical definitions, and explanatory claims. These represent different types of potential objects of evaluation. Although initially recognized in its own terms, each of these objects is juxtaposed relative to others in a broader frame of reference and its meaning is thus determined. Once they are properly interpreted, value objects are then judged. This is done with reference to the larger context, be it a system or a principled relationship, in which they are articulated. Critical to any systemically oriented judgment is the integrity of the system in question—its integration, coherence, elaboration, and basic stability. In this light, the value of an interaction, preference, or claim is judged by the role it plays in maintaining the system of which it is a part. The resulting judgments are essentially relative to the functional requirements of the individual or community in question. When principled concerns are introduced, evaluation extends to include a consideration of the requirements of cooperation and agreement. The resulting consideration of what is just or fair in the exchange between individuals or communities tends to suggest more universal social values. In either case, the evaluation is understood to be a constructed outcome, the product of reflection or argument.

Systematic thinking yields a relatively sophisticated understanding of argument and a capacity to use it for purposes of personal and social development. Argument is understood to provide a means whereby individuals may enter each others' reflections on their interpretations and evaluations and thereby contribute to the construction of a better understanding of truth and right. In this context, particular claims are understood to have little intrinsic meaning. As a result, the attempt to judge another's claims or to present one's own claims reflects a recognition of the need to address the broader concerns of one's own and the other's subjective understandings. Arguments are then crafted so as to bridge subjective differences and to create a common ground for constructive discussion. Whereas the aim is to come to agreement, disagreement is anticipated and respected where legitimate procedures of discourse and reflection are followed. Typically the latter is understood to require that individuals express themselves in a sincere, logical and coherent fashion and that their engagement with one another be conducted in an open, free, secure, and respectful manner.

In the following three chapters, these three types of thinking—sequential, linear, and systematic—are described in more detail. In each case, the description is offered in several parts. To provide the requisite foundation, description begins with a characterization of the mode of reasoning characteristic of each type of thinking and the general structure of understanding that this produces. In the latter regard, the focus is on the quality of the relationships that are constructed and the kinds of objects that are thereby related. Following this the nature of the substantive understandings generated by each type of thinking is addressed. First there is a focus on social reasoning. Of concern here is how social interaction, other people, and oneself are understood. Second, there is a description of political reasoning. Here the focus is on how the polity, power, institutions, and citizens are understood. In the final part, attention shifts from understanding to evaluation. Discussion here focuses on the way in which judgment and evaluation are conducted and the kinds of values this generates.

Chapter Three Linear Thinking

In this chapter I present an account of linear thinking. Although it is the second step in a developmental sequence, I begin with linear thinking because it is likely to be the most familiar. While it does not conform to the normative requisites of what may be designated fully logical or rational thought, linear thinking is probably the type of reasoning most frequently utilized in modern industrial societies. In this regard, the reader will find the account of linear thinking presented here to reflect a great deal of what is encountered in everyday life, including the preoccupation with fad, fashion, and social identity. Linear thinking is also evident in the conventionality and simplicity with which personal and political events are explained and judged.

For the reader who is aware of contemporary psychological research, the nature of thinking described in this chapter will appear familiar in another way. Linear thinking dovetails with much of the account of social cognition offered by social psychologists. In this regard, the description of thinking offered in this chapter reinforces and is reinforced by a vast amount of social psychological experimentation. That said, the characterization of thinking offered here differs in two critical respects. First, it suggests that the various aspects of social cognition researchers have identified are manifestations of a single form of thinking. Thus it is argued that there is a common structure, that of linear thought, underlying the apparently distinctive character of each of the various ways in which social psychological experiments have demonstrated that individuals attribute causality, deploy their schemas, balance their evaluations, construct their arguments, or have their social perceptions and identities mediated by social categories. Second, a central claim made here is that thinking takes different forms. This contradicts the dominant view in social psychology that all people think in basically the same way. The view presented here suggests that although a majority of adults in contemporary advanced industrial societies will think in a linear fashion most of the time, not all adults will do so, even in this single sociohistorical context. To the contrary, some will reason most of the time in a systematic fashion (as described in chapter 4) and others will reason in a sequential fashion (as described in chapter 5). In these cases, there will be little evidence of the cognitive consistency, attribution errors, social identifications, or arguments typically evidenced by the majority of subjects examined in the current social psychological research.

THE MODE OF REASONING AND THE GENERAL
STRUCTURE OF THOUGHT

Linear reasoning involves the analysis of sequences of action that are directly observed or have been recounted by other people. The focus is on concrete actions, the particular things that are done or said. These actions are abstracted from the sequential unfolding of events and are considered within an atemporal frame of reference. Several actions can thus be considered at the same time, and the manner in which each follows from or leads to another can be examined. The actions are understood by placing one in relation to another. The relationship constructed is imbalanced or unidirectional. It depends on the location of one action that serves as the conceptual anchor. Other actions are linked to this anchor and thus defined relative to it. As a result, the understandings produced by linear thought are ground in the concrete particulars of the actions to be understood and the specific active links that are observed or reported to connect one action to the next.

Operating in this manner, linear reasoning is oriented by three structurally equivalent kinds of questions. (1) What is the consequence or what is the antecedent of an observed action? This leads to a simple linear causal analysis. The observed action serves as an anchor. A search is then initiated for typically one antecedent or consequent action. This action is located either through direct perception or on the basis of verbal report and is then defined relative to the anchoring action as its cause or effect. (2) What actions are the result of the same cause or produce the same effect? This type of question leads to a categorical analysis. Linear categories are constructed by observing a specific action or actor, the conceptual anchor, over time. Specific attention is paid to those actions that lead to or follow from it. These actions are then grouped together to define the elements of the linear category of the anchoring action or actor. (3) What is the correct sequence of actions that should unfold in a particular circumstance? Here the focus is on a whole sequence of actions. The sequence is then considered relative to a preexisting representation of what sequence should unfold in the circumstances in question. The representation derives either from personal experience of what typically occurs or from others' statements of what should occur. This defines the normal order and content of the standard sequence. This standard or rule is then used to evaluate the appropriateness of the current sequence of actions under consideration. Characteristic of linear thinking, the analysis of what is and what should be coincide in this determination of the standards of correct action.

In answering these questions, linear reasoning relies on what is present (or is presented by other people) but goes beyond what is apparent. An observed sequence of events is readily decomposed into its constituent actions, actors, and objects. Through the observation of the active links between these constituent elements, the sequence is then easily reassembled. Metaphorically speaking, linear reasoning enables a person to take the motion picture of an event, analyze each frame into its elemental actions, and then reassemble the whole in light of the active links that lead from one frame to the next. In this sense, linear relations are analytical and synthetic. They isolate elements and place them relative to one another. These two activities, however, are not integrated. Analysis, guided by the qualities of the appearance or verbal report of the phenomena in question, abstracts the elemental actions (and actors). Subsequently synthesis, guided by the observation or report of the active links among the elements, then relates them to one another. Therefore, whereas linear reasoning goes beyond what is immediate, it remains anchored in the concreteness of the environment upon which it operates. It allows for imaginative recombination of the elements presented by playing with the active links observed. Examples of this would be adding or subtracting the actions associated with a given role (e.g., imagining a king taking orders, a boy flying like a bird, or a person having the body of a horse). However, linear reasoning does not allow for the construction of novel elements or the forging of relations that are inherently intangible or abstract.

The Structure of Thought: Unidirectional and Anchored

The conceptual relations constructed through linear reasoning abstract concrete actions from the flow of global events and then place them relative to one another in an atemporal frame of reference. The key property of these linear relations is their unidirectionality or imbalance. The relationship forged always depends on the location of an anchoring element and the relative definition of other elements associated with it.

To illustrate, let us consider the linear relation between an acting person, her action, and the action that follows. Let us take the example of Angele who initiates the action of writing that is followed by the production of an essay. In the linear reconstruction of this sequence of action, only one element in the sequence can be given priority; the others will be conceived relative to it. Where the actor, Angele, is the conceptual focus, the writing will be seen as an effect of her initiative and the essay will be understood as the effect of her action and, by implication, an effect of Angele herself. In this frame of reference, both the action and its outcome become attributes of the actor and are conceived relative to her. The writing is conceived as an element of the person, it is something that Angele does. It is not just "writing," it is "Angele's writing." Similarly, the essay is understood as something that Angele did. It is not just "an essay," it is "Angele's essay." Where the essay serves as the conceptual anchor, the writing and Angele will be conceived relative to it. The writing is viewed as an attribute of the outcome, it is what is done to produce an essay. Thus the writing is understood to be "essay writing." Similarly, the person doing the writing becomes an attribute of the outcome, the essay, and consequently may be viewed as "the person of that essay and the ideas it offers."

The general point here is that a linear relationship involves isolating one concrete action element and defining the other elements relative to it. The actions are not reciprocally related through some form of independently constituted relationship in light of which both are defined. Having this general form, the conceptual relations produced by linear reasoning have a number of distinguishing characteristics. They are concrete, general, singular, and normative. I will discuss each of these characteristics in turn.

Concreteness. To begin, linear relations are experientially based and concrete.

The construction of linear relations depends on the presentation of events as a guide to both the identification of the elements of an event and how those events will be linked. This presentation is a result either of direct observation or the description provided by other people. For example, consider the case of a student who rises in the middle of class and forcefully walks out. The appearance of the event focuses the observer on the student and what is done.[1] These become the conspicuous elements of the situation. Other students, the teacher, the classroom fade into the background. Moreover, other potentially significant aspects of the situation, for example, what had happened to the student before entering the classroom or what the student next to her just did, are not apparent at all. Therefore these other potential elements of the situation tend to be ignored. The appearance of the event also directs the observer's attention to the link between the actor and the action, usually a function of their contiguity in space and time. In this instance, the actor is the proximate cause linked to the immediately subsequent effect of walking out. Appearance may also dictate the nature of the relationship forged insofar as one element is observed to be more salient than others. In the case of the apparently disgruntled student, it is the student herself who dominates the visual field. As a result, there is a tendency to focus on her and therefore use her as the conceptual anchor in any relationship forged. Consequently, there will be a tendency to view her as the cause and the action as an effect and attribute of who she is.

The foregoing discussion of the grounding of linear relations in concrete experience brings to mind the "actor-observer hypothesis" proposed and tested by social psychologists (e.g., Nisbett et al., 1973; McArthur, 1972). This hypothesis suggests that actors and observers will tend to explain actors' behavior differently. This is accounted for in terms of their differing view of the same events and its effect on information processing. According to this analysis, the actors' view of the situation of their own acting tends to be dominated by the events impinging on them. As a result, these external factors receive greater attention and are more likely to be used as a basis for explanation. In the end, the actors have a tendency to view their own behavior as a reaction to the initiative of another person or to a particular external condition. Observers have a different view of the situation. Like the earlier example of an observer watching the student walking out, observers' view of a situation tends to be dominated by the figure of the person acting. This receives greater attention and therefore is more likely to anchor the understanding of the event. Consequently, observers tend to explain another person's behavior with reference to that person, her nature, or her intention. This account of the actor-observer difference is quite compatible with the view of linear relationships offered here. Because of the imbalanced quality of linear relationships, they are necessarily dependent on the concrete features of events as presented. This is evident in the identification of the relevant elements of the situation, in the choice of an element to serve as a conceptual anchor, and in the determination of those actions linked to that anchor. Indeed, I would argue that the actor-observer difference is a typical product of linear reasoning.

The actor-observer hypothesis has been supplemented by the "fundamental attribution error," which states that people tend to explain social behavior in terms of the qualities of the actor thereby underestimating the effect of circumstances. This is again accounted for in terms of the nature of the presentation of events. A similar view is adopted in research on the effect of salience and attention on social cognition (e.g., Taylor and Fiske, 1978). The argument here is that the manner in which situations are presented and then perceptually processed affects what aspects of the situation will receive greater or lesser attention. This will in turn affect which factors are emphasized in any subjectively constructed explanations. A good example of this research effort is offered by Shelley Taylor and her colleagues. In their studies, observers of a videotape were asked to determine which participant had the greatest impact in directing a conversation among a group of people arrayed around a table. The conversation was scripted in such a way that participants contributed in a roughly equal manner. In one study, the participants were people who were similar to one another in race and gender. The conversation was videotaped from different positions rendering one or two of the participants visible and the others only audible. The results indicated that the orientation of the camera led observers to attribute greater power and responsibility to the participants featured in the videotape (Taylor and Fiske, 1975). In a second study, the conversation was videotaped from above so that all participants were equally visible. One of the participants, however, was visibly quite different than the others (a women among men or an African-American among Caucasians). Following Gestalt psychology, the argument, confirmed by the evidence, was that element of the situation that was most visually distinctive would receive greatest attention and therefore would be attributed greater responsibility. Thus the single woman and the single African-American were seen as more influential in determining the conversations in which they participated (Taylor et al., 1977).

Here again the social psychological account of an aspect of social cognition is quite compatible with the view of linear relationships offered here. As in the case of the actor-observer difference, I would argue that the salience effect is a product of linear reasoning. This however raises a theoretical claim that importantly differentiates the view offered by the social psychologists and the one being presented here. Typically, social psychologists view the actor-observer difference, fundamental attribution error, or the salience effect as distinctive information processing techniques that are typically employed by all adults. I disagree with this characterization in several respects. To begin, I suggest that these different processes are in fact various expressions of specifically linear reasoning. In this regard, they share a common underlying structure. They reflect the imbalanced and experientially grounded quality characteristic of linear relationships. In addition, my argument suggests that these modes of information are not universal. People who reason in a linear manner will tend to explain action differently if they are actors or observers, will tend to overestimate the degree to which actors direct their own behavior, and will have the explanations generally oriented by the relative perceptual salience of the aspects of the phenomena they are observing. But not all people think in a linear fashion. According to the view posed here, people who reason in systematic manner will not explain events in the manner suggested by the social psychological research. People who reason in a sequential fashion may not be oriented to explanation at all.

Even when limited to linear thinking, an additional caveat must be introduced regarding this social psychological research. Linear reasoning is oriented by experience. This experience, however, is not simply a matter of the features of some physical environment or the qualities of perceptual processing of stimuli. It is also the result of social and cultural dictates. Linear reasoning is grounded in the concrete present, but this present is constituted by the linguistic construction of events as well as by objective qualities of events or the neurophysiological qualities of observers. Verbal statements affect a person's experience of events in a variety of ways. Perhaps most direct is the verbal injunction to attend to a particular element of a visual display. The command, "Look at what that person over there is doing," clearly orients the view of the listener and thus impacts what he will see at a particular time. Similarly, the narration of current events also emphasizes some aspects of what is occurring (obscures others) and creates the links between actions that the listener can then utilize as part of his subjective reconstruction of what has transpired. In everyday social cognition, this may serve to diminish any "natural" effects of perception in a manner consistent with the verbally communicated orientation provided by other people. A good example of this is provided by Reagan and Totten (1975) who were able to reverse the actor-observer difference by asking observers to empathize with the actor by "placing themselves in his or her shoes." On a broader scale, this is reflected in research on social cognition in cultures that are less individualistic than the American culture, in which most social psychological research is conducted. For example, research in Korea suggests that, guided by their culture, Koreans are significantly less likely than Americans to commit the fundamental attribution error of focusing on actors to explain how events unfold (Fletcher and Ward, 1988).

Beyond orienting attention to particular aspects of present events, narratives also serve as the source of information on events that have not been observed. Because linear reasoning largely depends on external presentation, another person's narrative may orient reasoning in two ways. More obvious, it provides the content of what may be understood by the listener to have occurred. This effect is likely to be particularly powerful when the listener has little other relevant information. More subtly, the other's narrative serves to focus the attention of the listener even when she disagrees. Thus even when rejected, the narrative provided by another person may nonetheless serve as a conceptual point of departure. It selects out a particular aspect of the universe of absent events, which then tends to become the focus of concern for the listener.

Generality. A second characteristic of linear relationships is that, despite their concreteness, they do have a certain generality. Relating specific actions to one another in the context of a specific event, linear relationships reflect the particulars of the initially observed situation. Once established, however, these relationships exist in an atemporal, simplified space of the subject's own construction and are thus freed from the specific circumstances in which they were initially experienced. As a result, the linear relationship established in one situation may be self-consciously applied in an attempt to anticipate or understand novel situations where the same actions or actors are involved. For example consider the case of an observed exchange. Chris gives Scott a gift. Scott reacts by showing pleasure and offering thanks. This scenario is reconstructed as involving the cause-and-effect relationship of two acts, the giving of the gift and the response of pleasure and verbal thanks. These actions and their relationship are readily abstracted from the specific situation of who gave the gift and who responded with thanks to create a relationship that may apply across the specific context of the giving and the particular actors involved. Thus the observer will expect Joe to respond with pleasure and thanks when given a gift by Mark. The specific relationship among the actions is generalized across the particular people or objects involved.

A direct consequence of the generality of linear relationships is a facility in integrating absence and presence in the understanding of events. Given the concreteness and specificity of linear reasoning, both absence and presence are conceived in relation to the experience of particular actions and actors. Once constructed and then cued in a particular situation, a linear relationship creates a definition of what is observed and an expectation regarding what will transpire. If the expectation is not fulfilled, an absence is noticed. This may then lead to a redefinition of what has been observed. For example, in the aforementioned example of gift giving, the presentation of a gift is linked to the evocation of pleasure in the recipient. In a new circumstance, Mark may be seen to be presenting an object to Joe. This may cue the already established relationship of gift giving and an appreciative response. In this light, it will be expected to cause Joe to be pleased. If, however, Joe reacts with displeasure, reanalysis follows. The focus will be on the unexpected reaction. To begin, this will entail a recognition of the absence of the expected response. This absence may then serve as an anchor for negating the initial definition of Mark's initiative. Because it did not produce pleasure, it may no longer be viewed as an act of gift giving. This may be followed by a utilization of Joe's reaction to redefine Mark's initiative as a provocation and, following on this, a redefinition of Mark as being an aggressive or annoying person.

As suggested by this example, absence is defined relative to presence. Presence is itself defined by reference to specific aspects of concrete experience. A limitation of linear reasoning is the relative inability to conceive of absence and presence relative to each other such that not only is absence the negation of presence, but that presence is the negation of absence. More broadly speaking, because they are indirectly defined with reference to a particular concrete presence, absences are not readily made sense of relative to one another. Thus in the context of linear reasoning about Harry's behavior, information that Florence's presence was associated with Harry's being more active is readily used to infer that Harry is energized by Florence. Contrary information that Florence's presence was associated with Harry being not active or that Florence's absence was associated with Harry's being active is also readily integrated. What is more difficult is the utilization of the confirming information that Florence's absence is associated with Harry's diminished activity as equivalent to the information that Florence's presence is associated with Harry's heightened activity. This difficulty in dealing with double absences or double negatives is nicely demonstrated in some early research on cognition (e.g., Smelsund, 1963).[2]

Extension. A third characteristic of linear relationships is that they may be extended or combined in ways not directly dependent on the manner in which concrete events are presented. Within the atemporal frame of reference constructed through linear reasoning, actions not directly linked in the unfolding of events as experienced or reported may nonetheless be related to one another. One such extension is categorical. This occurs when a conceptual anchor is identified and then considered over time. The actions observed or reported to be linked to the anchor are then combined to constitute a set of attributes associated with the anchor. An example would be the focus on an actor and the consideration of the various actions that lead to or follow from him. So Phillip may regularly be observed to harass his sister, help friends at school, wear his pants very low, and be complemented by his teachers. All these acts are aggregated together as defining attributes of the concrete category of the actor, Phillip. Alternatively, the focus could be on a specific action such as another person expressing pleasure (either verbally or nonverbally). The various actions producing this effect at different times, such as giving a gift, helping with an errand, or responding to a request, may be grouped together as attributes of the category of the action of causing pleasure or "being nice."

Linear relationships may also be extended beyond the presentation of present events in a causal linear fashion. Relationships that are constructed at different times may be linked together when they are observed to overlap with one another. This occurs when two relationships share a common action, but in one instance that action is an effect to a prior cause and in the other it is cause to a subsequent effect. In this manner, chains of linear causal relationship may be established. An example would be if the following relationships had been constructed in the course of experience at different times: (1) a person telling you secrets leads to the person feeling closer; (2) asking questions about a person's secrets leads to the person telling you secrets; (3) a person feeling closer to you leads to the person doing more of what you ask. Given the overlapping actions, these causal relationships can be linked to create the chain of asking questions about a person's secrets (2) leads to a person telling you secrets (2–1 overlap) leads to the person feeling closer leads to the person doing what you ask (1–3 overlap). This capacity to create causal chains enables linear reasoning to go well beyond the observed flow of events or the information given. This said, it is important to remember that while they extend beyond the specific manner in which events are presented, both causal and categorical extensions remain anchored in the concrete particulars of that presentation.

Singularity. A fourth feature of linear relationships is that they tend not to be utilized or understood in a reciprocal or mutually defining fashion. A linear relationship provides the means for thinking rather than constituting the object of thought. As a result, linear reasoning tends to involve the utilization of only one relationship as a basis for understanding a given circumstance. In this understanding, several specific actions (or actors) may be considered simultaneously, but not several relationships among them. For example, in a linear categorical analysis, the actions combined to form the category are defined relative to an anchoring action. They cannot at the same time be defined in terms of their relationship either to one another or to other actions outside of the category. Consider the case of several individuals who are grouped together because they all dress in the same manner. Their way of dressing anchors the category and each individual is included in the group by virtue of their choice to dress in the requisite manner. When thinking of this fashion group, other relationships tend not to be included. Thus, the relationships among the individuals (are they friends, do the converse regularly, do they conflict with one another) remain largely unconsidered. Similarly the connection of each individual actor to the various other actions she performs or other groups of which she is a member will also be ignored. In the relational context of the group, the individual person can only be thought of as a group member and therefore in terms of the characteristics of the group. This limitation is evident in the one-dimensional, stereotypical, and depersonalizing understanding of groups that is characteristic of linear thought.

The same limitation applies to the linear construction of chains of causation. Any given link in the chain is considered only as it overlaps and thus leads from or to another link. It is not considered in light of additional causal links with which it may be concurrently associated. As a result, systems of interrelated causal relationships that connect at a given moment as well as across time cannot be constructed. In this context, the conditional qualities of each step in the chain, that is, the other causal relationships that bear on it at the same time, are not readily considered. Similarly, the relationship among different chains of causation is not readily constructed. Let us return to the example of the causal chain consisting of [questioning a person about their secrets leading to [[him revealing those secrets] leading to [[[[him feeling closer]] leading to his doing what is asked of him]]]. Here we have a simple recipe for establishing control over another. Consider the middle relationship, the revealing of secrets leading to him feeling closer. In the present context, reasoning about this relationship tends to be limited to a consideration of that relationship's place in the chain. What is not considered is other known relationships that may bear on it, for example, that being close to a third person may prevent the target person from becoming close to the listener, that revealing secrets may lead to embarrassment and withdrawal, and so on. The absence of these other linear relationships leads to an understanding that is neither conditional nor naturally leads to an exploration of other relevant causal chains (such as might be used to construct a map of the personality of the target individual).

Normative quality. Finally, linear relationships have a distinctive normative and regulative quality. This is an extension of their generality. Once established, linear relationships have an existence and an order of their own. As such, they determine, as well as reflect, how actions are related to one another. Applied to subsequent specific experience, this determination of how actions *are* related becomes a standard for determining how they *should be* related. As such, linear relationships provide standards whereby that experience may be judged. These standards are based either on personal experience or verbal report. In either case, the initial conditions that lead to the formation of linear relationship typically generate only a weak link. If, however, the observed relationship is seen to hold across time or the reported relationship is confirmed by a number of other people, the cognitive link will be reinforced and thereby will come to be a standard of "normal" (in both senses of the word) behavior.

An example of this would be the experience of observing of people (Americans) cutting food by holding the fork in the left hand and the knife in the right hand, then resting the knife on the plate, shifting the fork to the right hand and using it to pick up the food. Seen repeatedly, this defines the "normal" way in which food is cut for eating. Alternatively, the same actions can be reported by others either as what is or should be done. The report will have greater impact depending on the value and/or power of the speaker. In either the case of observation or verbal report, the relationship established has a regulative quality —it constitutes a concrete rule of normal action. If new experience violates this rule, the rule itself generally will not be abandoned. Instead, the experience itself will be denied or denigrated. Thus the observer will simply tend to ignore the violating experience. Alternatively, she may recognize what has occurred and judge it negatively. In either case, the linear relationship is sustained despite contrary experience and is thus less susceptible to reconstruction. This is not to say that change will not take place, but it may require considerable contrary experience or verbal testament.

The regulative quality of linear thought referred to here is related to comparable claims regarding the nature of thinking made in the theory and research on schematic reasoning. In addition to being of considerable current interest, this research has a long history in both cognitive and social psychology.[3] Focusing less on the etiology of the phenomena than its result, this work has sug-

gested that people's representations of the world consist of chunks of information. They are referred to as schemas. Each chunk or schema consists of a more
or less elaborate set of associations. The focus of the schema research is on how
thinking is oriented by these chunks of knowledge. The strategy of the research
typically involves an initial cueing of a subject's preexisting schema and then
examining its effect on the subject's processing of new information. The hypothesis is that an individual's processing of information is oriented by the one
schema currently in use. Through assimilation of new information into the
preexisting schematic structuring of old information, there is a tendency for
distortion in a manner that is consistent with the schema. In this context, researchers have examined the effect of schemas on people's search for information (e.g., Snyder and Swann, 1978), their encoding of the information presented (e.g., Bruner, 1957; Bruner and Postman, 1948; Cantor and Mischel,
1977), their retrieval of past information (e.g., Bartlett, 1932; Wyer et al., 1982),
and their analysis of causal and categorical relationships present in the information collected (e.g., Chapman and Chapman, 1969; Medin and Smith,
1981). The results indicate that people tend to use preexisting schemas to assimilate information about the environment. This often results in a distortion of
the information presented by adding elements present in the schema but not
present in the event, by ignoring those elements that are present but are inconsistent with the preexisting schema, or by relating elements of what is presented
in a manner consistent with the schema even when the information dictates
otherwise.

The results of this research on schema use are certainly consistent with our
claims about the normative quality of linear thought and enrich our consideration of the linear construction of events and their subsequent retrieval from
memory. But again caveats must be introduced. In my view, the nature of the
schemas and the manner in which they are used will vary with the general quality of reasoning employed. Different kinds of schemas will be constructed and
different conditions will determine their initial genesis and subsequent use. Focusing more on the effects of schematic reasoning, researchers have paid little
attention to the quality of schemas—that is, to the nature of the associations
that constitute a schema rather than the concrete content of what is associated.
Practically speaking, their use of illustrative examples and their choice of
schemas to examine in empirical research clearly suggests that a schema consists
of either an aggregate of attributes associated with a common object or actor
(this is quite common in the person perception research) or a rather concrete
script for how one action will lead to another. This clearly suggests the kinds of

relational associations, either concrete categorical or linear causal, that are forged through linear reasoning. Moreover the strategy of cueing these schemas through the introduction of a visual stimulus or a statement of a concrete categorical or causal relationship also assumes a specifically linear use of schemas with its dependence on the contours of the immediate observed environment or the substance of a verbal report.

To conclude, it is likely that the majority of the schema research is applicable specifically to the consideration of aspects of linear reasoning. Its applicability to the understanding of sequential and systematic thought is not as straightforward. For example, systematic reasoning leads to analyses in which categorical and causal relationships are conceived relative to one another. In this light, specific subjectively constructed relationships and particular objective conditions are understood in a context dependent fashion. This will lead to a very different kind of schematic reasoning. First, schemas will be applied in a more tentative and careful way to novel circumstances. Hence there is less likelihood that there will be the same level of schema driven distortion as evident in linear reasoning. Second, schema evocation will not be so dependent on the specific contours of experience as it is observed or reported. Therefore, a subject reasoning systematically will not be particularly susceptible to the cueing strategies employed in most empirical research.

Units of thought. In addition to defining the quality of the relationships forged when coming to an understanding, linear reasoning also delimits the nature of the units that can be addressed. These conceptual units or building blocks are concrete, observable actions. Included here are: (1) physical moves like walking, hitting, or falling; (2) speech acts, the specific statements people make; and (3) acts of being, the concrete properties of how something appears, such as being red, tall, loud, or hot to the touch. These acts, physical or verbal, do not need to be actually seen or heard. It is enough that they are reported. In fact, linear reasoning may also consider action that is visible in its effect but is itself never observed. Included here are such actions as intentions or motives, be they the internal properties of persons or the attributes of unseen actors such as the gods or fate. While never observed, these actions or actors are often ascribed properties that render them observable. An example would be conceiving of the invisible god as a man or understanding motivation as internal voices or the demons within.

In this context, objects are a secondary, derivative concern. Action is the basic unit of linear thought. Accordingly, objects are defined by virtue of their relation to action. They are not conceived as "things-unto-themselves," but as "that-which initiates-action," as actors, or as "that-which-is-acted-upon," the objects of action. These action-units are extensive. Taken singly, they have objective qualities, but they are meaningful as they are related to one another. To create this meaning, a single connection will typically suffice. For example, consider the observation of a man falling to the ground. Unto itself, the act has no meaning. If attended to, it initiates a search for its unidirectional connection to some other act. This is satisfactorily completed when it is linked to either a preceding act, the man's foot hitting a stone embedded in the ground, or a succeeding act, his rolling in the grass laughing. If no linked act is observed, one will be inferred in a manner guided by a linear relationship constructed on the basis of prior experience or cultural narrative. In this manner, it may be concluded that bad luck caused the man to fall. The meaning of the fall will then be viewed accordingly. Thus, depending on the act with which it is related, the act of falling could be understood as tripping, playing or divine intervention.

Summary. Linear thinking involves the analysis of sequences of action. The focus is on specific concrete actions that are then placed in relation to each other. The link between actions is imbalanced. One act serves as a conceptual anchor and others are defined relative to it. This construction yields the conceptions of causality and categorization that are typical of linear thought. Regardless of the particular shape they take, linear relationships are concrete and ground in the specifics of one's own experience or that which has been recounted by other people. At the same time, these relationships do have a certain generality. Linkages between actions are assumed to hold across situations. Moreover when the linkage established has been reinforced, this generality may yield not only an expectation for what will occur, but also a normative standard for what should occur.

SOCIAL REASONING

Linear reasoning leads to the construction of a social world that is essentially active and dynamic. It is a world of concrete actions. This includes what is directly observed and what is reported by others, what is happening here or what is happening elsewhere, what is happening now or what has happened in the past or will happen in the future. As suggested by the structure of linear reasoning, this action includes what is done, what is said, and how things are or appear to be. This is the content. The focus of social reasoning is oriented by the apparent dynamic of social life. It orients to the causal anchors that initiate action and produce effects. As such, the social world is a world of actors, those entities that cause of action. This will include some people and, by the same logic, some animals. When a person is seen to command another to move and the other complies, or when a cat is seen to demand affection and get it, then both are regarded as fully social beings. It may also include natural forces such as the wind, current, and the sun. Where a concrete actor is not readily available as a plausible antecedent cause to an observed event, cosmic forces such as gods, spirits, or fates will be introduced. A good example of this is when unusual or fortuitous events are seen as the expression of the intervention of God or fate.[4]

The social world constructed by the linear thinker tends to exclude that which is simply the object or tool of action, such as those concrete elements of the environment that are inert (e.g., rocks, hammers, and lakes). In this sense, there is a fairly clear distinction drawn between the inanimate and animate worlds. However animate entities, such as people and animals, may also be regarded as objects when they are viewed primarily as the effects of action. When animals are merely regarded as beasts of burden or as a food source, then they are objects. Similarly, when people become ineffective and dependent or when they are targets of command, they too become objects. Examples of this are the diminished social status commonly ascribed to the handicapped or to housewives and children, and the social exclusion of slaves in Western history or of the untouchables in traditional Indian society.

Focus on Action, Efficacy, and Role

The dynamic of social life is understood by analyzing the flow of events into individual actions that are then related to one another. One essential way in which actions are understood is by the construction of a linear causal relationship. The concrete, specific actions that are observed or reported are abstracted from the flow of events (or the flow of the narrative) and linked to one another as an antecedent cause or consequent effect. This search for understanding is typically satisfied by the discovery of a single link, a single cause, or a single effect. For example, one may observe an interaction between Mark and Scott. To begin there is brief exchange of words and then Mark strikes Scott. The attack is unusual and therefore likely to be a focus of attention. Within the framework of linear reasoning, there is immediately an attempt to make sense of the act of striking, which then entails the search for an active link. This orients to what is salient, that is, either what is proximate in space or time or what is defined as relevant by prior experience or cultural prescription. In this case, the attack is viewed in the midst of the exchange with Mark and Scott, with their actions being most salient. Which of these actions will be the focus depends on the circumstance. If Scott had just demonstratively threatened Mark, then this may become the focus of attention and consequently be linked to Mark's attack and ascribed causal status. The threat provoked the attack that may now be seen as a defensive response. Alternatively, the attack may lead to Scott falling to the ground and bleeding profusely. The severity of the outcome might lead to a focus on it and an account of the attack in which it is linked to its consequence. In this case, the attack may be viewed as a brutal act of aggression. Finally, it may have been that just prior to the attack, Scott's threat was accompanied by an insult. In the appropriate cultural context, this may be seen as a cause that regularly leads to attack. Accordingly, the attack will be seen as a norm-governed response. The point here is that there is a tendency in linear thought to focus on just one causal linkage. Depending on which is invoked in this instance, the hit is understood quite differently—as a defensive, aggressive, or conventional act—and responsibility will be ascribed quite differently.

This causal analysis leads to considerations of efficacy and power. As causal analysis is central to the construction of linear understandings, so considerations of power are a central dimension of the linear conception of social life. Given the quality of linear relationships, power is concrete. It is located in a specific causal agent and is evidenced when one action can compel another. It is recognized when Lisa tells George to pick up the children and he does as he is instructed. It is also recognized when a storm creates waves that sink a ship. When extended through a categorical analysis guided by language, power can become an attribute of the agent. Lisa may be called powerful if she is observed to cause George to pick up children, cause her friend to come when called, cause a door to burst open with the kick of her foot, and so on. This view of her as powerful encompasses and specifically refers to these effects she produces. Lisa has the power to do specific things. (Note that built into this analysis is little appreciation of conditions or context.) It is important to recognize that the use of the linguistic term "powerful" when talking or thinking of Lisa carries its own associated concrete attributes. These may, incorrectly, be ascribed to Lisa. For example, it might imply that you do as you wish in the workplace, whereas there Lisa may dutifully follow her employer's instructions.

The observation of a specific act of power may also be extended through the creation of a chain of overlapping linear causal relationships leading to the construction of extended hierarchies of power. An example of such a hierarchy would be that of Lisa being able to command George to pick up the kids, which leads to George commanding his brother-in-law Clark to pick up the children on his way home from work. Clark may in turn tell Reena to replace him on the job while he leaves early to pick up Lisa's children. In this context, a hierarchy is established with Lisa at the top through George and Clark to Reena at the bottom. This result is typical of linear thought—the hierarchy is constructed on the basis of observing a particular concrete chain of causes and effects. The hierarchy is also specific to the actions in question. Additional relationships are not constructed. Thus, the conditions impinging on each step of the chain and contributing to its realization are not considered. Similarly, additional flows of causation, such as the simultaneous flow of power from the bottom up which may condition or delimit power as it flows from the top down, are not considered.

Actions are also understood categorically. Actions may be clustered together by virtue of their link to a common anchoring action. These links of several actions to a common anchor may be directly observed or simply recounted by other people. For example, living with another person, having children, and falling into debt may all be observed (or reported) to be linked to the anchoring act of getting married. Similarly, the assumption of a position or title, such as becoming a lawyer, may be associated with a set of effects, such as going to court, providing advice to friends, wearing a suit, and looking for prospective clients. This use of concrete categories configures action in such a way that a notion of role emerges as quite central to the linear understanding of social life. As suggested by the foregoing examples, roles are defined by a distinguishing act or by an orienting label. The role consists of both the set of actions observed to be associated with the role and, perhaps more important, those actions that are reported to be associated with it. It should be remembered that the actions that constitute role performance are concrete and specific. Moreover, while related to the anchoring action or position, they bear no independently meaningful relationship to one another.

Individuals: Person as Actor, Social Identity, and Self-Concept

Of course this categorical analysis applies to people, as actors, as well as to actions themselves. The individual actor may serve as the conceptual anchor. The category will then encompass the set of actions observed to be associated with the person over time. These will include concrete actions, aspects of being, and verbal statements, particularly those that recur over time. Consider Sarah. The category of "Sarah the actor" will include concrete activities she engages in, such as bicycling, speaking quickly, playing piano, listening to opera, and planning market strategy for a laser optics company. It will also include aspects of appearance, such as the fact that she has black hair, is thin, and wears dark clothing. In addition, the category of Sarah subsumes the statements she makes, such as "I believe in God" and "I feel distant from my sisters." A person serves as an anchor not only to those acts she initiates, but also those of which she is a target or effect. Thus, in the case of Sarah, she is also a person who was left by her husband, undermined by a coworker, and spoken well of by her friends.

In this context, it is interesting to note the implications of understanding a person as a causal agent. As with any anchoring cause, the associated consequent action is understood relative to that anchor as the cause's effect. It becomes an attribute or a property of the cause. Property here has a double meaning, both of which are implicated in the linear understanding of the relationship between a causal agent and the outcomes she produces. On one hand, the outcome is a property of the agent in the sense that it becomes her possession. A person owns what she causes or makes. Thus, if Sarah paints a picture, builds a house, or cultivates a patch of land, these are outcomes that are understood as her effects, in the dual sense of that term as consequence and possession. On the other hand, the outcome of an agent's action is a property of the agent in the sense that it becomes a defining characteristic. At the same time as you own what you cause or make, so that which you own becomes a defining property of who you are. In the case of the linear concept of Sarah, she is in part the land that she owns, the house she lives in, the car she drives, and the picture she paints.

Thus far in our example of Sarah, we have focused on how the conception of her as a person is based on the actions that Sarah has been observed to perform. While directly relevant, these actions are also significant insofar as they provide a basis for attributing actions to Sarah that are unto themselves inherently unobservable. Reference here is to Sarah's feelings and motivations. These "internal" phenomena have conceptual status only with regard to their relationship to the observable actions that they are seen to initiate. Thus feelings are understood with reference to the nonverbal behaviors, such as smiling, crying, or grimacing, which are associated with them. Consequently, the focus is on such visible emotions as happy, sad, and angry. Similarly, motivations are defined with reference to the specific action they produce. So when someone eats it is inferred they are hungry, when they work hard it is inferred they harbor ambition, and when they make a choice it is inferred they have a desire. The motives of hunger, ambition, and desire are thus defined in the terms of the observable actions to which they lead.

The category of a person is the sum total of all these associated actions. In the case of the casual observation of a stranger, this category may have few attributes. In the case of a closely considered friend such as Sarah who has been observed over a long period of time, the category of the person may become very elaborated.[5] In either case, the qualities of the category are the same: the attributes are concrete actions and statements, and these active attributes are only related to each other by virtue of their connection to the anchoring actor. Returning to the example of Sarah, the relationships among her statement of distance from her siblings, her husband's choice to leave her, and her devotion to the piano are not considered relative to one another. Thus there is no self-consciously interpretative reconstruction of the meaning of these attributes in light of their possible relationship to one another. In this regard, there is little understanding of subjectivity and the personal construction of meaning. People's beliefs, preferences, and behaviors may vary, but the actions and their associations are objective. They must simply be observed or reported. Similarly there is no self-conscious attempt to construct an integrative understanding of Sarah as a personality system. Sarah is understood as a collection of fragments. At any given moment in time, not all of Sarah's attributes will be considered together. Rather, one or a few will be cued by the circumstances at hand and she will be understood accordingly. Therefore at a dinner party, Sarah may be viewed as a piano player or someone who speaks quickly. Her belief in God, her bicycling, and her distance from her sisters may not be considered at all.

This said there is some, albeit limited, structure to a linear conception of a person. A person may be considered to possess one or more traits. This trait designation reflects the linear capacity to establish a concrete category of different actions that are linked to a common outcome. For example, paying for dinner, giving a gift, and helping with errands may be observed to elicit pleasure in another. This common outcome may then become the conceptual anchor of the concrete category of "being nice." Performance of one or more of these behaviors may then lead to the ascription of the entire category to the actor. The language is replete with terms to cover these kind of concrete action categories that are defined by their effect (and sometimes their cause). Included here are such trait terms as aggressive, generous, forgiving, subordinate, good-humored, and so on.

Social identity. A person's action may also serve as a conceptual link, which associates that person with a categorically constructed social group. In this context, all those acting in this manner may be defined commonly. For example, all those who pray on Saturday in the synagogue may be defined as Jews. If Sarah performs this action, she will be defined relative to her action and thus as a member of the category of Jew. Alternatively, all those who state they are against affirmative action may be defined as Republicans. If Sarah states that she is against affirmative action, she may be categorized as a Republican. Finally, because of her appearance, she may be defined as woman. This association of an individual with social categories or groups provides the person with social identities. They become part of the catalogue of who that person is. Thus apart from what she typically does, Sarah is also Jewish, Republican, and female.

Each social identification is itself a linear category that introduces its own concrete, specific associations. These may then become part of the cluster of attributes associated with the person. Being a Republican may itself be understood as a cluster of attributes, such as voting for George Bush Jr. in the 2000 presidential election, favoring the abolition of abortion, and dressing conservatively. It may also include definitions of what you are not, for example, a Democrat, and what you do not do, for example, favor greater government intervention. Having been identified as Republican because of her stated view on affirmative action, these other attributes of the group—Republicans—may then become associated with Sarah regardless of whether there is any evidence that she actually deserves these attributes or not. Again given the limitations of linear relationships, not all of these social identities would be considered at once and little connection among them may be established. Thus in one context, Sarah may be viewed as a Jew, in another as a Republican, and in a third as a woman.[6]

Self-concept. Apart from a concept of other people, linear categorization also facilitates the construction of a self-concept. This shares all the features of the conception of others. It is composed of an aggregate of concrete actions, appearance, and belief. The specific composition depends on observation and report. Thus one discovers who one is by observing what she does, what she says, and how she is identified. Like the other, the self consists of an aggregate of these concrete, specific attributes. Not all are evoked at any given moment; which is will be a function of context.

Although there are similarities between the linear construction of a concept of the self and another person, there may also be subtle differences. As already noted in conjunction with our discussion of the relevant social psychological literature, linear reasoning depends on the concrete contours of the situation as presented. When considering their own action, actors are more readily confronted with and therefore more aware of those factors impinging on them.

Their own role in the action is literally less apparent and therefore they are less aware of themselves as forces operating on the environment. A number of consequences follow from this. First, actors are more likely to focus on external forces and use them as conceptual anchors. They are commensurately less likely to regard themselves as anchors. Consequently, given the same amount of exposure, actors are less likely to attribute their actions to themselves than they are likely to make such an attribution when observing others acting in the same way. Individuals may therefore have a less elaborated view of themselves than of others. Second and following from the first, conceptions of oneself may be more dependent on others' accounts. Because we see less of our own role in what occurs, we see less of what we do and hence can rely less on our own observation of who we are. Linear constructions of the self potentially are therefore more dependent on the report and labels provided by others.[7]

Groups as Actors

The social world of linear reasoning is populated not only by individual actors, but by group actors as well. As suggested in our discussion of the linear construction of persons, an action rather than the actor may serve as a conceptual anchor. This may in turn lead to the construction of social categories or groups that are distinguished by their defining actions or action. Within this general linear framework, social groups may be fabricated variously. They may be based on the common behavior that the group members perform. This behavior may consist either of a concrete action or the expression of a specific statement. It may be performed once in a given context yielding temporary categorizations, or it may be a behavior that is regularly repeated. In the latter case, the behavior attains the status of ritual and may contribute to more significant and enduring social categorization. This may help explain the importance of ritual behavior for people who reason in a linear manner in maintaining both the social construction of the group and the relevant social identity of the individual participants.

Social groups may also be defined on the basis of a common cause of which they are an effect. Thus after a disaster, those who were commonly affected, the victims, may be viewed as members of a group. Similarly, those individuals who were produced by the same parents may be grouped together. This basis of social category formation is often drawn upon in group histories. In the case of people who are reasoning in a linear manner, the ascription of a common mythical origin or parentage may reinforce their perception of the status of the group. This will also reinforce their identification with the group. Additionally, those people who are treated the same way by others may be viewed as a group.

An interesting example of this is offered by Anne Schneider and Helen Ingram (1992) in their analysis of how public policy creates social groups by fostering a shared social identity among individuals who are the targets of a given policy.

In linear reasoning, physical appearance also serves as a significant anchor for the construction of social groups. Like doing the same thing, appearing the same way can provide a conceptual anchor for grouping individuals together. This close link between action and appearance as conceptual anchors is exemplified by social significance of people's apparel as part of their appearance. In this context, what one is wearing establishes one's social identity. This is clearly reflected in how individuals use clothing to identify themselves and others, either for the purposes of inclusion or exclusion in a group. Also significant are less readily manipulated aspects of appearance, such as gender or race. Gender and race are highly visible aspects of a person's appearance and thus are very likely to be used as bases for social group definition in a linear construction of the social world. Abstract ideologies may define individuals differently and thus reduce the political impact of such variables. If, however, the hegemony of these ideologies wane, such apparent bases of social distinction are likely to be strongly reasserted. Current examples of this include the rise of racism after the fall of the Communist regimes in Eastern Europe or the rise of "identity politics" in the face of the decline of liberalism in Western democracies, especially the United States.

The foregoing discussion focuses on the impact of direct perception on the linear categorization of groups. Also very important is the role played by other people and the language they use. By the way in which they refer to actors, other people may construct a linguistically based definition of a group. The use of a common label for a set of individuals accomplishes this most simply. The result is the label itself becomes an anchor that unites the various individuals to which that label is attached. Thus if confronted with a description of several individual people who are all "x," there will be a tendency to construct them as a group. Typically, these group designations constructed in language draw upon perceptual characteristics to reinforce their effect. These are not, however, necessary. This is interestingly illustrated by the experiments on the so-called minimal group effect (e.g., Tajfel, 1970, 1981; Brewer, 1979). In the research, a subject is told that she is a member of group that includes individuals she has never met and will never meet. She has no information on these individuals except that they are a part of her group (groups are usually designated by the use of a letter, e.g., "group A"). The research demonstrates that even in this minimal situation, a person assigned to the group may identify with it in a way that has significant social consequences. Again it is necessary to note that while this research is intended to illustrate how people in general construct group categories, here this is regarded as typical only of linear thought.

The role of language in linear thought is important, but action remains central. Although discourse can orient attention and emphasize some features of the environment and deemphasize others, its significance nonetheless depends on its capacity to reflect and affect action. Thus the strength of linguistic distinctions will depend in large part on their connection to concrete observable actions. To the degree that they are reinforced by observations of common origin, appearance, or action they will be stronger. So if a label is presented that defines a group whose members have a distinctive physical appearance (e.g., a particular skin color) and engage in a number of distinctive common behavior (e.g., speak the same language, eat the same food, and play the same games), it is more likely to be adopted and used in linear thought. If a label is presented that is not supported by such evident actions, it is less likely to orient a linear thinker's social cognition. The exception is where otherwise weak categorical distinctions are sustained by the deployment of social force. In this case, social rewards and punishments are utilized to reinforce the recognition and appropriate use of group distinctions where the concrete observable bases of these distinctions are few or unclear.[8]

Bosnia-Herzegovina of the early 1990s may provide a dramatic example of the social control of category formation and use. Apparent differences among the Bosnian Croats, Muslims, and Serbs were often not great. People looked similar, dressed similarly, their day-to-day behavior (especially among the more secular) was the same, and they all spoke a single language. In this context, the power of earlier ethnic group categorizations had waned as evidenced by intergroup commerce, friendship, and marriage. To reinvigorate them, the leadership of the various ethnic groups relied on force to reward those who sustained the distinctions and punish those who did not. The rewards included political favors and the punishments extended from the withdrawal of assistance to excommunication and the burning of homes.

Once constructed, a social group is understood in a way that has all the hallmarks of linear thought. As a social entity, the group is understood as an actor and hence is identified by what it does and has done to it. On one hand, this encompasses the typical activities that the members are observed or reported to perform. So once distinguished by a common birthplace and language, the category of Swedes may be extended to include commonly observed actions of singing during parties, trying to avoid being conspicuous (*logrum*) and expressing anti-American attitudes. On the other hand, the group is understood to act in the same sense as a person is understood to act. The group is itself an actor, that is, a monolithic entity that initiates action. In this light, the English as a internally undifferentiated group are understood to act uncooperatively when dealing with European Union. In similar terms, the Russians may be understood to threaten the Baltic republics and the Americans were understood to send a person to the moon. As actors, groups may also be ascribed intentions, feelings, and traits. In the latter regard, Canada may be seen as fair, Japan may be regarded as aggressive, and France may be viewed as proud.

As a concrete category, a characterization of a group applies to all its members. The individuality of the members as categories unto themselves is not be considered when the focus is the group. To the degree to which individual members are considered, they are simply ascribed the characteristics of the group. For example, it may be that a Spaniard thinking in a linear fashion may observe that there are people called gypsies that are dark skinned and live in caravans on the outskirts of the city. On this basis he may define them as a group. Having done so, he may then be exposed to prevalent reports that gypsies steal and are lazy. Although he may have had no direct interaction with a gypsy, he may nonetheless ascribe these qualities to the group and then view each of its members accordingly. Importantly, this view of gypsies is not readily altered by subsequent experience. His understanding that gypsies steal and are lazy is a concrete abstraction that is not easily changed by contrary experience, such as the observation of particular gypsies who do not steal and who do work hard. As suggested by this example, linear social reasoning leads to stereotyping of the kind often discovered in the research on prejudice (e.g., Allport, 1954; Brewer and Kramer, 1985) and the more recent schema theory work on group perception (e.g., Dovidio, Evans, and Tyler, 1986; Hamilton and Trolier, 1986; Linville, Fischer, and Salovey, 1989).

Although groups and their individual members are understood in terms of one another, linear reasoning allows only one level of consideration at a time. Depending on contextual cues, the focus may either be individual members or the group. Focusing on individual members, attention is paid to the unique attributes of the individuals and the various ways they act on one another. Focusing on the group, distinctions among individuals are ignored. The tendency to focus on either the group or its individuals is well illustrated by research on the effect of foreign involvement on presidential popularity in the United States (e.g., Mueller, 1973). One of the key findings is that the popularity of American presidents increases whenever the country is involved in an international crisis. With some limits that are not of concern here, this holds true regardless of whether the president is seen to respond well or badly. This seemingly strange result is readily understood with reference to the structure of linear understanding. When presidents are considered in the context of domestic American politics, they are regarded as an individual political actor in active relation to other actors and oneself. The result is potentially alienating and divisive for the observer. As a result, many citizens may disapprove of the president in this context. When considering international affairs, however, the focus tends to shift away from individuals to groups. In this context, the actor of concern is the nation-state, the United States, and the president is now regarded as a group member, as an American. More than this, the president may be viewed as emblematic of the country. In this light, the particular qualities of the president and the differences between the president and the observing citizen tend to evaporate or become irrelevant. Insofar as the citizen has a positive identification with her country, the associated positive feelings are likely to be attached to the president regardless of the specifics of the handling of the situation at hand.

Like individual actors, groups may be conceived relative to each other in light of the action they perform. This action may be used as a conceptual anchor that then serves as a basis for categorizing groups together. This yields a group of groups that is constructed on the same basis as a group of individuals, that is, on the basis of common action, belief, appearance, and so on. Examples include those groups who perform a common practice (Iraq, Germany, and the Mongols as aggressors), groups who have been commonly affected (Poland, Romania, and the Czech Republic grouped under ex-Soviet dominated countries), groups who have common appearance (the designation of Ethiopians, Zulus, and residents of Harlem as blacks) or groups who have a common territory (the designation of Apaches, Boston Brahmans, Kansas farmers, and San Franciscans as Americans). Alternatively, the action associated with a group may place it in active relationships to other groups. For example, one group may be seen to force another to comply with its demand for specific behavior. In this context, hierarchies of groups (again conceived as singular actors) may be constructed. A classic example is a simple understanding of the distribution of power in the military where generals command colonels who command majors and so on down the line. Most institutional structures are understood in these terms, that is, as a simple hierarchical array of internally undifferentiated groups.

Social Rules and Conventions

The social world constructed through linear reasoning is not only one of dynamic action and actors. It is also one of rules and conventions. This reflects the regulative quality of linear relationships. A linear relationship is constructed on the basis of the observed or reported connections among actions. The more frequently the connection is presented or the more salient the nature of that presentation, the stronger the relationship is likely to be. Once constructed, the relationship is then applied to novel situations in which these actions are involved. This application entails a determination of how these actions should be related, a determination that affects both one's own initiation of action and the understanding of the action of others. For example, one may observe that on greeting one another, Stergios and his brother Nikolas typically kiss one another on both cheeks. Moreover, one may observe that family members always greet one another in this manner. Based on these observations, a linear relationship is established, a specific rule of greeting. Subsequently, when observing such a greeting situation, one will expect that the family members will greet each other in the specific manner of a kiss on each cheek. This rule will also guide one's own greeting of family. Thus, while they are derive from the experience of how actions are connected, linear relationships provide a basis for defining how these actions should be related to one another. Characteristic products of linear thinking, these concrete rules or conventions of action are a ubiquitous element of the linear understanding of social life.

These linear rules have several specific qualities. First, they are concrete. They constitute regulations of particular action. In the case of the aforementioned greeting rule, the standard in question regulates the particular acts engaged when meeting family members. It is a guide as to what specifically to do. Second, linear rules or standards typically define the particular ways in which these specific actions relate to one another. The greeting rule used in the preceding example illustrates this well. Two family members are involved. They approach one another, embrace, and simultaneously kiss each other one time on each cheek. The prescription is exact. The nature and order of the action is clear. The kissing occurs during the embracing, not before or after. In this context, kissing is required and alternative behaviors such as a handshake or mere verbal greeting are disallowed. Moreover, the kissing behavior is clearly regulated. A kiss on just one cheek will be regarded as insufficient and three kisses will be regarded as excessive. A kiss on the lips or hand will similarly be regarded as inappropriate.[9] Third, linear rules tend to be generalized without regard to context. Thus it may be that the greeting ritual described is prevalent in one's own cultural environment in Greece, but not England (where you do not kiss at all). But if a Greek becomes a member of an English family, there will still be a tendency to apply the greeting rule and kiss initially startled and recurrently uncomfortable in-laws on both cheeks. This specific example reflects a more general tendency for those who reason in a linear manner to inappropriately apply conventions of behavior learned in one cultural context to others. This said, one should be careful not to underestimate linear reasoning. With experience and instruction, it can construct additional rules, each of which provides a concrete limit to unwarranted generalization. Given sufficient exposure of this kind, the result may be a rich collage of situation-specific rules of action that constitutes what we typically refer to as wisdom.

Finally, linear rules, by their very nature, tend to confuse what is and what should be. The observation or report of what is normal leads to cognitive practice that often effectively elevates what is usual into a standard for subsequent practice. To the degree to which the observed reality does not meet the standard, it will be manipulated to conform, denigrated, or simply ignored. Thus the degree to which a person's action does not conform to a rule, such as the greeting rule, it may be defined as vulgar, punished by excommunication, or simply offered no response. Claims that challenge conventional knowledge of nature (such as Galileo's defense of Copernican theory) or social behavior that violates accepted hierarchies (e.g., a plebeian dictating to an aristocrat) or categories (e.g., interracial or homosexual marriage) will similarly be rejected as unnatural and inappropriate. In this regard, rules are rather rigidly applied, typically showing little tolerance for deviation.

As the foregoing discussion suggests, linear reasoning is not only rule governed, it is also very conventional or traditional. The construction of linear relationships depends on the specific manner in which circumstances are experienced, either through personal observation or the other people's report. The experiential world into which a person who thinks in a linear fashion enters is not arbitrarily ordered. It is shaped by the structure of the larger social environment in which the person is located. That structure delimits with whom the person will interact, when they will interact, the circumstances under which they will interact, and the manner in which that interaction is likely to unfold. Derived from this experience, many causal and categorical relationships and the concrete rules that follow from them will reflect the substance of these socially structured interactions. They will therefore guide action in a way that tends to conform to and thereby reproduce the existing conventions of social exchange.

This conventionality is not only a matter of social structure. It is also a matter of culture. As it affects linear reasoning, a culture consists of a set of definitions, categories, and narratives that make clear how particular actions and actors relate to one another. Viewed from a psychological perspective, a culture consists of a vast repertoire of concrete schemata. As presented in mass media or as reported by other such agents of socialization as family and peers, these cultural dicta provide much of the material upon which the construction of linear relationships draws. Specific action is explained, anticipated, and categorized accordingly. Depending on her cultural context, a person who thinks in a linear manner comes to understand that the gods or invisible bacteria cause disease, that the stars or upbringing determine personality, that the corporations or the people control government, or that being born of Pakistani parents does or does not allow you to be English. Once internalized these causal and categorical understandings become part of the collage of concrete rules that will orient a linear conception of what does and consequently what should occur. As a result, linear reasoning leads to the subjective reconstruction of a culturally dictated vision, one that is likely to contribute to the reproduction of the culture itself.

THE LINEAR CONCEPTION OF POLITICS:
A SCRIPTED PLAY

Linear thinking does not spontaneously construct politics as a distinct dimension of social life. Although considerations of power, hierarchies, social roles, and groups are ever-present aspects of linear social reasoning, they are always embedded in the description and account of specific concrete action relations. As a result, no general understandings are abstracted such that power per se or the fact of hierarchy becomes the object of a specifically political analysis. Despite this limitation, a political dimension of social life will be recognized when society creates distinctively political institutions and the culture defines them in those terms. Thus although the notion of politics is not a cognitive invention typical of linear thought, cultural representations and social institutions that are presented as expressly political can be readily reconstructed in linear terms.

The focus of linear political reasoning is on action. Oriented by culturally provided labels that are presented both by other people and through the mass media, politics is understood as a particular category of social action. An observed or reported action may be identified as political when it is explicitly labeled in these terms. What action is labeled in this manner will of course depend on the cultural setting. Thus, in an American context, such acts as voting, passing a law, or giving a campaign speech on television are all typically presented as political and are therefore likely to viewed as such by people reasoning in a linear fashion. By virtue of their association with these acts, actors may also be viewed as political entities. Thus people who vote and the candidates they vote for may be seen as political actors. Similarly, legislators who pass laws and leaders who deliver speeches may be viewed as political. Other acts, such as choosing texts for school, refusing to wear a bra, or rioting in the streets, are often not presented as being political. Instead, in cases like the choice of school curricula, they may be presented as a matter of truth or practicality rather than of politics. Alternatively as in the case of refusing to wear a bra or rioting, the action may be labeled unconventional or criminal. Linear representations of these acts and their associated actors will not include an association with politics.[10]

The political domain is also constituted by those actors who at the outset are themselves labeled as political. For example, individual actors may be defined as political if they occupy positions or fill roles that are presented as political. In this context, monarchs, senators, and campaign consultants may all be viewed as essentially political actors. Action and other actors may then be defined as they are linked to these actors. In this vein, any action of a monarch or president may be viewed as political from the decision to go to war, to the choice of a spouse or automobile. Groups may also be viewed as political actors if they are identified as such. Political parties, such as the Social Democrats, the Conservatives or the Likud, typically present themselves in expressly political terms. Consequently these groups as well as most of the action they initiate or of which they are the target will be regarded as political. Other groups, such as Orthodox Jews, peasants, the electrical workers union, environmentalists, or feminists, may or may not be ascribed political status depending on the political culture.

Institutions, such as the Parliament, the town council or the army, may also be defined as political when they are explicitly labeled as such by others. In a linear frame of reference, these institutions are conceived in much the same way as groups. They are distinguished by what they do, by the specific action they take. The Parliament makes the law. The Department of External Affairs takes care of foreign policy. The federal government takes care of the country, and the provincial government takes care of local matters. Each of these institutions is seen as a group of individuals who are regarded as more or less identical when viewed in light of their association with the institution. Thus all parliamentarians may be ascribed one common set of concrete characteristics and all customs and immigration officials another set. As an organization, an institution is understood to have a hierarchical order. Considered in a broader context, an institution, like any group, is regarded as a monolithic actor. It is an individual writ large. In these terms, institutions are understood to have will, motivation, and purpose. They also have causal and categorical relations with one another. Thus, the relationship between can be readily comprehended, but only in the concrete and imbalanced or anchored terms of linear reasoning.

So identified, the domain of politics is concrete and active. It is inhabited by individuals, groups, and institutions who are conceived to be actors, each pushing in its own direction with more or less power to affect the others. A basic relation is one of causation with power attributed to those who are seen to initiate. In this context, the exchange between the actors is often represented as simply a matter of a succession of actions in which certain actors are causal and others are their instruments. This may be the case even when social structure dictates that the relationships are more complex and the culture clearly presents it as such. An example would be the rather complex division of power among the executive, judicial, and legislative branches of government that exists in the United States. The realities of this division are particularly evident in the battling that goes on between the Congress and the president. It is reinforced by the omnipresent high school civics instruction that focuses on this division of powers. Despite the exposure and the instruction, this structure of power is not easily assimilated within a linear frame of reference. The tendency is to reconstruct it in simple hierarchical terms. When questioned about this matter, respondents who reason in a linear fashion typically make some reference to the division of powers but ultimately tend to locate ultimate power either in the Congress or the president and define the other as a subordinate. In this vein, some suggest that the president is really the key figure in government and he basically tells the Congress what to do. Others may suggest that Congress is in fact the central authority and often view the president as a mere spokesman of congressional will. With specific training, the best that can be achieved within this framework is the recognition that in certain contexts the Congress tells the president what to do and in other contexts, the president dictates to the Congress. The result is still simple top-down hierarchy, but one that is now context dependent.

Political action can also be seen as an interaction between causal agents in which one affects another who in turn affects the first. This is most easily done in the case of two actors because monitoring what occurs over time is comparatively easy. The result is the construction of a chain of causation that emerges looking something like an account of a Ping-Pong match. This frequently occurs in linear construction of international relations. Consider the example of the following analysis of recent events in the Middle East. A typical reconstruction involves a focus on two groups, in this case the Jews and the Palestinian Arabs. Their interaction would be considered in the following terms. First, after World War II, the Jews came to Palestine thereby displacing the Palestinians. In response, the Palestinians fought to expel the Jews at the end of the British mandate. In response, the Jews defended themselves and created the state of Israel. In response to this, the Palestinians sought to regain their homeland and initiated terrorist attacks to pressure the Israelis. The Israelis responded with attacks on Palestinian refugee camps. And so it would continue, limited only by the knowledge of the person reconstructing the events.

As suggested by the foregoing example, the linear construction of political action is not only characterized by its focus on the power to initiate, but also by its emphasis on conflict. In a world of actors striving for their own ends, mutual obstruction and opposition are necessarily viewed as inevitable, indeed common. It is a world where another is irrelevant or she is your opponent. Those who occupy the same stage either are hierarchically organized and interact according to clear social prescription or the road to conflict is left wide open. This conflict is a simple one and so is its resolution. A struggle ensues that is resolved when one party is destroyed or subordinated to the will of the other. Where feasible, another possibility that may be considered is the permanent separation of the parties so they no longer come into contact with one another. To return to the example of the Israeli-Palestinian relationship, this limits the possible outcomes. For the most part, it will be viewed as a zero-sum game that can only end with one side as the winner and the other as the loser. In the language of the day, either the Jews are washed into the sea or the Palestinians are subordinated and policed. Viewed in these terms, it is easy to understand the powerful loyalties and enmities that conflict can engender. Another alternative is a relocation of the parties by placing the Israelis somewhere in Africa or integrating the Palestinians into a neighboring Arab state. In either case, there is little appreciation of the systemic context within which the conflict occurs and thus to the underlying forces, domestic and international, that sustain the antagonistic nature of the exchange.

The rather uncomfortable state of affairs of this Hobbesian world is alleviated somewhat by the linear complement to conflict, that is, alliance. Typically, the possibility of an alliance is perceived and then may be created when several actors share a common goal or interest. For example, workers in a factory may perceive that they have common interest in improved wages and working conditions and therefore unite to form a union. Also in this vein, two or more individuals or groups may be viewed as potential allies with one another when confronted by a third who threatens both. Thus the military alliance among countries as dissimilar as Japan, the United States, and Greece may be regarded as readily comprehensible in the face of a common threat from the former Soviet Union. Similarly, the electoral alliance among fundamentalist Christians and venture capitalists may be perceived as appropriate given their common aim to block the Democratic party whose platform is regarded as inimical to them both. Alliance may also emerge when the actors view one another as members of a group. Through their common identity, each may understand himself or herself to share in what happens to the others thereby creating a commonality of interests. These bases of alliance are often recognized by organizers and leaders and become part of the rhetoric of mobilization. "We all must breathe the same air. We must work together to keep it clean." "We in the West live under the specter of Communism. We must stick together to save us all." "We are Muslims. We believe and live differently than those in the Christian West. We must be loyal to each other."

However they are constructed, alliances are themselves regarded as groups. Viewed in relation to their opponents, alliances are seen as singular actors. In this regard, there is a tendency to view them as speaking in one voice and acting with one will. For example, at election time various ethnic and social groups ally for the purposes of trying to elect a Republican to national political office. This may include groups as diverse as fundamentalist Christians, Chicago School economists, Californians against immigration, and New England blue bloods. In the context of their electoral alliance, they are seen simply as Republicans. Their party platform, in reality a collage of all their policy preferences, is seen to reflect all their views such that each group is saddled with the views of the others. Viewed unto themselves, alliances are seen to have a rather simple structure. Typically the allies are regarded as having the same status or they are hierarchically ordered. So when considering the North Atlantic Treaty Organization, it is often assumed that the member countries simply act unanimously or that the most powerful country, the United States, simply leads and the others follow. Viewed from this perspective, it is perplexing and often frustrating to observe U.S. diplomats engaged in the complexities of cooperative policy formation and the mobilization of international support.

While fraught with power, struggle, and alliance, the political world constructed in linear thought is also rule governed. Action is not random but rather is perceived to be regulated by conventions of what is normally the case. Others' actions are understood in this light and one's own action is oriented accordingly. Even relations of domination and subordination are seen to have their rules that constrain the powerful as well as the powerless. Often many of these rules are encoded in laws. As reconstructed from a linear perspective, a society's laws, like any social convention, apply to the manner in which specific behaviors are to be initiated in particular situations. Where the state is successful, these laws are understood as norms of action. Obedience to the law is therefore regarded as necessary and beneficial, and individuals' actions are oriented accordingly.

Action may be rule governed, indeed possibly more effectively governed, without the explicit institutional regulation provided by law. When the state is unsuccessful in gaining acceptance for its laws or where no law has been established to regulate a particular behavior, the existing social norms of a community may operate just as effectively. Thus in countries like Greece, existing laws may be broadly ignored in the conduct of daily affairs, but social life may be powerfully regulated nonetheless by social norms and custom. Similarly in those countries where interaction within the family is subject to little legal regulation, what husbands can to do to wives or parents can do to children may be strictly governed by culturally dictated norms of acceptable practice. From the perspective of linear reasoning, social conventions are seen to reflect what is normal, that is, what is usual, necessary, and desirable. This is the basis of the influence they exercise.

The space and time of politics. The space in which political action takes place is a stage constructed out of the here and now of current considerations. This may be as immediate as what I am doing at this moment or as remote as the homeless living in another city five years from now. The geographical configuration is one of a center that extends out toward an ill-defined periphery. The stage is extended by the subjective introduction of either actions or actors who are known to be associated with present events or by the introduction of rules of action learned in other contexts. For example, focusing on me this afternoon, I may be worried about my ability to pay a mortgage bill. In this context, I may think about whether I will have enough money next month and then wonder where I will get the additional money I need. This may remind me of the fact that 35 percent of what I make goes to the government and not to me. I might wish I had more of my paycheck to take home. I heard a presidential candidate promise to lower the income tax if he gets elected. I might vote for him in the next election so that my taxes are less so that I will have the additional money I need to cover my bills. In this case, a concern with this month's mortgage bill projects into a future several months hence and defines a space that includes players as remote as a presidential candidate.

Later in the evening, I may be listening to a newscast about the homeless living in another city. The reporter talks of how the city is declining, industry is leaving, and the people are being left without jobs. Over the next five years, the number of unemployed is projected to increase and, as a result, so is the number of homeless. The newscast defines the center and point of departure of my construction of the meaning of what I have heard. Thinking about the report, I might focus on how hopeless the situation must be for many living in the city. This may cue a norm or rule I have learned, that it is the responsibility of a government to assist its citizens when they are in trouble. Following this precept, I believe that government should help to get the homeless jobs. This might require inducing existing industry to stay and other industries to enter. Alternatively, it may require providing retraining for adults and providing better education for disadvantaged young people. This will require money, money that the government may not have. If necessary, it may have to raise taxes to provide the help the people in this city require. In this example, my focus is initially on the poor in another city, but through the invocation of a norm, this quickly extends to include the national government and the action it must take over the next several years.

Finally, I might be talking to a friend who mentions that Germany is becoming the most powerful member of the European Community. I might wonder how this might be and remember hearing of how Germans are supposed to be very hard working. I may infer that they therefore produce more and are richer than the other European countries. Because they have money, they are able to exercise control over their less efficient neighbors. This may remind me that I have learned that Germany has always tried to control Europe, once leading to World War I and again leading to World War II. Then England stopped Germany, but England is weak now so Germany has no one in Europe to control it. Here the immediate concern leads to the inclusion of England, the character of the German people, and the mid-twentieth century as well as the early twenty-first century.

In all three cases, a domain is constructed by building out from present concerns. This includes going from the immediate concern to the inclusion of more remote players and from the present to the inclusion of a past or a future. The links are classically linear. This includes categorical associations (e.g., Germany to Germans are hard working and Germany always tries to control Europe), causal links (e.g., higher taxes will reduce my income, better education will lead to better jobs), and normative requirements (e.g., a government should help its citizens when they are in trouble). As is typical of linear construction, these various associations are based on past experience or report of the active connection between the concern at hand and these other considerations that are evoked. Linear thinking does not entail a consideration of the multiple links that may exist among actions and actors as they are articulated into a larger social or political system. In addition, this kind of thinking does not lead to a search for or construction of linkages that have not been either observed or reported. Therefore, while extended, the space in which political action is understood to occur is fragmentary. It consists of a set of stages upon which political actors are observed or reported to engage one another. Each stage is an arena unto itself. It has its own actors, norms of action, hierarchies, and conflicts. The stages themselves are not linked to one another unless the action on one is observed to spill out over the others in a fairly direct manner.

Consider the first two examples of extension immediately above, revolving around bills and taxes on one hand and the homeless and taxes on the other. In these examples, considerations began in two very different places, a bill with which I was confronted and the homeless in another city. In each case a political stage was elaborated quite separately from the other. This example is particularly interesting because the considerations may remain separate despite the clear overlap created by the consideration of tax policy in both cases. Often these arenas will remain subjectively isolated until information is provided that expressly makes the linkage between them. For example in the present case, it might be necessary for someone to tell me, "Look, if we start giving money to homeless, taxes are going to go up and you will have less take-home income and you won't be able to pay your bills." Of course, the consideration of German ascendancy is even more remote, requiring a greater number of links to connect this European phenomenon to the American economic situation and its possible consequences for taxation, employment conditions, and personal income. The net result is the construction of three fragments, three stages of political action that bear little or no relationship to one another.

Like its space, the time in which political action occurs is also fragmentary. The time constructed through linear reasoning is extensive; it builds from the present to a past and a future. This past, present, and future are not general frames of reference distinct from one another. Rather the present consists of the concrete action occurring at the specific moment under consideration. It provides a concrete point of departure out of which a past and future can be constructed. The latter consist of linear chains of particular causes and their effects that build backward and forward in a single trajectory of time. Each of these chains constitutes a history and a future, but these are specific to the particular action from which they extend. So rather than time being an integrated succession of epochs constituted by many actions both interrelated to one another and extending into the future, linear thinking constructs multiple, concrete, largely independent trajectories of particular sequences of action unfolding each in its own time. For example, there may be a consideration of events in the recent history of transportation from the ship and the horse-drawn carriage to the train to the automobile and the airplane. Additionally there may be an understanding of the development of population centers from villages on the seashore to densely populated urban centers to suburban sprawl. But although these histories are events occurring in the same place, they may not be considered relative to one another or in the broader context of social and technological change. Another politically interesting example of this is the terms in which a given country's conduct of foreign affairs may be considered. An individual may perceive that Saddam Hussein, as the leader of Iraq, has been engaged in an ongoing conflict with the United States. This has a history of the Gulf War, economic isolation, exchange of harsh words, and sporadic punitive attacks by the United States. She may also be aware that Saddam has been engaged in an internal struggle for control over his own country. This too has a history of defections, assassinations, and police actions. But unless instructed otherwise, it is quite likely that these two histories will remain quite separate and the so-called domestic-foreign nexus will not be part of the consideration of either foreign or domestic affairs.

Not only may several histories unfolding simultaneously not be related to one another, but also a potentially single history may be regarded as a set of discontinuous histories. Thus, when viewing a person, the events of adulthood and those of childhood may be regarded as completely separate from one another. This may be the result of several factors, such as the time of childhood being very remote from the present of adulthood, the structure of a life history in which work or travel displaces an adult from the context of his childhood thereby disconnecting him from it, or cultural definition that uses labels and rituals to demarcate adulthood as clearly separate from childhood. Similarly, when viewing the history of a group such as African-Americans, the events they experience today may not be related to histories of the antebellum South or the civil rights movement of the 1960s. In this case, the American Civil War or Martin Luther King may serve as separate anchors around which fragments of history are constructed. There is thus the history of slavery, abolition, and post-war exploitation that is constructed around the Civil War. There is also the history of politicization, rioting, and protest that is constructed around Martin Luther King. Finally there is the current history of high rates of unemployment and crime among the inner city poor and the growing conservatism of the black middle class. Although involving the same group in the same country, no links may be presented that connect these otherwise isolated chains of events. As a result it is likely that these histories will remain isolated fragments with little bearing on one another. Current events will not be seen in the light of slavery or the civil rights movements and the history of those movements will not be understood in the light of current events.

In sum, the space and time in which politics occurs is an aggregate of dissociated pieces. Whereas linear thought can move freely among the weave of connections that constitute any one of these pieces, it can consider only one piece at a time. To appropriate Robert Lane's language, linear thought is "morselizing" (Lane, 1962, 1973). Which piece or morsel will be considered is determined by what is being personally experienced or presented by others. The actors and actions involved will be made sense of in this context. For example, when a political discourse is presented that addresses drug abuse, the presentation may engulf the linear view of politics because it provides the conceptual anchor or point of orientation that then delimits the various subjective associations that are likely to be made. The latter may include considerations of the associated rise in violent crime, young adult unemployment, the decay in values, or the inability of government to address the problem. With a shift in the discourse, perhaps to a focus on the natural environment, the drug abuse issue will evaporate and the view of politics will be dominated by considerations of parks, air quality, and industrial development. As suggested by this example, the shifting focus of linear reasoning is powerfully oriented by external influences.

Recent research on the effects of mass media may be reconsidered in this light. Shanto Iyengar and Donald Kinder (1987) studied how television news could direct the attention of its audience away from some issues and toward others. In their research they manipulated the nightly news broadcast by regularly including an additional segment on a particular matter of national interest. Half their subjects saw a number of television broadcasts that frequently included a segment on the environment. The other half saw the same broadcast except the added segment focused on national defense. Subjects were then asked to rank policy concerns in order of importance. As predicted, subjects ranked the regularly added issue (either the environment or national defense) relatively important and ranked the issue not mentioned in the broadcasts relatively unimportant.

This "agenda-setting effect" of the broadcasts is precisely the kind of impact that mass media presentations would be expected to have on linear thinking. Working with a fragmented view of politics, linear reasoning tends not to construct associations between fragments when the requisite associations have not provided either through learning or current presentation. It is therefore largely confined to that arena of political action currently under consideration. If this arena is presented recurrently, it will receive more attention, become more salient, and therefore is likely to be regarded as more significant. Insofar as the nightly news is the individual's chief source of political information and that person reasons in a linear fashion, then that person would be expected to have his sense of political priorities set accordingly. Again it is important to note that our analysis here pertains to individuals who reason in a linear fashion. Those who think in a systematic manner construct their own context around such presentations and hence are less likely to be oriented by them (e.g., see Braunwarth, 1996; 1999).

Summary. It is apparent that linear political reasoning offers a limited understanding of politics. As reconstructed in linear terms, politics is something of a play, one already written by the gods, fate, or nature herself. The play has something of the quality of John Krizanc's experimental production of "Tamara" (1989). The action unfolds in several rooms simultaneously, but a member of the audience can observe only what is in one room at a time. From the perspective of linear reasoning, the action occurring in the different rooms is not integrated. Rather the play is a collage of fragments; each room has its own space and time. The events in a given room are understood relative to one another. They are related to events in other rooms only when the observer can actually watch how action in one room leads to or from action occurring in another.

Individuals and groups are the players in this fragmented play of politics. Some of these players are directly observed. Others are never seen but are only reported or inferred. The particular behaviors they enact are understood as reactions to another's action or as an expression of the goals, feelings, and needs inherent in the nature of the particular actor. Each room or stage upon which the play unfolds has its code of action, its norms. When conventions are apparent to the players, they engage one another peacefully and cooperatively. When conventions are violated or are unclear, the players follow their own interests typically leading to conflict. As revealed by what they are able to do to one another, it is apparent that some of the players have power and others do not. In some cases, this will indicate a hierarchical relationship among various individuals and groups. The conflict may also give rise to alliances among the players as they pursue common paths and move to help one another.

By paying attention to the play's script, the observer can learn the parts that she and others are intended to play, who they are supposed to be and how they are supposed to act in specific circumstances. This may enable the observer to feel as though the play is comprehensible and allow her to be an effective participant. Because political life is nothing more than the play itself, it is not the case that there are people who play parts and retain an identity apart from what they do. To the contrary, the people, individual and groups, *are* the parts they play. Similarly, the script does not simply direct the action of players; it defines what is real, necessary, and normal. Bound to this play and the particular concrete action of its many disconnected little plots, the observer has no sense of alternative scenarios or even of the underlying logic of the one being presented. To the degree to which critique is possible, the observer is limited to representing a criticism voiced by one of the players at some earlier point in time.

LINEAR EVALUATION: LIKING AND WANTING

Linear evaluation consists of liking and wanting. It is based on the experience of what is desirable, good, or normal. Consistent with the general structure of linear thought, the focus is on concrete actions and actors—that is, on the particular things that are said and done, and on the particular individual or groups who are the initiators or the targets. These actions and actors are abstracted from the flow of events and placed in relation to one another. The relationship thus constructed is imbalanced with one action anchoring the relationship. Apart from any defining characteristics, this anchoring action has value. This may consist of an immediate pain or pleasure or of some prior judgment. In either case, this value flows to the other actions with which the anchor is associated.

Operating in this manner, linear evaluation is oriented by two questions. (1) How desirable or likable is a given action (or actor)? The answer to this question is based on the pain or pleasure associated with a particular action, or on how that action is associated with specific other actions or actors that have already been evaluated. (2) Is this the correct or appropriate action to take in the present situation? The answer here reflects the direct or reported experience of the specific manner in which a series of actions normally unfolds in a given circumstance. Answers to these questions may also be culturally provided. In part, a culture consists of a vast storehouse of evaluations of the desirability or normality of specific actions. In the form of value labels and prescriptions for action, these evaluations are communicated to individuals through language and then may be applied by them when assessing the specific acts or actors in question.

The Primary Creation of Value

For purposes of description, linear evaluation may be viewed as a three-step process.[11] Initially there is a primary appraisal of a present and heretofore value-free action or actor. Evaluation at this point is conducted in several ways. It may be based on direct experience of the satisfactions or dissatisfactions associated with the action in question. For example, one may be asked to use a new machine on the job. Doing so, one may discover that operating the machine leads to a backache and consequently judge the use of the machine negatively. In a more political vein, one may be asked to declare a political identity. In response, one may state that "I am a Democrat." This declaration may be followed by others' approval. Consequently, the action is evaluated positively. This primary evaluation may also be based on other people's claims regarding the desirability of the action. Here no direct personal experience of the action is required. For example, one may be confronted by another's judgment that Gypsies are bad people. This may be sufficient to shape one's own assessment of the Gypsies even though one has had no personal contact with Gypsies. This social influence may extend to affecting the evaluations of actions or actors with which one does have experience. For example, one may find the act of voting to be unrewarding or even somewhat difficult. Others' statements about the positive value of voting, however, may be sufficient to override assessments based on one's direct experience. As a result, one may come to view the act of voting in a broadly positive way. In this manner, social influences and definitions can often outweigh personal experience.

Social influence on primary assessment is not limited to the effect of other people's report of their own experience. It also includes the effect of typical social practice either as directly experienced or as reported by others. When reconstructed in linear terms, this typical social practice constitutes a specific standard or concrete norm of what specifically to do and when to it. Insofar as the action in question matches this standard, it is judged appropriate and is evaluated positively. To engage in the action produces the subjective good feeling of having acted correctly. This reliance on normative standards of action extends from the apparently trivial (e.g., how to use one's knife and fork when eating or how to dress for croquet) to the possibly more consequential (e.g., how to address a superior at work or how to respond to another person's request for help). In each case, conventional behavior will be judged appropriate and therefore will be evaluated positively. In complementary fashion, unconventional and inappropriate behavior will be judged negatively. This interweaving of the conventional, the good, and the true is characteristic of linear thought.

The resulting primary evaluation of an action or actor is then abstracted from its specific context. Like other linear relationships, although they are concrete, evaluative links are represented apart from the particular circumstance of their construction and may be applied in other contexts. Consequently, if the evaluation of the action were based on personal experience of a consequent positive reward, that reward need not follow in a new situation for a continued positive evaluation of that action. Thus one continues to feel good about being a Democrat even when approval does not follow directly in subsequent situations. Similarly, if the evaluation is based on another's report, that other need not be present in order to evoke a positive evaluation of the action in question. Thus, one may continue to judge the Gypsies negatively even when one's friend is not present. Finally, one may continue to feel a behavior is appropriate and gain satisfaction from acting accordingly even when the social and cultural context of one's life changes. This is often the case with immigrants who continue to engage in the typical practices of their native land even when they are contradicted by the common practice of their new homeland.

The Secondary Creation of Value: Cognitive Balance, Prejudice, and Cultural Standards

The linear conception of action is extensive—an action or actor is understood only as it is related to other action. This extensive quality of linear relations leads to another step in the evaluative process, a secondary creation of value. The value of the action in question tends to flow to those actions or actors to which it is related. This relationship may be established through a causal link. Value, be it positive or negative, may be transferred to causes and effects of the valued action. For example, let us say that the action of assisting an elderly person across the street is valued positively. Any person observed performing that action will acquire value by virtue of causing the action. Like the act to which she is linked, such a person will be positively valued. Alternatively, we can consider the example of a negatively valued act, being struck by a car and badly injured. In this instance, a person who has been so effected will tend to acquire some of the value of the act and thus be more negatively valued. Most surprising, this will tend to be the case even when it is clear that the individual had no evident responsibility for the misfortune. This mode of evaluation is evident in social psychological research on the phenomenon of the derogation of the victim (Lerner, 1970).[12]

Not only do valued actions confer worth on actors, but also actors themselves may be valued. This in turn will affect the valuing of the action they perform. For example, if a valued friend decides to enter college, the act may acquire positive value because of its association with the friend. Similarly, if the friend voices a particular political opinion, that political opinion may be positively valued. The assumption that secondary value is created in this fashion underlies one common line of advertising strategy. Relying on the testimonial of screen and sports stars regarding the desirability of particular products, the advertiser is assuming that value the stars have for the viewer will transfer to the products they support. This transference of value from actors to action clearly obtains in the case of group actors as well. Thus the action of high prestige groups is likely to be positively valued and the action of low prestige groups is likely to be negatively valued. In a similar vein, the action of valued allies is likely to be positively regarded and the action of despised enemies is likely to be negatively regarded. This will obtain even when the action is the same in the two cases.[13]

Social categorization and out-group prejudice. Secondary value may be created through categorical as well as causal linkages. For example a category of action, say the role of being a surgeon, may be valued positively. This positive value will tend to flow to all the actors and actions associated with the role. Thus all individuals who are surgeons are likely to be more positively valued and all actions associated with performing the role, from wearing an otherwise unattractive surgical outfit to engaging in the otherwise unappetizing business of carving up a person's torso, are also likely to be more positively regarded. Value also flows from categories of actors. The value of a group is likely to flow both to all of its characteristic actions and to all of its members. Therefore if a group is regarded positively, for example Europeans, all individuals identified as European will tend to be well regarded as will all behaviors labeled as European. Similarly if a group is negatively regarded, for example Mexicans, then the members and their characteristic actions will tend to be negatively valued. This can lead to the otherwise curious phenomena of positively or negatively valuing the same behavior depending on which group is doing it. So Italian corruption may be viewed as harmless, French inefficiencies as part of the good life, and Greek family life as traditional and warm. On the other hand, Mexican corruption may be viewed as unacceptable, its inefficiencies as unbearable, and its family life as male chauvinist and authoritarian.

The result of this category-mediated transfer of value is that definition and evaluation often imply one another—common concrete identity or social categorization produces common evaluation. This has already been exemplified in the preceding discussion of Europeans and Mexicans. It is also interestingly apparent in the flow of evaluation that occurs between the self and the groups with which one is identified. As the evaluation of the group is conferred on its members, so it affects the evaluation of oneself. If one is a member of a well-regarded elite group, one's sense of self is enhanced. In a complementary fashion, if one is a member of a negatively regarded group, one's sense of self is commensurately diminished. This flow of evaluation can be reversed. This occurs when one's self is the anchoring category and social identifications become its associated elements. In this case, one's self-evaluation may affect one's evaluation of the groups to which one belongs. Thus a positive self-evaluation may lead to a positive evaluation of one's family, ethnic group, or nation. Negative evaluations will have the opposite effect. The latter phenomenon is well captured by oft quoted claim of the American comedian Woody Allen, "I would never want to be a member of any club that would have me."

In a related manner, social distinctions often produce opposite evaluations when one of the entities distinguished has clear value. This is especially true when the actors or groups involved are actively opposed to one another, such as enemies on the battlefield or opponents on a playing field. Here the opposing group, as well as all actions and actors associated with it, are denigrated. This direct opposition is a sufficient, but not a necessary condition for evaluation. Examples of how difference leads to negative evaluation abound, particularly where one's own social identity is involved. It is there in the lore of "the stranger" and the suspicion in which he or she is regarded. In the case of national identities, there is the negative concept of the foreigners. The British category of "wog" illustrates this nicely. In the case of ethnic identities, there is the outsider with its negative connotations. It is well illustrated by the Jewish category of the "goy." In the case of religious identity, there is the much-used category of the "infidel."

Insofar as evaluation and categorization imply one another, common evaluation may also produce common identity or social categorization. Action and actors that are positively valued may be swept into a single category. In the process, potentially meaningful differences may be diminished or eliminated altogether. In the case of action, different acts may be grouped together on the basis of whether they are positively or negatively evaluated. Thus, being discourteous, hurtling an insult, or physically attacking may all be defined as unfriendly or aggressive acts. Similarly, sneaking into a concert, stealing a small item from a store, breaking into a house, and striking another person may all be categorized as violations or crimes. One consequence of this categorization is that it may lead to a more extreme estimation of the negative value of the lesser acts in the category. In the case of actors, linear evaluation frequently leads to groupings of individuals and groups. For example, it is quite common to identify those people one likes and place them into a single group, for example, one's friends. Similarly, it is quite common that those who are disliked are placed into a single group as well. This is exemplified by the singular categories in which disliked others are placed, such as the "riffraff," "the undesirables," or the "*bas class.*" It is also evident in the construction of the out-group social identities mentioned above, that is the "goyim," the "wogs," and the "infidels," in which a host of otherwise dissimilar individuals are grouped together in a single social category because they are negatively valued. Of particular interest, these social categories are not applied to individuals who are members of valued out-groups and may be applied to devalued in-group members. For example, the term "wog" is generally not applied to individuals from high-status nationalities. In complementary fashion, a term like "goy" might be used to denigrate an in-group member.

It should be clear from the preceding discussion that linear reasoning and evaluation create fertile ground for the development for group-oriented prejudice. In this type of thinking, such prejudicial orientations as racism, sexism, and ethnocentrism flourish. As discussed earlier, linear reasoning naturally leads to the categorization of individual actors into social groups. Linear evaluation extends these discriminations by readily assigning value to the groups distinguished and thereby to all of the group members. Thus prejudicial evaluation accompanies stereotyping. This value can be generated on the basis of personal experience of group members. For example, the experience of being mugged by someone of dark skin color can readily generalize to an evaluation of all blacks. It can also be generated more subtly with the evaluation that accompanies definition in the case of one's own social identities. Insofar as one positively values one's own group(s), there will be a tendency to negatively value out-groups whose distinctiveness sustains the definition of one's own group. Thus relative to your family, you negatively value those "who are not blood"; relative to your team, you negatively value the opposing team; relative to your nation, you negatively value neighboring nations. Finally, group prejudice can reflect social influence and cultural dictate. Here the culture not only distinguishes a group, but ascribes it negative value. This negative ascription often brings with it the categories of being bad or less. This culturally provided evaluation is often extended through linear evaluation wherein evaluation leads to categorization. Negatively valued acts tend to be associated with negatively valued actors. In the case of the perception of negatively valued groups, this results in the same negative acts frequently being ascribed to otherwise very different groups. Thus all Gypsies, working-class people, southerners, and blacks are seen to be inefficient, untrustworthy, violent, criminal, and darkly sexual.

Again we have social psychological research that dovetails with the description of linear thought. During the late 1950s and 1960s, social psychologists were centrally concerned with cognitive balance and dissonance theories (e.g., Heider, 1958; Festinger, 1957; Abelson et al., 1968). Essentially all these theories suggest that people attempt to maintain a kind of consistency in their evaluation of entities that belong to a common category. So, for example, if you have a friend whom you positively value, it is cognitively consistent when that friend engages in positively valued acts, such as helping another or doing well on the job, or when that friend is associated with other people or groups that are positively valued, such as other friends. This cognitive consistency or balance is also maintained when entities that are valued in opposite ways are dissociated with one another. In the case of the friend, it is cognitively consistent when she does not do such negatively valued things as lose her job or is not associated with such negatively valued groups as one's own enemies. This relationship between categorization and evaluation clearly applies to perception of groups as well. Thus the members of favorably evaluated groups are themselves favorably evaluated. Similarly one's favorable image of oneself is maintained by favorably evaluating the groups with which one identifies or by choosing to identify with groups already positively valued. Importantly, this consistency effect extends beyond evaluation to the determination of social practice. Thus not only does one like one's own groups, but one also tends to act toward them in favorable ways.[14]

These cognitive consistency theories and the related empirical research are readily related to the structure of linear thought. As already noted, in linear thinking, evaluation and categorization imply one another. Actions and actors that are linked to an anchoring action or actor are not only defined relative to the anchor, they are at the same time evaluated in terms of it. Thus actions and actors that are causally or categorically linked also tend to be commonly evaluated. In this regard, the formal qualities of linear thought may be understood as providing the operational or structural underpinnings of the tendency toward evaluative consistency suggested by balance and dissonance theorists. Similarly, the evidence provided in their research and in later work on stereotyping and minimal group effects may be seen as wholly consistent with our understanding of linear thought. Again it is necessary to introduce the caveat that this body of research applies primarily to linear thought. Individuals reasoning in a sequential or systematic fashion should not evidence much cognitive consistency in their social judgments.

Cultural standards and morality. Apart from causal and categorical extensions, the secondary creation of value may occur in a third manner. This involves matching the valued action to a culturally explicit standard of correct behavior. Where such a cultural standard has been learned, the primary evaluation is placed in relation to an explicit rule of what should occur. The primary evaluation may or may not accord with this secondary evaluation. For example, one may experience an action that produces a satisfying effect such as having sex. However one may have been socialized in a culture where sex is regarded negatively despite its associated carnal pleasures. Alternatively, colleagues on the job may suggest that cheating the customer is permissible. But one may have been raised in a culture that explicitly condemns such cheating regardless of who approves or how profitable it may be. In both cases, the primary experience of value is extended by considering the activity and its immediate value relative to an express cultural dictum regarding desirable practice. To the degree to which the personal experience of rewards and the socially structured patterns of common practice are consistent with the cultural ascription of value, primary evaluation and this secondary introduction of value will complement and reinforce one another. To the degree to which they are not, they will conflict and one or the other will be ignored. Examples of this include both the denial of primary evaluation characteristic of ascetic, culturally dictated lifestyles, such as that of certain Catholic orders, and the denial of cultural dictates in favor of immediate pleasures evident among the young Scottish urban unemployed, such as those portrayed in film *Trainspotting*.

This mode of creating secondary value introduces a novel element into linear evaluation. It is a consideration of value based solely on a statement of what should be the case, one that is constructed without regard to what actually is the case. The result is an idealistic evaluation, one that does not necessarily derive from concrete or even common experience. Instead, the basis of this evaluation is a cultural imperative. Especially as it is opposed to what is real, this constitutes the expressly moral bases of linear evaluation. While idealistic, these moral claims are constructed in a linear manner. Like all linear relationships, they pertain to concrete and specific action. Good examples are such moral directives as found in the Ten Commandments: Thou shall not kill. Thou shall not use the Lord's name in vain. Thou shall not covet thy neighbor's wife. These are imperatives that by their very construction demand action that is contrary to common practices and immediate pleasures. Of course moral direction can be stated in more positive terms: Thou shall honor thy mother and father. This particular instruction is somewhat general. As with all linear reconstruction of more general cultural claims, it will be understood to require the enactment of a particular learned set of associated behaviors.

The moral dicta of linear thought are not spontaneously constructed and related to one another in light of some overarching evaluative system. Rather these rules of action are present in the culture and learned in a piecemeal fashion; they are understood in terms of their specific application rather than relative to one another. The limits of this construction are apparent when circumstances are such that moral imperatives collide. Such a collision, as typical of linear contradiction, is practical. It commonly occurs when two moral directives with different action implications are cued in the same situation. An example would be a decision to steal to help a friend. Here two common imperatives, that one help one's friends and that one should not steal, are introduced. Lacking an overarching sense of morality, linear thought offers no clear basis for deciding which is the appropriate course of action to adopt. A moral conflict may also occur when the situation is structured in such a way that any action simultaneously conforms to and violates a moral prescription. A dramatic example is provided by the title incident in William Styron's book *Sophie's Choice*. Set during the Third Reich in Germany, Sophie is at the train station where she and her two young children are being transported to what she realizes to be certain death at a concentration camp. Just before departure, a guard approaches her and offers to save one of her children, but she must decide which one. In linear terms, Sophie is confronted with an impossible choice, impossible because her action necessarily violates a moral at the same time that it conforms to that imperative: to save one child (a moral approved act) requires sending the other child to her death (a morally reviled act). Within the framework of linear thought, there is no satisfactory resolution of the conflict. In the book, Sophie makes her choice and is largely destroyed by its consequences.

Sophie's dilemma is one illustration of how linear morality lacks the higher order ethical frame of reference required to evaluate particular moral claims relative to one another. At best, moral reasoning at this level is open to specific instruction of how one particular claim can preempt another under certain circumstances. Thus one can learn that one cannot kill, except when under mortal threat from another or when following orders during military combat. Within the framework of the American Constitution, one can similarly learn that one has a right to enjoy and protect one's property, but this does not extend to the injury of others even when they trespass. In some cultural contexts, moral dictates are defined in quite general or abstract terms. Although this provides a basis for ethical integration, these abstractions are not readily assimilated. Instead it is translated into the terms of linear evaluation and becomes understood as a specific standard of moral evaluation. For example, a culturally defined norm of justice will be understood in the context of linear thought in terms of particular practices that are labeled as just, such as dividing rewards equally or giving all individuals a chance to apply for a job. Conceived in terms of the specific direction each offers and without regard for the higher order concerns in light of which they are justified, moral claims are not themselves typically subject to consideration.[15] They are merely applied, not criticized. In linear evaluation, there is consequently a tendency to reify moral claims—to regard them as natural and universal. They are applied without regard to cultural context or history. For example, a moral value learned in the United States, that punishment should be rehabilitative and humane, not vengeful and physical, is freely applied in the negative evaluation of punitive practices in Singapore or Saudi Arabia. Similarly, the moral value of family and community loyalties in the eastern Mediterranean is uncritically applied to the evaluation of specific examples of the individualist and meritocratic qualities of the American or German way of life.

Value Application

The third step in the evaluative process is one of application. Linear evaluations exist apart from immediate experience. This is true of both primary and secondary evaluations. As already noted, the primary evaluation is abstracted from the initial learning situation. The secondary creation of value occurs at an even greater remove from the ongoing flow of events. In both instances, the evaluations are mental representations of initial experience and its associations. These evaluations are then applied to subsequent experience involving the same actions or actors. These prior assessments tend to structure subsequent experience. In this sense, linear evaluations are strongly prejudicial. The effect is direct in that an already evaluated actor or action, when encountered again, will tend to be assigned the same value. Depending on the strength of the prior evaluation, this is likely to occur even when later experiences with the action or actor produce a neutral or opposite effect. Thus one's well-established dislike of another person is likely to survive incidents where that person behaves in a friendly or generally pleasing fashion. Similarly, one's denigration of women is likely to endure despite experiences of particular women's specific intelligent or effective action.

Linear evaluations are prejudicial in an indirect manner as well. Once established, the evaluation of actions and actors provides an anchor that may guide the later evaluation of other entities. To illustrate, consider the case where one likes Phillip and then discovers that Phillip plays volleyball. Because of its association with Phillip who is positively valued, volleyball will now tend to be positively valued. Assessed in a manner consistent with the evaluation of the anchor, these new secondary evaluations reinforce the first evaluation. Returning to volleyball, one may have had no attitude, but as a function of Phillip's play, one may come to like the sport. Volleyball may thus acquire a value of its own, which then reverberates back to support the positive evaluation of Phillip who plays this now desirable game. In sum, evaluations, primary and secondary, are applied in such a manner that they affect subsequent evaluation and are therefore likely to be maintained over time.

Constructed in this manner, linear evaluation can be reflexive, but only in a limited way. Prior personal judgments, social influences, and cultural dictates are generally the bases, not the object, of evaluation. A person typically does not reflect upon her evaluation that operating a machine on the job is hurtful and hence undesirable. This is simply the case and it orients subsequent judgment and choice. Similarly, she does not consider the fact that she has come to like volleyball because she likes Phillip who plays volleyball. She simply knows that she likes volleyball. Nor does she consider the value of the cultural imperative that you should help those in need. She just knows that this is a good thing and it ought to be done. While not typical, a limited mode of reflection is possible. Linear thought does enable the individual to objectify her action and thus reflect on it. This includes the evaluations she makes. In so doing, this activity, like any other, can be categorized or explained in the same manner as another's action. Similarly, the individual's evaluations can themselves be evaluated. This reflexive evaluation is conducted in the same manner as any linear evaluation, through a three-step process. Thus, the evaluation can be considered in terms of the value of the immediate consequences associated with it, how the evaluation is evaluated by others, and how common an evaluation it is. Secondarily, the evaluation can be examined in terms of value of other action and actors with which its causally or categorically linked or in terms of how it matches cultural stipulations of the value one ought to maintain. In this regard, reflection on one's evaluations is limited in the same fashion as the evaluations themselves. They are constrained by the concrete and specific quality of events as presented over time, be it personal experiences one has had, the experiences others have had and reported, the common practices and routines one has observed, or the values prevalent in the culture to which one has been exposed. In this sense, one is limited to the reproduction of what is personally felt, is socially structured, and is culturally defined. In this regard, linear evaluations, even when they are reflexive and critical, are oriented by the specific social conventions and cultural norms of everyday life.

Value Conflict and Resolution

For the most part, a single evaluative association orients linear evaluations. Once established in a given circumstance, there is little need to introduce additional considerations. For example, consider the case of Isaac who first meets Angela. Within a few moments he can observe that Angela is female, an African-American, and that she utilizes an extended vocabulary when she speaks. Reasoning in a linear fashion, Isaac will tend to evaluate Angela on the basis of the associated value of one of these characteristics. Which will be chosen will depend in part on the situation and in part on the particulars of the genesis of Isaac's values. Thus meeting her at a party, he may regard her as physically attractive and view her positively. In this context, he may choose to pursue her. Alternatively meeting her in a classroom, he may view her in light of speaking style and evaluate her positively. This may lead him to try to engage in further discussion or suggest that they work together. The key point here is that one characteristic will become an anchor that orients Isaac's evaluation of and subsequent behavior toward Angela in that context. If, as in this case, an attribute of Angela rather than Angela herself is the conceptual anchor orienting Isaac's evaluations at the time, no additional evaluations are introduced and no evaluative problem emerges. There is also no problem created when Angela herself becomes the anchoring concern if Isaac's various evaluations of the attributes linked to Angela are consistent with one another—that is, they all have the same positive or negative valence. In this regard, her attractiveness and articulate speech complement one another.

A problem emerges for linear thought when two evaluations of different valence (positive and negative) are actively linked to one another. Linear evaluation naturally leads to the construction of a single evaluation of an action and the other actions categorically or causally associated with it. The logic of linear thought is such that just as the members of a conceptual category must share common features so they must share common value. The introduction of inconsistent values creates a value conflict. In linear terms, the conflict is a practical one. An action cannot be good when it yields both good and bad consequences and an actor cannot be good if it has both good and bad qualities. When an action or actor is both good and bad, confusion ensues. Cognitive consistency theories refer to this as imbalance (Heider, 1958) and dissonance (Festinger, 1957) and later research provides convincing evidence that this cognitive confusion produces actual physiological discomfort (Cooper, Zanna, and Tavis, 1978). As noted previously, linear thinking lacks the overarching frame of reference in which potentially conflicting specific values may be coordinated relative to one another. Consequently different strategies, many of which are well documented in the research on cognitive consistency, are employed (e.g., Abelson et al., 1968).

One typical strategy for resolving evaluative conflict is to diminish the importance of some evaluations and bolster the significance of others. Returning to Isaac and Angela, a problem may be introduced by the fact that Isaac is racist and therefore regards African-Americans negatively. By implication he is led to evaluate Angela negatively while at the same time positively valuing her attractiveness and eloquence. Isaac is confronted with the unsatisfactory confusion that ensues. One way in which he can resolve the conflict is by diminishing her negative attributes. He can emphasize that she is light-skinned and of mixed racial parentage. At the same time he can inflate her positive attributes by regarding her as extraordinarily beautiful or intelligent.

Another related strategy is denial. Here the conflict is resolved simply by refusing to attend to the relevant dimensions of the action or actor in question. Let us return to hapless Isaac. Now he is confronted by the choice of working in the laboratory for the next several weeks and advancing the career he values, or he may go off to France in pursuit of a woman to whom he is attracted. So constructed, his plan of action necessarily has good and bad aspects: he either advances his career and loses the woman or he has the woman and his career stalls. The conflict may be eliminated through denial. Isaac can simply choose to deny one or the other effects of his choice. Thus if he chooses to stay and work, he can either deny or refuse to consider the effect on his prospects with the woman. Similarly, if he chooses to go to France, he can deny or refuse to consider the effect on his career.

Of course value conflict emerges in expressly political contexts as well. To illustrate, consider the evaluation of a political group, such as a party or country, with which one identifies. Such a group is likely to be very positively valued. Nonetheless, such groups are often reported to engage in activity that is negatively valued. A good example is the Israeli assault on Lebanon in the early 1980s ending in its complicity in the massacres that took place in two refugee camps. Israelis strongly identified with and had high regard for the moral integrity of their own country. Yet the incidents following the invasion of Lebanon presented them with evidence of Israel's involvement in action which was unambiguously unacceptable. For many Israelis, an evaluative conflict was created by the negative actions being attributed to a positively valued entity. This conflict was handled in a variety of typically linear ways in the attempt to render the evaluation of Israel more consistent. Some Israelis adopted the rather painful path of acknowledging responsibility and therefore lowering their evaluation of Israel and, by implication, of themselves. The result is many were left depressed and despondent afterwards. Some followed an alternative path of reducing Israel's connection to the action by emphasizing it was the Lebanese Christians not the Israeli Defense Force who were directly involved in the massacre, thereby limiting the relevance of the action for the evaluation of Israel. In a similar vein, still others sought to diminish the negative evaluation of the action by reducing the severity of its effect. They suggested that relatively few people were injured. Alternatively, the negative quality of the action might have been countered by a claim that both the action and its effect were normal. Those adopting this strategy suggested that death and intrigue were the inevitable accompaniments of war. The foregoing example refers to the evaluation of in-groups. Similar evaluative conflicts arise in a variety of political circumstances, such as when enemy nations achieve particular success, when respected leaders commit crimes, when disliked policy produces good results, and when despised ethnic groups do well. In the course of linear evaluation, the resulting evaluative conflicts are resolved either through attitude change or through denial, diminishment, and bolstering.

Summary

Evaluating the world around them in a linear manner, an individual emerges as a very distinctive social actor. She is preoccupied with concrete action and its consequences, categorical associations, and conformity to social conventions and cultural standards. There is a certain simplicity to the evaluative process. The aim is to determine what is desirable or undesirable, normal or aberrant, or good or bad. It is a basically a bipolar judgment where the key concern is less where precisely on some value line the object is located and more which side of a neutral midpoint it falls. To make that judgment, a relevant concrete rule, abstracted from prior experience, is invoked and applied. In the process, the determination of causal responsibility and the consequent attribution of blame or praise are central. Alternatively, considerations of categorical associations with roles or groups may be pivotal, resulting in the associated approval or disapproval of the action or actor in question.

Evaluation is conducted most comfortably when a single frame of reference, a single rule, guides the judgment. Where more than one is introduced, various strategies will be employed to simplify the situation by rendering the various bases of evaluation consistent and in this sense reestablish the practical singularity of the frame of reference. In this context, judgments of categories of action, such as roles, or actors, such as individuals or groups, are also simple. They are evaluated as positive or negative in a way that tends to engulf the judgment of all their individual aspects or members. Apart from their simplicity and internal consistency, the evaluations are also often unequivocal and enduring. In part this is evident in the loyalties and enmities that are so central to linear social evaluations. The result is strong friendships and in-group loyalties accompanied by equally strong dislikes and out-group disdain and hatred. The enduring quality of linear evaluation is also demonstrated by a resistance to change in attitude or practice. This leads both to dependability and to a rigidity of social and political outlook. It is often accompanied by an intolerant rejection of what is different or strange (as defined by personal experience or conventional social practice).

Overall, linear evaluation renders the individual susceptible to social influence and accepting of social convention. In part, this is because linear evaluation reflects the contours of experience as it is presented. Insofar as the social context shapes that experience, it will determine the values the individual will construct. This is in fact accomplished in a variety of ways. First and perhaps most obvious, the social context includes people who provide the individual with their reports of their experiences. These reports mediate the individual's direct experience of the objects in question and thereby influence her judgment of what is pleasurable or normal. This is especially true when these sources of information are themselves valued. Second, the social context affects the substance of the individual's experience directly. The social context normally has a structure evidenced in the regularity with which actions are initiated and in the way actions follow one another. This social structuring of action determines the kinds of consequences that actions generally will have. This in turn determines the pains and pleasures the individual will experience to be associated with various actions. In a similar fashion, the structuring of social action also affects the individual's construction of standards of normality. Existing patterns of social exchange delimit the sequences of action the individual is likely to experience as typical, thereby providing a standard for judging what is normal and therefore desirable or good. Finally, the social context is also cultural. As assimilated in linear terms, the culture consists of a set of prescriptions for how action ought to be conducted. These then provide the basis for the moral standards that an individual may employ. In sum, an individual who reasons in a linear fashion is an immediately, concretely, and intensely conventional social animal.

Chapter Four Systematic Thinking

Systematic thinking is the most sophisticated form of thinking of the three analyzed here. It emerges with the objectification of the concrete and anchored relationships constructed in the course of linear thinking. Reconstructed as objective interactions or subjective propositions, these specific relationships are related to one another either in the context of a broader system of relationships in which they are articulated or with reference to an abstract principle of relationship that they exemplify. Systematic thinking thus supposes that, apart from their intrinsic or concrete qualities, the particulars of interaction and discourse have a more essential, relational meaning. Integration, abstraction, and interpretation are therefore characteristic of this type of thinking.

Systematic thinking involves a high level of cognitive construction. In its most industrious and sophisticated elaborations, it yields very general theories of personal, social, and political life and very self-conscious and careful strategies for observing, interpreting, and judging events. As such, it may be used not only to describe the more informal efforts of everyday analysis, but also most contemporary social science. As a result, in the description of systematic thinking presented in this chapter, occasional reference is made to particular social science theory and research as exemplars of systematic thinking.

Two cautionary points regarding the quality of systematic thinking should be made here. First, systematic thinking, like all forms of thinking, requires effort. It may therefore be conducted in a more or less methodical and elaborate manner. Where there is less effort, the result will be conceptual systems that are partially or loosely constructed and principles that are less abstract and less carefully deduced and applied. Although deficient, the basic quality of thinking and the structure of the understandings and evaluations in such cases are nonetheless systematic. Second, even when it is more carefully conducted, systematic thinking is not the final step in a developmental progress or the most advanced form of thinking attainable. The view of development being advanced here is neither teleological nor ahistorical in the manner of many psychological theories of development (e.g., Piaget or Kohlberg). Rather it is assumed that cognitive development is a social psychological process and thus very much subject to the social structure and culture of specific historical periods. Therefore it makes no sense to posit a final stage of development. In this chapter, a type of reasoning beyond systematic is alluded to at several points when discussing the intrinsic limitations of systematic thought. This "metasystematic" form of reasoning is not itself an object of analysis. In part this is because the empirical research suggests that this form of thought, even in its crudest manifestations, is very rarely evidenced in the population at large.

THE MODE AND STRUCTURE
OF SYSTEMATIC THOUGHT

Systematic thinking is an essentially interpretative activity. It involves making sense of events by juxtaposing the relationships among interactions and propositions. In this manner, a number of observed actions and assertions of fact or preference may be considered simultaneously. These phenomena may be treated inductively or deductively. When the concerns being addressed are novel and not readily assimilated into existing understandings, reasoning will be inductive. In this case, the observed interactions and propositions are placed relative to one another in an empirically determined manner. On one hand, this juxtapositional effort may be oriented by the attempt to make sense of the systemic context in which the observed phenomena are occurring. This involves examining the multiple ways in which the relevant activities are interrelated to one another. On the other hand, this induction may be oriented by the attempt to discover an underlying principle of relationship. In this vein, interactions or propositions are first classified and then regularities in how exemplars of the specific classes relate are observed.

When the concerns being addressed are assimilated into an existing interpretative framework, systematic reasoning proceeds deductively. This may begin by identifying an already constructed system in which the specific activities being considered are then located. This provides a conceptual frame of reference for determining the relative meaning and functional significance of the interactions observed or propositions expressed. Alternatively, deduction may begin by invoking a principle of relationship. This provides a basis for a more abstract or ideal conceptualization in which the specific matter being addressed is understood as an exemplar of a class of interaction or proposition that stands in principled relation to some other class of activity. An understanding of what is occurring and complementary assumptions regarding what happened before and what will happen next are crafted accordingly. In either inductive or deductive modes, specific interactions and assertions are conceived as manifestations or outcomes of underlying principles or broader contexts. Understanding therefore requires unearthing these larger or more abstract concerns so as to determine the nature and dynamic of what one is observing.

Proceeding along these lines, the questions that orient systematic reasoning often revolve around considerations of interpretation and judgment. This may be a matter of drawing upon underlying principles or systemic contexts. Consider first questions of principle. Where possibly relevant principles are assumed to be unknown, induction leads to questions of the following kind:

> What kind of interaction is being observed and how may it be observed to be objectively related to other kinds of interactions?

> What type of proposition is being made and how may it be observed to be sensibly or validly related to other types of propositions?

In the first question, the focus is on a reality that is understood to be objectively constituted. The answer depends on the observation over time of empirical regularities in the relationship between different sets of what are defined to be equivalent interactions. In the second question, the focus is on subjectively or culturally constructed claims. The answer in this case depends on the consideration of equivalent responses or initiatives and evidence of how they are linked to one another in reflection or discourse. In both cases, the aim is to reveal regularities of association or juxtaposition from which underlying principles of connection may be inferred. Although very much a matter of empirical observation, it is important to recognize that this inquiry also consists of and is understood to be a definitional activity. Reasoning begins with a self-conscious decision as to which particular interactions or propositions are to be regarded as essentially the same. This then structures subsequent empirical inquiry by determining what specific phenomena are relevant and in what way.

When possibly relevant principles are known, deduction leads to the following kinds of questions:

> What is the relevant principle of social interaction? Once this is determined, how does it define the terms in which the observed interaction must be understood and how it is related to other kinds of interactions?

> What is the relevant principle of reflection or discourse? Once this is determined, how must the considered proposition be defined and its connection to another class of propositions or action be specified?

The answer here requires the application of a principle—that is, fitting the definition of elements abstractly constituted in the principled relation to the particular character of the situation observed. The result is again an interpretative reconstruction of the particular interactions observed or the propositions expressed as specific instances of a more general case.[1]

As in the case of underlying principle, considerations of systemic context may alternatively adopt an objective or subjective frame of reference. Where the broader context in which the interaction or the proposition occurs is not yet established, induction leads to the following questions:

> What other interactions are observed to be linked to the interaction observed and how are these other interactions linked to one another?

> What other propositions or claims are observed to be associated with the one made and how are these other propositions linked to one another?

The answer to these questions depend on directed observation where circumstances are explored over time in order to discover the apparent concomitants of the activity of concern and its place in a weave of interrelationships. The investigation is thus very much an empirical one. Here again, however, the empirical investigation is self-consciously delimited by a prior conception of what the boundaries of the yet-to-be-understood system are.

Where the systemic context is already constructed, deduction leads to questions of the implication or meaning of the interactions or propositions observed. Focusing on the interrelationship among interactions and propositions leads to questions of the following kind: If an interaction or proposition is or might be observed, what others must also have occurred, are occurring or will occur? Alternatively, the concern may be the consequence of the action for the larger system of which it is a part. In this vein, the question would be: What function does a given interaction or proposition serve or what role does it play in the overall performance or maintenance of the system? Considering a specific relationship among interactions across systemic contexts may give rise to the question: What are the conditions, real or hypothetical, under which a given relationship will hold? The answers to these questions involve utilizing a subjectively constructed map of the system of interconnections to locate the place of the activity in question and trace its correlates. This interpretative map may be of either an objective system of action or a subjective or cultural system of meaning.

Systematic thinking generates a certain self-consciousness of its own activity. Any reasoned attempt to answer the foregoing questions is consequently regarded as a propositional activity like any other and therefore as a product of principles that regulate and of systemic contexts that enable and constrain. For example, when the answer to a question requires observation, the consequent observations are understood to be embedded in a context that shapes what is seen. On one hand, this context is understood as objective. The observed connections among actions at any given moment are understood to occur in a broader context and thus may reflect the specific circumstances in which they are observed to occur. In recognition of this, systematic reasoning leads to observational strategies in which the interactions being explored are examined over time and across circumstances in order to determine whether the connections observed are a mere matter of the moment or are more enduring and fundamental. On the other hand, the act of observing is also understood to be embedded in the context of the observer. A person is a weave of interrelated preferences, beliefs, and purposive acts, each of which is facilitated and limited by its relationship to many others. Woven into this fabric, the act of observing is understood to be potentially affected by impinging beliefs and values and may therefore be prejudiced accordingly. In recognition of this subjective context of observation, systematic reasoning leads to empirical strategies that extract the act of observing from its personal context and render it less idiosyncratic. These include specific rules of how to conduct one's observation and the demand for a reliance on the observations of more than one person.[2]

Where an abstract or principled understanding is already in place, answers are obtained through interpretative reconstruction and definition. Like observation, this interpretative activity is viewed as an action and therefore occurring in a context. Here, however, the only context is that of the interpreter. To regulate her activity, principles of inference and definition are introduced. These stipulate forms of logical connection and standards of coherence and noncontradiction. When applied to subjective construction and reflection, these principles are intended to address psychological concerns regarding personal bias, insufficient elaboration, and lack of integration. Applied to intersubjective construction and argument, the principles are extended in light of social and political concerns regarding possible constraints on participation in the discourse. In this light, guidelines for free and open debate are introduced. In sum, systematic reasoning is reflexive in the sense that it generates a set of methodological considerations that apply to observational and interpretative bases upon which its understandings are built.

The Underlying Structure of Thought:
Systems and Principles

When making sense of events, systematic reasoning involves juxtaposing the phenomena observed in an actively constructed subjective frame of reference. It thereby allows for the simultaneous consideration of a number of the elements of the present situation in light of some broader external framework of which they are regarded to be a part. This is done in two ways. On one hand, it may involve isolating key elements of the situation and interpretatively reconstructing their apparent nature or meaning by redefining them as exemplars of a particular principle or abstract rule. In this manner, systematic reasoning breaks down a situation into its component parts and, at the same time, redefines those parts relative to some a priori concept that they are understood to reflect. The process is one of coordinated analysis and synthesis in which the general is induced from the particular; the general is conceived in its own abstract terms, and then is used to define particulars and deduce how they will relate to one another in specific instances. On the other hand, systematic reasoning may involve considering elements of a situation and then locating them in the context of a large systemic whole of which they are a part. In this process, the situation is also broken down into its component parts and, at the same time, these parts are considered relative both to one another and to elements of other related situations. The process is again one of coordinated analysis and synthesis, but here the whole is constructed out of the parts and then is defined and elaborated in its own terms. This elaboration involves not only considering a number of observed connections in relation to one another, but also constructing connections that the systemic whole seems to require but that have not yet been observed. In this context, the multiple known consequences of action can be traced out and the conditions under which novel consequences would occur may be deduced.

Systematic relations. A product of the juxtapositional and self-consciously constructive quality of systematic reasoning, the conceptual relations characteristic of systematic thought are bidirectional. They establish a reciprocal relationship among units. In this context, each unit is defined relative to the relationship that encompasses them both. Unlike the relations of linear reasoning, they are not grounded in the particular manner in which one unit bears on another. Interposed between units, systematic relations are not anchored in any one unit. Thus, they are not defined with regard to concrete, specific action. Instead, the relations of systematic reasoning are defined either relationally (relative to other relations) or abstractly (relative to some higher order defining principle).

To illustrate, let us compare linear and systematic conceptualizations of the case of Pamela marrying Kobi. From the linear point of view, this consists of one person acting on another. Constructed in a linear fashion, the relationship is concrete and specific. It consists of Pamela choosing Kobi. The focal actor, Pamela, then serves as an anchor whereby the other actors and actions are defined. Other actors are regarded by virtue of their anchored or imbalanced relation to her. In this instance, Kobi becomes her husband. His definition is dependent on her. This readily extends to related conceptions of him as subordinate to her, as her property, and as an element of her character. With regard to how the marriage unfolds, the focus is on specific action outcomes associated with one or both of the actors. Any one of these outcomes is then explained as the effect of an actor's particular initiative or reaction. So it may be observed that Kobi and Pamela are happy with one another, and this effect may be explained in terms of Pamela's action, say her considerate, easygoing manner of behaving. Normative views are also constructed in these concrete terms. There is a tendency to understand what the marriage requires either with regard to what typically occurs in the specific case of the marriage of Pamela and Kobi or with regard to cultural guides as to how husband and wife behave in any marriage.

From the systematic perspective, the case of Pamela and Kobi is understood quite differently. The two of them have entered into a marital relationship. This relationship is conceived at its own level and is thus defined in one of two ways. On one hand, it may be defined relative to other social relationships with which it is variously associated. For example, the definition of marriage may involve its negative association with an uncommitted sexual relationship. At the same time, it may also be defined in terms of its implicative association with the relationship of parent and child. On the other hand, the marital relationship may also be defined abstractly, that is with regard to some higher order principle of social relationships. For example, marriage may be viewed as belonging to the category of social relationships that are defined by the principle of voluntary contract. Alternatively, it may be conceived of as an example of a property relationship and defined accordingly. Whether it is thus defined in relational or abstract terms, marriage is not conceived with regard to the concrete specific nature of a particular party to the marriage or to the concrete specific things he or she might do. Instead the martial relationship is understood in its own abstract terms, and this then becomes a basis for defining and explaining what specifically transpires in the particular marital relationship in which Kobi and Pam are engaged. Viewed from this perspective, both Kobi and Pam, as individuals, are understood to be transformed by the relational context in which they are engaged. Similarly, any action Pamela and Kobi direct toward each other is understood as an interaction that is oriented and delimited by the relationship in which they find themselves.

As suggested by the foregoing discussion, the bidirectional relationship constructed in the course of systematic reasoning has certain formal qualities— that is, there are various ways in which it operates so as to relate its units or elements.[3] In other terms, there are various forms of association that may be established. For example, there is a relationship of identity whereby one unit is determined to be essentially the same or equivalent to another. This may be an empirically based claim, but it can be definitional as well. In the latter regard, apparently dissimilar units may be viewed as identical if they are regarded as equivalent expressions or manifestations of an underlying abstraction. Thus, the marital relationship and a relationship between a prostitute and his or her client may be regarded as comparable expressions of the abstract relation of voluntary contract. Alternatively, dissimilar units may be regarded as performing a comparable function relative to the performance of a system. Thus suicide and betrayal can be viewed as essentially the same insofar as both undermine the ability of a community to command the necessary loyalties of its members.

Another form of a bidirectional systematic relationship is negation. Here one unit is defined as the opposite of the other. This is not a matter of practical conflict as in linear thought, but rather a matter of conceptual coordination in which each unit contributes to the definition of the other as its own negation.

In this sense, negation does not produce tension—to the contrary, it is one of the elements of coherent system-building. An example already provided is how the marital relationship and an uncommitted sexual relationship may stand in relationship of negation. Criminal actions are typically regarded in a negative relationship to proscribed social norms of behavior. Again, both units stand in reciprocal relationship—each is defined by virtue of their negative association with the other.

A third form of association is one of implication. In this case, the units are related in that each suggests, depends upon, or leads to the other. Conceived in linear terms, such an association is a linear causal relationship in which cause flows into effect or effect into cause. Here one unit becomes defined as part of the other. In a systematic relationship, this association is reconstructed such that the flow from one unit to the other moves in both directions simultaneously. Both units are then defined in terms of the connection that joins them. For example, consider the case of a power relationship in which one person tells another what to do. Viewed from a systematic perspective, this relationship does not consist simply of the assertion of one over another. Instead, it is understood to be a compact between the powerful and the powerless within which the possibilities and limits of the exercise of power are constructed. In this context, the assertion of power and the subordination to power imply one another.

Systems. Although general in nature, systematic relationships are often conceptualized with reference to a particular substantive domain of inquiry. The result is often the construction and use of a system of interlocking relationships. Each systematic relationship is an association between units. Where these units are involved in more than one relationship, they provide an evident basis for a relationship among the relationships. A more limited form of this occurs in linear thought. A relationship between a causal action and its consequent effect establishes an imbalanced or unidirectional relationship. This may be extended insofar as the effect is observed to be a cause to a further effect or the initial cause is observed to be an effect to a prior cause. In either case a linear chain of causation is established. In systematic reasoning, units are juxtaposed in the context of balanced or bidirectional relationships. In this instance, the tie between a causal action and its consequent reaction is not simply anchored in either one but is seen as a reciprocal relationship between the two: each implies the other. Because one unit is not defined in terms of the other, both units are retained as bases of conceptualization. Several of the relationships between the base units and other units may therefore be considered at the same time. The result is not a construction of a chain that builds from one link to the next in a single direction, but rather is a construction that simultaneously extends from a center outward through a number of links leading in various different directions and contracts from these peripheral points back to the center. The result is the weave of a system of mutually implicative relationships rather than a linear chain of cause and effect.

These distinctions can be illustrated in the case of Annalee's issuance of a directive to her sister Catarina to go to the store to buy milk and Catarina's departure to the store. From a linear perspective, we have a straightforward case of a causal action, Annalee's directive, and its effect, Catarina's departure. This explanation is extended by building on the chain. Moving backward, Annalee's directive may be viewed as an effect of Annalee's intentions. In this instance, she will be seen as the cause of her sister's departure and hence as exercising power over her. Moving forward in time, it may be noted that Catarina's trip to the store may lead to her having an accident and injuring a pedestrian. In this case, Annalee's power and responsibility may be extended to the pedestrian's injury.

From a systematic perspective, the exchange is viewed as an interaction consisting of the initiative by Annalee and the complementary acquiescence by Catarina. Considered on its own, the meaning of the interaction is regarded as intrinsically ambiguous. To clarify matters, its place in a system of interactions is explored. Thus, Annalee's issuance of the directive may be linked not only to her intentions, but also to her feeling that she is responsible for making sure the family household is maintained, to the fact that she cannot go because she has another errand to run, and to the fact she enjoys exercising control over Catarina. Similarly, Catarina's acquiescence may be linked to several other relationships, such as that she already intended to go to the store to buy cigarettes, that her brother had said they ought to be helping their older sister Annalee more, and that she enjoyed pleasing her sister. Thus the specific interaction between the sisters is understood as the point of intersection of a number of relationships impinging on both Annalee's request and Catarina's response. Where cause and effect are the concern, this leads to a clear understanding that a given interaction is often the effect of multiple influences and, in complementary fashion, is likely to have multiple effects.

If circumstances warrant, reasoning does not stop here. Where there is a certain density to the interactions and sufficient interest in understanding their dynamic, the full weave of interrelationships may be explored. The causal influences linked to the specific interaction between Annalee and Catarina and the consequent effects flowing from it may themselves be examined. In this light, it may be that they are discovered to be interactively related not only to yet other interactions, but to each other as well. Thus, by shifting one's considerations from one focal interaction to another and juxtaposing the results, a whole weave of interrelationships may be constructed. In the case of the sisters, this may lead to a consideration of different interactions between the two sisters, to interactions each has with their brother and a third younger sister, to their relationship to their father, and so on. In the end, a systemic understanding of the family may emerge. This would provide a basis for understanding the implied causes and consequences of any given interaction that occurs within the family. It also provides a framework that can be elaborated so that new, heretofore unobserved interactions can be inferred. For example, it may be that the interactions between the siblings are observed, but the interaction of any one sibling with the father is not. Nonetheless, inferences may be drawn. Observation may reveal that the siblings regularly are involved in requesting one another to do things. From this it may be inferred that insofar as direction is frequently negotiated between the siblings, they are not receiving much guidance from their father.

Once constructed, systems may themselves be divided into subsystems. Like the broader systems, subsystems are distinguished by the relative density of overlapping interaction within their boundaries. For example, a society may be regarded as an integrated system. Within that society, arenas of interaction and collections of individual actors may be perceived to be particularly intertwined and thus come to be regarded as subsystems of interaction. In this regard, the workplace, the family, or a region may be viewed as a subsystem embedded in a larger society, but having a somewhat distinct organization of its own. Subsystems may also be distinguished on the basis of functional distinctions that are constructed. In this regard, a class of interactions may be defined by virtue of the common function they serve in a system. For example, in the case of society, different functions such as that of production or regulation may be identified and the related classes of interactions and actors that constitute the domains of the economy and the polity may be constructed. These functionally distinguished domains are not regarded as systems at the outset. Once distinguished, however, there may then be an attempt to discover not only whether indeed these domains are functionally distinct classes of interactions, but also whether they are organizationally integrated subsystems.

Principles. Systematic reasoning also leads to the construction of principles of relationship. Here the focus is on the relationship between classes of action.

Construction is a two-step process. To begin, interactions must be identified as members of a common class or category. In the case of linear reasoning, such classes are defined by their anchored relation to a single common outcome or cause. In systematic reasoning, the anchored linear relationship is transformed into a balanced one. Both linked actions are interposed between prior causes and subsequent effects. For purposes of classification, defining outcomes and causes are considered simultaneously. The resulting general classification and the specific interactions included in the class also retain a balanced relationship. In linear thought, the defining criteria of the classification and the concrete elements included in the class are collapsed onto one another. In systematic thought, these two levels imply one another but retain a certain conceptual independence. Because of their independence, each level of a classification is not only related to the other, but can be related to comparable levels of other classifications. Because of their mutual implication, these external relationships at one level of classification have a binding effect on relationships inferred or observed at the other.

The next step involves a determination of whether one class of interactions bears any relationship to another and, if so, if there are principles that appear to govern the relationship between these two classes. This may require an empirical examination of how specific interactions of one kind actually are linked to specific interactions of the other kind. Where regularities are observed, an underlying principle or law of relationship may be inferred that links not only the actions observed, but also the two classes of interaction to which those actions belong. Alternatively the considerations may be more formal. Rather than a focus on the specific members of one class as they relate to the members of another, this entails a consideration of the two classifications themselves. Here there is a consideration of the degree to which they may be formally related to one another through operations of identity, negation, implication, and so on. Where such a formal relationship is stipulated, a principle of relationship may be established that links not only the two classifications, but also the specific exemplars of one class to those of the other.

Principled relationships also emerge through the consideration of the relationship between a class of interactions and a system of interactions. Here the interactions of the class are considered relative to their effect on the overall ability of the system to meet its requirements of internal coordination and its external relation to other systems. Like the relationship between classes of action, this may also be explored in either an empirical or substantively oriented manner or in a theoretical or formally oriented fashion. Where observation suggests there in fact is a regular functional relationship between system outcomes and the performance of a class of actions or where formal deduction suggests there must be such a relationship, an underlying principle or law may again be constructed.

Given the manner of their construction, systematic principles are twice removed from the specifics of observed concrete action. Whether they link two classes of interaction or a class and a system, they consist of a relationship between two relationships. They are thus doubly abstract and therefore tend to be quite broadly applied. Unlike principles, systems are constructed through considerations of the weave of interrelationships within a specific domain. The resulting interpretative structure therefore tends to yield analyses and interpretations that are relative to the context in question. Principles are constructed by abstracting interactions from their context. First the interactions are abstracted from their particular circumstances as they are included into classes that are defined according to general criteria which typically are not specified relative to any particular context. Then these interactions, now viewed as exemplars of one class, are examined with regard to how they relate to interactions of another class. This relationship is itself considered across particular contexts and thus the ensuing conclusion is abstracted from any one. As a result, the principles inferred tend to yield analyses and interpretations that are context free or universal in nature.

To illustrate, let us consider a systematic construction of a principle of relation between two classes of individual's behavior, aggressive action on one hand and rigidity of action on the other. As suggested above, first there is the issue of defining these classes of interaction in the bidirectional or balanced terms characteristic of systematic thought. In the case of aggression, the interactions included are those that express or realize the explosive, angry feeling of the individual actor in a way that is intended to cause harm to a target. In this context, the cause, the release of a feeling, is understood to be reciprocally related to the specific effects, the attempt to harm, it produces. The actions included are defined by both simultaneously. They are not a matter of being hurtful (thus being defined solely by the effect) or a matter of being explosively angry (thus being defined only by the cause). In the case of the rigidity of action, the interactions included reflect the individual's desire to submit to specific ways of acting that are conventionally or normatively prescribed. Here the actions are included in the same class if they are both caused by the individual's desire to submit and if they have the effect of conforming to conventional prescription.

Thus submissive responses to another person's initiative or those actions that only follow prescribed conventions will not be included.

Once identified, the possible relationship between these two kinds of inter-actions may be explored. This may be done empirically. The behavior of various individuals will be examined in order to see whether particular examples of aggression are regularly associated with examples of rigidity. Evidence of four kinds of relationships between aggressive and rigid action would be considered: (1) where aggressive action was found to be associated with rigid action, (2) where the absence of aggressive action was found to be associated with the absence of rigid action, (3) where aggressive action was found to be associated with the absence of rigid acts, and (4) where the absence of aggressive action was associated with the presence of rigid action. Conceived relative to the claim that there is a positive association between aggressiveness and rigidity, the first two kinds of evidence would be considered equivalent and confirming and the second two would be considered equivalent and negating. The relative frequency of the four kinds of evidence would then be considered. When the combination of re-lationships (1) and (2) dominate, it will be inferred that aggressiveness and ri-gidity of action are positively related to one another in principle. When the combination of (3) and (4) dominate, the inference will be that aggressiveness and rigidity of action are negatively related—the existence of one precludes the existence of the other. In either case, a formal relationship between the classes is inferred. When neither combination is apparently dominant, then no princi-pled relationship between aggressiveness and rigidity will be inferred. Any con-nection is thus regarded as random rather than principled.[4]

The relationship between the two classes may also be explored formally. Rather than empirically examining concrete exemplars of the classes, this involves a theoretical determination of how the classes are related. Unlike in linear think-ing, a formal connection cannot be straightforwardly assumed when the ele-ments of one class appear to overlap with elements of another. The problem here is that the elements that appear to be the same may be defined differently when they are absorbed into two different classifications. An example of this might be rigidity and self-subordination. Assuming the latter consists of pur-posive acts of submitting to the desires of others, the overlap with rigidity is clear. This may suggest a connection, but it may be unwarranted if the sub-stantive overlapping element, submissive action, is constituted differently in the two categorical constructions. In the case of rigidity, it may be self-protecting, a way of securing one's position in a social context. In the case of self-subordination, submission may be self-destructive, a way of using others to eliminate one's self.

As suggested by the foregoing example, the establishment of a relationship between classes of interaction depends on a prior theoretical understanding of how these classes are integrated. In the case of aggression and rigidity, this may consist of a theoretical understanding of the individual as a personality. In this context, it may be asserted that a person needs to act so that a variety of her needs, those felt now and those felt later, can be served. This may require a certain level of control in one's purposive action at any one moment. In this context, aggression and rigidity can be defined and their relationship deduced. Aggression becomes one type of uncontrolled purposive action where the feelings of the moment obliterate other considerations. Rigidity of action becomes understood as a way of drawing upon external resources—for example, a cultural specification of how to act when—to provide balance for one's actions. So defined, the theoretical relationship between the two becomes clear. Aggression becomes a symptom of a lack of necessary control and rigidity becomes a means for reestablishing that control. Thus, given the theory of personality, a principled relationship between these two classes of action can be deduced. Where such a formal relationship is specified, particular expectations or hypotheses can be formulated regarding how evidence of exemplary actions of one class will be linked to exemplary actions of the other.

Integrating systems and principles. Thus far, we have discussed the two types conceptual relations, systemic and principled. Typically these two types of relationships are constructed independently of one another, but in the most elaborated systematic theorizing, one may be used to order the products of the other. For example reasoning may lead to an attempt to establish systemic relations among a set of principles of interactions that are assumed or observed to be intertwined. An example might be a set of principles of social interaction such as the mutual obligation between individuals, the complementarity of the roles people assume, and the primacy of the community. When these principles are recognized to apply to an interconnected set of behaviors, or when they are observed to be voiced by a single individual or to be dominant in a single culture, the relationships among them may be explored. An attempt is made to further understand these principles by determining how they stand in relation to one another in some encompassing abstract context. They are thus located in a system of principles that constitutes a particular political ideology or social philosophy.

Alternatively systematic reasoning may lead to a consideration of the principled relationships that govern the interaction of systems of action that impinge on one another. For example, an individual may be understood as a system of propositions and purposive actions, that is, as an internally organized set of thoughts and deeds. Insofar as it is recognized that individuals must regularly interact with one another, the question is then raised: What principles govern the relationship among individuals? Like all issues of principle, this may lead to empirical inquiry or theoretical deduction. In the first instance, the effect of the social interaction on the systemic qualities of individuals involved (e.g., their coherence, elaboration, etc.) may be observed. In the second instance, understanding of the systems requirements of individuals as personalities or biological organisms may lead to deductions of how they will engage each other and with what consequences.

Systematic units. Systematic reasoning not only defines the quality of the relationships forged when coming to an understanding, it also defines the nature of the units that will be addressed. An objectification of the relations of linear reasoning, systematic units consist of the relationships among actions and beliefs. These concrete relationships are of course not only objectified, but they are also restructured in systematic terms. Thus, the relationship among actions is bidirectional and focuses on the specific quality of how each constituent action relates to the other. The basic units of systematic thought are manifest in two forms. One speaks to the nature of action. Here the unit is an interaction in which two or more concrete acts are defined in terms of the relationship in which they are joined. Whereas in linear thought, one action is understood to produce a second, in systematic thought, this relationship is seen to be an interactive one, itself a particular example of a more general type. For example, when viewed systematically, the case of Scott who offers money to his friend Mark, who then accepts that money may be understood as an interaction. It consists of the offer of the money that is interposed between Scott's intention to give and Mark's intention to receive. The meaning or nature of that interaction is interpreted with reference to the context in which it occurs. Thus, it may be viewed as an episode in a relationship of loyalty and mutual obligation and be considered an example of a supportive interaction. Alternatively, the interaction may be viewed as a step in a strategic exchange and be considered an exercise of power.

Subjective phenomena, such as preferences and beliefs, are viewed in similar terms. Unlike in linear reasoning, they are not defined solely in terms of the actions they produce or the object to which they refer. Rather, these subjective phenomena are defined relative to one another as well as to objective circumstances. Here the basic unit is a proposition or judgment. For example, consider the case where Richard states that he dislikes his ex-wife Marilor. Viewed in linear terms, this is a preference which is understood as an attribute of Richard or alternatively of Marilor. In either case, it is understood in its own concrete terms. Viewed from a systematic perspective, this expression of preference is understood as a judgment. It is constituted at the intersection of Richard's preferences that relate to Marilor such as a predilection for trustworthiness and caring in others and Marilor's qualities as a person such as her infidelity and self-preoccupation. Statements of belief are conceived in similar terms. Thus they are regarded as proposals of fact that stand at the intersection of the proponent's perception and the qualities of the object. Thus Marilor may claim that her ex-husband Richard is egomaniacal. This claim is understood as complexly determined by her perception of Richard, her feelings toward him as they affect that perception, Richard's behavior, and the factors that affect how Richard behaves in relation to Marilor. The meaning of her assertion is interpreted accordingly.

As suggested by the preceding examples, the units of systematic thought, be they interactions, propositions, or judgments, are complexly constituted. On one hand, they do have an intrinsic or objective identity. On the other hand, these objectively constituted events are rendered meaningful only when they are placed in relation to one another either in the context of a system or with reference to a principle of interaction. Thus the observation or assertion of a unit is significant only as it is interpreted in some broader relational context.

Given the separate and relational aspect of the construction of units, systematic reasoning also lends itself to the definition of subunits of analysis which are completely abstract. These subunits, specific concrete actors or acts, can be specified but generally are not. When constructing a class of interactions such as an aggression, it is defined at the intersection between the specific intentions of the aggressor and specific consequences for the victim. The aggressor and the victim, while defined with reference to specific persons, need not refer to any one person in particular. Moreover they do not need to be specified for reasoning to progress further. In this regard, they may be conceived abstractly, as placeholders in the system of relationships or the principle of relationships being constructed. In this regard, any specific actors may be regarded as essentially equivalent or interchangeable. For another example, consider an analysis of an organizational environment such as a production line. The line may be understood as a system of interrelated tasks involving particular aspects of providing materials, assembling, and testing. These activities may be considered in relation to one another in light of the overall task at hand. In this frame of reference, individual tasks may be redesigned or repositioned relative to one another. All of this may be accomplished without any reference to the concrete individual workers involved (e.g., Chris, Scott, Mark, Molly, or James), despite the fact that the tasks require these workers to perform them. Rather there is an abstract notion of "the worker" that operates as a conceptual placeholder in the analysis of the production line. Here "the worker" is conceived as an abstraction that is only defined relative to the work requirement of the tasks in question.[5]

As suggested by the preceding examples, the relationship between the conceptual relations and the conceptual units of systematic thought is complex. One consequence of this complexity is a certain tension that is characteristic of reasoning of this kind. It is a byproduct of the very manner in which the relations and units of systematic thought are constructed. On one hand the conceptual relations are primary and the units derivative. Systematic relations may be defined relative to one another and therefore without reference to the units related. As such, these relations are self-constituting and independent. At the same time, they provide a context in which the identity of the units related may be defined. In this regard, the units of systematic thought are derivative entities. Some of the distinguishing qualities of systematic reasoning reflect these features of its underlying structure. The independent and defining nature of its conceptual relations provides a medium for the directed abstraction and theory-building characteristic of systematic thinking. The derivative quality of the units insures that the theories constructed apply across a range of specific interactions, including novel and hypothetical ones as well as those already observed.

On the other hand, the relations and units of systematic thought are so constructed that the units are primary and the relations are derived. The units of systematic thought have an intrinsic identity (defined by their concrete or objective particularity) that remains constant across the various relational contexts in which they may be articulated. In this sense, the units are self-defining and independent. Moreover, their evident association with one another provides an empirical base from which conceptual relations may be abstracted. With this reversal of the primacy of units and relations, we see another aspect of systematic thought. Because the units are assumed to be defined independently of their interrelation, it insures that all general claims—and by implication all theories, cultures, and subjective points of view—will be based on a common identification of the particular interactions or specific proposition to which they refer. Consequently, the different relational definitions constructed in the varying subjective, cultural, and theoretical contexts will share a common empirical foundation. This in turn provides a common ground upon which various theories can be tested and through which intersubjective, intercultural, and cross-theoretical discussion can be conducted.

Insofar as either conceptual relations or units may be ascribed primacy in the construction of a given systematic understanding, two forms of this construction are common. As described earlier, one is based on assumption, theoretical elaboration, and definition. The other is based on observation and empirical abstraction. The point here is that the two activities are not well coordinated relative to one another. In general there is a tendency for construction of one kind to envelop the other and reduce that other to its own terms. One result is the dualism that is at the heart of systematic thought. In its most elaborated form, this dualism is best exemplified and accentuated by the epistemological debates between the idealist and empiricist philosophers of the eighteenth century. Apart from such reductions, the best coordination of the complementary but separate activities of deduction and induction achieved is a simple matching to test the compatibility of claims generated in one way with those generated in another.

The relationship between the units and relations of systematic thought is complex in another sense as well. The issue here follows not from how the units and relations are constructed, but from the fact that they both share a common form. Both conceptual units and relations are bidirectional or balanced and associative. This structural parallel facilitates the taking of conceptual relations as the objects of thought. These relations may themselves be related in the context of higher order principles or systemic integrations. The result is a reflection on the terms of one's own thinking. This reflection is readily accomplished in a manner consistent with the structure of systematic reasoning and is indeed a characteristic feature of this kind of thinking. This reflective construction of the relations among relations may be extended such that relations may be constructed at a number of different levels of generality or inclusiveness. Each level is formally the same as those above or below. Each consists of a relation among units that are, at a lower level, themselves relations among units. The relation itself is a unit that is related to others at a higher level. Proceeding in this manner, systematic thinking creates a pyramidal vision of the world as layers of abstraction. Taken to its extreme, this peaks in a concept of the self as the one who thinks (that is, the one who constructs relations) or in a concept of the other as self-regulating and self-defining. The latter is well exemplified by notions of God as implicit in the organization or lawfulness of the universe.

THE NATURE OF SOCIAL REASONING

The social world of linear reasoning is dynamic, an arena where action produces reaction and actors collide. Systematic reasoning builds upon and transforms this understanding. The social world thus constructed is homeostatic—the active element is retained, but it is now orchestrated. In this construction, the manifest dynamism of the linear social world is contained within a systemic organization and principled regulation. But more than this, the dynamic of social action is also understood to be enabled by the possibilities that organization opens up and regulation creates.

Oriented by this understanding, systematic social reasoning always moves from the observation of a social act to a consideration of the nature and meaning of that act in light of the broader context in which it occurs or the underlying principle which it follows. Thus the act is ultimately defined and explained with reference to its location in a broader array of social interactions. The organized social context in which social action is thus located may be extensive, encompassing a broad panorama of actions and actors, or it may be localized, circumscribing the action or actor in question rather narrowly. In either case, it always includes the possible (as hypothesized) as well as the actual (as experienced). The social world in which action is placed is also understood to be lawful. These laws may be more or less abstract and thus regulate the connection between broader or more narrowly defined concerns. Regardless of how they are cast, these principles of social interaction consist of what is underlying and essential (as deduced) as well as what is present and apparent (as observed). This organization and regulation of social interaction is not only conceived as a matter of objective facts, but also as one of created meanings. In this regard, it is understood that individuals and cultures represent and relate the elements of social life and thereby render them meaningful. This subjective activity is assumed to be lawful, reflecting the principles that govern how individuals or cultures make and connect propositions. Systematic social reasoning is also self-reflective. It is aware of its own meaning-making activity. In this light, it is aware of its tendency to assimilate objective concerns into its own subjective frame of reference with the consequent potential for distortion and bias.

In this systematic construction, the social world is conceived to have a substance that is in some sense independent of the relational frameworks in which it may be located. On one hand, this substance consists of objective social interaction. In part this is a matter of what an individual does. This does not, however, simply consist of the act that the individual performs. Rather, the individual's action is always considered relative to her intention, motive, or goal. As such, what an individual does is not conceived to be a simple observable behavior, but a *purposive action*. Social interaction is also considered in terms of how people engage one another. Again this does not consist of simple behaviors, that of one person's behavior and the behavior of another which follows. Behaviors such as these are conceived with regard to each other and thus as a *social interaction*. In this context, action and reaction imply one another. On the other hand, the substance of social life also consists of propositions, what is thought or what is said. Unlike in linear reasoning, a statement made by an individual is not conceived in isolation, but with reference to other statements with which it is related. Thus the substance of what a person says is not to be found in the particularity of an isolated statement but in its *subjective intent*. The substance of what is said is also conceived in terms of what people say to one another. Here the particularity of one statement is placed relative to the particular statements of others to which it is related. In this sense, the social world is understood not to consist of people speaking at one another, but as communicating. The focus is thus on the *intersubjective or discursive exchange*.

As units of systematic reasoning, these elements of social life—purposive action, subjective intent, social interaction, and discursive exchange—are complexly constituted. In part, they are defined independently of any relational context in which they are articulated. In this regard, these social elements are understood to be substantial, that is, to have a quality or nature of their own. It is also in these terms that social life is understood to have a material reality. There are the facts of what individuals intend to do or mean to say as there are the facts of what people do and say to one another. These social facts have an intrinsic quality quite apart from any extrinsic qualities with which they may be imbued as they are articulated in some personal or collective arrangement of action. For example, the same purposive act, writing a book for publication, may mean one thing to Harry who is insecure and writes to capture the recognition of others and quite another thing to David who is secure and writes simply to communicate ideas he regards to be worthwhile. Although the act of writing has a different significance in these two personal contexts, it still has a certain quality of its own, for example, putting words to a number of pages with the intent to publish. Similarly, the same social interaction—two people agreeing to meet at a certain hour at the end of the week—may signify very different things in a Greek context, where such an agreement is commonly subject to ongoing confirmation and modification during the time prior to the appointed meeting, and in a Swedish context, where the commitment is regarded as largely inviolable. Again despite variation in its cultural meaning, the interaction, agreeing to meet at a certain hour, retains a substantive quality of its own.

This definition of elements has important consequences for the systematic understanding of social life. It suggests that despite variations in personality, subjective understanding, social structure, and culture, there is a dimension of social life, its substance, which exists independently of the relational contexts created by individuals and communities and therefore has a quality that remains the same across contexts. This insures that although individuals and cultures may vary in how they arrange or organize actions and statements, they all operate on a common ground. This ground, the substance of what is said or done, provides the avenue through which a person may enter the relational systems different than her own. Through careful observation of how the elements of social life are organized in any given context, all individuals and societies may understand each other.

At the same time, the elements of social life have a relative identity. They are conceived in a context, one in which they are in a dynamic and mutually determining relationship to one another. Thus, these social elements are defined as they are articulated into a system of relationships or as they express an underlying principle of relationships. Placed in a systemic context, the elements of social life are conceived as points of intersection in the weave of a social system. Placed relative to a principle, the elements are viewed as members of a class of social interaction or discourse. In either case, substantive concerns are eclipsed by a focus on the relative meaning of the interactions or propositions being considered.

Systemic Contexts: The Individual
and the Community

In systematic thought, systems of relations among interactions and propositions may be constructed at a variety of levels and with greater or lesser compass. These may extend from the single individual, to a relationship between individuals (e.g., a martial relationship), to small groups (e.g., a family or a work unit), to large groups such as whole societies or communities. The most basic concerns, however, are typically the individual and the community. Conceived as a system, each may be understood as an organizing force that creates order and coherence in social life and as a defining force that gives that life meaning and value.[6]

Individual as thinker and personality. In linear thought, the individual is defined in relation to action. As a categorical entity, she is a collection of the actions she initiates and those of which she is the target. In systematic thought, the individual is conceived as an organizing, defining force. On one hand, this is evident in the individual's capacity to think, to create meaning by virtue of the connections among propositions of fact and value she is able to construct. Over time, the person constructs her own system of meanings. The result is a subjective frame of reference that orients her interpretation and evaluation of events. On the other hand, the individual does not simply construct meaning, she also provides an organization of her own action. In this sense, the individual is not only a thinker, but a personality. Her initiatives and reactions, her motives, and her goals are all understood in relation to one another as they are integrated into the system of action that she is. What she does, cannot do, or might do are understood accordingly.

Let us consider the example of Richard. From a linear perspective, Richard is a set of actions and roles. He is male, a Wall Street lawyer, short, and articulate. He tells jokes, works long hours, has a few close friends, and has a tendency to associate with women who demean him. Together, these attributes constitute the collage of what Richard is. From a systematic perspective, this does not provide an understanding of Richard. Rather, it provides a provisional definition of actions from which such an understanding may be constructed. On one hand, a systematic conception of Richard requires a sense of the kinds of understandings Richard crafts. This requires attention to the statements he makes and more particularly to the connections he makes among them. For example, Richard may talk of his being a lawyer. In so doing, he may refer to the specifics of what he does in facilitating mergers and acquisitions. He may connect this to the broader economic consequences of his activity and the larger societal and political effects of the effort to which he contributes. At the same time, he may discuss the effect of being a lawyer on his own and others' conceptions of himself. Considering the connections Richard is making, one may conclude that Richard's thought is rich or complex in the sense that a given claim is actively related to a number of others. Similarly, conclusions may be drawn regarding the coherence, elaboration, and creativity of his thought.

As the connections Richard forges are mapped out, the meaning of specific claims or preferences he asserts may be determined. This involves locating a particular proposition relative to others in the system of understanding Richard has constructed. Thus Richard may state that being a lawyer provides wealth and social status. On its own terms, the statement has a certain intrinsic meaning by virtue of the specific realities to which it refers. This substance of the claim is, however, only a point of departure for the systematic interpretation of its subjective meaning. The latter only becomes clear when the assertion is considered relative to other related propositions. In Richard's case, these include the following: (1) Good lawyers are generally bright people who did not have the imagination or initiative to do something else. (2) Wealth is an object of illusory value—it simply allows you to have what others dictate you should want. (3) Social status is a trap forever confining those who seek it to obsequiousness and conventionality. In this context, the meaning of the original claim becomes clear. As understood by Richard, it criticizes the profession, wealth, and status and construes all three as mutually reinforcing forms of self-subordination. Following this further, inferences may be made regarding how Richard is likely to view certain concerns, such as fashion, or other careers, such as that of doctor or professor. Continuing, this may also lead to inferences regarding statements Richard might make about himself and his own career trajectory.

Not only can Richard be understood as a subject, he can also be understood as a personality. The focus here shifts from connections that Richard self-consciously crafts among his own representations and preferences to the connections that exist among his initiatives and reactions. This may include what he says as well as what he does, but the focus is on connections as they are objectively perceived to be rather than as they are subjectively represented by Richard. In this light, a number of Richard's actions may be considered relative to one another. For example, these might include actions such as: (1) his decision to be a lawyer, (2) his efforts to aggrandize considerable wealth, (3) his choice to get involved with women who try to undermine him, and (4) his tendency to interact with acquaintances and colleagues through constant sarcasm and humor. It may also include such statements as: (1) Good lawyers are generally bright people who did not have the imagination or initiative to do something else. (2) Wealth is an object of illusory value—it simply allows you to have what others dictate you should want. Juxtaposed to one another, these purposive acts and meaningful statements are understood to suggest something of Richard's personality system. An interpretative reconstruction of the meaning of these actions in light of their interrelation is initiated. Several of the actions may be seen as attempts to achieve what is commonly understood to produce a positive image of one's self either in one's own eyes or the eyes of others. This would include the career choice, the accumulation of wealth, and the securing of the love of others. The positive value of each of these actions, however, is tempered by the apparent falseness of what is achieved. It is as though Richard is reaching out for approval that he regards to be empty or artificial. His action may be interpreted accordingly.

This emerging understanding of Richard's personality also provides a context in which his statements can be understood as purposive acts that have personal significance. In this light, these assertions are not simply subjectively meaningful statements of fact or opinion. They achieve a purpose, that of diminishing Richard's achievements, so that the uncertain view of himself and his relationship to others can be sustained. Taken together, these may be viewed as a pattern that reflects Richard ambivalence regarding his personal worth. Richard has a sense of his abilities—reflected by his willingness to put forth the effort to succeed in work and love—and yet there remains an uncertainty with regard to the basic value of what he does and who he is for others and for himself. In this context, Richard's strategy of dealing with others through humor and sarcasm can be viewed as another strand in the weave of his personality. Juxtaposed to some of his actions, this can be understood as an integral part of a personality racked with ambivalence. Richard is sociable and engages people frequently and confidently, but this apparent reflection of self-worth is counterbalanced by a defensive strategy of humor and sarcasm that allows him to maintain a self-protective distance from others.

As suggested by the foregoing example, systematic reasoning leads to a construction of the individual as a subject and an object. As a subject, the individual consists of the understandings that she creates. The focus here is on the kinds of connections she self-consciously establishes among the propositions she asserts and the purposes she actively pursues. As a personality, the individual exists as an objective organization of her own purposive actions and subjective intents. The focus here is on an internal emotional life that constitutes who she is as a self, both for herself and in relation to others. In this context, the connections exist even if they are not recognized or understood by the individual in question. Whether a thinker or a personality, the individual is presumed to be an internally orchestrated system.

Self and social identity. This understanding of a person, as a subject and as a personality, applies to the systematic construction not only of another person but also to one's self. When reasoning about individuals, the focus is on relationships among a person's purposive actions and subjective intents. This evidentiary base can just as easily consist of one's own actions and intents as those of another person. Self-understanding then involves weaving this elemental evidence into a system of interrelationships. As in the understanding of another person, the resulting conception of one's self consists of a system of meanings and an organization of action. Once constructed, these two contexts provide a frame of reference for interpreting the meaning of one's own action and explaining the dynamic that drives it. In sum, the self is constructed as an other, one that varies from the rest insofar as the relevant substantive information tends to be more directly accessible and more generally available.

The result is a conception of the individual as a self-constituting entity and therefore one that may be identified largely with reference to itself. This is very different from the linear identification of people in terms of their active, external connections to social entities outside themselves. In the linear conception, one's locale or territory, the particular rituals one performs during the day, the things one owns, or one's specific appearance are attributes of one's identity. To change one of these external links is consequently a self-transforming act. In systematic thought, the specifics of location, ritual, property, and appearance are epiphenomenal. What one typically does or where one lives are simply one or two among the many activities, preferences, and beliefs that are incorporated in to the whole of a person's identity. Moreover, the sense of any one of these aspects of the self are meaningful only as it is integrated into and defined relative to the self-system. The significance of these concrete and external links is thus not only diminished, it is a matter of personal construction. They are objects of definition and use whose conceptual and practical meaning is determined by their location in the self-system. Thus, I am not where I live, what specifically I do, what I own, or how I appear. Instead, my choice of locale, action, property, and appearance may mean various things to me and may be self-consciously utilized to achieve particular purposes.

The decreased significance of specific concrete external relations for a systematic conception of identity is also interestingly reflected in the meaning of group membership. In linear thought, group identification is a central component of self-identification. Group membership can constitute a concrete category that subsumes the self and provides definition to it. Thus Sarah, who was described as Jewish, may be defined by both herself and others as a Jew with the collection of attributes (rituals, appearance, etc.) associated with the group, Jews. In systematic thought, this tends not to be the case. First, the self is defined as a set of component purposive acts and meaningful statements that are internally related to one another. In this context, association with a group becomes an aspect of the self that is subjectively defined and personally organized relative to the other things the individual does (and to the other groups with whom she may be associated). Second, a social group is never conceived as a categorical entity composed of elements that share the same characteristics. As we shall see shortly, a group is a complex integration of a variety of actors and actions that complement rather than are identical to one another. Consequently, to be located in a group does not confer a categorical or stereotypical identity as much as it places an individual at a locus of a complex set of interactive associations. In sum, group association is less central to a systematic conception of self.[7]

Community as organization and culture. As individuals are understood as subjectively constructed and objectively constituted systems, so communities are understood in a similar fashion. In linear thought, the focus is on groups conceived of as collections of individuals defined by common concrete attributes (e.g., territory, ritual, appearance, or identifying label). In relation to other groups, a given group is an actor, a monolithic entity that acts and is acted upon. In systematic thought, the focus shifts from groups to communities, from categorical units to integrated systems and from the unself-conscious observation of concrete action to the interpretative consideration of social interactions and discursive meanings. In this light, a community, like an individual, is an organizational and definitional force. This is manifest in the integration of the system of interactions that constitute the structure of a society and the system of discursive meanings that constitute that society's culture. In this construction, the elements of the community are not specific acts or actors nor are they identical to one another. They are relational entities, interactions and intersubjective meanings, which are substantively different from one another but are interrelated as complementary parts of a whole. The meaning and dynamic of social exchange and communication are understood accordingly.

Again let us illustrate with an example. Consider the case of Greek society. From a linear perspective, Greek society consists of a collage of what one can see, islands floating in an azure sea, the Acropolis, the grime of urban Athens, the picturesque low standard of living in the villages, the dark hair of the people, the late night entertainment, and the unruly driving habits. There are also the distinctive sounds of the bouzouki, the rhythm of the language, the smell of an arid landscape, or the flavors of lemon and olive oil in the food. From a systematic perspective, the foregoing all pertain to Greece and Greeks but give little sense of Greek life. Such a sense requires insight into the interactions as they are intertwined in the fabric of the social structure and in the understandings that are characteristic of the culture.

To make sense of the organization of social life, it is first necessary to observe the various interactions that are typical of day-to-day exchange. In the Greek case, it may be observed that: (1) social encounters between family members and close friends are very open, direct, and frequently emotional; (2) people spend the majority of their free social time with family and perhaps one or two close friends; (3) the vast majority of Greeks have a relatively low income; (4) regardless of income level, there is a tendency to spend what one earns— there is little emphasis on savings or investment; (5) there is a prevalent belief that one must recognize that life, along with its joys, is filled with frustration, defeat, and catastrophe. In a systematic conception, these various interaction patterns and cultural propositions regarding the nature of life are interrelated and must be interpreted accordingly. In this vein, these aspects of Greek life may be understood to exist in a mutually supportive fashion. In the face of the potential for disaster, to reduce current expenditure in order to save and thereby control a future that is inherently uncontrollable makes little sense. In complementary fashion, a hand-to-mouth lifestyle insures that living will necessarily be a precarious activity. At the same time, this circumstance makes one's dependence on others all the more important. Moreover, these ties cannot be frivolous, a matter of causal friendship and entertaining acquaintance. These must be social connections that run deep, where loyalties are strong. To this end, contact must be open and frequent. In a complementary fashion, this kind of contact fosters an emotional vulnerability and the concomitant life fraught with conflict and tragedy thereby reinforcing the sense of the inevitability of crisis. In the end, the various social facts first noted are now better understood as they are interwoven in the fabric of Greek social life.

Separate from this consideration of social structure is the attempt to also understand Greek culture. Here the focus shifts from the objective connections among facets of Greek life to the discursive meanings of how Greek culture represents that life. Here one begins by collecting proposed beliefs and advocated preferences as they are communicated in daily life. They may be found in common discourse and in the artifacts of the popular culture (e.g., popular books, film, televisions, and music). A number of observations may be made in this regard: (1) There is regular and direct conversation about each other's health and its fragility. (2) Capitulation—surrendering to the failed career aspiration and settling for the common fate—is commonly regarded as acceptable, even noble when the height from which one has fallen is great enough. (3) The denigration of those who show unbridled optimism or good humor as childish or foolish is also common. (4) Greek literature is replete with stories of failed enterprise and love at the hands of capricious fate. Taken together this suggests a dark side to Greek culture, one in which tragedy is both expected and accepted. Concerns for health, the denigration of optimism, the belief in the maliciousness of chance, and surrender to failure may all be understood as mutually defining expressions of this Greek sense of the tragic.

Systemic Construction of Social Life:
Limits and Confusions

The foregoing discussion of systematic social reasoning gives something of the flavor of a systematic construction of social life. Two basic organizing forces are identified, that of the thinking individual and that of the coordinating community. Each of these operates so as to place interactions and meanings in a dynamic and significant relationship to one another. At the same time, each of these systemic contexts is dually constituted. Both consist of a subjective construction of understanding and an objective organization of action. In this light, systematic reasoning engenders a relatively complex, integrative, and self-consciously interpretative analysis of the psychological and social conditions of daily life. At the same time, this tendency to construct interpretative frames of reference and to do so in an integrative manner also defines two of the conundrums typically engendered in systematic thought. These highlight some of the limitations of systematic reasoning.

Social object vs. social subject. The first conceptual difficulty emerges in light of the divide between the objective and subjective organizations of personality and social exchange. In the case of the individual, the construction of who a person is entails the definition of two domains. One is the domain of the objective facts of how an individual's initiatives and reactions, verbal as well as nonverbal, are interrelated with one another in a personality system. The other is the domain of the subjective meaning of a person's statements and actions as they are self-consciously related to one another in that person's own understanding. In this conception, these two systems of understanding and of personality are understood largely apart from one another. At the same time, they are recognized to operate on the same ground, that of a particular person's concrete thoughts and actions. Given the evident circumstance of their frequent if not constant intersection and the integrative tendencies of systematic reasoning, the question arises: What is the relationship between the system of subjectively constructed understanding and the system of the objectively integrated personality?

Given the structure of systematic thought, there is a tendency to construct related phenomena as systemically integrated. Therefore, the tendency is to conceive of two organizations of the same phenomena as parallel and thus as essentially the same. In the present context, the manner in which this may be achieved is by stipulating that personality and understanding are the same and then conceiving of one in terms of the other. In this vein, it may be assumed that the personality system is largely transparent to the reflective actor, as it is to an observer, and therefore that it is subjectively understood and orchestrated. In this light, the individual is understood to be essentially a reasoning being. Possessing considerable self-insight, the individual is also basically a self-organizing and consequently a self-directing force. So defined, the individual is regarded as ultimately responsible for her own condition as well as for her interaction with others. Alternatively it may be assumed that understanding is an integral part of the personality system and is therefore objectively organized. Moving in this direction, the parallelism between understanding and personality is sustained by collapsing the former on the latter. Viewed from this perspective, the individual reasons and constructs meanings, but not in a manner that is particularly self-aware or consciously regulated. Here the individual is assumed to have relatively limited self-insight, and what insight is crafted is presumed to be distorted by the biases and needs typical of her personality. In this conception, the individual is still regarded as a self-organizing system, but one that is a product of character rather than self-conscious reflection and judgment.

A problem arises when this construction is confronted with the evidently more complex circumstances of the person observed. Sometimes on the basis of limited exposure, but more frequently where exposure is relatively extensive, it becomes apparent that there is a disjuncture between an individual's understandings and her personality. For example, let us return to the case of Richard. Richard has been observed to deal with friends and lovers in a manner that reflects a personality system that is ambivalent and self-protecting. Given the intensity of the associated feelings, Richard often unself-consciously construes his personal contacts as pawns who are defined and engaged in light of their place in Richard's internal emotional struggles. At the same time, Richard is reflective and actively constructs an integrated conception of who he is and the meaning of what he does. He will assert that he is aware of the meaning of his actions and that they are responsive to the particular qualities of the specific individual with whom he is dealing. Most difficult is that this is, in part, evidently true. Thus it appears that Richard's actions are not only organized by his personality, but also by his self-consciously constructed self-understanding.

Matters become even more difficult when it is apparent that not only is Richard's self-understanding constructed somewhat independently of the organization of his personality, but that this self-understanding may connect to his personality in a manner that has no impact. Thus we may observe that Richard is self-reflective and aware of his personality dynamics, but this is of little consequence. Even when he is clearly trying, he cannot change his personality-governed behavior in a way that is more consistent with his subjectively constructed sense of who he truly is or should be. In an essentially mysterious way, it appears that the relations of his personality elude those of his subjectively constructed understanding at the same time that they are comprehended and thus subjectively integrated.

The conceptual problem that arises for systematic reasoning is that there is an apparent separation and lack of coordination of the two systems of the self. They are not similarly organized and yet operate on the same concrete matter—how Richard engages and reacts to others. Consequently, they will necessarily create conflicting organizations of individual action. Through this they will generate an internal tension both between and within the personality system and the subjective understanding of self. Lacking the structural cognitive resources to come to an integrative understanding of this, systematic reasoning can only note this disjuncture of necessarily integrated systems. At best, this may be extended somewhat to observing that in particular circumstances, one system seems to operate more powerfully than the other. In any case, however, no systemic understanding of the disjuncture can be achieved. One consequence of this is a recognition of the limitations of one's own cognitive functioning. In its most elaborated form, this often leads to certain forms of epistemological skepticism concerning social matters.

A similar issue arises in the systematic understanding of community. Like an individual, a community is conceived of as having two organizing aspects. One is its objective organization. This is evident in the facts of social structure, in the regularities of who interacts with whom, when, and in what way. The other aspect is subjective, a realm of culturally constructed representations of the interrelation among interactions and the discursive meaning of communications. Each of these two domains of the collectivity is conceived largely independently of one another. At the same time, they are understood to operate on the same phenomena, in this case the relationships among social interactions and discursive meanings. This leads to a consideration of the relationship between social structure on the one hand and culture on the other.

As in the consideration of the individual, the systematic analysis of intertwined systems that orchestrate the same activities leads to the presumption that the two systems essentially do or will parallel each other. To understand the relationship between them, one system is effectively reduced to the terms of the other. One way in which this is accomplished in the analysis of a community is to assume that a culture comprehends its social realities. It thereby integrates the particulars of those realities in its intersubjectively organized terms. In so doing, the culture provides both an organization and a direction to social interaction. This view suggests that social realities are regulated according to cultural determinations. Concomitant with this view is a certain faith in social engineering and public policy. The alternative conceptual strategy is to assume that the organizing force in social life is to be found in the material realities of social interaction. The emphasis here is on the observation of existing patterns of exchange. Cultural representations are often regarded as epiphenomenal and derivative. The logic and signification of discursive meaning is grounded not in any inherent qualities of discourse or language, but in the socially structured exchange that communication reflects and in which it is embedded. In this view, culture is merely a reflection of social structure.[8]

Either of the preceding ways of reconciling cultural and social structural organizations of social life is satisfying because it offers an understanding that is consistent with the form of systematic thought. The problem arises when systematic observation of a community suggests a discontinuity between these two domains—when cultural definitions and representations of social life contradict or fail to reflect patterns of actual social practice. Here it is apparent that the two systems of the community are not coordinated and do not parallel one another. They organize the same interactions and discursive understandings—the particulars of how people interact and what they agree to be true and desirable—but do so in ultimately incompatible ways. The result is confusing as each aspect of the community seems to reorganize the other and the particulars of social exchange seem burdened with double and incompatible meanings. It creates an ill-understood tension between and within the culture and the structure of the community being considered. At times and in certain situations, it may appear that one or another dimension of community life is more dominant, but no overarching understanding of this contradictory relationship between them can be constructed. As in the analysis of individuals, this may in turn lead to an awareness of the limits of reasoning and an epistemological skepticism.

Individual vs. community. Apart from the difficulties of reconciling the subjective and objective dimensions of social life, the systematic construction of social exchange also leads to conceptual difficulties regarding the relationship between the individual and the community. Again the issue is conceiving the relationship between related but different systems, but here the systems conceptualized exist as different levels of organization. In systematic thought, individuals and communities both tend to be conceived as loci of organization of action and meaning. Conceptual difficulties arise because although the individual and community are understood as two different levels of organization, they interpenetrate in fundamental ways. On one hand, the organization of the community delimits what individual members of that community can do and who they can be. The social structure of the community defines a system of interaction that both enables and constrains how individuals can act, and its culture provides the system of signification through which an individual can meaningfully express her own beliefs and understand the beliefs of others. Conceived in this context, individuals are derivative entities. Unto themselves, they are indefinite forms that function as interchangeable placeholders in a weave of relationships. Individuals are regulated, located, and thereby defined by the social system in which they are integrated.

This perspective on social life orients much of Anglo-American sociology with its focus on the conditions of interaction and cultural orientations. In this sociological view, the individual is an effect of social life, a product of the socializing forces of the interactive environment and cultural context in which she is located. Created and shaped in this manner, the individual is a collage of the actions that she performs in the various interactive settings into which she is regularly integrated. Added to the mix are the orienting purposes, propositions, and identities the individual internalizes from the culture to which she is exposed. In sum, the individual is an amalgam of social effects, a mere construction. It is not a meaningful or coherent entity unto itself. Like a piece of a puzzle, the individual acquires definition only when seen in the context of the systemic whole of community life.[9]

On the other hand, there is the countervailing construction that suggests that the reasoning and personality of individuals delimit what the community is and can be. In this vein, it is assumed that individuals enter the social arena and pursue their purposes in a manner orchestrated by their personalities and understandings. This then organizes and delimits the ways in which they will interact with one another. The social force here is the individual's attempt to engage others in a personally organized and subjectively comprehensible manner. The relationships that emerge between individuals are an outgrowth of these attempts. To endure, social relationships and institutions must organize interaction in a manner that is consistent with the personalities and understandings of the individual participants. In this light, the hierarchical quality of prewar German social institutions may be explained with reference to the authoritarian personality prevalent among individual Germans. Similarly it may be suggested that the various dominant narratives in a culture are consistent with one another because the thinking of individuals is integrative and therefore creates a demand that cultural representations cohere. Whether the frame of reference is personality or reasoning, this psychological analysis renders interpersonal relations derivative, a product of the individuals' organization of their own actions. Social phenomena are interpreted and explained accordingly.

Both this psychological view and the preceding sociological one offer an understanding of social life that is, in systematic terms, coherent and satisfying. The problem emerges when the two perspectives are considered relative to one another. There is a clear tension inherent in the resulting dualistic vision of individuals and communities as at once organizing and self-directing, and organized and determined. This is avoided by the reductionism of either the sociological or psychological perspectives or by claims that these two independent systematizing forces parallel one another and therefore do not conflict. Whereas these views exert some influence in the academic world, they often appear unwarrantedly narrow and simplistic when making sense of relationships and people (including one's self) in one's own immediate environment. Here close observation often confronts the conceptual apparatus of systematic thought with the apparent complexity and ambiguity of a social world that is culturally defined and personally construed, and collectively organized and personally orchestrated. An example is the case of modernity discussed in chapter 1. This ambiguity is not readily comprehended within the framework of a mode of thinking in which units have a relative but definite meaning within the system of relations in which they are embedded.

Principles of Social Relationship

The systematic construction of social systems is complemented by the construction of underlying principles or regulations that are understood to govern the dynamic of social life. As rules of social exchange, these principles are conceived quite differently than the specific, reified social rules or norms of linear thought. They differ from linear rules both in what is related and the form of that relationship. Whereas linear rules speak to action, systematic principles pertain to classes of interaction. An example of a class of social interaction would be cooperation. In systematic thought, specific social interactions would be designated as cooperative insofar as they involve the intention of both parties to act toward one another in a manner that meets the jointly recognized demands of a mutually defined task. The classification is not based on the unidirectional concrete relation of a cause to an effect, but on a mutual or bidirectional relationship between specific interactions. In the case of an interaction between Phillip and Angele, it is not enough that Phillip intends to help Angele. She must view Phillip's action as helpful and be willing to accept it. In a complementary fashion, it is not enough that the Angele views Phillip's action as helpful; that must actually be Phillip's intention. Constructed in this manner, this class may include a number of ostensibly different interactions, such as an argument in which the participants provide information and reasons to each other with the aim of coming to a common understanding, or a business arrangement in which different tasks are defined and then allocated to the partners so as to produce the desired product.

The form of the principled relationship between these classes of interaction is also different. In the case of linear rules, the relationship is concrete and specific. The conceptual relation and the concrete elements related are collapsed on one another. The concept and the reality to which it refers are confused such that each directly evokes the other. In the case of systematic principles, the principled relationship and the classes related are both connected and independent of one another. The principle regulates or determines the relationship between the classes of interaction, but there is a divide between the concept of the regulating principle and the interpretative description of the classes of interaction regulated. Theoretical inferences regarding laws of relationship and empirical accounts of those relationships therefore bear on one another and yet are self-constituting. Knowledge of principle leads to deduction regarding empirical realities, or conversely, knowledge of empirical realities leads to induction regarding principled relations.

To illustrate, let us consider a systematic construction of the principles governing the relationship between two types of social interaction, cooperation and the exercise of power. First there is the task of identifying those interactions that properly belong to one or the other of these two classes of cooperation. The class of cooperative interactions has been addressed in the preceding paragraphs. The class of interactions of power is constructed in a similar manner. It depends on the interpolation of action between causal influences beginning with one person's intentions and extending to her behavioral initiatives on one hand and effected outcomes beginning with the other's behavioral response and extending to the meaning of that response for the other. Here a definition of power somewhat akin to that of Robert Dahl (1956) may be constructed. An interaction of power entails one person's intention to operate on another so as to produce a desired result with the other person acting as required when she initially intended to do otherwise. As in the case of cooperation, the meaning of the power is not grounded in the concrete sequence of action, but rather emerges in the reciprocal relationship between flows of action emanating simultaneously from the powerful and the powerless.

Having defined the two classes of interaction to be considered, the question then is how are they related. Given that each class is defined in its own terms, this relationship may be explored empirically. This empirical exploration is self-consciously guided by the tentative assumption or hypothesis that there is a relationship between cooperation and power. This involves the search for the relationship between how specific interactions of one type, now considered as exemplars of a class, are related to specific interactions of the other type. This may be carried out in a variety of venues. Thus, various contexts might be explored, such as particular friendships, research groups, families, or governmental bureaucracies. Throughout, there is an attempt to observe the extent to which cooperative interactions and interactions of power co-occur. The evidence is then interpreted in light of the hypothetical claim of relationship. In this context, the presence and absence of each in relation to the other is considered. This leads either to the conclusion that power and cooperation are related to one another (either they imply or preclude one another) or to the conclusion that there is no (or a random) relationship between them.

The relationship may also be explored more formally. Here there is a reflective attempt to determine whether there is any theoretically necessary relationship between power and cooperation. In this vein, it might be assumed that communities exist and endure by virtue of their coherence or integration. This then lays the foundation for a deductive analysis of the relationship between power and cooperation. Thus it may be determined that both classes of interaction order social exchange. Therefore in any well functioning social system, it is likely that both cooperation and power will be evident.[10] Whereas the general contours of systematic thought provide the foundation for a deductive analysis, they do not determine the specific result of that analysis. Different considerations may be introduced leading to different deductions. For example, in the present case, it may alternatively be deduced that power and cooperation are contradictory modes of social integration and therefore will be negatively related. The potentiality for alternative theory and deduction is always recognized in systematic thought. As a result, there is a characteristic openness to argument and reflection as modes of inquiry and revelation.

Constructed in this manner, social principles have a number of distinctive features. One is the tendency toward universality. In this regard they differ from the conceptualization of social and personality systems. The construction of these systems consists of a weaving together of the specific interactions that are related to one another in a given context. The concrete dynamic of action evident in a given system, for example, cause and effect relations, and the particular meaning of action are thus understood to be specific to that system. Explanations and interpretations are therefore relative to the person or community in question. The resulting claims are not universal.

Although also the result of juxtaposing interactions, principles are not articulated in a context-specific fashion. Classes of interaction are the units that are related by principles. The construction of such a class does depend on an initial interpretation of specific interactions that is sensitive to their contextual meaning. The class into which these interactions are incorporated, however, constitutes what is essentially its own context. It consists of a set of interactions that are included, that is, they are juxtaposed to one another, because each has an identical meaning relative to the defining features of the class. Thus whereas these class members have meaning in particular systemic contexts, the classification in which they are incorporated creates a juxtaposition among them free of any of the particular contexts in which they were initially recognized to be embedded. In this sense, the members of the class are defined independently of a particular social and cultural context and can therefore "be discovered" in a wide variety of contexts. Any relationships between these context-free juxtapositional classes are therefore also likely to be cast without reference to any particular systemic context, personal or social.

The overall result is that the systematically constructed principles of social life tend to be cast in universal terms. In the consideration of individuals, this yields principles of psychology. Examples of such systematically constructed psychological principles include assertions that frustration breeds anger, that aggression is related to rigidity, or that insecurity is related to withdrawal. In each case, a claim is made regarding a relationship which is characteristic of an aspect of human nature. It is a principle that is understood to apply to all individuals. The consideration of communities produces a similar result: principles of sociology. Examples of systematically constructed sociological principles include assertions that the power of a government depends on the support of the people, that religious faith is related to social cohesion, or that the form of authority prevalent in one domain of social interaction will parallel that which is prevalent in other domains. Here again the claims made are universal, albeit in this case they are intended to apply to all communities or interpersonal relationships.

Contradictory experience and systematic skepticism and relativism. This tendency to universalize can be tempered by experience. Although cast abstractly, principles do apply to observable relationships between specific instances of the classes of interaction being considered. This can lead to the recognition of contexts in which the principles do not apply. In this vein, the examination of people may lead to the observation that there may be cases when the principled relationships claimed to obtain between types of purposive actions or subjectively constructed meanings do not hold. Similarly, cross-cultural or historical experience may provide evidence of places and times when principled relationships between types of interactions do not appear to be in force. Instances like these are ill understood and confusing. Sometimes they are discounted as exceptions, random events, or the result of additional unrecognized factors. When the evidence is accepted, typically the principle is abandoned. Over time, this can lead to an epistemological skepticism akin to that accompanying the recognition of endemic incoherence in the functioning systems. Here this leads to the presumption that either the dynamic of social life is not lawful or, at the very least, these universal laws are sufficiently obscure that they cannot be comprehended by the understandings that persons or theorists produce. Such a position is nicely exemplified by late seventeenth- and early eighteenth-century conservative and romantic rejections of the systematic conceptualization of thought and social life offered by earlier liberal philosophers.

An alternative solution is to import higher order (meta-systematic) theoretical claims that assert the relativity of principles of thought and interaction, and then to understand this relativity in essentially systematic terms. This approach is evident in much contemporary social science theorizing. It is exemplified in the psychological literature by the simplified reconstruction of Piaget's dialectical conception of cognition in Jerome Bruner's influential adaptation (1958) and in the social psychological work on cognitive complexity (Schroeder, Driver, and Streufert, 1967). In both cases, the authors explicitly acknowledged the evident insight of the theory but find it unnecessarily "difficult, abstract and obscure" and therefore recast it in "simpler, more familiar and comprehensible" terms. The same tendency is evident in the analysis of communities, albeit generally less self-consciously, in the simplified representations that are often provided of poststructuralist visions such as those of Michel Foucault (1979) and Jürgen Habermas (1984, 1987). The result here, as in the case of psychology, is a reduction of structured and theoretically specific definitions of forms of knowing, valuing, and communicating to particular sets of generally meaningful propositions regarding specific knowledge claims, moral assertions, or standards of reflection and discourse. In a typically systematic fashion, these propositions are understood systemically, that is, as they are observed to be associated with one another in the particular vision of the theorist being considered.

POLITICAL REASONING

Systematic reasoning leads to the definition of politics as a distinct domain of community life. It consists of a functionally differentiated set of interactions and discursive meanings that relate to issues of governance. In a systematic frame of reference, governance is conceived in two ways. On one hand, it is a matter of organizing social interactions so as to sustain the basic integration or coordination of action characteristic of a given society. On the other hand, governance is a matter of effectively reinforcing the need for cooperation and mutual respect among the individuals or groups that interact with one another. In the first case, political life is conceived in relation to a social system. In the second case, political life is conceived in relation to basic principles of social interaction. We will consider each of these two aspects of systematic political reasoning in turn.

Political System

Like the linear view, the systematic view of the political domain centers on the issue of power. In the present context, however, power is conceived very differently. In linear thought, power is manifest in the concrete and specific instances in which one actor is able to force another to comply with her wishes. In systematic thought, this concrete power remains a concern, but it is conceived in a very different way. The capacity to control others and dictate their responses is understood in the broader context of the system in which it is embedded. In this context, a particular individual's capacity to affect specific acts in a given situation is itself understood to be an outcome, a result of a system of interactive relationships that effectively distributes and regulates such specific instances of the exercise of concrete control. In this systematic conception, power is conceived at two levels. The first and less consequential is a matter of control, the specific capacity to affect another's response. This control is understood to be conditional and constrained. For example, the employer's capacity to command the employee is clearly limited to the confines of the workplace and to the range of commands that are deemed appropriate in that context. Similarly, the control exercised by monarchs or presidents is delimited by the political context in which they operate. This then leads to the second and more essential level at which power is conceived. This is the level of the collectivity itself. At whatever level this collectivity is conceived (from an institution through to the whole community), it is understood to operate as an organizing force. It constrains and enables the more concrete and specific exercises of control. As the source and condition of this specific control, this organizing force is regarded as central to the understanding of political life.

The focus of a systematic conception of politics is thus on the organization and culture of control. With regard to organization, the focus is on the specific way in which control is distributed in a society. To paraphrase Harold Lasswell, the issue here is who gets to do what when. This leads to a consideration of the organizational means whereby concrete power is distributed through allocation of roles and the creation of hierarchies. In this context, these roles and hierarchies are not understood as natural or essential. Instead they are viewed as artifacts or political outcomes—the result of present organizational forces. In the systematic conception, politics is not simply a matter of the organization of interaction. It also entails the organization of meaning. This constitutes the culture of power, political culture. It distinguishes social categories and prescribes the role prerogatives or action possibilities associated with each of them. In so doing, the culture provides beliefs and understandings, and determines what will be regarded as relevant interests. Like roles and hierarchies, specifications of belief and interest are also understood as political outcomes and thus as objects of manipulation and vehicles for the exercise of organizational power or governance.

Political institutions and the organization of interaction. Because society is viewed as a system, a key concern that emerges is the coordination of the interaction between the members of the society. This coordination sustains the integration of the community and thereby assures its very existence. For the most part, this integration is achieved organically. Where perturbations occur, they are assumed to invoke their own correction through a host of local, barely detectable shifts and compensations. Where such a natural reintegration does not occur, a governmental function is invoked. This requires institutions of power that regulate interaction within the community so as to facilitate and maintain that community's internal coordination. This involves the specification and enforcement of rules or laws of how individuals may engage one another. These laws both define particular roles and behavioral conventions and, at the same time, determine how those roles will be allocated and which behavioral conventions will be required under what conditions.

Unlike the simple, reified hierarchies of linear thought, the systematic conception of these governmental institutions is quite complex. Power and influence operate in a number of directions simultaneously. Not only do they flow from the top down, but also from the bottom up. In this view, the impact of the powerful depends on the cooperation of the less powerful. The action of the powerful is oriented accordingly. Similarly, at any given level in a hierarchy, it is understood that there is internal division among players at that level. Consequently, power and influence are understood to move laterally as well as up and down. Finally, institutions are understood to operate within a larger political context. This includes other governmental and nongovernmental institutions. Examples of the latter may include political parties, labor unions, or special interest organizations, such as Amnesty International or Greenpeace. Thus power and influence are not only manifest within an institution, but across institutions as well.

Political culture, ideology, and the organization of meaning. As conceived in systematic thought, society not only provides an organization of action; it also generates a framework of meaning. Complementing the organization of action in a community is the integration of its culture. The presumption here is that the meanings, representations, and purposes communicated within the community cohere. In part, this coherence is understood to depend on consistency among these various elements of the culture. As noted earlier, cultural claims of truth and value are presumed to be intertwined through specific linkages based on identification, negation, and implication. In the case of any particular claim, this opens up a set of inferences that link that claim to others. The key is to insure that this process does not produce internal contradictions. In this view of culture, the emergence of contradictions leads to confusion in the specific case and is destabilizing for the broader system of meanings as a whole.

In this view, the coherence of a culture depends not only on its internal consistency, but also on its commonality. The meanings, representations, and purposes incorporated in conversation (or included in the monologues of mass media presentations) must be commonly understood. This provides the common sense and shared norms of discourse required as a backdrop for meaningful communication. The importance of this is clear if we consider the discussions regarding public policy that emerge between religious fundamentalists and citizens with a secular orientation. Whether it is a debate over abortion in the United States or an argument over territorial concessions in Israel, communication between fundamentalists and secularists is obstructed by different assumptions about the nature of the world, how that world can be known, and how differences between people may be legitimately resolved. For the fundamentalists, the world is essentially divine, knowledge is a matter of insight, and differences must be resolved through recourse to some form of divine authority. For the secularists, the world is more physical and human, knowledge is tentative and a matter of discovery, and differences can only be resolved through open negotiation and compromise. Given these differences, there is very little common ground for meaningful discussion between the two groups. More generally, it is clear that this lack of common ground and the attendant failures to communicate will undermine the cohesiveness of a community.

This systematic understanding of cultural claims and the role they play is very different from the linear conception. In the linear view, discursive claims that are common in one's own culture are understood to be both essentially normal and true. In the systematic view, these claims are understood to be social creations. At the level of interpersonal relations, discursive claims are understood to be negotiated between individuals against the backdrop of a shared culture. At another level, they are understood to serve a systemic function of sustaining a particular cultural community. In this light, the categorical definitions and explanatory claims that orient linear social reasoning (e.g., race, gender, or nationality) are understood to be social products that serve social purposes. As social constructs that perform social functions, a culture's categories, explanations, and conventions may also be viewed as objects that may be manipulated to meet the needs of a specific community. This raises specifically political issues.

In the systematic conception, the coherence and commonality of meaning, like the organization of action, is assumed to be a natural characteristic of communal life. However, as in the case of the organization of action, it is recognized that circumstances may arise which introduce elements that challenge the coherence of a culture. This may involve the emergence of new ideas, either as they percolate up within the culture itself or as they are introduced from outside or foreign sources. In the current international context, this typically consists of the penetration of American ideas and values into other domestic cultures. A good example of this is the introduction of American views of economy and politics into third world countries such as China. According to a systematic understanding, such a penetration of foreign ideas will often be dealt with organically. The meanings of the ideas will be recast in the domestic context. Thus American notions of citizen participation get framed within the authoritarianism of China's Confucian culture. Participation becomes a matter of solicitation, request, and limited protest. Where such an organic assimilation does not occur, there is a need for governance. Institutions must be mobilized that interpret new ideas in a manner consistent with the culture at large. In the Chinese case, this involves massive use of mass media, the institutions of public education, and the police.[11]

Perhaps even more important than the problem of insuring the coherence of the culture in the face of new ideas is the need to insure that existing ideas are commonly understood. Again there is the assumption that a community will typically solve this problem in its own organic way. Where there is an isolated, homogeneous community, the process is a simple one. New entrants to the culture, that is children for the most part, are simply taught the significance of things by those around them. Matters are recognized to be far more complex in large nations that, at the outset, are not a single cultural community, but a cluster of more or less related communities. In this instance, the governmental function is again invoked in the cultural sphere. To this end, institutions are created that essentially socialize people into the common culture. Institutions of this kind are central to government. Where a society fails to sustain and disperse a common culture, a government must create cultural authorities that can do so. The preeminent modern example of such an authoritative, socializing institution is the public school. Of course, depending on the manner in which the community is organized, mass media may also come under the purview of government and be utilized in a similar manner.

In the context of our discussion of culture, it is also important to note that governance has not only an organizational dimension, but a cultural one as well. Reference here is to that aspect of the culture that pertains to issues of organization and control. In systematic reasoning, this constitutes the political culture or ideology of the community. Like the culture more broadly, this subsystem of meaning consists of representations of the structure, dynamic, and purpose of social life. Here, however, the focus is limited to questions of government and governance. For example, it indicates who can govern or participate in government, how government can be organized both unto itself and relative to the community at large, what goals government may pursue, and how it may pursue them. Political ideologies or cultures are differentiated on this basis. For example, in a systematic analysis, medieval European political cultures and later liberal enlightenment ones may be defined and distinguished along all the aforementioned lines. Medieval political cultures may be viewed as having prescribed that only the appropriately born should govern, that the monarch was the government and the community was in a certain sense a mere extension of the monarch, and that the government should pursue the interests of the monarch in whatever manner seemed necessary. In contrast, liberal en-

ishments. Supplementing this would be the utilization of existing institutions of enforcement such as the police and the creation of new ones such as family oversight agencies.

The second dimension of the solution is cultural. Depending on the context, this may be seen simply as a need to resort to new means to assure the dispersion and reassertion of traditional meanings. To this end, institutions of socialization may be mobilized. This might include the use of the mass media as conduits for a program of parent socialization and for mobilizing neighbors and teachers to take greater and more proactive responsibility for monitoring childcare. This effort may be supplemented by the use of schools to inform children regarding the parenting practices they should expect and those that are expressly forbidden. The cultural problem may also be seen to require the introduction of new meanings to support the flagging old ones. This may involve an attempt to redefine the parent-child relationship by dissociating it from its traditional conception as a property relationship and by actively recasting it as a relationship between individuals. In addition, there may be an attempt to redefine child-training practices by disassociating them from notions of corporal punishment and by linking them to the idea of education. Throughout the aim is to insure that these attempts at redefinition cohere, both unto themselves and with the broader culture.

Culture-structure dualism and public policy. As discussed earlier in the description of social reasoning, a culture-structure dualism is a characteristic product of systematic reasoning. This is evident in political reasoning as well. There is a distinction drawn between political culture as a system of meanings and political structure as an organization of action. These two systems, however, are understood to operate on much of the same ground; meanings reflect, refer to, and direct interaction and interactions include discourse as an element of the exchange. Moreover, culture and structure are understood as operating in the same domain, that is, both are dimensions or subsystems of the larger society or community. Thus for purposes of political analysis, systematic reasoning typically assumes that the political culture parallels the objective realities of social exchange; it reflects and comprehends those realities and thus may have an impact on them. It is this assumption that renders the whole project of governmental intervention and public policy plausible.

When it is evident that governmental interventions fail despite the best intentions and the greatest efforts, the simple parallelism and connection posited in systematic thought is called into question. The perception that public policy failure is ubiquitous tends to engender a political skepticism premised on the notion that culture and social structure do not parallel or reflect one another. Systematic reasoning based on this uncomfortable assumption leads in the following direction. To the degree to which the culture is disconnected from the structure of social exchange, it is likely that representations of social realities will be distorted. In this case, there can be no presumption that social problems will be adequately detected or properly interpreted. In addition, there is no guarantee that the public policies which follow will be appropriately crafted or that their implementation will produce the desired impact. The overall conclusion is that government intervention is likely to be ill conceived and its effect will be largely unpredictable.

Many elements of the typical presumptions and the skeptical rejections generated by systematic political reasoning are to be found in the classical debate between eighteenth- and nineteenth-century liberals and conservatives. The liberal view reflects much of the initial result of systematic political reasoning with its assumption of systemic integration and its concomitant faith in the appropriateness and efficacy of governmental intervention. This is reflected in the writings from John Locke to John Stuart Mill. The conservative rejection of the liberal view of public policy initiatives in the face of the evident failures of government in the late eighteenth and early nineteenth century may, in part, be understood as an example of the systematic political skepticism that such failures typically produce. This is apparent in Edmund Burke's work on the French Revolution and the writings of such English romantics as John Keats and Thomas Carlyle.

The space and time of politics. Thus far the discussion of the systematic conception of the political system has focused on its function as a governance mechanism. Here we supplement this discussion with a consideration of the arena or stage upon which this political activity is played out. This political arena may be characterized in terms of its space and time. In the systematic view, the space of politics is an integrated one. Every activity is understood as a point on a larger integrated map of social and political action. On this map, the points bear on one another; the location of each is suspended between the locations of the others. This map or space not only includes interactions or activities that have been observed or reported, it also includes others that may be inferred. In this respect, the systematic construction of politics is very different from its linear counterpart. Cast in linear terms, political activity is understood within the narrow confines of its immediate circumstance and some other associated circumstance that is identified as a cause or an effect. As such, the understanding of the political domain is fragmentary—activity in one context does not link to activity in other contexts unless an evident active connection is present. This domain is also limited to what was observed or reported. The cognitive apparatus of linear thought does not allow for systematic deduction and true hypothetical claims.[12]

The time of politics constructed in systematic thought is also quite different from that of linear thought. In the linear conception, time is also fragmentary. It is caught in the unfolding trajectory of specific sequences of action that are isolated from one another except insofar as they are identified with one another or are causally related. In the systematic conception, time is integrated. The various linear trajectories of concrete cause and effect are interrelated within the relative timelessness of a reciprocally sustaining weave of interactions. In other words, the various times of particular substantive actions are now interrelated with one another. Cause and effect, the specific moment of one and the moment that follows of the other, are now located relative to a host of other causes and effects in an integrated system of moments. Thus as the place of an action is located as a point in a systemic space, so the moment of that action is located as a point in a systemic time.

The time and space of the systematic political arena are not only internally integrated dimensions, they are also integrated with one another. In a sense, the integration of time into space is implicit in our discussion of systems. Insofar as a system coordinates different interactions relative to one another, it effectively interrelates their times within the space of the system. In this regard, time is contained within the social space. The integration of time and space can also be understood as space configuring time. In the systematic conception, time is not bound simply to the flow from action to reaction. It is expanded to subsume the space of the system of connections among interactions. In this understanding, time is not only the passing of the specific moment, it is also embodied in the duration of a system that directs the passing of moments. In this latter regard, time is configured as an epoch or period. Each particular epoch is distinguished by the character of the system of interactions (their substance and arrangement) of that time. An example would be an attempt to understand recent political history by dividing it into two periods, the cold war and the post–cold war. The patterning of global interaction differentiates the two periods. In the first case the interaction may be understood to have been primarily between nations and arranged according to bipolar military alliances. In the second case, the interaction may be understood to involve nonnational economic entities that engage one another in a multipolar system.

In this context, we can differentiate linear and systematic concepts of political change. In the linear conception, political change is anchored in the concrete contours of specific actions, actors, and norms. Political change occurs with the fall and rise of political leaders. It is denied with the enduring quality of concrete symbols (e.g., the crown) and locations of power (e.g., Buckingham Palace or the Houses of Parliament) and the repetition of the specific rituals of power (e.g., the Queen's opening of Parliament, celebrations of such national victories and sacrifices as Remembrance Day or Guy Fawkes Day). In a systematic conception, political change and stability are not anchored in specific leaders, symbols, places, or rituals. Unto themselves, these concrete entities are regarded as relatively meaningless or indeterminate. The dynamic and form of political life is found in interactive relationships and discursive meaning. Thus it matters little if the reigns of power are in the hands of the Social Democrats or the Christian Democrats or if the capital is Bonn or Berlin, or even whether West Germany expands to include the GDR. What is key is the institutional structure of the German government and the broadly democratic cultural frame of reference within which political issues are discussed. The specific party in power or the size of the polity has a certain limited significance, but the core reality of the political system is the institutional and discursive rules that define the political players and delimit how they may interact with one another. Insofar as these rules remain the same, the political system is presumed to remain essentially the same. If these rules change, the changes are assumed to reverberate through the political system. The result is a broad transformation or political revolution.

One important consequence of this is systematic reconfiguration of the space and time of linear reasoning is that the agenda-setting effect discussed in connection with linear reasoning is less likely to occur in the case of systematic thinking. As the reader will remember, the fragmentary quality of the political space and time of linear thought left reasoning of this kind very open to external direction. The integrative quality of systematic reasoning renders it less susceptible to framing or agenda-setting effects. For example, in the case of the Iyengar and Kinder study discussed earlier, the potential agenda-setting effect of changing the content of the television news presentation would be muted by the tendency of systematic reasoning to assimilate that content into an already constructed map of politics. The specific content of the news presentation is located within the broader context of a preexisting subjective conception of the political system. Thus the presented issues are placed relative to absent issues even when the newscast itself makes none of the necessary connections. This has two relevant consequences. First, the issue as presented is actively interpreted with reference to its place relative to other issues. Second, the emphasis the presentation places on the issue is diminished as other issues are invoked and thus are also made salient.[13] In sum, someone thinking systematically is less vulnerable to the worrying effects of mass media that are demonstrated in some empirical research and are often a matter of concern to politicians and political philosophers.

Political conflict. As constructed in linear thought, political conflict consists of a simple clash of interest between opposing parties. It is a natural state of affairs, the result of individual parties pursuing their own ends. Each intends to do something that obstructs the action of the other. The parties may be individuals, groups (nations), or alliances of groups. In any case, the parties to the conflict are monolithic actors that are conceived relative to the specifics of the conflict. As a result, the conflict between the two parties is a total or encompassing one, and a resolution depends on the subordination or destruction of one of them.[14]

The systematic construction of political conflict is quite different. Whereas linear thought tends to conceive of conflict in bipolar terms, systematic thought considers it to be a potentially multipolar phenomenon. The parties themselves are similarly complex. They consist of a number of actors and institutions that relate to one another as well as to the opposing party. Thus a given party's action must be understood not only to be a response to its opponent, but also the product of internal political activity. In addition, the parties are no longer regarded solely with reference to the conflict itself. It is recognized that the relationship between the parties is multifaceted. Consequently, while they conflict along one line, they may be in agreement along another. In this regard, the alignment of parties, the way in which alliances and oppositions configure, will vary with the specific interactive conditions being considered. Conflict is thus no longer regarded as total. In this context, the perceived magnitude of the conflict is reduced and the destruction of the other seems a less sensible resolution than one that entails a better coordination of the relationship between the parties.

Thus far the systematic construction of conflict has been presented as a complicating of essentially linear concerns. This is not enough. The systematic understanding of conflict is constructed in basically different terms. Political interaction is understood systemically. Conflict is thus conceptualized in the broader context of an otherwise integrated system, perhaps that of the national political system in the case of domestic conflict or that of the world political system in the case of international conflict. In this broader context, conflict is not regarded as a natural or enduring state of affairs. Rather, the natural state is one of integration and coordination. In light of this natural integration, conflict may be understood in two ways. The conflict may be regarded as more apparent than real in the sense that it is systemically structured in a manner that maintains the integration of the system at large. An example of this would be the self-consciously designed and systemically regulated conflict among the executive, judiciary, and legislative branches of government in the United States. Conflict of this kind is regarded as nonproblematic, a mere type of integration. This notion of conflict as means of integration is very difficult to assimilate to a linear understanding of the world. One example of this is the dissatisfaction and unease that the conflict endemic to democratic politics produces in people that reason in a linear manner.

Insofar as it is regarded to be real, the conflict is understood as a breakdown in some aspect of the integrative force of the system in which the conflict occurs. The difficulty is typically regarded as a localized problem. The particular circumstances of the interaction between the conflicting parties result in an essentially deviant form of exchange. A product of the conditions of interaction, the reduction of conflict requires the transformations of those conditions. This may be achieved through a change in the objective conditions of the exchange, such as by altering the material resources or technological means available to the conflicting parties. It may also be achieved through a change in the subjective perception of the exchange. This may entail a recasting of the relevant beliefs and perceived interests of the parties. The presumption is that the system will generally self-correct because of the host of pressures, internal as well as external to the conflictual relationship, that operate to maintain more conventional and rule-governed interaction. Where this does not occur, governmental action is necessary. The resolution of the conflict, be it the result of organic self-correction or governmental intervention, is understood to consist of a renewed coordination of the exchange thereby reintegrating it into the larger system of political relationships.

To illustrate, let us consider the example of the Israeli-Palestinian conflict discussed in chapter 3. When constructed in linear terms, the conflict is viewed largely in isolation. It is understood specifically with reference to the parties and their conflicting territorial claims. Therein lies the problem—both want the same piece of land. Within the confines of this conflict, each side is viewed simply and completely as the enemy of the other. The conflict plays itself out as a succession of initiatives and responses, something in the style of a Ping-Pong match between two players. The boundaries of the conflict may be extended somewhat to include allies associated with each of the parties. Thus, the United States may be included as an ally of Israel and the other Arab states may be included as allies of the Palestinians. Despite this expansion, the two sides are conceptualized in the same way—as monolithic actors that in a broad sense are enemies to one another. How can this conflict be resolved? There is only one fundamental solution—one side or the other must be subordinated or destroyed. Thus, the Palestinians must be policed or dispersed among other Arab lands, and the Israelis must be washed into the sea. This view of the conflict is somewhat simplified, but it reflects the essentials of a linear construction of it.

When viewed in systematic terms, the Israeli-Palestinian conflict is understood very differently. To begin, the conflict is understood in the broader context of the international system. In this context, the conflict may be understood to be exacerbated by the cold war politics of the forty-five years after World War II. The world was organized into a bipolar system of oppositions in which local contests were incorporated into the broader geopolitical concerns of the opposed parties. Thus, the Israeli-Palestinian conflict can be understood as one that was appropriated by the United States and the Soviet Union. They helped define the conflict as a multifaceted one involving not just territory, but ideology and identity. In this context, the Middle East conflict was integral to expressing and sustaining the broader world system. Its significance and dynamic must be understood accordingly. With the collapse of the Soviet Union, the world system has changed and with it the context of the Middle East conflict. The bipolar arrangement has dissolved and national antagonisms grounded in ideology are diminishing. Emerging in its place is an order that is multipolar and operating on the narrow basis of trade and economic growth. In this context, much of the support for the Israeli-Palestinian conflict has collapsed. Where once international pressures sustained the conflict, now they are forcing it to a close. This is complemented by cultural pressures as well. Part of the new international culture is a focus on economic advancement. This is seen to be dependent on peace and cooperation. The pressure for the Middle East to be reconstructed according to these understandings is clear. The cultural pressures coincide with the structural ones in demanding a resolution that will allow business to continue in a way now defined as normal.

At the same time, the conflict can be viewed more narrowly in terms of the particular parties most immediately involved. In this light, a number of considerations emerge. First is the multidimensional nature of the relationship between the parties. The Israelis and Palestinians are not only related by an interest in a common territory. They are also related in a variety of other ways. They have interdependent needs for security and maintaining the integrity of their own national groups. In complex ways this operates to undermine as well as sustain the conflict. The Israelis and Palestinians also depend on one another economically, both at present and in the future. Because of the conflict, each is a target of a certain amount of aid. At the same time, however, economic resources are diverted toward military buildup rather than to social and economic development more broadly. The conflict also discourages international investment and the emergence of regional cooperation that would benefit Israelis and Palestinians alike. This consideration of future possibilities introduces hypothetical concerns into the analysis. Second, there is the complexity of how the two sides are organized. Each side subsumes a diversity of governmental, religious, ideological, and economic entities. These entities have separate agendas and interact with one another within the context of the group, Israeli or Palestinian. Moreover, these domestic political forces also interact directly with elements of the opposing group and outside international forces. In this light, the initiatives and reaction of each side is understood to be complexly determined. To understand the dynamic of the conflict, all these dimensions of the Israeli-Palestinian relationship must be considered.

The requirements of resolution are understood in this light. Interaction among the conflicting parties must be coordinated in a manner consistent with both broader international imperatives and the particulars of the conflict. This sets the demand for a coordination that is consistent with conduct of Western style international business. This will require altering the conditions of exchange between the conflicting parties so that exchange is more subject to and consistent with the broader international regulation. This may include changes in the objective conditions, such as aid and trade predicated on progress toward peace rather than on continued military engagement. The new coordination will also require the transformation of local understandings. This may include a subordination of national identifications as Israeli or Palestinian in favor of the redefinition of both players as Middle Easterners or as "the special bridge" between the West and the Arab world. This may also include a change in perceived interests wherein Arabs and Israelis both deemphasize the importance of territorial and religious claims in favor of considerations of long-term security and economic growth. The result would be a mutual accommodation, commonly recognized and valued, and with it a new stable equilibrium.

Individual as social product and citizen. Thus far the consideration of the systemic dimension of systematic political thought has focused at the level of the community. This is complemented by the conception of the individual as a product or a pawn. Where the notion of the systemic integration of the polity frames the understanding, the individual citizen is considered as she is articulated into the political system. The individual's place in the system determines her social identity and, in a complementary fashion, the limits and potentialities of how she may participate in social life. As the individual's social location changes, so will her social identity. For example, when Talma rises at home in the morning she is a mother, when she arrives at work she is a clinical psychologist, when she reads the newspaper report of the California proposition repealing affirmative action she is Hispanic, and when she goes out to a social event in the evening she is a woman. Talma's identity is not constructed by her but by the contexts that envelop her.

Conceived in these terms, an individual does not constitute an appropriate focus of social or political analysis. Individuals may be considered, but when they are, they are understood to be the products not the producers of organization and meaning. Thus the sense and dynamic of social life must be sought elsewhere. Much of the ostensibly psychologically oriented research in contemporary political science adopts this perspective. One example is the research on individuals' belief systems that follows in the tradition of Philip Converse's early study of the American voter (Campbell et al., 1960; Converse, 1964). Converse focuses on individuals but quickly discounts any explanation of the interrelationship among their beliefs in terms of any inherent qualities of individuals. Instead, he turns to the individuals' exposure to the political culture in order to explain how their beliefs cohere. A similar explanatory strategy is adopted in most of the extensive empirical research on childhood and adult political socialization (e.g., Easton and Dennis, 1969; Jennings and Niemi, 1974; Sigel and Hoskin, 1981; Ichilov, 1990).[15]

This concept of the individual is radically altered when she is regarded as a system unto herself. In this alternative frame of reference, the individual is understood to be an organizing and defining force. She is the producer of her actions and the author of her subjective understanding of the world. Transposed into a political context, the individual is self-defining and self-directing, an agent-citizen in the full sense. Thus she cannot be conceived as a social construct, a mere target of manipulation and thus peripheral to political analysis. Rather the individual must be viewed as the key force in political life. By directing her own action and crafting her own meaning as she engages others, the individual necessarily contributes to the structuring of exchange and the defining of discourse in which she participates. The concept of the citizen thus shifts from one that focuses on membership, regulation, and obligation to one concerned with individuality, participation, and rights.

The implications of this alternative view of the citizen for the understanding of society and politics will be deferred to the following discussion of principles of political interaction. For now it is sufficient to note that the construction of systematic thought yields different levels of political analysis. Analysis at one of these levels is formally equivalent to the analysis at the next level. When related to each other, however, the understandings generated at the different levels frequently contradict one another or produce irreducible ambiguities. For example, when the results of two levels of analysis of the nature of the individual are juxtaposed we find that the individual is self-determining and determined, a coherent system and a collection of externally constructed fragments, an epiphenomenal product of political action and its essential cause.

This "levels of analysis" problem is also evident in the analysis of international politics. The formal structure of the reasoning is the same, just the specification of the levels change. The higher level becomes the international or world system and the lower or individual level becomes the nation-state. Thus transposed to the analysis of international politics, the focus of systematic reasoning may shift back and forth between the level of the world as an integrated system and individual nations as internally coordinated systems. In the first case, the world order is understood to organize the interactions between groups. It determines what can be done and when. In this regard, the international order not only defines action, but also the nature of the actors. Depending on the order, the players may be constituted by kinship relations (tribes), territory (nations), culture (e.g., the West), or material interests (e.g., business corporations, ecological groups, etc.). Examples of analysis at this level include the neo-Marxist theorizing of Wallerstein (1979) and the international regime arguments of Haas (1989) and Klotz (1997).

When the level of analysis shifts to nation-states, the understanding changes dramatically. In this frame of reference, the individual players are self-constituting systems. This suggests that they are not defined and oriented by a world order, but are instead self-defining and self-directing entities. Pursuing their purposes in the context of other nations, nations are constrained by each other. Consequently, it is the nations themselves (or other specified players) that determine the kind of international relationship they have with one another. A contemporary example of this is the "neorealist" approach to the study of international relations (e.g., Buzan, 1991; Keohane and Nye, 1979).[16] As the internal structure of nations change, so will their purposes and therefore their international relationships. Such an understanding is illustrated by the claim that the cultural and economic character of some nations are changing thereby transforming the relationship these nations have with one another from one determined by the strategies of war to one determined by the requirements of trade.

Principles of Political Interaction

Thus far in our discussion of systematic political reasoning, we have focused on one way in which political life may be constructed, that is, as a system of interactions and discursive claims. Politics may also be conceived in a second way, as it is ordered by underlying or higher principles. Here interactions are not juxtaposed relative to other interactions with which they are connected in a system. Rather they are defined relative to a particular type of bidirectional or mutually defining relationship of which they become specific examples. Interactions are thus abstracted from the specific systemic context in which they might otherwise be viewed. Classes of interaction are then juxtaposed relative to one another in a formally determined or empirically driven manner in order to establish the nature of the principled relationship between them. This juxtaposition is formulated without reference to particular concrete systemic contexts. Whether it is generated deductively or inductively, the principle is conceived in an abstract or disembedded manner, thus producing general or universal claims of association.

The construction classes of interaction and the principled relationship between them have been amply discussed in our earlier account of social reasoning. There the process was illustrated by the example of cooperation and control. The systematic construction of principles of relationship applies to expressly political interactions in the same way it does to interactions that may be designated as social. Arguably the earlier example of control and cooperation is as much political as social. Two other examples of systematically conceived principles are claims that: (1) there is a relationship in principle between a class of interactions involving mutual and voluntary commitment and a class of interactions involving trust (this claim is central to Robert Putnam's analysis of social trust, 1993), and (2) there is a relationship in principle between the distribution of control among interacting agents in nonpolitical social interactions and the distribution of control among interacting agents in expressly political interactions (this claim is central to Harry Eckstein's analysis of authority structures, 1968).

Our analysis of the principled dimension of systematic reasoning can be extended to a consideration of the role it plays in the conceptualization of the relationship between systems, where the systems in question are individual citizens. In this frame of reference, systems are considered as they extend outward toward their environment. Given the understanding of individuals as systems of personality and subjectivity, this extension consists of the purposive acts individuals initiate and the subjective meanings they express as they engage another person. In this context, a person is no longer regarded as a system that is conceived in light of her particular internal weave of connections. Instead, she is an agent and is conceived relative to a class of interactive engagement. This class may be constructed such that it consists of purposive acts and thus defines the individual as an actor, or it may be constructed such that it consists of expressions of meaning and defines the individual as a subject. In either case, the classification depends on the consideration of the focal type of engagement (purposive action or expression of meaning) as it is exemplified across particular situations involving the particular things specific individuals say or do to one another. Thus the class itself is constructed by grouping together concrete, embedded interactions into a conceptual context that is itself inherently disembedded or abstract. The result is a conception of "the subject" or "the agent" as an abstraction. By the very nature of its construction, this conception is free of the particulars of any given individual or any particular social environment that individual is attempting to engage. This of course is very different from the person-specific interpretations and contextual explications that are part of the systemic conception of the individual. Relative to the determinism of this systemic conception, the abstract, principled conception of the individual is in a sense liberating. In principle, the general manner in which individuals engage in social interaction or conversation is common to them all, however the specific things they say or do are understood to be largely indeterminate. Consequently, when considering the specifics of their interaction, there is a tendency to regard individuals as relatively free agents.

Principled relationship between agent/subjects. Given this principled conception of a system as a class, the problem of the connection between individuals is reconceived as one of the relationship between classes of interaction. Depending on how the classes themselves are defined, this relationship may be an interactive one between two actors or a discursive one between two subjects. The principle constructed, like all systematic principles, both embodies and reflects the particular classes related and transcends and regulates the interplay between them. To illustrate, consider the relationship between two individuals, each of whom is defined as a class of actor oriented to the another. On one hand, the principled relationship between them is understood to reflect the activity of each of the actor-classes. Drawing on a conception of the individual as a system as a point of departure, it may be deduced that (1) all purposive acts are deployments of the personality (as the organization of action) of the actor (as a general classification), (2) as such, all purposive acts share in common this attempt to assimilate the environment into the existing personality system thereby maintaining the integrity of the system relative to that environment. This general aim, *maintaining the integrity of one's personality,* which is true of both actor-classes is then embodied in the principle of the interaction. While thus reflecting the basic characteristics of the classes related, the principle of their relationship also transcends the particularity of each. Here this entails considering the meaning of an interactive relationship between forces, each of which is attempting to sustain the integrity of its own personal organization of the interaction between them. This may readily lead to a conclusion that *cooperation* is an essential principle of the relationship between purposive actors.

Reasoning proceeds along similar lines when considering the relationship between two individuals conceived as subjects. Again the principle is constructed in a manner that embodies and transcends the qualities of the classes related. Each individual (considered as a class of interactions) is regarded as a subject who expresses meaning in the attempt to lead another person to understand what she, the subject, has said in a manner consistent with her subjective understanding of her own claim. In this regard, the expression of subjective meaning consists of an attempt to assimilate the other's understanding of that expression to one's own terms of understanding thereby maintaining the coherence of one's own system of meaning. In this understanding of individual subjectivity, all particular expressions of meaning share in common this attempt to maintain the coherence or integration of one's subjective system of meanings. This general characteristic of both classes being related, *maintaining the coherence of one's subjective understanding,* is embodied in the principle of communication. At the same time, the principle is conceived in such a manner that it transcends the particular nature of the classes related. The result may lead to some notion of *agreement* as an essential principle of the communicative relationship between expressive subjects.

Conceived in this manner, the notions of cooperation and agreement are quite abstract. How they are utilized to define a specific instance of interaction will be a matter of interpretation. To illustrate, let us consider the example of an abusive social relationship in which one party's purposive acts aim to harm and the other party's purposive acts aim to incur harm. To the degree to which such relationships are evidenced over time and across different sets of people, they must be understood not as an accidental or chance phenomena, but as exemplars or manifestations of an underlying social principle. In the present context, it may be regarded as an example of cooperation, even if a highly counterintuitive one, and be interpreted accordingly. To this end, the particular interactions constituting such an abusive relationship are understood to be conducted in such a manner that they are consistent with each party's attempt to regulate the exchange between them according to the organization of their own personality. Thus both abuser and abused are understood as cooperating in producing interactions that sustain the sadistic personality organization of the abuser and the masochistic personality organization of the abused. The two actors are thus understood to contribute to the definition of the relationship that then regulates them both.[17]

Given the quality of the systematic construction of social principles, notions of cooperation and agreement and with them the allied considerations of personal integrity and coherence are likely to figure quite centrally in any social or political analysis. Several points should be made here. First, the social principles constructed in the course of systematic reasoning are very abstract. They only become consequential when they are used as a basis for making sense of particular interactions and discourses. At this level, the interpretations or explanations they suggest will vary with the conditions of their application. Most important, the parameters of cooperation and agreement will vary given prior assumptions of the meaning of integrity or coherence in the case of the individuals related. This is already illustrated by the foregoing characterization of an abusive relationship as a cooperative one. It is also illustrated in an earlier discussion of control as cooperation between the powerful and the powerless. In either case, the relationship is understood to be cooperative or a matter of agreement and, by implication, one that sustains the integrity of both parties.[18]

Second, once elaborated in particular conditions, the social principles identified are assumed to govern the dynamic of social interaction and discourse. Where individuals do not engage one another in the prescribed manner, it is assumed that the relationship will break down. This is true even where control ostensibly is in the hands of the one of the actors, for example, the powerful or the more understanding. Where the terms of cooperation are violated and the integrity of the personality system of the powerless is challenged, the powerless will either undermine the relationship (to the point of explicit rebellion) or leave it. Similarly where the terms of a mutually comprehensible communication are broken and the coherence of the subjectivity of the less understanding party is violated, the less understanding party will work to subvert the communicative relationship or abandon it altogether.

Third, the elaboration of social principles of cooperation and agreement are socially and historically relative. Systematic reasoning occurs in a social context. Central to such a context are social determinations of how different sorts of individuals can act and cultural definitions of what different kinds of individuals are like. Different societies may present systematic reasoning with a social reality in which people's personalities are configured differently and with a culture in which those personalities are represented differently. This will affect the systemic reconstruction of individuals as systems and therefore the prior assumptions upon which the construction of principles of relationship between individuals are based. Thus even if systematic reasoning is oriented by concerns of cooperation, integrity, intersubjectivity, and coherence, the elaboration of these concerns in the understanding of the specific dynamics of social life will be strongly affected by the social context in which the reasoning occurs.

The dependence of principled systematic reasoning on the cultural context can be illustrated by those instances in which the culture identifies certain categories of people as somewhat less than fully human. In the European and North American traditions, this has been done in a way that has relegated people of color, native peoples, and women to a secondary status. Systematic analysis of individual members of these groups builds on these culturally prevalent definitions producing a conception of them as less fully integrated personalities or less fully coherent subjects than their white male counterparts. Thus people of color, native peoples, and women are typically viewed as impulsive and irrational. This necessarily affects the conceptualization of the basic quality of the social relationship that can exist between a member of one of these groups and a white male. The typical result is to confer some respect for the integrity of these relatively incompetent individuals, but only in the context of a caretaker relationship in which they become part of the "white man's burden."

Fourth, by virtue of the manner in which they are constructed, social principles tend to evoke ever greater abstraction and generality. When put to use, a principle is elaborated in a more substantive context. At the same time, however, there is a reflective tendency to try to understand and justify the principle relative to yet a higher order principle that it expresses. The result is the tendency toward constructing principles at the highest level of generality and in what is understood to be their most essential form. This is evident in systematic political theory and jurisprudence where there is an attempt to ground any explanations or regulations on the basis of a few very abstract and essential principles of social life. A concept of constitutional law, that is, law that constitutes the essence of the polity, follows from this. Commensurate with this abstracting essentialism is a tendency to regard individuals in increasingly abstract and disembedded terms and therefore as essentially equivalent or equal.

Fifth, the systematic construction of social principles is self-conscious and therefore tentative. Systematic reasoning is self-aware in that it recognizes that the principles it infers to be true are nonetheless a subjective product. As such, social principles are not regarded as objective facts or necessarily true, but rather as hypothetical claims that are being advanced as true but might prove to be incorrect. Thus, unlike the certainty of linear reasoning regarding the truth and correctness of its construction of social norms, the systematic construction of social principles has an inherently provisional quality. Claims regarding how to best explain or interpret a situation that are based on a particular principle may be drawn quite conclusively. At the same time, however, there is a recognition that the underlying principle is itself only the best one to have been generated thus far. A better underlying conception might emerge and then conclusions so clearly drawn on the basis of the superseded principle would have to be abandoned.

Sixth and related to the fifth, experience can lead to the rejection of principles. Understood as hypotheses, conclusions regarding social principles are not only used to interpret concrete exchanges between people, they are also tested against them. Insofar as these exchanges suggest that people do not interrelate in the manner hypothesized, doubt is cast on the principle in question. The greater the number of principles affected or the more basic the principle that is called into question, the more significant the doubt created. One result can be the genesis of a broad skepticism. This can manifest itself in general claims that the social universe is not governed by principles of cooperation and agreement, but rather is simply anarchic—a world in which those with advantage exercise control for the moment. Alternatively and somewhat more optimistically, it may be assumed that there must be an order to social life, but this order is too complicated or profound to be known. This view of life as mystery typically involves some culturally oriented leap of faith. A third option is to assert the existence of basic principles but suggest that they are conditional. In this vein, it may be claimed that principles do operate but only in a culturally or historically relative manner. In other words, they are system specific. Despite their quality as rejections, all three of these constructions—the anarchic, the mysterious, and the conditional—are nonetheless systematic. They are negations and as such they are derivative; their meaning depends on the meaning of the systematic principles they reject.

Implications for a general view of politics. Whether systematic reasoning adopts a systemic or principled approach has important implications for the ensuing sense of politics. When a systemic approach is adopted, the focus is on society as an organic entity. It orchestrates interaction and discourse so as to maintain its own integrity. Articulated into the social system, an individual is regarded as derivative and fragmentary, a collage produced by the various social contexts in which she is embedded. Consequently, considerations of personal integrity or the social impact of individual self-direction makes little sense when posed in this frame of reference. When a principled approach is adopted, the view of social life is dramatically different. The focus is on the natural relationships that exist between individuals. Although these relationships dictate how individuals are interrelated with one another, they are also understood to reflect the nature of the individual as a participant in interaction who actively pursues purposes and expresses subjective understandings. In this context, society is viewed as a set of arrangements somehow produced by or reflecting the requirements of its individual members.

With this shift from a systemic to a principled approach, the sociocultural system thus evaporates and is replaced by a set of principles of interpersonal relationship. Society and politics are conceptualized accordingly. Society is no longer an organizing system but rather a collective outcome. It consists of crafted social arrangements, the product of interacting individuals. Although manifest in particular ways in a given sociohistorical circumstance, these arrangements are understood to be bound by basic principles of social life.[19] It is thus presumed that societies that are organized in a way that contradicts those principles will necessarily fail. At the same time, it is recognized that particular people interacting in particular circumstances may engage one another in a deviant manner. This requires that otherwise very abstract and unstated principles be elaborated in a clear and relatively concrete manner so that they may be understood by all. It also requires means of enforcement to insure that the understanding leads to appropriate conduct. This defines the domain of politics.

Constructed in this way, politics consists of establishing basic principles of relationship between individuals that are then elaborated as a set of rules that speak to how individuals may relate in specific contexts. The basic principles reflect a most general attempt to make sense of the manner in which the integrity of individuals may be sustained in the context of the necessity of their relationship with one another. Given prevailing assumptions regarding human nature, this yields claims regarding the basic parameters of interpersonal conduct that are conducive to the achievement of cooperation and agreement. These are typically elaborated as a set of first principles or constitutional laws of the polity. These are expressed in very general terms. Conceived abstractly, these laws are often assumed to apply universally. This leads to a tendency to assume that basic constitutional arrangements may be readily exported from one social setting or country to another. In any particular setting, first principles are given more specific elaboration through their deductive application to more specific situations. This typically gives rise to the construction of a considerable number of more specific rules or laws such as those that govern business transactions, family relationships, or property.

The adoption of a principled conception of politics also affects the view of the political process. The understanding of this process reflects the quality of the systematic construction of principles themselves. These principles both transcend and embody that which they interrelate. This is reflected in the systematic conception of the political process as consisting of two reciprocally related aspects, governance and representation. Governance reflects the manner in which a principle transcends that which it relates. In terms of the political process, the issue becomes one of the regulation of the interaction between individuals. In its principled conception, governance consists of the rule of law. The exercise of the rule of law entails two activities. The first consists of the application of law. The problem here is interpretative. Conceived systematically, principles of relationship, even those that are elaborated in context and are therefore more delimited in scope, are defined in general terms. They refer to the relationship between classes of interaction. Therefore, the application of laws to specific situations involving particular people who have initiated particular acts toward one another will necessarily require interpretation. This will consist of properly characterizing the exchange to understand what classes of interaction are involved and therefore which law is applicable. In addition, the application will require an interpretation of how the general law applies in the particular case. This may include a consideration of the specific application with regard to the execution not only of the particular law, but also of basic principles or constitutional laws as they may be relevant to the case in question. As the aspect of government that is responsible for this task of application, the judiciary assumes a central role in a principled conception of political life.

Once interpreted, the rule of law also requires enforcement. Whereas it is assumed that properly defined laws reflect underlying propensities of human engagement, it is also recognized that deviation may occur. This suggests the need to police the law and punish violation. Particular circumstances will determine how policing and punishment are designed. In this principled vision, however, enforcement is itself always understood to be constrained by basic principles and thus by a concern for cooperation and individual integrity. This requires the adherence to constitutional and more specific law as much as possible, even when policing those who violate them. Punishment is understood in a similar light. In addition to being constrained by a basic respect for the integrity of the criminal, the aim of punishment is to insure compliance with basic and essentially natural laws. The goal is to prevent self-directing, understanding actors from deviating in the future. In this light, a legitimate response to violation is regarded less as a matter of punishment (conceived as retribution or restitution) and more as a matter of rehabilitation (consisting of education and therapy).

Apart from governance, the principled conception of the political process also entails the complementary activity of representation. As the notion of governance flows from the conception of a principle transcending what it relates, the understanding of representation follows from the conception of a principle as the reflection of that which is related. In the latter regard, it is assumed that the principles and laws of the polity, in part, embody the demands of integrity and coherence characteristic of the individual citizen. Insofar as they do, the law will naturally prove effective. Where problems arise, the political process is understood to provide means for the correction of incorrect rules and the creation of new ones. To insure that the requirements of individuals as actors and subjects are properly introduced, the political process is typically assumed to involve participation of some kind. Whereas the specific nature of this participation will vary across polities, it necessarily will involve means for both individual political action and individual political expression. Through these means, representation complements governance to insure appropriate and effective regulation. It is in this context that freedom of speech generally emerges as a central concern of principled systematic reasoning. It is understood as the vehicle for allowing individuals to express their aims and dissatisfactions with current conditions and regulations. The concern here is not simple self-expression without regard to purpose. The activity acquires practical political significance only insofar as it is oriented to reaching agreement with others as to how people can cooperate and thus how laws should be constructed and applied. For this reason, an interest in constructive debate typically complements an interest in free speech.

One very good example of a principled construction of politics is the understanding of politics offered by classical seventeenth- and eighteenth-century liberal political theory. Liberal theory begins with the need to determine the basic qualities of the individual, in this case "man." This is achieved through a thought experiment in which the individual is abstracted from any social system so as to determine his general qualities. The result is the conception of the individual in the state of nature. This abstract individual was conceived as a system, that is, as a coherent, self-directing entity, and in this regard as essentially equal to all other individuals. This then provided a conceptual basis for attempting to induce general principles of social relationship, principles that reconcile the social necessity of a reciprocal relationship with the psychological demands for the integrity of the individuals related. The result was a rule-based conception of political life. This was understood to require the elucidation of essentially natural laws of human cooperation as a balance of rights (reflecting systemic requirements of individuals) and obligations (reflecting regulative demands of cooperation). These then were regarded as providing the basis for elaborating a more specific set of legal applications. Alongside this view of politics as the rule of law was a consideration of the processes of governance and representation that such a rule necessarily entailed. Whereas liberal philosophers differed from one another in working out how governance and representation could be realized in a practical and effective manner, they shared the same basic principled view of politics.

Of course principled systematic political reasoning can yield conceptions of political life that are quite different from those of liberalism. This may be the result of rejecting basic elements of the liberal construction. On one hand, this may entail the rejection of the presumption that individuals are internally coordinating or coherent entities. Whether drawing on experience or cultural premises, systematic reasoning can lead to the conclusion that most individuals, as actors and thinkers, are in reality more like the insane or children than the ideal constructed through systematic reasoning. People are therefore assumed to be generally unable to act or think on their own behalf. In this instance, the conception of cooperation as caretaking is not an exceptional application of the general principle, but rather is central to any understanding of political relationships. The result is a very maternal and undemocratic view of the polity. This said, the actions of the polity are still constrained by basic notions of cooperation and respect for the integrity of its not fully competent citizens. We see evidence of such a view in nineteenth-century conservative rejections of liberalism's "naïve" idealism in the face of mounting social problems.

On the other hand, a rejection of the principled constructions of liberalism may focus on principled relationships themselves rather than on qualities of individuals. What is rejected is the assumption that there are basic principles of association that can be known and applied. Drawing again on cultural claims or experience, it may be assumed that the world is either anarchic or mysterious. In either case, individuals either alone or together cannot know the underlying principles of natural association. Such a view can lead in several directions. One is a wholesale epistemological skepticism. This entails a rejection of the search for the knowledge of basic principles and, by implication, a denial of the very activity of politics itself. Instead there is a move toward connection based not on reason, but on emotion and feeling. One arrives at what is natural through intimacy and thus must limit oneself to small-scale association with a few other persons or retreat from society altogether and return to nature herself. Such tendencies are exemplified in the nineteenth-century romantic movements in England and Germany. The irony of course is that this rejection of principle remains inescapably principled. This is evident in the call to consider people as concrete entities that are unique unto themselves.

Variations in the principled systematic construction of politics not only involve some form of skeptical rejection. They may simply reflect a switch in the level of analysis and the reconstruction of agents and principles of their relationship at that new level. For example, this may lead to a multicultural view of politics. In its systematic construction, this involves regarding a group rather than a person as the individual unit of analysis. As in the postmodernist case, the group is thus regarded both as an organizing and defining force that is realized in its own internal coordination of interaction and in the coherence of its culture. In this frame of reference, it is recognized that groups necessarily exist in relation to other groups. This invokes considerations of principles of relationship. As in the case of individual people, groups are considered as agents who engage one another with purposes to pursue and meanings to express. Defined in these abstract terms, groups and their specific organizational and cultural products are regarded as essentially equal. Similarly, the relationship between these group actor-classes is conceived in light of basic considerations of cooperation and agreement as both regulating the exchange and embodying the basic aims of the groups interacting. In this light, politics is still seen to revolve around the rule of law and involve processes of governance and representation. What is distinctive here is that the voices to be represented are those of groups, not individuals. This in turn leads to the specification of different procedures for ensuring this group participation in the definition and interpretation of basic principles of intergroup association.

To conclude, let us briefly consider the relationship among the various systematic analyses that may be conducted. As suggested in the foregoing discussion, it is clear that principled reasoning may focus at different levels of analysis. Broadening the context somewhat, it is also clear that these principled analyses may be supplemented by systemic ones that may also be conducted at various levels. The conduct of any one of these analyses, be it principled or systematic and at whatever level, typically requires a bracketing, at least initially. This bracketing has two aspects. On one hand, it entails a choice of analytical orientation. This includes a decision as to what kind of analysis will be conducted, systemic or principled, and at what level of generality or inclusion. On the other hand, this choice is complemented by an elimination of other possible considerations of the matter in question. Thus, in order to consider principles of international relations, systematic reasoning entails the exclusion of considerations of such subnational entities as cultural groups or individual citizens. In addition, it excludes a systemic orientation to the question premised on the notion of an integrated world order. In a similar fashion, systemic considerations of human personality typically bracket out social psychological considerations of principles of social interaction and systemic or principled considerations at the level of groups, states, or the world system.

The logic and consequence of this bracketing is evident in much of the division of the various disciplines of the social sciences and humanities. While this tends to be sustained by the institutionalization of academic departments, the juxtapositional quality of systematic thought nonetheless suggests the need for some higher order or more essential integration. In academia, this is reflected in efforts to bridge the divide between the individual disciplines. In so doing, systematic reasoning leads beyond the limits of its own capacity to understand. Thus while aiming for integration, the resulting efforts typically involve either some form of theoretically oriented reductionism, or a more empirically oriented approach that draws on various levels and types of understanding in a largely atheoretical manner.

Conclusion

Systematic reasoning generates a relatively powerful and integrative conception of political life. The focus is on specific political interactions, but these are always understood in a context, either that of a broader system of interactions or of an overarching principle of relationship. These contexts are regulative and definitive; they determine the dynamic of the relationship among interactions and the meaning of any one interaction. Consequently, the analysis of a political event always requires interpretation. There is an ever-present awareness that the initial perception of the concrete nature of events yields only a tentative and ultimately inadequate view of their social and political nature. To understand the dynamic and meaning of events requires a self-conscious attempt to view those events either as an element of a larger social system or as the particular expression of an underlying general principle.

To continue the metaphor introduced in chapter 3, systematic reasoning, like linear reasoning, yields a conception of social and political life that may be likened to a theatrical play. The systematic construction of this play is, however, much more complex. The play is not simply a matter of the actors and what they do to one another. More fundamental, the play is an organic whole, an expression of the intentions of the author. The author has an understanding that she wishes to elaborate and this defines the basic organization of the play. It determines the identities that will be conferred on the actors and the specific manner in which they will be allowed to interact with one another. Consequently, particular actors and interactions must be understood as symbols whose meaning must be interpreted in light of the underlying themes being conveyed by the play. Implicit in this understanding is a recognition that the actors could have been identified and led to engage one another differently—a different play could have been written. Therefore interpretations of the nature of actors and their interaction must be relative to the particular play in hand.

This understanding of the play is further complicated by the introduction of additional considerations. In its systematic conception, the play may also be understood to have a very modern form, one that provides a medium for the self-expression of the actors as well as the author. As in the efforts of the contemporary British film maker Mike Leigh, the script provided is viewed as a mere starting point, one that may be adapted by the players in directions intended to match their own desires and understandings of what the trajectory of the play should be. This project extends to the audience as well. All present become involved as authors in the writing of the play. As a result, there is a double focus, both on the play being written and the means—the rules and procedures—whereby agreement will be reached as to how to script the action. The specific play produced is understood to be contingent. There is a tendency, however, to understand the process of cooperative writing to be an essentially human activity and its underlying rules to apply quite generally. In the end, the systematic construction of the play is a difficult one. Indeed, it tends to reach beyond the limits of its own capacity to understand.

SYSTEMATIC EVALUATION:
FUNCTION AND PRINCIPLE

Systematic evaluation is a matter of interpretation and judgment. The focus is on specific interactions, behavioral norms, expressed preferences, categorical definitions, and explanatory claims. These represent different types of potential objects of evaluation. Although initially recognized in its own terms, each of these objects is juxtaposed relative to others in a broader frame of reference. The meaning of the object is thus determined. On one hand, this juxtaposition of value objects may involve locating them in the appropriate systemic context, typically that of the personality or subjectivity of an individual actor, or the structure or culture of a society. On the other hand, value objects may be viewed as exemplars of a class of interaction or as expressions of one system interacting with another. Here the value objects are understood relative to a principle of relationship.

Once they are defined, value objects are then judged. This is done with reference to the larger context, be it a system or a principled relationship, in which they are articulated. Critical to any systemically oriented judgment is the integrity of the system in question—its integration, coherence, elaboration, and basic stability. In this light, the value of an interaction, preference, or claim is judged by the role it plays in maintaining the system of which it is a part. When principled concerns are introduced, evaluation extends to include a consideration of the requirements of cooperation and agreement. The value of an interaction or preference is judged relative to the degree to which it conforms to the particular principle invoked.

Proceeding along these lines, systematic evaluation is oriented by a number of characteristic questions. When the frame of reference is that of a system, the following questions are posed:

> Observing an objective interaction: How does this interaction affect the maintenance of the social system in which it occurs? In the case of an individual, how does it affect the maintenance of that individual's personality system?

> Considering a discursive exchange: How does the discourse affect the coherence of the culture? In the case of the individual, how does it affect the coherence of that individual's subjective understanding?

In both instances, value is assessed in functional terms and is essentially practical. At issue here is the systematic construction of the nature of the good.

Evaluation may also be conducted in a principled frame of reference. In this case, value is assessed in light of basic rules of relationship and is implicitly, if not explicitly, idealistic. Here the issue is the construction of the nature of distributive justice or fairness. The orienting questions are thus different:

> Observing an objective interaction: To what extent does the interaction conform to the requirements of some basic or natural law of society or of human nature?

> Considering a discursive exchange: To what extent does the discourse conform to some basic or natural laws of argument? In the case of an individual's subjective construction, to what extent does the relationship among the claims made conform to some basic or natural laws of logic or meaningful relationship?

In answering these questions, systematic evaluation is generally oriented by culturally prevalent assumptions regarding the natural qualities of individuals and society. Despite these foundations, principled considerations may nonetheless lead to a critique of particular conventional practices or norms. The resulting evaluations are somewhat tentative. They are recognized as the result of a subjective process of interpretation and judgment. As such, they may be flawed and therefore must be regarded as provisional. This is true both in the case of the more relativistic evaluations of what is good for a given personal or social system and in the case of the more universalistic claims regarding what constitutes fairness in an interpersonal or international exchange.[20]

Processes of Evaluation:
Systemic and Principled

Let us now consider this evaluative process more closely. It begins with the consideration of an object. This may be an individual's purposive action or a social interaction. Examples of individual's purposive action would include a person's ambitious pursuit of a career, the decision to marry someone less able than oneself, or the act of hitting another to force compliance. Examples of social interaction might include responding to a friend's request for assistance with help or protesting a government's rejection of the results of a free election. Alternatively, the object may be value laden, such as an individual's expression of a desire to smoke or a preference for "workfare" as a substitute for welfare. At a social level, the valued object may be a social convention or ritual of exchange like having tea in the late afternoon, burning a living wife on the husband's funeral pyre, or casting a vote on election day.

Systemic evaluation. Each of the aforementioned actions, preferences, conventions, and norms is understood to have no intrinsic value. To be properly understood and judged, they must be placed in a context. In the case of a person, the object to be judged is juxtaposed relative to other purposive acts, subjective claims, and preference of that person. Insofar as the object contributes to the maintenance of that individual's personality system or the coherence of her subjective understanding of the world, it will be judged favorably. Thus in the case of Sarah, the decision to work sixty-five hours a week is judged relative to other aspects of her personality system. Thus it may be related to her (1) low estimation of herself, (2) doing favors for others, (3) reacting strongly to others' judgments of her, and (4) difficulty controlling her own emotions. In this context, the apparently workaholic behavior may be seen to serve as a compensation for her low self-estimation insofar as the hard work secures the approval of others to which Sarah is so sensitive. At the same time, it creates the disciplined lifestyle conducive to self-control. Overall, the behavior integrates well with Sarah's personality and contributes to the integrity of that psychological system. As such, working long hours would be judged good for Sarah. As suggested by this example, the value of the object is judged relative to a specific person. If the person in question is Mark, who has high self-esteem, is strongly attached to his family, and is critical of capitalist social values, the same work behavior may be judged incompatible with Mark's personality. In his case, the decision to work long hours would be regarded as dysfunctional and bad.

In the case of a community, any particular social interaction, discursive exchange, behavioral convention or cultural preference is judged relative to its place in the social structure and culture of that community. Consider the example of the social convention that women's primary responsibility is in the home. In the case of linear evaluation, such a norm provides the basis for evaluating any specific woman's behavior. But in the case of systematic evaluation, the norm is the object, not the basis, of consideration. For purposes of judgment, this convention must be placed relative to other conventions, patterns of interaction, and cultural definitions in order to determine its practical value for the society at large. Thus it may be related to (1) women providing personalized domestic services, (2) women being available to provide diverse emotional support, (3) men not having to devote energy to their own personal maintenance, (4) men not developing diverse emotional skills, (5) men being defined and judged as workers in the public sphere, and (6) work roles consisting of demanding, relatively unidimensional tasks oriented solely by the criteria of productivity. In the context of this particular community, the relegation of women to the home may be understood to have clear social value. This would be the case insofar as this convention is judged to be consistent with the existing organization of labor in which women provide the necessary practical and psychological support for men who must conform to the narrow strictures of the workplace. In this interpretation, the convention in question is judged to have clear practical value—it is good for the social system in question.

As suggested by the foregoing remarks, systemic considerations tend to produce a culturally relativist orientation to evaluation. First, the value of any cultural norm or social practice cannot be judged in the abstract. Its importance can only be judged relative to the nature and needs of particular communities. Therefore, value must necessarily be relative to the community in question. Second, judgments of value in one cultural context cannot be generalized to another. The function performed by the same practice, definition, or norm in one community may be quite different than the function that it performs in another. Therefore, the values and practices of each community must be assessed in its own terms. Most particularly, one must be careful to avoid the tendency to rely on values that have proven practical and comprehensible in one's own community when judging any other community.

Principled evaluation. Systematic evaluation may also revolve around principles of relationship. These principles rather than a particular personality or social system then provide the context for interpretation and judgment. The issue here is the relationship between personalities or between social systems. To illustrate, let us continue with the example of the evaluation of the convention of women remaining in the home and its position relative to other aspects of the cultural definition of women and the complementary definition of men. Rather than being juxtaposed relative to other elements of a particular social system, the conventions and definitions in question may be viewed as particular instances of the general case of how individuals ought to relate to one another. In a contemporary Western society, such a consideration is likely to be premised on the notion that all individuals are basically equal in their capacity to represent their interests and direct their action. Building on such a foundation, principles of social relationship are likely to be predicated on free and equal participation in the construction of the terms of any specific forms of social cooperation. Moreover, these terms should not preclude the possibility of further free and equal participation. In this context, a social convention that categorizes adults according to gender and relegates social roles to them on this basis may be regarded as a violation of principle. It imposes a limiting definition on individuals thereby unwarrantedly restricting their own attempt at exploring and elaborating their self-system. The convention defines how men and women will interact and thereby prevents them from engaging one another cooperatively for the purpose of creating arrangements that are acceptable to both. In this regard, the convention will be regarded as inherently unfair or unjust.

Based on general claims regarding human relationships, there is a tendency for principles and the evaluations that follow from them to be applied across personal and cultural contexts. Consider the preceding example. There the evaluation is based on the late twentieth-century Western view of individuals as essentially equal in their capacity to know and represent their interests. This leads to a principled understanding of relationships as cooperation predicated on open negotiation and agreement. Defined in the abstract, there is a tendency to apply this principle to the evaluation of non-Western as well as Western communities, both as these communities exist now and as they have existed in the past. Thus such practices as polygamy, the veiling of women, and female circumcision are likely to be viewed as violations without regard for cultural context. Similarly, nondemocratic political rule is likely to be universally condemned for obstructing the just process of the open and free participation of individuals in the determination of the laws that govern their exchange.

Despite this universalizing tendency, principled systematic evaluation is nonetheless culture bound. The premises upon which such an evaluation is based are certainly specific to the cultural context in which the reasoning takes place. Thus the foregoing evaluation builds on culturally and historically relative assumptions regarding the nature of individuals, most specifically the essential equality of men and women. Another cultural context may provide definitions of male-female differences that characterize women as being more diverse in their thinking, more expressive in their emotions, and more likely to form attachments. Men may be assumed to be commensurately more narrow in their thinking, less emotionally expressive, and more solitary. Operating in such a context, systematic reasoning may yield a very different understanding of the demands of personal integrity for men and women in which the placement of men in the workplace and women in the home is regarded as an appropriate or good distribution of roles. This said, the evaluation of the justice of this distribution still depends on the manner in which it is decided. Even where there are basic differences among the parties involved, a systematic understanding tends to demand that these parties be able to represent their different interests by participating in a process of deciding the terms of their cooperation.

This general concern with the process whereby the manner of cooperation is determined does not, however, necessarily lead to a prescription for open and equivalent participation. Such a principle is only constructed in cases where individuals are assumed to be equally capable of entering into the essentially political process of negotiating terms of engagement. If the culture leads to the assumption that certain individuals or categories of individuals have limited capacities to know and present their interests, the principle of participation will vary and the responsibilities for representing those individuals may fall on others. For example, even in liberal societies, it is generally assumed that children and the insane are less able to know their interests and effectively participate in social negotiation. Therefore, in principle, it is just that they become wards of their parents, families, or the state who in turn become responsible for operating on their behalf. This view of the limited capacities of individuals may be extended much more broadly. For example, in classically conservative visions, it is generally assumed that most, it not all, individuals are generally unable to know their interests or effectively realize them through attempts at social engineering. Consequently, there is a principled negative evaluation of full participation of all people in crafting the rules that govern their exchange. This principled evaluation of participation is also reflected in much of the post–World War II democratic theorizing that follows in the tradition of Schumpeter (1942).

Three Levels of Value: The Desirable, the Good, and the Ideal

Proceeding in this manner, systematic evaluation generates three levels of value: (1) what is desirable, (2) what is good or just, and (3) what is ideal. The first two are clearly distinguished in any systematic evaluation. The third, the ideal, is implicit in the second and often not fully recognized on its own terms.

The desirable. The first level of evaluation is a matter of preference. It includes the concerns that orient linear judgment, the preferences one expresses, and the social norms and rituals of behavior. These preferences are understood to reflect the particular satisfactions and dissatisfactions of given individuals and the regularities and prejudices of particular communities. In this light, preferences are viewed as having value, but one that is a property or element of the individual or community in question. As such, they are recognized to be important to those individuals and communities and to be consequential for action. At the same time, they are regarded as very relative and carrying no broader evaluative imperative.

Considered in this manner, preferences and conventions are dealt with very differently than in linear evaluation. In linear evaluation, an established personal preference or a recognized social convention dictates how a relevant act or actor will be judged. Typically, a single evaluative parameter frames the issue at hand. The resulting evaluation tends to be certain and global. It encompasses associated acts and actors and is readily generalized across social contexts. Thus once linear evaluation has recognized a social convention and therefore concluded, for example, that a man allowing a woman to enter a room first is good, behaving in this manner is seen to be completely desirable regardless of the cultural context. Similarly, once the experience of adverse consequences leads to the evaluation that compromising with an aggressor nation is bad, the act in question is viewed as capitulation and as completely undesirable.

In systematic evaluation, preferences and conventions are handled quite differently. A number of experiences, preferences, and social conventions of different value may be considered together. Thus the judgment of a person or community is likely to include some aspects that are seen to be undesirable and others that are desirable. This is not understood to be contradictory or problematic. For example, when considering a country like the United States, one may find its lack of community and commercialism undesirable and, at the same time, comfortably regard its openness to innovation and standard of living as desirable. When considering a person, one may similarly find her wonderfully generous on one hand and torturously uninteresting on the other. In linear terms, such systematic considerations of desirability are likely to appear ambivalent or multivalent (rather than univalent) and, as such, will be viewed as confusing or indecisive.

Not only are a number of preferences considered simultaneously, but they are also considered in relation to the context (an individual or a community) in which they emerge. The bases of preference vary with the individual and circumstances in question and therefore the desirability of an act or statement is therefore always regarded as contingent. As a result, someone reasoning in a systematic fashion certainly has preferences and desires that affect her evaluations, but the latter will be premised on the recognition that those preferences, like any other person's preferences, are personal and cannot be assumed to correspond to the wants and desires of anyone else. One consequence of this understanding of preference is that she will be less likely to demand that others share her preferences or to derogate those people who do not. In a complementary fashion, she will be less subject to the influence of either the preferences that others express or the behavioral norms that social convention dictates. In the language of social psychology, systematic evaluation is such that, unlike its linear counterpart, it does not operate according to the principles of cognitive consistency or dissonance.

The good and the just. The second level of evaluation is basic to the systematic construction of value. Here the goodness or justice of interactions, discourses, expressed preferences, cultural conventions, and behavioral norms are determined quite apart from the preferences an individual expresses or the prevalent norms of social interaction. In the case of the good, the key is the practical or functional value of the issue in question for the person or the community as a whole. This may be clearly at odds with personally experienced satisfactions, expressed preferences, or stipulated cultural norms. For example, Talma may clearly enjoy the stability and company that marriage to Isaac offers and express a desire to remain married. Reasoning systematically, however, she may also recognize that the marriage imposes patterns of interaction which erode the integrity of her self. Despite the particular satisfactions it confers, she may judge the marriage to be bad for her as a person.

Consider also an example at the level of a community. There may be a cultural norm in the United States that an individual should receive what the free marketplace is willing to pay for her services or goods. A systemic evaluation of this convention would largely ignore the degree to which this norm was broadly accepted. Rather the key concern would be the effect of this norm on the maintenance of the social integration or cultural coherence of American society. One concern may be that the income differences not become too great in a society that advocates basic equality. In this light, it may be suggested that wages of the already relatively low-paid unskilled segments of the labor force are likely to decrease because they must increasingly compete with still lower-paid workers in other countries. In this context, the free market norm of income distribution, if followed, may lead to sufficiently great income disparities such that coherence and internal harmony of American society is undermined. As such, the prevalent norm may be judged destructive and bad.

It is important to note that these systemically oriented evaluations are relative, but not in the full sense that preferences are. In the systematic understanding, preferences can only be decided by the individual affected. She is the clear arbiter of what feels satisfying or frustrating to her. Notions of what is good for an individual or a community are also relative. What is good for one person or community may not be for the next. However, judgment of the good, unlike determination of preference, is not an inherently private matter. Anyone can enter into the consideration of the broader systemic consequences of a given activity or discourse for an individual or society in question. The only advantage that individual or a member of that society has is that of potentially (but not certainly) greater access to information. But with information in hand, outsiders can, in a warranted fashion, enter into the task of interpretation and judgment. Indeed, there is the recognition that an informed outsider's analysis is less likely to be clouded by the strength of lower level preferences that may pertain to the activity being evaluated.

Beyond systemic considerations, this second level evaluation also includes matters of principle. In social and political matters, the key concern is the relationship between systems. This may be a matter of the relationship between persons or of the relationship between social systems. The concern here remains the integrity of individual systems, but this is now understood to be dependent on the quality of the relationship between them. The relationship itself thus comes to have value. The related systems are then evaluated by the degree to which they conform to or violate the basic parameters of that principled definition of their relationship. The net result is an extra-systemic basis for evaluating the activity of systems. For example, the systemic considerations of individuals may lead to a clear recognition of the very general value of each individual maintaining the integrity of her self. At the same time, it may also be recognized that individuals in society necessarily engage one another in the course of maintaining their own individual personalities and understandings. As such, each individual penetrates the attempts at internal coordination of every other. They are interdependent. On this basis, some form of cooperation is likely to be valued. It then provides a basis for judging the interaction between individuals. By implication, this also provides a basis for judging the initiatives and responses of an individual apart from its effect on her own integrity. In this manner, notions of justice emerge in relation to, but independently of, notions of the good.[21]

The foregoing example of a principle of relationship that focuses on individuals is of course reflective of classically Anglo-American liberal constructions of social relationships. Once the preserve of theory, it has been increasingly reflected in social representations of everyday life. A very good example of this is the evolving cultural definition of intimacy. This is nicely discussed in Anthony Giddens' *The Transformation of Intimacy* (1992). Of greatest interest given our purposes here is the transformation, still ongoing, from a definition of intimate relationships in which modes of engagement were conventionally prescribed to a definition in which the manner of engagement is open for negotiation. The more traditional form often involved culturally specified roles of man and woman and commonly valued rituals for manifesting intimacy such as a man bringing flowers, a woman cooking special dinners, and the two engaging in an exclusive sexual relationship. This traditional form of relationship is being replaced by one in which individuals are required to recognize each other as very distinctive loci of meaning and desire. In this light, intimacy depends on conversation oriented toward mutual discovery and enabling an open and cooperative determination of ways of being together. In our terms, the traditional form of relationship is linear and the emerging form is systematic.

The relationship between systems may also be a matter of collectivities. This is often constructed in much the same manner as the relationship among individuals. In a multicultural society like Canada or India, or in a multinational entity like the European Community, each cultural or national community is viewed as its own source of organization and meaning. As such, the integrity of each community becomes a prime, or irreducible, evaluative concern. In the broader political context, however, it is recognized that the communities must regularly engage one another practically and culturally. Therefore, it is apparent that the integrity of each community is linked to the integrity of the others. Thus the evaluative focus shifts to a consideration of the relationship upon which these interacting social systems depend. Again this leads to the related notions of open participation, free agreement, and cooperation. In the present case, however, the entities that must be allowed to represent their interests and understandings through participation are communities rather than individuals.

Given the manner of their construction, notions of justice tend to be defined in more universal rather than context-specific terms. By implication, this tendency to universalize principles extends to the conception of an individual's (or group's) responsibilities and rights as participants in a relationship as well as to the nature of the relationship itself. To illustrate, consider a principle of relationship that stipulates the value of voluntary cooperation of individuals based on open and freely achieved agreement. Concomitant with such a principle of relationship is a set of implied rights and responsibilities of participants in such a relationship. Among their responsibilities, it may be deduced that individuals are required (1) to represent their interests and understandings in a manner that maintains their integrity as persons, (2) to respect the freedom of others to voice their demands, to disagree and to disengage, and (3) to cooperate along the terms agreed. Among their rights, it may be inferred that individuals should be allowed (1) to freely express themselves, (2) to disagree, and (3) to choose not to participate. These various points set up criteria for individual behavior which, like the evaluative principle itself, tend to be defined universally.

The ideal. Underlying these second level evaluations is a third, if not completely separate, level of evaluation. This consists of ideals. Rather than being explicit and self-consciously asserted, these ideals are largely implicit in the second order evaluations of the good and the just. This third order of value is to be found in the very logic of systematic evaluation. In the case of systemic judgments of the good, there is an implicit presumption of coherence and integration, or at the very least the tendency toward these states, which underlies both the interpretation of meaning and the judgment of value. In the case of principled judgments of the just, there is an implicit presumption of the abstract lawfulness of the world and, in the case of the relationship between systems, this revolves around notions of cooperation and agreement.

Inherent in the very quality of systematic evaluation, these implicit ideals of coherence and lawfulness are constructed somewhat independently of culture and context. As already noted, the manner in which they are elaborated depends on the dominant ideology or cultural assumptions of a given community at a particular historical juncture. The manner in which these cultural assumptions are subjectively represented, however, remains an artifact of the logic of systematic construction. Regardless of the cultural context, systematic reasoning orients to the discovery and construction of coherent systems of interaction and the meaning or lawful principles of relationship. Even in its most skeptical manifestations, it is bound to this form of understanding. The furthest systematic thinking can deviate is to suggest a negation in which the social world is characterized by incoherence, disintegration, lawlessness, and conflict. This suggests that any second order concerns with justice or goodness are meaningless. The result is a form of incomprehension and amorality that generally cannot be sustained. Thus this skepticism is often adhered to in a playful or admittedly inconsequential fashion, but it is not applied to the practical exigencies of personal life or public policy.

Systematic evaluation has considerable capacity for social critique. The quasi-independence of conceptions of the ideal extend this even further, opening up the possibility of partial critique of even culturally based determinations of the good and the just. In second order judgments of the goodness or justice of particular conventions or preferences, systematic evaluation is limited because it necessarily begins with the presentation of a socially structured array of behaviors and a cultural definition of how they interrelate. The interpretative and integrative activity of systematic thought, however, provides the means to go beyond the information thus presented. Drawing on existing cultural definitions of the systemic and principled quality of social life, systematic evaluation readily leads to a rethinking of the presumed meaning and value of specific aspects of social exchange or cultural prescription. The result is the potential to construct novel and hypothetical juxtapositions that may lead to interpretations and judgments that may differ substantially from the specific assessments dominant in the culture. For example, what is understood to be good for an individual may reflect a cultural emphasis on the need for individuals to be responsible for the integrity of theirselves. This second order conception of the good may then be subjectively applied to a rethinking of cultural norms that stipulate the value of loyalty among friends or family members. In this context, conventions of loyalty may be understood to undermine efforts to maintain the integrity of the self-system and thus be judged to be bad.

The logic of the ideal implicit in these second order evaluations allows systematic critique to penetrate the culture even more deeply. Systematic interpretation and judgment is oriented by the logic of systems and principles. Its subjective reconstruction of the objective nature and cultural definition of social life will therefore tend to explicitly or implicitly assert the existence and value of the systemic and principled quality of social interaction. Where cultural assumptions are inconsistent with these systematic constructions, the tendency will be to reject those assumptions as incorrect, illogical, and immoral.[22] For example, it has already been argued that principled evaluations tend to be subjectively structured such that principles of free cooperation emerge as central. As a result, even where authoritarian political norms are dominant, systematic reasoning is likely to generate a critical assessment of arrangements that preclude participation or otherwise fail to respect the basic integrity of the individuals involved. Culturally prevalent notions of what is good and just may thus be called into question. This criticism will necessarily be grounded in the dominant understandings and values of the society, but it will nonetheless tend to reach beyond them toward the ideals of coherence and cooperation that are inherent in the very structure of systematic reasoning and evaluation.[23]

Value conflict. As suggested by the foregoing discussion, systematic thinking generates a plethora of value-laden concerns that may be considered together at any given moment. Thus value conflict and resolution is central to the activity of evaluation. Value conflict occurs within a level of evaluation. At the level of preferences, conflict is a practical problem of maximizing interests. Systematic thinking allows for different aspects of the same person or community to be liked differently. A value conflict does emerge, however, when one's preferences are at odds in a pragmatic sense, when the attempt to satisfy one preference interferes with the attempt to satisfy another. Preference conflict is thus viewed as a practical issue. It is resolved by initiating some satisfying coordination strategy or by establishing priorities and making choices. Alternatively, a certain ambivalence may be recognized and endured as endemic to the circumstance.

At the level of judgments of what is good or just, value conflicts are handled very differently. Conflicting determinations of what is good or just raise problems of interpretation and judgment. They are adjudicated by considering the appropriateness of the interpretation of the interaction, definition, preference, and so on at issue and the adequacy of the judgment of its consequences for the individual or community being considered or its connection to the relevant principle. These considerations are either a matter of personal reflection or interpersonal argument. For example, it may be that Jeremy's desire to do a first degree at Cambridge is being evaluated. On one hand, it may be judged a good thing because it provides a context for Jeremy to develop his reasoning abilities and to explore who he might become in the relative freedom of college life. On the other hand, it may be judged a bad thing because Jeremy's sense of self and his way of being are deeply rooted in the culture and day-to-day exchange of his working-class, immigrant family. The very different culture that dominates in the university may introduce meanings and practices that are disorienting and destructive. To decide the issue, second order systematic evaluation leads to a further examination of the adequacy with which the choice is being interpreted and its consequences judged. This leads to a further consideration of Jeremy's way of understanding the world and his personality. In this vein, one may suggest that Jeremy has the capacity to understand the context-specificity of particular practices and the strength of character to assimilate those external influences that are consistent with his nature and reject those that are not. On this basis, one may decide that the view that university life poses dangers is based on an incorrect interpretation and that, overall, its effect on Jeremy will be a good one.

The process of conflict resolution may also be illustrated by an example of a conflict of principle. Consider the following scenario. A farmer finds that his chickens are frequently being stolen from his barn. He tries various means of preventing the theft or catching the thief but all fail. In the end, he rigs a rifle to the door such that the rifle will fire at knee level when the door is opened. The ploy works and the thief is shot and disabled during his next attempt. Is the farmer's response justified? Two very different answers may be offered. On one hand, the principle of a right to property may be asserted. In this vein, it may be suggested that cooperation oriented to the maintenance of the integrity of individuals implies that one person must not act so as to intrude on those aspects of the environment that are integrally a part of another person. Those aspects become property of the person. To tamper with them without permission is to violate a basic social principle of cooperation. Therefore, in stealing, the thief was acting unjustly. The farmer, in protecting his property, was justified in doing what was necessary to stop the thief. On the other hand, the principle of right to life may be asserted. In this light, it may be suggested that cooperation is predicated on protecting the physical well-being of those involved. The farmer was therefore acting unjustly by harming the thief to protect his property.

In such a case of conflicting principles, systematic evaluation leads to additional interpretation and judgment. The focus shifts from a judgment of the activity in question relative to particular principles to a consideration of those principles with regard to the more fundamental premises or principles upon which they are based. In the present example, the key underlying premise is that social interaction must be conducted in a way that maintains the integrity of the parties involved. Claims regarding the value of the rights to life and property as principles for judging social exchange are justified with reference to this premise. This fundamental premise also provides a basis for judging the relative importance of these two derivative principles and thus the relative severity of their violations through stealing and shooting. In this vein, it may be argued that a person's health is more central to their being and integrity than any particular things which that person may own. Therefore the principle of the right to life is more important than the right to property and would take precedence over the latter right in any conflict between them. Insofar as this is true, the violation created by the theft could not provide adequate justification for the response of violating the health of the thief.

In sum, systematic evaluation, like systematic reasoning, is a juxtapositional activity. As a result, interpretation and judgment are central to the exercise. Specific events, interactions, claims, preferences, conventions, and rituals are considered with reference either to the relevant individuals and communities or to the relevant principles of social exchange. The systemic considerations of coherence and integration lead to evaluations of the good that are essentially relative. They are crafted with regard to the particular functional requirements of the individual or community in question. The principled considerations of what is just or fair in the exchange between individuals or communities tend to suggest more universal social values. In either case, the evaluations are understood to be a constructed outcome, the product of reflection or argument. As a result, the conclusions drawn may be strongly asserted, but this is tempered by an awareness that further consideration may yield better judgment.

Chapter Five Sequential Thinking

Sequential thinking is embedded in the immediacy of present circumstances and is intertwined with the unfolding of passing events. The most primitive of the three forms of reasoning discussed here, sequential thought emerges prior to linear and systematic thought. It is distinguished by its shifting focus, its dependence on appearances, and its relative lack of clear causal or categorical considerations. At its core, sequential reasoning is a synthetic tracking of events as they unfold. It produces conceptual relations that have the temporal concrete quality of these episodes both as they are observed to transpire and as they are felt to satisfy or frustrate.

Although the most elementary form of reasoning, sequential reasoning is perhaps the hardest to understand and the most difficult to accept. There are several reasons for this. To begin, sequential reasoning is relatively distant from the everyday experience of the reader. The reader typically engages the materials presented in a systematic manner, or alternatively, with some advanced form of linear reasoning. Consequently, the qualities of sequential reasoning and the understandings it generates are incommensurate with the structure of the reader's own understanding. As a result, it will seem more strange and hence more unlikely than the two other forms of reasoning already presented.

The relative unfamiliarity of sequential thought also reflects bias in the reader's exposure to the thinking of other people. In a manner we often underestimate, social structures delimit who will interact with whom. Apart from cursory and largely ritualized exchanges with people who provide services—the butcher who serves meat in the store, the mechanic who works on your car, the conductor who takes your ticket on the train, or the waiter who serves you in the restaurant—the people with whom we interact tend to have education, experience, and opportunity comparable to our own. While not simply determining, these factors can affect the development of reasoning. Consequently, it is probably the case that the people with whom the reader speaks openly or at length reason, like the reader, in a systematic or well-trained linear manner. Comparable exposure to people who reason in a sequential manner is commensurately rare.

Unfortunately research in political science and psychology does not alleviate matters much. In the case of political science, it is rare for research to explore how people reason in any depth. The depth of inquiry into individuals' opinions and behavior is sacrificed in order to achieve a more valued breadth of inquiry. Oriented to national sampling and comparative research, studies of political behavior are largely limited to survey research.[1] Although quite valuable for certain purposes, such an approach is not particularly helpful in exploring people's thinking. As I have argued elsewhere, surveys explore the results of thinking, the particular attitudes or beliefs people express. Thinking itself and thus the meaning the individual gives to the attitudes expressed are not examined. Instead, this basic meaning and the related qualities of the logic of the connections people forge are taken as given and provide the epistemological foundation for the interpretations made regarding the survey results. Proceeding on this basis, the political attitude research has discovered that most people's attitudes do not seem to be reliable (when one might assume they should) and do not seem to cohere (as one might assume they logically should). Indeed, a substantial number of people seem to barely have any political beliefs or attitudes at all. Given the assumptions guiding the research and its consequent limits, there is little conceptual space to give an account of the quality of the reasoning that could produce such a result. Instead motivational and circumstantial factors are typically invoked and the otherwise anomalous results are explained as the result of a relative lack of interest or relevant exposure. The net result is that a familiarity with the political attitude research does relatively little to reveal the nature of reasoning that differs from our own, particularly reasoning as different as sequential thinking.[2]

Psychologists of course are less concerned with large-scale cultural or historical phenomena and happily sacrifice the political scientist's breadth of inquiry for greater depth and care in probing individual cognition. But here too a methodological problem limits the research. My own empirical research and my speculations regarding the circumstances that facilitate and inhibit cognitive development suggest that sequential reasoning is most likely to be found among those people who have relatively limited exposure and opportunity. They are the ones whose work is largely physical and repetitive. They are also the ones who are partly or completely illiterate; in general they have not completed their school education. Although people who share this background do not necessarily reason sequentially, many tend to do so. In any case, these people are certainly not the adults who are the participants in the typical experimental research on cognition. For the most part, the people who are studied are the hapless undergraduates who are the captives of first- and second-year university psychology classes. Even when attempts are made to broaden the research population by advertising for subjects, it is unlikely that such a net will catch many of the people who by conventional measures of power and opportunity are in the bottom 25 to 30 percent of the population of society. As a result, the nature of sequential reasoning remains relatively unexplored in psychological research.

Apart from issues of exposure, there is another matter that makes the claims regarding sequential reasoning difficult to accept. The issue here is ideological—specifically the liberal ideology of the Enlightenment, which permeates Western industrial society. Liberalism carries with it an epistemological and political imperative—that is, that all people reason in the same fundamentally rational fashion. Claims regarding sequential reasoning violate this imperative on two counts. First, it suggests that some people differ quite dramatically in how they reason. Second, it suggests that people who reason sequentially are clearly not thinking in a manner that is consistent with the conventional notion of rationality. Understood in these terms, the claim of the existence of sequential reasoning is a politically threatening and noxious one. In liberal philosophy, the distribution of rights is contingent on the capacity for rational thought (children and the insane have their rights limited on this basis). Claims regarding sequential reasoning therefore imply that some people, probably a very significant number of people, do not reason in a manner that meets the standard for allocating full social and political rights. Guided by a liberal vision, we are thus inclined to disbelieve and to reject on principle the claim that a large number of adults reason sequentially.[3]

I mention these factors to alert the reader to his or her own assumptions and inclinations that are likely to render the asserted qualities of sequential reasoning to be strange or unacceptable. My hope is thus to reduce their prejudicial effect, at least for the duration of this chapter and the following one, which presents the results of the empirical research.

MODE OF REASONING AND THE GENERAL
STRUCTURE OF THOUGHT

Sequential reasoning involves the tracking of events as they transpire. The focus is on the immediate and present events observed and the memories of earlier ones evoked. These events are connected to one another by overlaps in time as they unfold in a sequence, in space as they exist along side one another, and in memory as they share aspects of similar appearance or feeling. In each case, one event flows into and becomes the next. The events are thus fused into sequences that have an order but not true causality, and into identifications that are based on some commonality but are not true categories. Experience is encoded in these terms and subsequent reasoning proceeds accordingly. In the latter regard, sequential reasoning consists of a reenactment, in actual fact or in subjective representation, of learned sequences and identifications. Operating in this manner, sequential reasoning is oriented by the following questions: What does this look like? What do I do now? What happens next? The answers to these questions depend on the direct observation of one's own or another's experience and the memories this evokes.

Sequential reasoning consists of the initial construction and subsequent working through of learned sequences. This mode of reasoning is reflected in the structure of the relationships and objects of sequential thought. Sequential relationships have an essentially active quality. They are mediated by the observation and hence the appearance of present events. The relationship forged has the qualities of the observed flow of events as they are occurring. The connection thus depends on overlap in time, space, or sensation. Such an overlap in any one dimension may be sufficient to yield a subjectively constructed connection, or several dimensions may be involved at the same time. Where the connections among events reflect a contiguity in time, a sequence is constructed by events that are observed to flow from one to the next. For example, if one observes that placing a ladder next to a plum tree, stringing netting, and then vigorously shaking a branch will bring the ripe, sweet plums that have a pleasing taste, a relationship may be established among the series of observed events or activities.

Contiguity can also be a matter primarily of spatial relations. Thus objects or actions that occur in the presence of one another can come to be associated with one another. Again it is a matter of a flow that yields an overlap. Thus as the eye passes over a scene it creates the subjective basis for an unfolding connection among the objects observed to coexist with one another. The result is a collage of what has been observed. Returning to the preceding example of the plum-gathering activity, the texture of the sequence is elaborated by the observation of the events transpiring. Thus the initial experience may be of circumstances in which a particular costume is worn for the activity or a particular incantation is shouted when shaking the branches. Whereas linear or systematic reasoning might entail a consideration as to whether these embellishments are necessary to produce the desired effect of having the sweet plums, this does not occur in sequential thought. Insofar as they are observed to be part of the global events unfolding, they are understood (largely unselfconsciously) to be integral aspects of the events and will be included in any subsequent reenactment.

Synthesis Without Analysis

The connections made through sequential reasoning tend to be largely synthetic ones with relatively little counterbalancing analysis. As a result, the relationships constructed consist of a fusing of the events that are strung together. In the case of a learned sequence of events, there is a tendency for each event to fuse with those that precede and succeed it. Whereas the whole of the sequence may have some loosely defined meaning in terms of its end, there is little consideration of the moments of the sequence as distinctive and separate events, each of which may be defined unto itself. Instead the meaning of each unfolding moment is a function of its place in the sequence, that is, as it emerges out of the preceding event and leads into the next. This quality of sequential relations is evident in the otherwise incomprehensible need which those who are reasoning sequentially have to insure that all the steps of the sequence are reenacted, even if they are not, in any strictly causal sense necessary to the outcome. Indeed, given the understanding constructed, there is no anchoring focus on the outcome. It is only an ill-differentiated element of the global, unfolding sequence of which it is a part. Thus for the young child who is reasoning sequentially, the understanding of the experience of eating an ice cream that tasted so delicious is embedded in and includes the larger sequence of which it is a part. Therefore it is important that the recreation of the experience include going with one's father to the particular shop at which the ice cream was purchased.

The identifications of sequential thought produce a similar fusion of the events related. Identification occurs when a present observation cues a memory of an event. This occurs because of some kind of subjectively sensed overlap between the present event and the remembered one. This may be the result of certain common apparent characteristics. For example, the smell of the air may evoke scenes from one's childhood in which a similar smell was detected, or being in an automobile at night may evoke the memory of a traumatic car accident in which one was involved. As suggested by the examples, the identification does not necessitate any complete commonality or categorical similarity. Just one or a few overlapping features, features that may or may not be central when viewed from the perspective of linear or systematic reasoning, may be sufficient to construct the identifying link. Once constructed, the identification fuses the events connected. In this limited context, the present becomes one with the past and the meanings of each flow freely back and forth. Returning to our examples, the current smells produce the feelings and inclinations of the childhood memory with which they are identified and the night ride in the car evokes the terror of the earlier accident. In this manner the past invades the present. But the reverse also occurs. For example, with repeated experiences of pointedly pleasant trips in the automobile, the negative past associations with driving may be overwhelmed by the positive present ones. The result is not only that driving is now no longer frightening, but also the terror associated with the memory of the accident is diminished.

In this synthetic fusion of sequences and identities, there is little analysis of the particular aspects that are related to one another. They are not abstracted from the relational context in which they are embedded. As a result, the whole of a relation among elements is not easily considered apart from each of the specific elements related. One consequence of this is the confusion of part and whole, which is typical of sequential reasoning. Because of the linguistic environment, sequential reasoning is frequently forced to consider categorically defined relations. In this context, there is a demand to consider wholes (the category) without specific reference to any part (specific exemplars of the category). Unable to construct relations of this kind, there is a tendency to fuse the categorical label with a specific present exemplar to which the label refers or to a memory of an exemplar that is evoked. Thus if asked to consider the qualities of the French while being presented with a specific French man who is wearing a white linen summer suit and is seated eating scallops, there will be a tendency to consider not only his facial features, mannerisms, or language but also the particular clothes he is wearing and his preference for scallops.

Lacking a clear distinction of part and whole, sequential reasoning does not generate even the anchored categorical relations of linear thought. This said there is a type of "proto-categorical" construction that does go on. This is evident in the identifications described earlier. They are constructed on the basis of an overlap between a feature of a present event and a remembered one. This construction also occurs in the grouping of present events. This is nicely illustrated by an early experiment of L. S. Vygotsky (1962). Vygotsky asked his subjects, children, to divide an array of objects into different groups. The objects varied in size, shape, and color. At one developmental stage that Vygotsky describes, the subjects create groups on the basis of what I would refer to as a chain or flow of identifications. Thus in creating a group, the subject might begin with a large red square and then add a large blue circle. Following this she might include a small blue circle and then a large blue triangle. This nicely illustrates the process of identification as a flow of connection based on overlap that proceeds from step to step with little attention to any overarching whole that might be or ought to have been constructed.

Moving away from Vygotsky's children to the adult sphere, we find a similar example of protocategorization suggested by Freud's discussion of the unconscious in his *The Interpretation of Dreams* (1913). For Freud, dreams provided examples of the prelinguistic or sublinguistic operations of unconscious adult mental life. Among various instances of this unconscious functioning are such relational activities as projection and condensation. Viewed in the present context, these activities are readily understood as examples of sequential reasoning. In each case, associations are made which are strange because they ascribe a common identity to entities that are not properly members of the same categories. In the case of condensation, one object is identified with another when only a few nonessential attributes among many are shared in common. In the case of projection, this occurs where one of the objects is oneself. In both cases, the boundaries between the entities thus identified are rather fluid and the meanings associated with each tend to flow back and forth between them.

In this context, I would argue that the unconscious and relative incomprehensibility of these dreamlike associations could be readily explained with regard to the structural pragmatic theory I am developing. Reconstructed in these terms, dreams are largely sequential constructions. Most of our conscious reflections on dreams, however, are typically linear or systematic. The problem here is that dreams are being represented in a way that is inconsistent with their initial construction. In form and therefore in substance, dreams are essentially nonlinear and unsystematic and therefore cannot be readily understood in either of these ways. Deviating from traditional Freudian interpretation, I would therefore conclude that the meaning of dreams is rendered unconscious, not because of active repression (although this may be operative as well), but rather because of their structural incompatibility with either linear or systematic consciousness.

Another illustration of the protocategorical quality of the relations of sequential thought is offered by the qualities of the tools used with more or less success in relatively primitive tribes. Typically the tool is used as part of a sequence that is presumed to result in a desired outcome. Some of the efficacy of the tool is to be found in its partial resemblance to the anticipated outcome of the sequence. For example, in British Columbia, there is the traditional implement used by the Kwakiutl Indians to call orcas. The implement is a hollow piece of wood with a handle. The hollow portion is filled with nuts or small stones and sealed thereby creating a noisemaker. To call the orcas, one shakes the noisemaker over the surface of the ocean. What distinguishes this particular implement is that it is carved in the shape of the killer whale. Part of its magical efficacy is derived from this. In sequential thought, where distinctions are loose and the boundary between representation and reality is readily crossed, the visual similarity of the noisemaker to an actual orca calls forth both the subjective sense and the reality of the outcome desired.

The inability to separate part and whole is also reflected in the lack of any true causal considerations. Even in its linear form, causal relationships depend on the abstraction of cause and effect from the flow of events and a consideration of one in terms of the other. The result is a connection that stands apart from either the cause or the effect but regulates the link between them. Because of the independence of the linkage, linear reasoning facilitates a consideration of the cause or the effect of a present event when neither has been observed. Sequential relations are active, flowing ones. There is a sense of the order of events, but they are not analyzed into causes and effects nor is there a sense of the independent and regulative quality of the link that binds them together. Therefore there is little tendency to speculate about antecedent events that have not been observed or consequent ones that extend beyond the last event in a sequence already established. Thus sequential reasoning does not produce a concern for why things happen. Rather there is just an awareness that they do and the question is how.

Temporality, Immediacy, and Mutability

A rather direct reconstruction of the subjective perception of the flow of events, sequential relations have an essentially temporal quality. Unlike linear relations, sequential relations are worked through in real time. They unfold. Like the passing present that structures them, sequential relations consist of the representation of one event actively passing to the next. In this regard, the whole of the sequence is not held in the mind at once. Rather it is cued by the introduction or memory of a constituent event and then the rest of the sequence is reenacted, primarily through actually watching or participating in the events or secondarily through storytelling. While retaining a sense of where the sequence is leading, the sequential reasoner is largely caught in the present step, and the arrival of the next is a mix of quiet surprise as well as anticipation. This can be seen in the otherwise mysterious pleasure that is taken in the repetition of familiar activities or the retelling of familiar stories.

The tendency to be caught in the present moment of the sequence as well as having a sense of its trajectory contributes to the relative mutability of sequential relations. The sequence is teleological, but only in a loose sense. The orientation to the present opens the door to circumstances that may shift the view of what is currently occurring and thus facilitate the introduction of alternative trajectories of events. This is readily exemplified by the manner in which younger children are readily distracted from a course of action by the introduction of novel stimuli, such as a different toy or person. In this manner, sequential reasoning is readily redirected and the relations it constructs are therefore relatively mutable. Even when a sequence is valued and well ingrained and there is therefore some resistance to redirection, the blocking of the anticipated course of events will not yield a sense of violation. Such a sense depends on the clear separation of the regularity of what is anticipated as a rule that stands apart from the specific events to which it is applied. In such an instance, the rule is readily juxtaposed to the overall sequence of what is occurring and the latter can be denied as false or wrong. The relations of sequential thought are embedded in—rather than abstracted from—the passing of current events. Thus unanticipated changes are more a matter of surprise and perhaps frustration than a sense of violation.

The immediacy of sequential relations is also evident in their lack of generality. These relations are a function of learning how events transpire under loosely apprehended but particular conditions. Therefore the subsequent use of these established relationships constitutes a reenactment of the sequence under conditions similar to those in which it was originally learned. Some generalization does occur through a process of identification. Identifications effectively equate different event-states such that sequences can be initiated under varying circumstances. These identifications depend on the observation of apparent, partial similarities between one circumstance and another. Thus generalization is limited, irregular, and visually mediated. Sequential relations lack the abstraction and categorical qualities that facilitate the construction of general understandings, which can then be broadly and intentionally applied across particular settings or situations. The construction of relationships is therefore dependent on specific learning, on the experience of new associations that either extend or modify old ones. In this regard, the structure of sequential learning is a piecemeal phenomenon, very much like the learning described by the psychological research on classical conditioning (e.g., Pavlov, 1927), operant conditioning (e.g., Skinner, 1953) and imitative learning (Bandura and Walters, 1963; Bandura, 1973).[4]

Conceptual Units

The units of sequential reasoning are the event-states that follow one another in the course of what is observed to transpire from moment to moment. These events are apprehended through the senses of sight, smell, and touch. As such, they are constructed as concrete and immediate entities. In the context of sequential reasoning, events are constructed in two ways. First, they are objectively presented. The event occurs before the individual and becomes the object of her regard. Alternatively, events may be subjectively represented. This occurs when the event is stored in memory as part of a sequence or as an identification and is cued accordingly. The represented event then begins to fill the individual's view of what is occurring. Consequently, while sequential reasoning is powerfully rooted in the immediate environment, the line between existing and represented events is easily crossed such that representations achieve some of the force of reality. This is reflected in the "reality" that imaginary events and episodes in stories can have for individuals who are reasoning in a sequential manner.

As objects of sequential considerations, individual events are fluid entities. This is true in two senses. On one hand, they are conceived as transient phenomena; they are thought of only as they flow into the next event in the sequence or the other event with which they are identified. In this regard, events are meaningful in terms of where they lead. Of note, this focus on the passing presence of events leads to relatively little consideration of the past of events, that is, where they originated. This is evident frequently in the retelling of something that has been observed or reported to occur. Where the story begins is rather random; it simply needs to get started so that subsequent events can be reported. Another result of this preoccupation with where things are going rather than where they originated is that the common concern with "why" in modern society is rendered irrelevant or relatively insignificant in the context of sequential reasoning. On the other hand, events are fluid even when the focus is on a relatively static present. Sequential consideration of the event follows the path of the individual's roving eyes and the occasions of the fleeting intro-duction of sounds and smell. The result is a loose collage, a string of associated sensations that circle back on one another within the confines of the unchang-ing scene being experienced.

These fluid or transient qualities of events are reflected in the fact that several events or the several apparent elements of a single event are not readily held in the mind at the same time. This has a number of important consequences for sequential thought. Meaningful only as moments in a sequence, events (or any object of thought) are not considered out of this context and thus in their own terms. This limitation is evident when someone reasoning in a sequential fash-ion is asked to describe a particular object or event apart from any particular se-quence in which that object is embedded. A natural consideration within other modes of reasoning, the concern is ill fitting and regarded as odd from a se-quential perspective. As a result, the tendency is to ignore such a question or to answer in a perfunctory fashion with a reference to a single aspect of the object of concern. For example, in sequential thought, there would be little consider-ation of John the next door neighbor as an abstracted object of concern. John is the person who is in the house over there who can be seen tending his garden when I go walking, who stands up with a groan and says, "Fine afternoon today. How are you?" and I say, "Good. How are you?" and he says nothing bending back down and I continue on. Alternatively, John is the man who can be heard shouting at his wife at night followed by a slamming of the door and the roar of a car engine. Here we have two Johns, ostensibly the same person, but an event or an element of an event that is significant in two wholly dissociated contexts. John is not conceived as "the person John"—an anchoring concern or categor-ical entity whose various aspects are collected and considered in relationship to him. Therefore a consideration of John out of the context of the sequences in which he is articulated is neither natural nor particularly meaningful. At best, it will elicit a response that offers a description of two or three such random characteristics as "He has black hair and he shouts." There is no concern for completeness or adequacy of description.

As noted earlier, events can be identified with one another. This is a matter of overlapping apparent aspects and of one event being fused with the other with which it is identified. This is a reflection of the fact that several events are not represented at once. Similarly, sequential reasoning does not facilitate a full comparison of events by a consideration of the several aspects of the one event relative to the several aspects of another event. More limited forms of comparison, however, do occur and these are facilitated by the extent to which the events considered are apparently similar to one another. Thus quantitative judgments of more and less or big and small are also readily made when the objects of focus are otherwise the same. Qualitative comparisons, judgments of similarity and difference can also be made. Given the nature of sequential reasoning, these judgments are unreliable. Depending on circumstances (subjective as well as objective) different aspects of an event may be accentuated. As a result, its comparability to other events will vary. These comparisons are not only unreliable, but they are unstable. There is a tendency for two objects that are seen to be similar to be collapsed onto one another. This reflects the sequential tendency to synthesis without analysis and, in this case, the consequent fusion of one event with another with which it is identified. An example of this in my own personal experience comes to mind. A few years ago, I went on a lecture tour in Europe. Because I had small children, I typically did not leave home for more than several days at a time. On this occasion, however, I would be gone for two weeks. My son Phillip, then eight years old, was not at all happy about the impending absence for what must have seemed to be an eternity for him. In fact, it seemed to me that in part he was afraid I might not come back at all. At the time, I had a favorite pen that I used for note taking and personal correspondence. Wherever I was, the pen was not far away. Before leaving, I gave Phillip the pen. It had a surprisingly calming effect. While I was gone, he kept the pen in the back of his desk drawer and would bring it out to soothe himself when he missed me. The pen was an aspect of me. Having it, he had a piece and hence all of me.

Summary. In sum, sequential reasoning involves the tracking, representation, and reenactment of sequences of events and the matching of current events to remembered ones. Operating in this manner, it is intimately engaged in the ups and downs, twists and turns of what is happening here and now. To this it adds the memories of other "heres" and "nows" that are evoked and thus rendered present also. In the resulting melange, the line between the present reality and a represented or imaginary one is readily confused. The products of this mode of reasoning, sequential relationships are active, a matter of the actual working through of sequences either through de facto or represented reenactment. The result is a synthetic fusion of the events related with little analysis of them as individual entities existing apart from the sequences and identifications in which they are embedded. Consequently, there is little causal analytic or categorical thinking. Events, the objects of sequential thought, are fluid, transient entities that are meaningful only in terms of the subsequent events to which they lead.

SOCIAL REASONING

The social world constructed through sequential reasoning is an active one. It is a world of happenings, a world filled by doings, comings and goings. All of this activity is occurring on the stage of an unfolding present. The players may include people, animals, and even the natural surroundings. Whether they are active or inert, actors or acted upon, these various entities are understood as they are implicated in transpiring events. When viewed from the perspective of other forms of thought, sequential reasoning appears naturalistic and sometimes anthropomorphic. This is something of a misstatement. It is not that nonhuman entities are ascribed human characteristics, but rather that all entities, human and otherwise, are conceived in the same way—that is, relevant to their specific place in particular sequences of events. The sequential social world is also a fluid one. There are regularities and a comfort in that repetition, but there is no law or necessity. In this sense, there is also no violation or falsehood. Rather there are simply anticipations and the associated realization or frustration of expectations. Throughout, the boundaries between the subjective, intersubjective, and objective dimensions of events are ill understood and readily transgressed. As a result, the social universe constructed by sequential reasoning is a magical one in which memories are present realities, and not only sticks and stones, but words can break bones.

Temporal and Spatial Parameters

The time of sequential social reasoning has limited duration. Social life revolves around what is happening now and the imminent future to which it leads. As noted before, this is reflected in the enthusiasm and tension with which scenarios can be reenacted or stories retold. It is all still exciting because thought is focused on the present as it unfolds even when the overall scenario is well known. A familiar example of this is the seemingly endless pleasure younger children evidently experience in the regular retelling of stories they know so well they could easily recount the stories themselves. In an adult context, this is nicely illustrated, if somewhat speculatively, by the early pagan customs of Germanic and Scandinavian Europe. Although there was the recurring cycle of the seasons, the people apparently remained uncertain as to whether the cycle would in fact recur as it had in the past. Thus when the harder seasons passed, the arrival of mild ones were the occasion of considerable celebration. Also in the midst of the harsh winter with its ever longer nights, the people needed some visible reminder that there was something beyond what they were now experiencing. To this end, a custom emerged of taking apples, the surviving evidence of a time beyond winter, and hanging them on trees around the time of the winter solstice. The probable efficacy of such a custom can best be understood with reference to sequential reasoning. In this light, the custom can be seen as a response to the fears that emerged in the limited time frame of a darkening present. The response was effective because it evoked the memory and thus "re-presented" or introduced a reality that was not winter.[5]

A matter of a passing present and the memory of related presents now part of an ill-differentiated past, sequential social time has the structure of recurring episodes. It is not a subjectively constructed abstraction that imposes a linear trajectory on events from an ever-receding past through the momentary flash of a present into a infinitely extended future. Rather, sequential time is a matter of the sequences that are currently being enacted and their connection to earlier sequences that unfolded in the same way. In this sense, time is framed in repetition, a matter of reoccurrence in which the present invokes and repeats a past. In the process, the past is both recalled and collapses onto the present reenactment. In contrast to the construction of linear thought, the past of sequential thought is thus not held apart nor is it enunciated as a proper history that leads to, but is not, the present. The extent to which this basic structure of repetition through reenactment gets elaborated very much depends on the extrasubjective structuring events. The culture of a group may serve to resurrect the past and sustain its presence through the various rituals of daily life. Alternatively, objective realities themselves structure events within the recurring cycles of day and night, the changing phases of the moon, and the seasons of the year. A part of events themselves, these externally constituted cycles both extend and anchor the succession of actual and remembered presents of sequential thought.

While cultural rituals and natural cycles provide a common or an intersubjective ground for the temporal constructions of sequential thought, the sense of time remains essentially substantive and personal. The time of sequential thought is not an empty time marked by some abstract measure. Instead it is constituted by substantive events and passes with them. These events are the moments of the experience tracked by the individual who is reasoning sequentially. Consequently, time is constructed out of the experience that is present to the individual observer. It consists of what is occurring to her. Depending on the circumstances and the conditions of her receptivity, time has different tempos; it passes at different speeds. As well as its cadence, time's structure is also a personal matter. It reflects the individual's past experience that the present evokes and thus the substance of her personal rhythms and habits. One manifestation of this notion of time is the relative irrelevance of abstracted time, clock time, to sequential reasoning. The lack of attention to clock time in rural areas of some third world countries may be explained in these terms. The irrelevance of clock time as a marker of appointments was apparent in my own early research experience. A preliminary indicator of the quality of reasoning of a prospective interviewee was the reliability with which appointments were kept at my office. Typically, those subjects who later proved to reason sequentially failed to keep appointed times at all. Often three or four meetings with a number of accompanying reminders would have to be scheduled to succeed in having a single interview. Of additional interest was that when an interview was finally held, there was a total lack of recognition that any violation had been committed. Given the concept of time and the relative lack of necessity inherent in the concept of social action, this is not at all surprising.

Like its time, the space in which social life takes place has a structure that reflects the qualities of sequential reasoning. It is limited to what is immediately apparent and to the various locales to which current sequences may lead. In this sense, the natural social space that frames sequential considerations is the local neighborhood—its personally traversed streets and country paths. This natural space also includes the inhabitants who pass through those routes and paths and the sights, sounds, and smells of foliage, buildings, and activity encountered along the way. Not that this need be constrained to a single locale. The circumstances of life may lead an individual to regularly inhabit two or more locales depending on the demands of work or the seasons. The focus, however, will be on the present locale and the memories of other places the current one evokes. The structure of any one of these spaces is simple and fragmentary. Sequential reasoning, with its relations of unfolding events, constructs routes through the space. Oriented in these terms, the individual moves through the local space by again moving from one place to the next thereby reenacting trips that have been encoded in memory in this manner. Like so much of sequential reasoning, traveling such a route is very much embedded in the present location and the next one to which the present path leads. A sense of final destination is retained, but the considerations are focused on where one is now.

Cast in this manner, the social space constructed through sequential reasoning is a focused, moving one. Rather than a space separated from time, the two are joined in the trajectory of what is occurring now. Thus, sequential space is not an atemporal two-dimensional construction in which all the various routes can be placed and then related to one another. Consequently, sequential reasoning is not cast in terms of maps—these are not spontaneously created nor readily utilized when provided. Lacking such an abstracted frame of reference, sequential social space is also not stable. It is a matter of ongoing evocation. The stimulus may be objective—a function of what is actually present in the environment—or it may be subjective—a result of some mood, feeling, or internally generated sensation (e.g., hunger). Thus, sequential reasoning may be engaged in working through the spatio-temporal trajectory of one sequence, perhaps following a particular path to accomplish a specific task. Then hunger may strike evoking a new place and the path to be followed to get there. In the process, a new trajectory with its sequence of places is adopted and the prior one largely evaporates.

Social Action

Social action, what is being done or said, is embedded in the global, diffuse totality of events unfolding. As noted earlier, sequential reasoning involves little causal analysis. Consideration of a current event does not entail any search for antecedent causes. Instead, the focus is on what will happen next. As a result, action is understood in terms that give it an almost magical quality. Events, particularly those not intended as a successive step in a sequence, just appear on the scene. They are not explained. To the degree to which they are understood it is in the terms of the sequence that they evoke and hence where they will lead. The social world of the sequential thinker is thus a world of consequences rather than causes.

Operating in this manner, sequential reasoning accords little attention to what or who is responsible for what is occurring. Consequently issues of blame or credit are not particularly meaningful unto themselves. Confronted with others using this vocabulary, terms relating to responsibility may be used. But their meaning is transformed as it is incorporated into sequential terms of understanding. Thus, the positive or negative values associated with credit and blame are learned, but their causal meaning is not properly assimilated. These terms may be invoked, but more often they reflect the pain or pleasure attached to salient moments in a sequence rather than any attempt to locate causal responsibility.

Instead of the social world of causes and responsibilities, sequential reasoning leads to the construction of a world with recurring sequences of action—of familiar patterns and rituals. Situations and sensed needs evoke representations of sequences that are then enacted. Reasoning in this manner, the individual moves to the places where the sequence leads and attempts to include the people, animals, and inert objects that are salient aspects of the successive event-states called forth. The focus is on the current activity that is understood in the context of the sequence in which it is embedded. Specific action is not abstracted from the context, generalized to novel circumstances, and then applied to them.

An example of embeddedness of social action in a sequence of global events is offered by the case of the social activist and the workers residing in a poor Appalachian mining town mentioned in chapter 1. As the reader will remember, the activist resided in the town for a period of six months to a year. During this time, he demonstrated to the local residents what they needed to do in order to obtain local government cooperation in rectifying certain situations, such as installing a traffic light at an otherwise dangerous intersection. As part of the instruction, several of the residents were involved in a given project and, with the guidance of the activist, they worked their way through the whole process from problem identification through solicitation of government action to witnessing the generally positive results. Toward the end of the activist's stay, the local residents were able to follow through an initiative with only minimal input from the activist. The activist left feeling that he had altered the social and political life of many in the town. The unexpected outcome was that very little of the behavior learned during the activist's stay was sustained after his departure. This largely incomprehensible result may be readily understood in the present context. It may have well been that most of the residents involved reasoned sequentially. If this were the case, their understanding of what transpired during the activist's stay consisted of various largely independent sequences in which the activist himself was a salient aspect of many of the constituent events. When he left, the texture of events were changed—he was no longer a part of them. As a result, the learned sequences involving the activist were less likely to be cued and, if cued in other ways, they became much more difficult to follow through.

In sequential reasoning, a single sequence frames the consideration of a given event. Consequently, several courses of action are not considered simultaneously. An event may be a complex collage of elements. Insofar as the individual's focus varies, different sequences may be evoked and the individual may waver between alternatives. But the operation of holding both in mind and considering them in their entirety relative to one another is not readily achieved. As a result, it is often difficult for someone who is reasoning sequentially to choose between two alternative courses of action. This is particularly the case if neither scenario follows naturally from the current flow of events. Readers who are parents of younger children will readily recognize this phenomenon. Given the choice among pleasant but substantively different alternatives, such as going to the zoo or spending the day at the park, a child reasoning in a sequential fashion is often simply unable to decide. If a decision is forthcoming, it is usually a matter of some aspect of one alternative becoming salient and with it the subjective representation of an entire scenario. One consequence of this reasoning in terms of single sequences is that there is not a true conflict of action in sequential reasoning. When another's action trajectory is incompatible with one's own, the matter is considered relative to the sequence in which one is currently engaged. The other person, what she is doing, and what she introduces is understood simply as an obstruction, an obstacle blocking one's own path.

Oriented by the current sequence of unfolding events, the consideration of action is restricted to context-specific identification. Sequential thinking is thus limited in two important respects. Lacking abstraction, there is little categorization of action. Rather actions are understood by virtue of their place in the passing events and representations. As a result, sequential reasoning does not naturally give rise to the notion of "role" as a set of related behaviors performed by individuals of a particular status. Whereas such a concept is quite central to linear thinking, it is largely irrelevant or inadequately understood from a sequential perspective. In the latter regard, a verbally identified role is fused with the example of the particular role-holder and what she does in a specific situation. Thus the role of king is confused with the person who is king and what he does.

The failure to abstract action from the sequences in which it is performed also underlies the limits of a sequential understanding of social regulations. The inability to abstract a concept of a sequence and represent it apart from its concrete instantiation inhibits a consideration of a rule independently of its enactment. Thus the necessity associated with a rule and its application gives way to the relative uncertainties of the manner in which a given sequence will unfold at any particular time. The latter opens the door to varying focus and novel externalities that may redirect the trajectory that events follow. This becomes evident in the weak meaning which social conventions or role prescriptions have for those who reason in a sequential manner. Guided merely by currently cued anticipation, a person is readily led astray by the otherwise peripheral distractions of the moment and conventions are consequently violated with relative ease and lack of self-consciousness.

The Concept of Persons:
Embedded and Fragmentary

As reconstructed within the framework of sequential reasoning, people are understood in terms of a given sequence of events in which they are implicated. As such, a person is her appearance and activity as they are observed in a specific context. She is not constructed as an abstracted identity that is sustained across the specific sequences in which she is signified. In other words, a person is not constituted as a categorical object—that is, one which serves as an conceptual umbrella for the various things she is, appears to be, or does in the various circumstances in which she is involved.

Conceived in these terms, a person is an accoutrement of events rather than a director or cause. Individual people are therefore not a particular focus of sequential reasoning. They occupy a place in the events experienced and may often serve as landmarks for recognizing or recalling the associated sequence of events. However, unto themselves and thus abstracted from context, people are not a matter of concern. This is evident in sequential speech. When recalling events, the focus is on what is generally unfolding. Individuals are mentioned as part of the events, but they are one of the many aspects and little special time or attention is devoted to them. In this regard, no attempt will be made to stop the line of the story to provide a description of particular individuals. To the degree to which any description is offered, it typically revolves around characteristics that are directly relevant to the unfolding of the event currently being discussed. So if the story were focused on the particular moment of a man removing a large boulder blocking the road, some passing comment may be made regarding the man's size and strength. The sequential conception of people is further demonstrated by the response offered to a conversational intervention in which a description of an individual in the story is requested. Typically the question is greeted with a certain impatience. After all, from the perspective of the speaker, the point of the storytelling is to work one's way through the sequence of what transpired. Detours demanding a focus on aspects of an event that are otherwise not particularly salient are understood to be irrelevant and obstructive. If a desired response is forthcoming, it is short and fragmentary. It may include a passing reference or two to an aspect of a person's appearance (he is tall or has graying hair) or to some particular act they have performed (he moved the boulder or he pulls sheet metal at the factory).

Given this understanding of what a person is, it should be clear that sequential reasoning does not lead to the spontaneous construction of social identities. A social identity requires placing a person relative to either a role or a social group. As noted earlier, roles are not readily constructed and thus do not provide a basis for defining individuals. The same is true of social groups. Individuals are considered relative to their present or remembered place in the unfolding of a sequence of events. The social world is thus framed by the "here and now and where it is leading." Individuals are not considered relative to some nonpresent and hence abstractly conceived group of which they are a member. As a result, sequential reasoning does not lead to the kind of social categorization typical of linear reasoning. The world is not divided into groups distinguished by the origin, typical practice, appearance or ownership.

As members of societies in which group distinctions are important, people who think in sequential terms do not readily assimilate the relevant cultural imperatives. They may learn to use the group labels current in the society, but these are assimilated into the terms of sequential understanding. Thus rather than the individual being an exemplar of a categorically defined group which has a particular name, that name becomes an aspect of the person being considered, much like her hair color or her driving a red car. When conversation forces the otherwise unusual focus on the individual and her group membership, there is a tendency to identify the label with the person. The result is a collapsing of the social category onto to the present exemplar and confusing the former for the latter. Given the irrelevance of group distinctions, those who reason sequentially readily ignore the socially relevant divides. In a group-stratified society, people who reason sequentially must be frequently monitored in order to insure their behavior respects these social divisions in the manner required.

A final concern here is the self-concept engendered by sequential thought. Typically there is little sense of one's self. Part of the problem is that like a concept of another, a concept of one's self demands some kind of categorical construction. Sequential reasoning does not foster such a construction. Consequently, the self, like any person, is typically considered only in the context of a currently unfolding sequence of events. For sequential reasoning, however, the problem of self-conceptualization is even more difficult than that of conceptualizing another person. Social reasoning is a matter of observing events as they transpire. As viewed through one's eyes, these events generally consist of external circumstances and other people. One's own self is largely invisible from this perspective. Consequently, one's own person is even less likely to be an object of self-conscious consideration than any other person.

Given this relative lack of self-reflection or a consciousness of a categorical self, it is difficult to distinguish the one's subjective sense of what is occurring from its objective reality. Sequential thinking thus engenders a subject-object confusion. One's own images and feelings become aspects of the event that evokes them. Thus as objective circumstances constitute one's subjective being, those same circumstances are infused with one's imagining and feeling. The result is that one's sense of self and one's sense of external conditions are the same—both are intermingled in a sense of being. Of course this sense of being is not a matter of abstraction and reflection, but rather one that is realized in the familiarity of the regularly recurring sequences of daily life.

In chapter 2, personality was discussed as a layered construction in which each layer consists of the experiences encoded according to the quality of the individual's reasoning during that period of her development. For a person who develops the capacity to reason in linear or systematic fashion, the sequential sense of being constitutes an early layer in the development of the self. Given the unreflective and noncategorical quality of its sequential construction, this layer of the person's personality is largely inaccessible to the language mediated and categorical modes of later reasoning. As such, this sequential layer of the self is largely subconscious. Rather than an object of conscious consideration, it is simply manifest in the current reenactment of the myriad of isolated, concrete sequences learned during an earlier period of one's life.

One example of this sequential construction of personality is provided by the difficulties encountered by people who are reasoning in a linear or systematic fashion when they self-consciously attempt to change their "self." The desired transformation may involve a change in character or a change in the way one engages in relationships with others. The decision to change may be a matter of personal resolution or it may be a response to friendly advice or psychotherapy. In any case, one's current beliefs, intentions, and consequently one's practice are rejected in favor of a different orientation. The problem that often arises is that whereas a new orientation may be adopted, many of the relevant behaviors may continue to be reenacted as before. In the present terms, the suggestion is that this difficulty can be traced to the fact that the attitudes and behaviors addressed self-reflectively or in psychotherapy are conceived in the categorical or interpretative terms of reasoning that develops after sequential thought. Many of the relevant behaviors, however, may be embedded in sequences that were experienced and learned in the concrete and immediate terms of sequential reasoning. To the degree to which this is the case, the behaviors in question were not conceived in a categorical or causal way and thus elude a self-monitoring that is carried out in these terms. Thus honest efforts to follow through on self-conscious decisions to change behavior rooted in earlier experience are quite likely to fail. The suggestion here is that change at this level is most effectively achieved when the relevant sequences are unlearned in the same manner they were learned—that is, one at a time through concrete, immediate experience.[6]

A second complementary example deals with personality change that is not self-induced but is circumstantially dictated. A person who is reasoning in a linear or systematic manner may have a stable sense of who she is as a person. This will include character traits and may extend to interpretations of overall personality and ways of thinking. The difficulty is that this construction of the self generally fails to take into account the sequential level at which one's self is constructed and therefore the embeddedness of the self in the little rituals of everyday life. This becomes apparent when these little everyday sequences are disrupted. The effect is surprisingly unsettling and potentially anxiety-inducing. This is evident when one moves from one city to another or goes abroad for the first time. In these novel contexts, the familiar largely unnoticed little routines of one's normal existence can no longer be reenacted. One is often surprised by the extent of the discomfort one feels and the difficulty one has "being one's self." Taken to the extreme, the total disruption of the little routines of daily life can seriously undermine one's sense of self and ontological security with devastating effects on one's personality. Part of the effect that the concentration camps in Europe during World War II had on their victims may be understood in these terms.

Routines Rather Than Rules

A person who reasons sequentially acts in routine ways. She does not think about the routines and sequences as such. They constitute the terms of her considerations rather than their object. In this regard, a given sequence is not reconstructed as an atemporal abstraction that can be held apart from events which are currently unfolding. As a result, sequential reasoning does not lead to the construction of rules or standards of action that have general meaning and various particular applications. This is not to say that sequentially directed behavior cannot be socially regulated and regular. However, this is not achieved through cultural stipulation, nor is it maintained through conscious self-monitoring. Rather, the regularities of daily life for someone who reasons sequentially are sustained by the substantive, concrete regularities of the contexts in which she finds herself. In this sense, it is concrete, local social structures rather than cultural definitions and imperatives that regulate the interaction among those who reason sequentially.

While rules like those of linear thought are not constructed and linguistically mediated social demands thus have relatively little force, this is not to suggest that they have none at all. As noted earlier, learned sequences can be subjectively represented and then presented linguistically. The latter consists of storytelling. It is an active process whereby the represented sequences are actually worked through in the course of the telling. The story does not abstract the sequence from the time and substance of the succession of events being retold. Therefore the story does not function as a parable that may apply across a variety of concrete life situations. This said, a linguistic mediated reenactment of experience can be used as a means, albeit a limited one, for the social regulation of behavior. Through instruction and example, a story can be integrated with a particular sequence of events. The various points in the story thus become understood as aspects of the events with which they are associated. In fact, the next point in the story can act as a stimulus to the evocation of the substantive event with which it is associated. In this way, individuals can be taught to talk their way through a particular performance of an activity. The limit here is the talk does not exist apart from events and direct them. Rather it as an accompaniment to what is occurring and proceeds with much of the uncertainty of all sequential constructions.

Given the relative lack of understanding of or concern for social conventions and rules, people who reason in a sequential fashion will violate social norms with relative frequency and a commensurate lack of concern. As a result, social compliance depends on a close structuring of the environment to sustain the concrete contexts in which the desired behaviors are stimulated. Typically, this is bolstered by severe and very visible punishment for violations. It may well be that the logic and relative efficacy of certain social institutions may be understood in these terms. For example, royal recourse to a very public and brutal form of physical punishment in seventeenth-century France may be seen in this light as a necessary and effective means of controlling a large illiterate public. Similarly the introduction of confession by the medieval Catholic Church might be viewed as an astute maneuver to sustain the reach of the church into the daily life of people, most of whom probably reasoned sequentially. In this context, confession provides a vehicle for the regular repatriation of a flock who would inevitably and regularly fail to follow prescribed behavior. Continuing in this vein, I would suggest that the force of the argument of the Grand Inquisitor in the Dostoyevsky's *Brothers Karamazov* can be understood in these terms. In the story, confronted by Christ returned, the Grand Inquisitor defends Church practice and, in so doing, emphatically rejects God's law. In the present terms, the Grand Inquisitor is arguing that God's law is constructed at such a level of abstraction it could only possibly be understood and adhered to by a few people thereby leaving the vast majority of humanity without direction or salvation. With its myths, specific dicta, threats of punishment, and opportunities for confession, the Church misrepresented divine law. But it did so in order to meet the needs of the ignorant (essentially sequential) masses of people who were otherwise abandoned by a God bereft of understanding or compassion.

POLITICAL REASONING OR STARING AT THE NIGHT SKY

Politics and political considerations are not really a significant part of sequential reasoning. There is little awareness or sense of what is remote. Therefore the distant realities of national, regional, or even city politics are not readily comprehended from a sequential perspective. They may acquire some significance only insofar as they enter into everyday life of the individual in some concrete fashion. This may occur in two ways. On one hand this may be a matter of circumstance. For example, someone who reasons in a sequential manner may be confronted with other people discussing politics. But the words she hears are likely to have little meaning except insofar as they become associated with the events transpiring when they were uttered. Thus for a child who is reasoning sequentially, particular statements—such as claims of support for the right to abortion or for affirmative action—may become a recurring part of family dinner conversation. These statements are understood less with reference to the political issue or leader to which they refer and more as a part of the general atmosphere of the family dinners. When questioned directly about a particular policy preference, this will invoke the dinner conversation and the child is likely to parrot what has been heard. This response may be quite reliable even if the child has no sense of the specifically political meaning of the statements she is making.

The mass media also serves as a source of contact with a more remote political world. For the most part, the information presented is abstract as well as remote and cannot be understood. It thus has little personal relevance or meaning for someone who is reasoning sequentially and is therefore ignored. However, when the events focus on specific individuals and the concrete things they do or have happen to them, they can attract attention. The result is the internalization of a fragment of a story—that is, the particular concrete events observed in the two to five minutes of television exposure. The story then is understood and reproduced in typically sequential terms. It is an isolated fragment that has an internal meaning that is elaborated in its unfolding. In winter 1997, there were thus many adults who reasoned in a sequential manner who were aware of and could reiterate some of the events surrounding the life and death of the British Princess Diana. But these same people might have had little or no sense of why the paparazzi were willing to chase her car to get a picture, not to mention a clear idea of what England is.

This introduction of political events through circumstantially determined exposure may be complemented and extended subjectively. An event in a political story may be identified with another event with which it has some overlapping characteristics and then cue the sequence with which that second event is associated. This might explain some of the unusual stories that children who are reasoning sequentially tell about national leaders. In an early political socialization study, Fred Greenstein (1960) reports how children who were asked what it is that the president of the United States does responded by describing how he pushes them while they are on the park swing. Although the children's responses were not sufficiently probed to allow for any confident interpretation, it is probably the case that the president may, at that moment, have been identified with another adult male, perhaps the child's father. The question regarding the president thus may have cued the memory of a recent sequence where the father pushed the child's swing, except now the president is doing the pushing.[7]

Given the nature of sequential understandings, much of the constitutive elements of political life are simply not readily constructed or understood from a sequential perspective. Thus in addition to a relative inability to make sense of remote events, sequential reasoning allows little sense of a political entity such as a nation-state. For sequential reasoning, the space of events is a shifting ground centered on what is presently occurring or remembered. It is a field limited by what is seen at any given moment. At most, it consists of the spaces linked together through the sequence of travel. In this context, the stable and extended geographical space of a nation is not naturally constructed or well understood within the context of sequential thought. In addition, sequential thought does not think of people in terms of social groups. As a result, an alternative formulation of a nation in terms of its "people" also is not readily assimilated in sequential terms. Exposed to nationalist concerns, sequential reasoning imports what is most readily experienced in concrete terms. Thus the national geography is understood in terms of one's own immediate surroundings, and the nation itself is often confused with its concrete symbols. Thus, the national flag may be understood as the nation itself, and it may be reasoned that destroying the flag actually physically harms the nation or hurts the people. With training the associations with the nation may be increased, but they still constitute an ill-understood collage. This is illustrated by an interview with an adult who spoke of national government by discussing something that Congress did. When asked what Congress is, the adult appeared slightly confused by the question and responded by saying, "it is a big building up over there."

Other key elements of politics are also not consistent with a sequential conception of social life. Lacking a concept of groups, sequential reasoning can make little sense of the collective entities that are central to most political action. Races, classes, and political parties are not readily considered and therefore typically generate little interest or attention. When circumstances require a focus on groups, sequential reconstruction will generally lead to the characteristic confusion of part and whole and thus to an understanding of a group in terms of a particular present or recalled member. Often political groups are understood in terms of their leader. Thus discussion of Germany may call to mind one's German neighbor or talk of Russia may call to mind television images of Vladimir Putin. Similarly, having little sense of causality or role, sequential reasoning does not lead to the construction of hierarchies of the kind around which political life typically revolves. Confronted with a discussion of such a hierarchy of status or power, sequential reasoning typically yields a two-step hierarchy in which one person is able to tell another what to do.

Overall the understanding of a complex polity engendered by sequential reasoning compares to its vision of the sky at night. In sequential thought, the night sky is comprehended as it appears. It is a blackness punctuated by a host of stars. The stars themselves are simply there and do nothing. Occasionally, there may be a shooting star. This will be noticed and the trajectory of this un-usual event may be remembered. Whatever happens up there, however, is never really a part of the immediate events of daily life. The night sky is thus a remote world, one that is rarely a matter of any particular consideration. At most, a particular configuration may be identified with the visual image of some re-membered other event. This may lead to an introduction of the stars into a fan-ciful story. If forced to think about the stars, sequential reasoning will generate little understanding. Left to its own machinations, the stars will not be consid-ered at all. The only thing that can be understood is that the stars are there next to one another in the blackness above. From the perspective of sequential rea-soning, politics is the domain of the night sky.

THE NATURE OF EVALUATION:
FEELING AND NEEDING

In the same way that sequential reasoning revolves around observing and reen-acting sequences of events, so sequential evaluation is a matter of experiencing and recalling the feelings evoked. Through the experience of the various sensa-tions associated with the unfolding events of a sequence, these sequences come to have value. When the valued sequence is cued, the resulting anticipation is not only a matter of expected outcomes, but also involves expected sensations as well. Until they are realized, these expectations constitute needs to continue or avoid the impending flow of events. Cast in these terms, sequential evalua-tion is oriented by the following questions: (1) What does this feel like? (2) Do I want this to happen? The first question is answered by reference to what one is currently feeling or by the memory of what was felt before. The second ques-tion is answered by drawing on the answer to the first to determine the desir-ability of the current course of events.

Evaluative Relations

Conducted in this manner, sequential evaluations consist of learned associa-tions. Sequences of events occur that evoke subjective feelings. If the feelings are particularly traumatic or are regularly evoked by the sequence in question, they may become an integral element of the experience. For example, it may be that going to a weekly religious service as a child entails a number of sensations, including the discomfort of putting on formal clothing, the warmth of sitting close to one's parent, the wonder at the spectacle of sights and sounds, and the pleasing tastes of the special meal that follows. A regular part of this recurring set of events, these associated sensations and feelings become intertwined with the events themselves. They become part of the anticipated sequence that is cued with the announcement that it is Saturday morning and it is time to go to the synagogue. Just as one expects to see the rabbi draped in ceremonial garb at the pulpit so one expects to feel the warmth of one's parent sitting in the next seat. Indeed, the relatively unpleasant moment of putting on the scratchy woolens or the starched cotton is offset by the anticipation of the pleasures to which this leads.

In this evaluative connection between subjective sensation and objective circumstance, the feelings are united with the events with which they are associated. In typical sequential fashion, there is a synthesis without a counterbalancing analysis. Again there is a subject-object confusion. Here it is a confusion of personal feelings and objective events. As the events are imbued with the texture and value of the personal feelings that are evoked, so those feelings acquire the objectivity and specificity of the events to which they are attached. Neither the unfolding feelings nor the unfolding events are abstracted from one another. Instead they are united in the totality of the experience of the event. Thus the feelings associated with the meal after the religious service are not abstracted sensations of particular flavors or satiation. They are "the-tastes-of-the-traditional-food-eaten-on-Saturday-at-home-with-family-after-which-I-felt-so-full." It is because of this union of feeling and event that either readily can evoke the other. Thus when one is an adult, the discomfort of woolen pants or a starched shirt collar may evoke memories of dressing for synagogue as a child and cue the sequence of Saturday morning. Alternatively sitting in a synagogue as an adult may evoke the childish wonder felt so many years ago and something of the now distant comfort of nearby parents.

Part of an unfolding of experience, evaluative relations have an immediate quality. They are very much of the here and now. Particular feelings are evoked in response to what is currently occurring. At the moment of their evocation, they constitute the totality of what the individual is feeling just as the current event constitutes the totality of what they are thinking. As a result, the feelings of sequential thought are unmitigated by the crosscutting considerations often introduced in linear or systematic evaluation. Whereas the evaluative relations of the latter kind are abstracted from events and thus constitute standards of judgment, sequential evaluative relations are immediate and concrete and therefore consist more of spontaneous expressions of affect. To the observer, sequential evaluations therefore appear relatively pristine and genuine and more directly felt. They also appear to be fleeting. Bound to sequences, feelings last as long as the relevant event or sequence. Thus feelings associated with a pleasant sequence may disappear with the introduction of an unpleasant sequence and the particular feelings it evokes. The result is that sequential reasoning produces the rapid changes in affect associated with moodiness or emotional instability.

Although an aspect of the present moment, evaluative relations unfold over time. Like the events to which they are attached, one feeling evaporates into the one that follows. Feelings are not static associations abstracted from the flow of experience. Like the sequences of which they are part, the feelings unfold. Thus they are attached to one another as well as to the objective circumstances of the successive events. In the flow of feeling, different feelings become comingled in the unfolding experience of a given sequence. As a result, otherwise distinct and perhaps even incompatible feelings readily coexist. For example, consider the sequence in which an otherwise inattentive parent regularly follows the activity of screaming and hitting a child with a remorseful show of physical attention and tenderness. For the child, an affectively loaded sequence is learned in which terror and pain lead to warmth, security, and pleasure. The various feelings coexist, and indeed the terror and pain are understood as the route to warmth, security, and pleasure. The result is that terror and pain are, in this context, infused with feelings of security and warmth.

Evaluative Units

The objects of sequential evaluations are sensation-event states. They are concrete, immediate, and passing. These states are not abstract but are part of what is occurring to the evaluator now. As a result, sensation states are highly specific to the particulars of the event to which they are attached. As such they have a different structural quality than the categorically defined feelings referred to in the discussion of linear thought and therefore cannot be adequately assimilated in those terms. This failure to assimilate is evident in the difficulty we have trying to capture the raw sensations of experience in linguistically mediated reflection. The contextuality and specificity of the particular feelings create an irregularity that confounds the categorical distinctions inherent in the language we use to describe them.

At the same time that sensation-event states constructed in the course of sequential evaluation are highly specific, they are not well differentiated. They are not held apart from the sequences in which they emerge and given separate identification. This is true in two respects. As suggested by the discussion of linear evaluations, the boundaries between sensation-event states in an unfolding sequence are highly permeable. The feelings of earlier events are permeated by the anticipation of later ones, and the feelings of those later events bear their traces. At the same time, the identity of the early events being evaluated is intertwined with the meaning of the events that follow. Thus Richard the father who is racing toy cars with Max and Richard the father who obstructs Max's attempt to order Sprite at lunch are two different event-states ("my-daddy-playing-cars" and "my-daddy-disallowing-Sprite") and two different sensation states ("my-daddy-whom-I-like-to-play-cars-with" and "my-daddy-who-makes-me angry"). In one instance, the child will be pleased with father. In the other, the child may express anger and, with full sincerity, tell the father that he hates him.

These context dependent evaluations are equally evident in adults who reason sequentially. It can be seen in the volatility of emotionally charged relationships between intimates in which one partner may display affection and pleasure in one context and act violently in the next. It is also apparent in the changing affiliations and alliances that are typical of sequential interaction. Friendship and personal loyalty are circumstantial. Sometimes a constancy of affective response can be observed. This is not, however, the product of a considered judgment overwhelming present circumstances. Rather it is the result of the stability of those conditions, internal as well as external, that evoke feelings. Thus, if the conditions of interaction are such that one engages the other in only pleasurable sequences, the feelings toward that person will remain constant. Alternatively, if the initial feelings attached to a sequence involving the other are sufficiently strong, they may be cued whenever the other is present. Thus the same feeling may overwhelm the context specific sensations that are or might have otherwise been elicited.

The lack of differentiation of event-sensation states is also evident in the sequential connections made through the process of identification. As discussed earlier, one event may be identified with another on the basis of one or only a few elements, which both the original event and the one identified with it share. Once established, the identification tends to fuse the two events into the present one being considered. As just discussed, the feelings associated with an event are one of its aspects. Thus a strong sense of warmth one feels with someone now may evoke the warmth one felt with a parent earlier. Cued with this overlap, an identification may occur evoking earlier experiences and fusing them with present ones. Of course all of this occurs within the largely unconscious domain of precategorical experience that was largely not mediated through language. The result is that in the immediate situation, the adult begins to feel about the other in a manner cued by the earlier sequence of feelings and events. If the adult is thinking in a linear manner, this present feeling is an object of reflection and categorization. It may thus be sustained over time.

To illustrate, consider the earlier example of a child who has had the repeated experience of an inattentive parent who, at times of punishment, screams at the child, strikes her, and then responds to her tears with affection and tenderness. As noted earlier, strong feelings of terror, pain, warmth, security, and pleasure comingle in this learned sequence of sensation-events. The terror is laced with the anticipation of affection and the affection bears the residue and intensity of the terror. The years pass and the child is now an educated adult who thinks in a linear manner. In her conventionally shaped and categorical lexicon, feelings of terror and pain are incompatible with feelings of security, warmth, and pleasure. And yet she may find herself incomprehensibly attracted to men who are not only affectionate, but also scare and abuse her. While it does not make sense to her, she does not experience anything like this intensity of emotion with men who provide the affection free of any fear or pain. Of course the apparent nonsense of her reactions is a linear phenomena. Considered in sequential terms and thus with reference to a layer of emotional memory and meaning largely inaccessible to her now linear considerations, her reactions make perfect sense.

Although sensation-events are not abstracted and then systematically compared to one another, evaluative comparisons are made. Typically this occurs when the sensation-event itself is of varying intensity. This may be a function of variation in the apparent quality of the aspects of the event itself. Thus events or aspects of events that capture more of the visual field will produce a more intense reaction. The greater the quantity of a preferred item, be it beads, edible delicacies, or cattle, the more intensely it will be desired. Similarly, the larger the item will produce a more extreme affective response. Thus a giant killer that is ten times one's size will be feared more than an equally deadly killer that is only half one's size. In the same manner, the severity of an offense will be judged relative to the amount of visible damage done. Thus if one knocks over and breaks a large vase, this is regarded as a much more serious act than if one breaks a drinking glass.[8] Similarly an injury is more serious the more visible it is. The last formula underlies the sequential understanding of degrees of punishment.

Egocentrism and Social Influence

The basic structure of sequential evaluation can be seen in the qualities of the social judgments it engenders. To begin, the evaluations and preferences of sequential reasoning reflect a profoundly egocentric point of view. This is true of both the cognitive and affective aspects of sequential social reasoning. On one hand, the experience is defined as it is personally observed. The perspective taken is necessarily one's own and thereby excludes others' view of the same events. On the other hand, evaluations reflect the sensations that those events produce in oneself. Apart from the empathic response discussed below, others' affective responses are irrelevant except insofar as they have a direct impact on one's own experience. Thus the otherwise personally pleasing sequence of events will be unaffected by the fact that another person may be visibly annoyed. If, however, that annoyance leads to shouting that is fear inducing, then the other's feelings may affect one's own.

The egocentric quality of sequential thought makes an individual who reasons and evaluates events in this way a relatively asocial being. That said, sequential reasoning is readily socialized, albeit in a manner that is consistent with the qualities of sequential understanding and evaluation. As already noted, sequential evaluations are embedded in and evoked by the unfolding of personal experience. This experience is not solely a subjective construct. To the contrary, it is in large part socially defined. A society or subsystem of a society delimits the kinds of interactions that regularly take place and the consequences they have. In this manner, there is a social determination of the particular pleasures and pains that are associated with different sequences of events. This in turn impacts sequential evaluations and subsequent responses. In the latter respect, an attempt will be made to avoid sequences that are punished and to initiate those that are rewarded. In this manner, socially desirable evaluations are made and socially appropriate behavior is likely to follow.[9]

There is a second route whereby social influence may be exerted on sequential evaluations. This involves an empathic response to another's feeling such that the same feeling is invoked in oneself. This has sometimes been regarded as something of a mystery for developmental psychologists who study younger children. These children are understood to be egocentric in their understandings and thus largely unable to reason in a way that allows them to set aside their own understandings and feelings and take the perspective of another. Yet in more naturalistic studies that observe the child's interaction with significant others at home, empathic response is frequently observed. Thus a mother's tears may evoke sadness in the young child even if they do not interfere with the activity in which the child is currently engaged.[10]

In my view, this empathic response is best understood in terms of the subject-object confusion that is characteristic of sequential evaluations. When another person is an object of attention and that person displays the signs of a readily recognized emotion, this emotional display may be identified with the observer's own similar display of emotion and thereby cue that emotional response in her. Consider the example of the observation of another person sobbing. In sequential terms, the sounds of the sobs and the sight of tears may overlap with sensations associated with one's own crying. An identification may follow in which the other person's crying is fused with one's own. In turn this may cue a memory of an unhappy or painful sequence of events during which one cried. This past sequence, complete with its emotional associations and the display of those emotions, may then be evoked by the present observation of the other person crying. Of course all of this transpires in a quick and largely unself-conscious manner. The result appears to be an empathic response in which one feels another's pain. In fact, one is simply feeling one's own painful response to other circumstances.

The subject-object confusion typical of sequential thought also opens another avenue of social influence. The concern here is less a communication of feelings and more a transmission of behavior patterns. A person who is reasoning in a sequential manner may observe a series of events involving the actions of another person. In certain cases, the events may evoke strong evaluative associations (positive or negative) for the observer or they may include clear displays of feelings by the actor involved. If the resulting sensations are strong enough, attention will be paid to the sequence. Moreover, the observed rewards or feelings may be identified with one's own. In this case, rather than the subject-object confusion leading to an introjection of another's response into one's own remembered sequences, confusion leads to a projection of one's self into the observed situation. The events are evaluated or felt personally and are learned accordingly. The net result is imitative learning with all the dynamics and characteristics described by learning theorists (e.g., Bandura and Walters, 1963) who have focused on this phenomena.[11] Of course it should be remembered that whereas this type of learning does provide an effective avenue for social learning, it is limited to what is concrete, immediate, and thus readily observed.

A final means for the socialization of sequential understanding and evaluation is linguistic. Whereas language may be an essential part of the social environment, it is somewhat peripheral to the sequential experience of the world. That said, certain specific labels or phrases may acquire significant value if they regularly accompany events whose affective associations are strong. In the diffusion of value across the event, these labels are associated with the affective response. In the end, they may be able to cue that affect themselves. A typical example of this would be the way in which the words "good" and "bad" are used as accompaniments to the rewards that follow or are a part of particular sequences of behavior. As the word "good" is repeatedly associated with pleasurable events and the word "bad" is repeatedly associated with discomforting or painful events, these words will acquire some of the penumbra of the feelings associated with the events they evoke. This then gives a speaker leverage over the evaluations of a listener who is reasoning in a sequential manner. By attaching the label of good or bad to a sequence, the speaker may be able to cue feelings in the listener that thus become a part of the experience of the event in question. Given the nature of sequential reasoning, this will be more effective if the events in question are currently occurring. Even here the effect may be mitigated if those events are already evoking a different feeling in the individual. Thus telling someone who is reasoning sequentially that something that tastes bitter to them is in fact "good" is likely to have little effect on their evaluation of the experience of eating that particular food.

In sum, despite the relative egocentrism of sequential thought, sequential understandings and values are readily subject to social influences. By their very nature, social contexts and the people in them exercise some control over the reinforcements associated with various sequences of action. They also regularly provide examples of what to do in specific situations. In addition, there is a regular use of linguistic labels to reflect the personal consequences of past events and to affect the evaluation of present ones. Through these means someone who reasons in a sequential manner can be socialized. The learning is piecemeal and its effects are often somewhat unreliable. With experience over time and across situations, however, sequential reasoning can provide the basis for competent and appropriate participation in the concrete and specific routines of everyday social life.

CONCLUSION

Sequential reasoning and evaluation are clearly very limited. They are very much bound to the here and now and the temporality of this passing present. Sequential understandings are thus very concrete and circumscribed by context. There is no abstraction and little categorization or causal analysis. Sequential evaluation is also intertwined with the unfolding sequence of events. It consists of the feelings evoked by the here and now of a present (or re-presented) sequence. As such, evaluations tend to be ephemeral. They also tend to be felt relatively intensely. Despite the concreteness, specificity, fluidity, lawlessness, and egocentrism of sequential reasoning, it still provides the basis for the development of considerable social competence. Within the confines of recurring contact with the same people under the same circumstances, sequential reasoning can accumulate vast and detailed experience of the variety of events and the sequential trajectories of which they are part. Consequently, in such a delimited social context, the demands of interaction can be handled quite deftly and desired results can be readily produced.

Chapter Six Epistemology, Methodology, and Research Design

The question addressed in this chapter is how best to study the way in which people evaluate social and political life. The approach I suggest is rather different from that adopted in most political and psychological research on cognition and evaluation. To clarify the nature of this difference, the chapter opens with a discussion of epistemology and method. The basic point made here is that one's conception of appropriate empirical method depends on the epistemological position one adopts. In other words, one's approach to the conduct of research will reflect one's underlying, often only implicit, assumptions about the nature of knowledge and the process whereby it is acquired. Insofar as the structural pragmatic view of thinking offers an alternative epistemology, the methodological considerations it raises will necessarily differ from those orienting most other contemporary research. Following this general discussion of methodology, the remainder of the chapter is devoted to a presentation of the design and methods of the empirical research reported here. This includes a description of the subject population and the in-depth interview technique used to study it. The chapter closes with a discussion of the way in which the interview texts were analyzed.

EPISTEMOLOGICAL ASSUMPTIONS
AND METHODOLOGICAL ORIENTATION

The structural pragmatic view of social and political thinking is based on several key epistemological claims: (1) that thinking is an activity; (2) that this activity has a form which determines the underlying structure of the kinds of understandings and evaluations that are produced; (3) that thinking is both subjectively determined and intersubjectively oriented and this creates a dynamic that may lead to the transformation of both reasoning and social regulation; and (4) because of differences in social conditions different individuals may come to think in qualitatively different ways. These epistemological claims not only have consequences for psychological and political theory. They also have important implications for the design, conduct, and analysis of empirical research.

Liberal Social Scientific Inquiry

The vast majority of research on social cognition and public opinion is based on a different understanding of thinking and therefore is oriented differently. The view adopted is essentially the seventeenth- and eighteenth-century liberal epistemology upon which traditional scientific method is based. The critical claim made here is that all individuals perceive, represent, and reason about an objective world in the same and essentially correct way. Even in its earliest conceptions, this somewhat sanguine view is tempered by the recognition that human cognition is subject to distortions. These are produced by hasty judgment, the complexity of what is being observed, deceptive circumstances, honored social conventions, and personal motivation and prejudice. As a result, we often ignore certain features of the environment, unduly emphasize others and infer felicitous but inappropriate connections among persons, actions, and events.

While these distorting influences clearly interfere with the drawing of correct conclusions, the understanding of these influences leaves the liberal epistemological vision intact. First, it should be noted that although the substantive consequences of the various distorting forces vary with the particular observer and the specific circumstances and subject of inquiry, it is assumed these forces all operate on us in the same manner. Thus the liberal assumption of universal cognition and its concomitant denial of significant differences in the ways in which different (normal) people perceive, represent, and reason is retained. In our mistaken judgments as well as in our correct ones, the basic quality of the representations we construct and the connections we craft remain the same. Second, it is assumed that these distorting factors are external to cognition itself. We may think about the world in a manner that is influenced by partial exposure, personal interest, or social convention, but how we think—the basic manner in which we perceive, represent, and reason—remains at its core unaffected. When the distorting influences are removed, thought once again becomes rational and produces correct judgment.

In this context, the problem of empirical inquiry becomes one of creating procedures for eliminating the impact of these extracognitive factors that impair our judgment. The general solution to this problem is the scientific method. Its prescriptions are designed to prevent or counteract the operation of distorting influences. For example, the potential influence of personal motivation or prejudice is addressed by a procedural demand for the clear specification of technique. The aim here is to enable others to replicate the research. The assumption is that insofar as different researchers (with their different biases) achieve the same results, these results will be free of the bias of any one of them and therefore will be correct. Similarly, the potentially distorting influence of partial or hasty observation is countered by the demand for careful recording of data and an assessment of the reliability of measures across time.

These epistemological considerations not only pertain to the conduct of scientific research in general. They also have specific ramifications for research on social behavior and cognition. The issue here is the special problems raised by studying objects, in this case people, which are also subjects—that is, entities which are themselves thinkers and thus create meaning and purpose for their action. The question is whether the observer's interpretations correspond to the actor's intentions. In a liberal epistemology, this potentially serious problem is rather straightforwardly handled by recourse to the assumption that thought has a universal or common nature. One critical implication is that not only will a given object be commonly understood, a matter of representation, but so will the meaning and purpose a person gives to her statement or action, a matter of presentation. As a common form of thought yields a shared understanding of what is objective, so it yields a shared means of expressing what is subjective. The net result is that a speaker or actor and her audience will share a common understanding of the particular things she says or does.

Again there is a caveat. Whereas the commonality of reason insures that the formal or qualitative nature of the understandings of the observer and actor will be the same, the question remains regarding how much of the substantive meaning of what is said or done is shared. The problem here is that substantive

meaning and purpose depend on the specific connections that are drawn between a particular statement or act and other statements or actions. These specific associations are a matter of exposure and learning. As such they reflect the
particular individual's experience of the world around her. Thus, although we
all think similarly, our capacity to understand one another's actions or statements properly will depend on the degree to which our experiences, direct and
indirect, are the same. Thus we may feel considerable confidence when dealing
with others of the same culture and even more when dealing with others who
share the same position in that culture (e.g., the same gender, class, ethnicity,
age, etc.).

Conventions of social science research have emerged in this light. Apart
from the more general methods adopted by all scientific research, social science
has developed additional procedures for dealing with the fact that the objects of
its inquiry are themselves inquiring, reasoning beings. Unlike an object, a person actively makes sense of the environment, including the stimulus situations
that a social scientist may introduce or the questions she may ask. This raises a
unique and important methodological concern: Is the stimulus or the question
understood by the various people being studied and by the social scientist in
the same manner? Given the possibility of varying background experience, the
same object may be associated with different other objects and therefore understood differently. When subjects inhabit a largely common social and cultural world and the stimulus situation or question is an integral part of that
world, common understanding is generally assumed. Even here, however, it is
considered prudent to conduct exploratory pretesting with a small sample of
the population to be studied. The aim here is to insure the stimulus used in the
study does not evoke unexpected associations and thus come to be defined by
all or some subjects in a different manner than the experimenter or surveyor intends.

Most sociological and political science research proceeds on this basis. As a
result, there is little attention to the process of thinking itself. Its nature is
more a matter of assumption than research. Either it is viewed as rational and
logical (both concepts are generally underspecified), or it is viewed as purely
associative, a matter of learning connections as they are presented in the social environment. In this light, the focus turns to the products of thinking;
that is, to beliefs, attitudes, and behavior. Because reasoning itself is not a primary concern, these products are most often considered relative to their
broader social causes and effects rather than in relation to one another. Thus
they are examined either to determine their ramifications for collective out-

comes or to discover the cultural and institutional conditions that foster their production.

Under the rubric of studies of ideology, some political science research has been done on the relationship among attitudes. Also relevant here is social psychological research on the relationship between attitudes and purposive behavior. In both cases, the work examines the correlation among these various cognitive products, among attitudes themselves, or between attitudes and behavior. Given the assumptions of rationality or learning that orient the design of this research, the results are surprising and provocative. The evidence suggests that attitudes do not correlate with one another in a manner that is either rational or reflective of how the attitudes are related in the culture at large.[1] In a similar manner, attitudes do not appear to be rationally or conventionally related to subsequent behavior.[2] Overall, the products of thought are not related to one another, as is conventionally assumed, in either a rational or culturally determined manner. This result cannot be readily or straightforwardly interpreted. The problem is that the liberal epistemology that orients both the research and the subsequent interpretative efforts assumes the very formal rationality and substantive learning which is called into question by the evidence. Theories cannot readily assimilate evidence or claims that contradict their core assumptions.

For the most part, researchers operating in this tradition have chosen not to view the evidence in this light and therefore do not search for alternative theoretical perspectives. Instead they attempt to save the basic orienting vision. This is not surprising given that this vision structures the terms in which they make sense of their data. In this vein, they have argued that the lack of rationality, coherence, or proper learning is the result of distorting influences that affect either the people being studied or the person studying them. Reference is made to such intervening factors as insufficient motivation, inadequate information, or simple mismeasurement.[3] From the structural pragmatic perspective, the evidence is not so surprising or incomprehensible. It only appears to be so because the theoretical conception of the process, thinking, that produces these attitudes, beliefs, and behaviors, is incorrect. If people are assumed to reason in different ways and thus to reconstruct cultural definitions and social phenomena in their own subjective terms, it is not at all surprising that any attempt to discover the coherence of their views in singular and in publicly or culturally defined terms will fail.[4]

Unlike the more collectively oriented sociopolitical studies, psychological research, particularly the work on cognition and social cognition, has taken thinking as its focus. Rather than examining externalities (although these too are considered), there is an emphasis on the activity of thinking itself. As a result, this work has direct implications for the core assumptions of liberal epistemology. The research here has been largely experimental. The recurring result is that people often do not think in a manner that is logical or rational. Nor do they appear to experience their environment in a direct, unmediated way. These results clearly constitute a direct challenge to the liberal epistemological vision. Although most psychologists studying social cognition generally accept the substantive results, their methodology remains unaffected. These psychologists continue to rely on an essentially liberal vision to guide their research and theorizing. Even when rational processing is called into question, rationality remains the standard or benchmark whereby thinking is conceived.[5] At the same time, the assumption of universal cognition is retained. This leads to an orientation to research in which cognition is described in terms of its deviation or adherence to the norm of rational processing and, even in their deviation, all individuals are presumed to cognize in the same ways and employ the same sets of strategies.

Such an orientation is evident in the design of the mainstream research on social cognition conducted during the 1960s, 1970s, and 1980s. Typically the research addressed a hypothesis regarding the particular mistaken or irrational way in which all individuals would reason when confronted with a certain kind task. A subject population was then assembled. Usually this consisted of the most available people, college undergraduates. The use of this otherwise unrepresentative group was considered theoretically justifiable because it was assumed that all people reason in basically the same manner. In the experiment itself, subjects were presented with an indicative problem or choice and asked to make a judgment. In evaluating subjects' responses, it was assumed that there was a rational or logical way of approaching the problem that would yield a correct or best judgment. In this light, there was also the expectation that subjects would come to a different, mistaken judgment—one that reflected the particular irrational, subrational, or bounded cognitive mechanism hypothesized.

This negative strategy of specifying the various particular ways in which cognition deviates from the norm of rational processing is best exemplified by the influential research on the attribution of causality. This work captured the center stage of the social psychological research on cognition in the 1970s and 1980s. It received much of its initial impetus and guidance from the theorizing of Harold Kelley in the early 1970s. Kelley (1971) described a normative model of attributing causality, one which depicted rational processing as an essentially multivariate statistical operation. Two decades of research followed that attempted to chart the various ways in which people deviated from this model due to common errors in perceptual and logical processing.

The assumption that all people cognize in the same way is also evident in the approach to data analysis typically adopted in this attribution research and other work on social cognition. In the analysis, responses are defined relative to the single cognitive mechanism hypothesized. The majority of responses are thus viewed as either confirming or disconfirming this hypothesis. The remaining responses, the reactions of a minority of subjects, are regarded as experimental error, the result of the vagaries of the experimental condition. Neither at the point of hypothesis formulation nor at the time of data analysis is there any consideration of variation in how people cognize. Given the universalism of the guiding epistemological orientation, this is of course not surprising. But taking into account that most researchers are also teachers and therefore have extensive and ongoing classroom experience of significant individual differences in how students think, the failure to consider individual differences in their research is more interesting. Indeed, it is suggestive of the power of the epistemological and social forces which guide and constrain research.[6]

Apart from its presumption of universality, the adoption of a liberal epistemology also tends to foster an atomistic analysis of thinking. An inherent attribute of all thinking, rationality constitutes the basis of inquiry rather than the object of liberal thought and scientific research. We all share a "common (rational) sense" and thus have an always ready and publicly recognized means for understanding others and for judging the coherence and validity of their claims. Because we all have it, use it, and recognize it, there is little need to specify its underlying or general nature to understand its workings or results. Rather we only need to use our rationality to determine when thinking is operating incorrectly. Thus concern focuses on the products of thought, our specific claims of fact and value. We can "sense" when these are incoherent or self-contradictory and we can observe when they are wrong. Moreover, we can account for why these claims are wrong by consideration of the various distorting influences that come into play in any particular circumstance. Thus the mode of analysis shifts from the holistic and formal to the atomistic and specific. We focus on particular claims and judge their evident logic through reflection or their evident truth through observation.

The atomism of liberally oriented psychological inquiry is evident throughout the research on social cognition. A good example is the work on causal attribution discussed earlier. In addition to adopting rational processing as its conceptual benchmark, this work focuses on the various particular mistakes people make. The result is not an integrated conception of the quality of irrationality, but rather a catalogue of the various types of errors people make. Even later work that ambitiously attempts to chart a more positive course by depicting cognition without reference to the debunked concept of rationality remains atomistic in its orientation. A good example of this is the otherwise interesting research on heuristics or cognitive short cuts initiated by Tversky and Kahneman. In their work, they present a set of experiments, mysterious in their origin, that reveal various examples of the interesting and odd (nonrational) ways information is processed. Theorizing consists of empirical generalization. To the degree to which subjects' responses to certain experiments seem to share common features, a type of heuristic is identified. Initially this yielded three types of heuristics. As additional and more diverse experiments are conducted, additional types of heuristics are postulated. With time the list has thus been extended, but no overarching conception of the quality of thinking has been offered.[7]

In sum, psychologists have retained much of the basic methodological orientation dictated by a liberal view of thinking even as their research questions the adequacy of this epistemological vision. Evidence of the apparent irrationality of the inferences people make raises questions about the nature of the process that generates these associations. The focus turns back from the various products of thought to the nature of the thinking process itself. The concern is a very general one—given that our conception of thought as essentially rational appears to be incorrect, what must the overall nature of thinking be such that these various experimentally generated examples of nonrational or irrational associations are its product. In essence, the evidence demands theory building that can replace the general claims of rationality and a commonly sensed coherence with an alternative understanding of cognition. At the same time, as the basic understanding of thinking is subject to reconsideration, so must the methods used to study it. Insofar as a liberal conception of thinking is called into question, so must the guidelines for empirical research that such a conception engenders.

Given their atomism and related empiricism, psychologists typically lack the intellectual tools to handle such a problem. Trained in a liberal tradition, they are expert in the application of the liberal scientific methods of careful, self-aware, nonprejudicial, systematic observation. In this context, theorizing is a matter of empirical generalization. Essentially this consists of making inductive inferences from observed associations, the primary data, and then inferring various rules that describe the regularities observed. As a result, they are largely limited to producing conceptions of cognition that are neither general or interpretative. They are therefore ill equipped to offer overarching theory or to suggest alternative guidelines for empirical investigation.

The Structural Pragmatic Approach

The research presented in chapter 7 is guided by a structural pragmatic understanding of thinking. Consequently it is not based on an epistemological assumption of a universal rationality, nor is it oriented by an atomistic approach to the study of thinking. To the contrary it is assumed that thinking has an overarching structure and this may take various forms. Different people may therefore reason in qualitatively different ways. This alternative epistemological frame of reference suggests different kinds of methodological concerns and caveats than those that typically guide more liberally oriented research.

First, in recognition of potential variation in how individuals reason, an attempt must be made to study a population of individuals who are diverse in ways that are likely to produce differences in cognition. Furthermore, what constitutes diversity cannot simply be a matter of intuition, conventions of research, or good guesses. It must make sense relative to the theory of cognitive development. Structural pragmatics indicates which social conditions are likely to broaden the temporal and spatial range of the decisions one makes, and what social influences may introduce increasingly complex behavioral strategies and increasingly abstract rhetorical considerations. In this context, it is clearly inappropriate to study only undergraduates at one's own university. Because of their similar age and occupational status, they are likely to be exposed to similar demands and opportunities for making choices and directing their behavior. Because of their common education, they are likely to be exposed to the same level of rhetoric. Consequently, such a group is unlikely to exhibit the full range of types of thinking present in contemporary society.

Second, the research must be designed so as to allow for an investigation of the differences in the quality of the meanings people construct. The assumption of structural differences in cognition eliminates the relatively safe ground of liberal research. One can no longer assume a commonality of reasoning among subjects or between any one subject and the researcher even when they share a common cultural context. Therefore research must be designed on the assumption that the investigator does not comprehend the meaning of subjects' statements but rather tends to assimilate them to her own framework of understanding. To avoid this, the researcher must create the opportunity to observe a number of a subject's interrelated statements and/or behaviors. This allows for an easier determination if that subject is making inferences that systematically differ from those that the investigator would make. As well as alerting the investigator to the existence of this basic difference, it also provides the rich weave of inferences necessary for an interpretation of the quality of the connections the subject is making.

Viewed in this light, the use of close-ended survey items or standard experimental techniques are clearly inadequate. They do not take into account differences in either how subjects interpret the stimulus materials or how they ascribe meaning to the response they make. Similarly the concern over the control of the stimulus, which is critical in this research, is regarded as a secondary matter. In conventional methodology, control over the stimulus is crucial because it is recognized that variation in the substance of what individuals are presented with may influence the content of their responses. In structural pragmatic research, the focus is on the structure rather than the content of a subject's responses. Consequently variation in the stimulus situation, which may produce differences in the content of subject's responses, is not regarded as necessarily significant. For example, changes in question wording or even in the focus of the question are generally not presumed to affect the structure of the respondent's thinking. Given the desire to observe a respondent make a number of related inferences or claims, the research is designed to insure that the respondent is sufficiently interested and engaged to actively think about the question or task posed. Thus, the methodological concern shifts from controlling the stimulus across subjects to tailoring the stimulus to each individual respondent.

Third, the analysis of results must be interpretative. Given the absence of the assumption of a common understanding shared by the researcher and her subjects, this interpretation begins with preliminary observation. This is predicated on a self-aware and tentative determination of the qualities of the subject's statements and actions and the form of the connection among them. This then establishes a basis for further observation, now driven by this tentative conception, to determine if statements and behaviors cohere in the manner anticipated. To the degree to which they do not, basic conceptions of the nature of the quality of the subject's connections must be reformulated and observation must commence anew. At each step in this iterative process of theory construction and empirical research, the investigator is self-aware in her attempt to describe the substance of what she observes by reconstructing it in terms of her theorized understanding of its formal qualities. The result is not an atomistic or fragmented conception of the individual's thinking. Aspects of how an individual thinks may be addressed separately, but each aspect is always conceived relative to the overarching understanding of the structure of the individual's thought. In the structural pragmatic research presented here, this exercise is guided by the theoretical definitions of sequential, linear, and systematic thought.

SUBJECT POPULATION STUDIED

Given the research methods used, a large number of subjects could be studied only with a prohibitive expenditure of time and money. Therefore no attempt was made to select a representative sample. An attempt was made, however, to select subjects in such a manner so as to ensure that the full range of types of thinking would be represented. To this end, several indicators of the social circumstances of subjects were used in combination as selection criteria, including level of education, income, and responsibilities on the job. These were chosen for two reasons: ease of assessment and potential relation to cognitive development. In the latter regard, the guiding assumption was that at their lower levels, each of these indicators would point to a social environment that presents the individual with greater limitations and constraints. It was assumed that at the lower levels of education, income, and job responsibilities the individual's choices and practical decisions would tend to revolve around what was immediate, concrete, repetitive, and orchestrated by other people. To the degree to which this was in fact the case, such an environment would be unlikely to facilitate development. Indeed, it might discourage the emergence of more integrative and abstract forms of thinking. In complementary fashion it was assumed that at the higher level of these indicators, the individual would be confronted with an environment that is both more extended and open. With wealth, higher education, and greater job responsibilities, it is assumed that the individual would be required to make his or her own decisions about people and situations which are remote in space and time and which may require the creation of novel responses. Such an environment would be likely to create demands on the individual to develop to higher levels of thought.

The aforementioned demographic variables are assumed to be indicators of the pragmatic quality of an individual's daily life, but only rather poor ones. It cannot be assumed that these indicators, even in combination, necessarily reflect the kinds of differences in environments that may affect cognitive development. Wealth, education, and a high-level position are realized in everyday interaction in a variety ways. Depending on their specific realization, they may or may not open up possibilities and require novel thinking. In addition, there are important aspects of experience that are not tapped at all by these three demographic measures. For example, migration can be a very challenging experience that exposes one to new truths, demands new ways of interacting, and thereby fosters development. Finally, the demographic measures do not incorporate any consideration of the conditions under which possible environmental challenges are presented. If life's challenges, be they a matter of work, school, or immigration, are presented as opportunities for exploration and gain without too great a risk, they are likely to stimulate development. If, however, these challenges are presented (or perceived) as threatening and fraught with the risk of self-abasement or destruction, these challenges are likely to foster some form of individual or collective withdrawal rather than any structural change in thinking.

With these considerations in mind, forty-eight subjects were interviewed as part of the study. They were selected in order to create three groups of sixteen subjects. The first group consisted of the relatively dispossessed and disadvantaged. Subjects selected for this group had a high school education or less, earned less than $20,000 per year and, if they were employed, had relatively little control over the tasks they performed or over any other person at work. The second group was generally speaking drawn from the middle of American society. Subjects included in this group had some college education, earned between $25,000 and $35,000 per year, and did have some flexibility in short-term task planning as well as some control over a few colleagues. The third group was composed of relative elites. Members of this group had at least some postgraduate education, earned over $60,000 per year, and had long-term planning responsibilities, considerable control over how tasks were to be performed, or control over larger numbers of people.

METHOD OF GATHERING DATA

Each subject was interviewed individually. Initially subjects were asked a number of questions that were answered in a close-ended fashion. These included questions regarding age, ethnicity, level of education, income, occupation (with some elaboration where the meaning of the job was in question), political ideology, and party identification. Answers to these questions were recorded in writing by the interviewee. The core of the interview consisted of the open-ended exploration of the interviewee's understanding and evaluation of three issues: a personal one, a domestic political one, and one involving foreign policy. To orient the reader, I offer a brief overview of this in-depth part of the interview. This is followed by a more complete description of the questions addressed and the probing strategies used.

Discussion of the personal topic focused on a significant other chosen by the interviewee. Once this person is selected, the interviewee is asked to describe this person and discuss their good and bad points. Afterwards, the central issue addressed is whether the interviewee would be willing to give up her life's savings or even steal to help the person if she were chronically ill and in considerable pain. In the second part of the in-depth interview, the subject is asked to consider a domestic social and political topic. The focus here is on the controversial photography of Robert Mapplethorpe and the attempt of one Midwestern city to ban a public display of his work. The question addressed is, given the conservative values of the city, whether or not this art should be displayed. The third part of the in-depth interview focused on a foreign policy issue. The question presented is whether or not the United States should continue its involvement in Bosnia. The two political topics, one revolving around a domestic policy issue and the other focusing on a foreign policy issue, were chosen because survey studies of citizens' views across these two domains indicate that people reason differently or better about domestic politics than they do about foreign politics (e.g., Converse, 1964). Thus a comparison of reasoning across the two political issues provides a particularly rigorous test of the singularity of the structure of an individual's reasoning. The inclusion of a personal issue involving a person who is well known and very important to the interviewee makes the test even more stringent.

In the in-depth interview regarding the domestic and foreign policy issues, subjects were given a brief description of the facts relevant to the cases at hand. If additional information were requested or apparently became necessary, the interviewer provided it. Subjects' evaluation of all three issues was probed extensively. This included the use of follow-up questions directly probing expressed values and associated justifications. This typically involved such questions as "What do you mean by ____?" and "You mentioned that ____ is important to you. Why is it so important?" It also involved the introduction of additional concerns or alternative scenarios to clarify and challenge the subject's values. These were designed to ensure that value considerations at all levels—sequential, linear, and systematic—were introduced during the course of each part of the interview. This was done in an attempt to frame each problem in such a way as to open up the possibility for a subject to reason at different levels during the interview. Again this was to further test the structural consistency of subjects' evaluative reasoning.

The overall interview required between two and three and one-half hours to conduct. The average interview was about two and one-half hours. The interview was conducted in one or two sessions depending on the circumstances and interest level of the interviewee. Whereas demographic questions were always administered first, the order of the issues discussed in-depth was randomly varied from interview to interview. The interviews were conducted by myself and five graduate student research assistants.

In-depth interviewing is a demanding exercise in the structural exploration of a subject's reasoning. Throughout interviewers must pursue the interview with two concerns in mind. On one hand, they must be responsive to the substance of what the interviewee is saying and do so in a manner that will generally be seen as comprehensible and natural to that interviewee. On the other hand, they must also always guide the interview so as to insure that the meaning of the various claims the subject is making is rendered as clear as possible. The aim here is to have the subject provide a sufficiently rich set of related assertions and responses so that inferences can be made regarding the underlying structure of the interviewee's reasoning. Often these two concerns are at odds. This is particularly true in the case of those interviewees who are not inclined to speak much at all. Here the task is to make the interviewee as comfortable and interested as possible in the "conversation." Equally difficult are the interviewees who are inclined to go on and on, quickly shifting from one topic to the next without making clear their understanding of any one. Here the task is to arrest the interviewee's progress and lead her back to further discussion of the points initially raised.

As the foregoing description of the task suggests, successful interviewing requires extensive training. Part of this involves becoming familiar with the structural pragmatic conception of thinking, particularly with its claims regarding the underlying quality of thought and the different forms it takes. In my experience, a basic understanding of the issues of structural theorizing and analysis is necessary to enable an interviewer to conduct an interview with sufficient sensitivity to facilitate a subsequent interpretation of the formal qualities of the meanings and evaluations expressed. To this end, interviewers were involved in classroom style training that involved the close reading of relevant theoretical materials, including work by Jean Piaget, L. S. Vygotsky, G. H. Mead, Lawrence Kohlberg, and Jürgen Habermas, as well as my own related work. After this classroom instruction, interviewers conducted several practice interviews.

After each interview was completed, it was closely analyzed and critiqued. This review was done in a group that included the trainees, two quite experienced interviewers, and myself. (I should note that all of us benefited from these sessions.)

To guide the interviewer, an interview manual was provided. It contains all sections of the interview, including close-ended as well as open-ended questions. As a reminder regarding procedure, general instructions are reiterated at the beginning of the packet. As the manual has been provided to researchers with whom I do not work personally, the instructions are quite general. The substance of the manual is presented below.

Objectives and Administration of the Interview

The aim of the interview is to explore the nature of an individual's values. The interview protocol has been designed in light of a structural pragmatic theory of cognition. This theory suggests that different people may understand and evaluate circumstances in fundamentally different ways. They may utter the same sentences or invoke the same values, but the meaning of what is said may vary significantly. With this in mind, the interview focuses on the nature of the underlying structure or coherence of different evaluations made by the same individual. To this end, open-ended questions are posed. Probes intended to reveal the meanings and understandings implicit in the interviewee's responses follow. Often, alternative considerations or scenarios are then introduced. These are intended to lead the interviewee to address evaluative concerns defined at different levels of development (sequential, linear, and systematic). This allows for a rather stringent test of the singularity of the structure of an individual's evaluative reasoning.

Methodological Concerns

1. Order of Presentation. Personal and demographic information on the subject is collected first. The interview always begins with the Political Belief Systems Section and is then followed by the Personal Issue Section. The Community vs. Individual and Foreign Relations Sections are presented in an order that is randomly varied from interview to interview.

2. Political Belief Systems Section. This is standardized. Consequently, there is no freedom to vary the presentations or the question format. Please follow the protocol exactly.

3. Personal Issue, Community vs. Individual, and Foreign Relations. These

three sections of the interview are interpretative. The success of these sections depends on two factors. *First, you must initiate your own probes of the meaning of the values the interviewee asserts.* One way to do this is to ask: "Why is this important?" and "What do you mean by this?" This is critical in obtaining sufficiently elaborated statements to allow for subsequent assessment of the interview. Additionally, when a subject reverses a position by introducing new concerns, probe the importance of the new value relative to the old ones apparently abandoned. *Second, you must also be guided by the interview protocol.* Whereas you will need to go beyond the specific questions included in the interview protocol, you must also ask all the questions provided in the protocol materials. Note: The interview is a clinical one. Although the protocol does provide considerable guidance, interview training is advised.

Following these general instructions, the various parts of the interview, including the questions to be asked, are presented. These are described in the following sections.

The Political Belief Systems Interview

The questions posed here are the open-ended, short-answer questions that are regularly a part of the National Election Studies. These questions are intended to explore the interviewee's political ideology. Responses are generally evaluated in terms of Phillip Converse's levels of conceptualization (1964). The questions are as follows:

I'd like to begin by talking about American politics. Specifically I would like to ask you what you think about the Republican and Democratic Parties.

1. Is there anything in particular that you like about the Democratic Party?
   a. (If no answer) Is there anything at all you like about the Democratic Party?
   b. Is there anything else?
2. Is there anything in particular that you don't like about the Democratic Party?
   a. (If no answer) Is there anything at all you don't like about the Democratic Party?
   b. Is there anything else?
3. Is there anything in particular you like about the Republican Party?
   a. (If no answer) Is there anything at all you like about the Republican Party?
   b. Is there anything else?

4. Is there anything in particular that you don't like about the Republican Party?
   a. (If no answer) Is there anything at all you don't like about the Republican Party?
   b. Is there anything else?

Now I'd like to ask you what you think are the good and bad points of President Clinton.

5. Is there anything in particular about Bill Clinton that might make you vote for him in the next presidential election?
   a. (If no answer) Is there anything at all?
   b. Is there anything else that might make you vote for him?
6. Is there anything in particular about Bill Clinton that might make you vote against him?
   a. (If no answer) Is there anything at all?
   b. Is there anything else that might make you vote against him?

Because the interviews were not conducted during a presidential campaign, interviewees were asked to evaluate only President Clinton. No questions about a Republican leader were posed.

Personal Issue: Evaluating Another Person and Breaking the Law to Help a Friend

This part of the interview begins by asking the interviewee to identify a person who is close to her. Typical choices include family members, best friends, and lovers. The interviewee is then asked to evaluate that person. The specific questions asked are:

I'd like you to think of someone very close to you, perhaps a lover, spouse or best friend. Tell me the name of that person.

1. What do you like most about *name?*
(Probing each favorable item mentioned:)
   a. What exactly do you mean by _____?
   b. Why is _____ so important to you?
2. What do you dislike about *name?*
(Probing each negative item mentioned:)
   a. What exactly do you mean by _____?
   b. Why is _____ so important to you?

Critical to the success of this part of the interview is that there be adequate follow-up probing. The prescribed probes are a point of departure. Just asking these questions may or may not be enough to lead the interviewee to provide sufficient definition or justification for her claims. It is at points such as these where the interviewer must rely on her judgment to determine when and how to press further.

Upon completion of the exploration of the interviewee's attitudes toward the significant other, a dilemma is posed. The interviewee is asked to imagine a situation in which the significant other named is very ill and in need of her help. The situation is presented in the following way:

Let us consider a hypothetical situation. *Person named* develops a serious chronic illness—an illness that will stay with him/her for the rest of his/her life. The illness causes recurring pain—*person named* is always uncomfortable and occasionally suffers severe pain. He/she is generally confined to his/her bed. To his/her surprise, he/she discovers that a research scientist has just produced a drug which completely cures the illness. He/she calls the scientist and asks to purchase the drug. The scientist states the drug will eliminate the disease and agrees to sell the single dose required for $30,000. The charge is this high because of all the years the scientist devoted to the development of the drug and the difficulty with which it is now made. *Person named* does not have the money and cannot raise it. He/she comes to you for help. He/she wants you to help him/her get the drug.

The presentation of the dilemma is followed by several questions that are intended to reveal the interviewee's decision and elicit the reasoning underlying it.

Introductory questions:

1. If you had the money, but it represented all your savings, all the money you had in the bank, would you give it to him/her?
    a. Why or why not?
2. If you did not have the money and could not raise it, would you be willing to steal the drug for *person named?*
    a. Why or why not?
3. *(If interviewee responds yes to 1 or 2 but not to both)* Why would you be willing to (give the money/steal) but not (give the money/steal)?

Again the probing that follows the interviewee's response is critical. This may include such questions as: "You said you would do X, because of Y. What do you mean by Y? Why is Y important? Why is the reason you just gave a good or an important one?"

After this initial step, the interviewee's evaluations are further probed by the introduction of alternative scenarios. Different scenarios are posed depending on how the interviewee responded to the introductory questions. These scenarios are constructed with two aims in mind. First, these scenarios facilitate the further exploration of the interviewee's judgment. By presenting a consideration that contradicts the interviewee's evaluation, further justifications and relevant evaluation may be elicited. Second, the scenarios allow for a more stringent test of the claim of the structural quality of the individual's reasoning. The scenarios are designed not only to introduce contradictory concerns, but also ones that are likely to evoke considerations of qualitatively different kinds. Of course they may not. Indeed, the theory suggests that subjects will restructure the concerns introduced in the terms of their own way of thinking.

Follow-up questions include:

If Unwilling to Give Money or to Steal:
1. Let us assume that even if you give away your savings, you will still have enough money for yourself. You have a good job that pays as much as you need to live on comfortably.
   a. Would you still be unwilling to help?
   b. Why or why not?

[Sequential Manipulation]

2. If you don't help your friend, he/she will feel betrayed. He/she will no longer like you or be with you in the way you have enjoyed.
   a. Would you still be unwilling to help?
   b. Why or why not?

[Sequential Manipulation]

3. Friends are supposed to help one another. After all that is a central aspect of what friendship is all about. Sometimes helping requires sacrifice—a willingness to do what you really don't want to do. Even though you do not want to give away your savings, as a friend you really should help.
   a. Would you be willing to help?
   b. Why or why not?

[Linear Manipulation]

4. One might argue that the real issue here may be your own selfishness. *Person named*'s health and well-being are more important than your financial security. Quality of life is more important than property. You should help.
   a. Would you be willing to help?
   b. Why or why not?

[Systematic Manipulation]

(N.B. If interviewee is convinced to give money at a certain level, probe his/her willingness to steal at that same level by using the appropriate questions (4–6) from the section below entitled "If willing to give money but not steal.")

If Willing to Give Money but Not Steal:

1. You are willing to give away all your savings. Would you still do so if you knew you were going to lose your job? Without your income or your savings, you would no longer be able to pay your bills. Your life would be greatly affected—you might have to give up your home/apartment, your car etc.

   a. Would you still be willing to give your savings?

   b. Why or why not?

   [Sequential Manipulation]

2. Let us suppose you and *person named* are not so close as you used to be. You have argued and you don't get along well anymore.

   a. Would you be willing to give your savings?

   b. Why or why not?

   [Sequential Manipulation]

3. Let's assume that if you did steal the drug, you would never be caught. No one except *person named* would ever find out.

   a. Would you be willing to steal the drug?

   b. Why or why not?

   [Sequential Manipulation]

4. What if you had other people depending on you. For example, you have small children. They depend on you. Without your job and savings, you would not be able to take care of them properly. A parent has a responsibility to take care of their children.

   a. Would you still be willing to give your savings?

   b. Why or why not?

   [Linear Manipulation]

5. Friends are supposed to help one another. After all that is a central aspect of what friendship is all about. Sometimes helping requires sacrifice—a willingness to do what you really don't want to do. Even though you do not want to steal, as a friend you really should help.

   a. Would you be willing to steal the drug?

   b. Why or why not?

   [Linear Manipulation]

6. One might argue that the real issue here may be the druggist's selfishness. *Person named*'s health and well-being are more important than the scien-

tist's ownership of the drug. Quality of life is more important than property. You would be perfectly correct in stealing the drug to help.

   a. Would you be willing to steal the drug?

   b. Why or why not?

[Systematic Manipulation]

If Willing to Steal but Not Give Money:

1. Let us assume that if you do steal the drug, the police will certainly trace the theft to you. It is grand larceny. You will be convicted and go to prison for several years. Prison is a terrible, terrifying place to be.

   a. Would you still be willing to steal the drug?

   b. Why or why not?

[Sequential Manipulation]

2. Let us suppose you and *person named* are not so close as you used to be. You have argued and you don't get along well anymore.

   a. Would you still be willing to steal the drug?

   b. Why or why not?

[Sequential Manipulation]

3. Stealing is a bad thing to do. We are all told we should never steal. Bad people steal. The situation with the scientist is a bad one, but stealing, doing yet another bad thing, is not the answer.

   a. Would you still be willing to steal the drug?

   b. Why or why not?

[Linear Manipulation]

4. Stealing is not the answer. Stealing is regarded as wrong for a reason. Society depends on agreement regarding the basic way in which we deal with one another. Together as a community and a culture we decide what it means to be a person and how people should deal with one another. We create a morality and it is reflected in our values and our laws. Individuals do not have the right to simply decide what is right and wrong on their own, without going to their community. Considering this,

   a. Would you still be willing to steal the drug?

   b. Why or why not?

[Systematic Manipulation]

If Willing to Give Money and Steal:

1. Let us assume that if you do steal the drug, the police will certainly trace the theft to you. It is grand larceny. You will be convicted and go to prison for several years. Prison is not a pleasant place to be.

   a. Would you still be willing to steal the drug?

    b. Why or why not?

[Sequential Manipulation]

2. Let us suppose you and *person named* are not so close as you used to be. You
    have argued and you don't get along well anymore.
    a. Would you still be willing to steal the drug?
    b. Why or why not?

[Sequential Manipulation]

3. Stealing is a bad thing to do. We are all told we should never steal. Bad peo-
    ple steal. The situation with the scientist is a bad one, but stealing, doing yet
    another bad thing, is not the answer.
    a. Would you still be willing to steal the drug?
    b. Why or why not?

[Linear Manipulation]

4. Stealing is not the answer. Stealing is regarded as wrong for a reason. Society
    depends on agreement regarding the basic way in which we deal with one
    another. Together as a community and a culture we decide what it means to
    be a person and how people should deal with one another. We create a
    morality and it is reflected in our values and our laws. Individuals do not
    have the right to simply decide what is right and wrong on their own, with-
    out going to their community. Considering this,
    a. Would you still be willing to steal the drug?
    b. Why or why not?

[Systematic Manipulation]

Again throughout, interviewees' responses to the questions are subject to further probing. It should be noted that this may lead the interview considerably
astray as the interviewee introduces subject matter not addressed in the protocol.
Interviewers are instructed that this is perfectly acceptable. Indeed this has the advantage of insuring that the interviewee is addressing subject matter that is of importance to her. It also has the additional advantage of giving the interviewee the
feeling that their views and concerns are important and are being addressed. This
is in stark contrast to the experience of most interviewees who feel straitjacketed
and ultimately ignored when responding to close-ended surveys.

Domestic Political Issue: The Controversial
Display of Homoerotic Art

The focus here is on the issues raised by the display of homoerotic art in the city
museum of a conservative community. In many respects, the problem is a clas-

sic one confronting democratic societies when the rights of the individual conflict with those of the local community. Of course, the interviewees do not necessarily frame it in these terms. The interview begins with the presentation of the dilemma.

I would like to discuss with you a problem that arose several years ago in the city of Cincinnati. Cincinnati is a middle-sized city in Ohio. It is an unusually homogenous city. Most of the people who live there share similar beliefs and values. For the most part they are conservative. They tend to have rather traditional views on social and political issues. Recently, the director of the city's art museum organized an exhibition of the work of a well-known American photographer, Robert Mapplethorpe. Mapplethorpe photographed a wide variety of subjects, but sometimes his work is explicitly sexual, often homosexual. Several of these photographs were included as part of the larger exhibition of his work. A public outcry followed the opening of the exhibition. People were very upset by the photographs of homosexual activity. Several members of the city council judged the photographs to be obscene, clearly violating the values of the general community. They demanded the offending photographs be removed from the exhibit or the entire exhibit be shut down. The director of the museum disagreed. He argued that the photographs were part of Mapplethorpe's art and should be displayed along with the rest of the work.

Introductory question:

1. What do you think? Would you want the photographs displayed or not?
   a. (If not) Why not?
   b. (If yes) Why?
   (N.B. At this point the interviewee will mention certain concerns or values. The meaning of each should be probed with questions such as: What do you mean by this? Why is this important?)

As with the personal dilemma, the initial probing of the interviewee's evaluations are followed by the introduction of concerns that contradict her judgment. Again these contradictory concerns and alternative scenarios are designed to potentially evoke considerations at each of the levels of thinking, sequential, linear and systematic. These follow-up questions are presented below. Follow-up questions if the interviewee supports the exhibition.

1. Let's say that you go to the museum yourself. You see the pictures and decide that they are really revolting. Would you still want the pictures to be shown?

[Sequential Manipulation]

a. Why or why not?

(N.B. If any new concerns or values are introduced at this point or in response to subsequent questioning, the meaning of each should be probed with questions such as: What do you mean by this? Why is this important?)

2. Let's pretend you live and work in Cincinnati. One day your boss tells you of a promotion that will be available soon and that she intends to offer it to you. During the conversation, she also mentions the art exhibit and how she finds the whole thing immoral and strongly believes the exhibit should be canceled. She also makes clear that she could not respect or associate with anyone who was willing to allow such obscene pictures to be publicly shown. A few days later a special committee of influential members of the community that is deciding whether to support or oppose the exhibition approaches you. They respect your judgment and ask for your thoughts on the matter. Your boss is a member of the committee. What would you say? Why?

[Sequential Manipulation]

3. (If continues support) Let's also assume that your friends also live in Cincinnati. Unlike you, they are very upset by the exhibition and feel very strongly that the photographs should be banned. They make it clear that they think people supporting the exhibition are irresponsible, immoral, and arrogant. They will respect you less and withdraw from you if they discover your opinion. Knowing this what would you tell the committee? Why or why not?

[Sequential Manipulation]

4. Let us assume that one way in which the city tries to deal with the controversy is to bring in a group of respected art experts and civic leaders to view and evaluate the photographs. They decide that the photographs really are vulgar and do not have any real artistic value. They suggest that the photographs be removed from the exhibition. What would you suggest? Why?

[Linear Manipulation]

5. Cincinnati is very different from Los Angeles. Here in Los Angeles we live in a constantly changing community filled with different groups. Perhaps for this reason we believe in people expressing themselves in whatever way they like. We also believe that change, what is new and different, is good. Cincinnati is a smaller quieter city, where people are more similar to one another. Changes there occur more slowly and less often. Perhaps because of this, the people in Cincinnati believe more in traditional values and keeping things they way they are. The photographs go against their community's beliefs and values and they don't want them shown. Given this, don't you think that

it might be a mistake to allow the exhibition of explicitly homosexual photographs? Why or why not?

a. What if there is a referendum and an overwhelming majority of the citizens of the city vote to ban the exhibition. Would you still want it to be shown? Why or why not?

b. Does not a community have a right to define its own identity and protect its own values? Why or why not?

[Systematic Manipulation]

6. Let us assume the situation was different. Let's say the art museum is in Santa Ana, a mixed community of whites, African-Americans, and Hispanic-Americans, and the plan was to have a display of contemporary American art. The work included some of the famous artists of the day. This included some work that was surprisingly racist. Racial minorities were shown to be stupid and ugly. The pictures were clearly degrading. The community was outraged and demanded that the offending pictures be removed or the exhibition canceled. Would you want the pictures to be shown or not?

a. (If pictures should not be shown) The museum director complains. He says the works are of artistic value—they are beautifully done. In addition there is the artist's freedom of expression that must be respected. He argues that the exhibition should continue. What do you think?

[Systematic Manipulation]

Follow-up questions if the interviewee prohibits the exhibition:

1. Let us say that you have the chance to go to the museum yourself. You see the controversial pictures and are quite surprised. You find them very beautiful and enjoy seeing them a lot. In fact you would like to return again. Would you still want the exhibition to be banned? Why or why not?

[Sequential Manipulation]

(N.B. If any new concerns or values are introduced at this point or in response to subsequent questioning, the meaning of each should be probed with questions such as: What do you mean by this? Why is this important?)

2. Let's pretend you live and work in Cincinnati. One day your boss tells you of a promotion that will be available soon and that she intends to offer it to you. During the conversation, she also mentions the art exhibit and how she finds the attempt to control art and the artist's freedom to be immoral. She also makes clear that she could not respect or associate with anyone who supported the attempt to ban art and control expression. She certainly would not want to work with them. A few days later a special committee of

influential members of the community that is deciding whether to support or oppose the exhibition approaches you. They respect your judgment and ask for your thoughts on the matter. Your boss is a member of the committee. What would you say? Why?

[Sequential Manipulation]

3. Your friends also live in Cincinnati. Unlike you, they are very upset by the attempt to ban the exhibition. They make it clear that they think people supporting the ban are irresponsible, immoral, and arrogant. They will keep distance from you if they discover your support of the banning of the photographs. Knowing this, would you tell them your opinion if they asked? Why or why not?

[Sequential Manipulation]

4. Let us assume that one way in which the city tries to deal with the controversy is to bring in a group of respected art experts and civic leaders to view and evaluate the photographs. They decide that the photographs really are of artistic value. Also they state that although the content is controversial, debate should be open and the photographs should be shown. Would you respect their suggestion and support it? Why or why not?

[Linear Manipulation]

5. Let us assume the city council decides to hold a town referendum, a vote on the problem. Almost all the citizens of Cincinnati turn out and vote. To everyone's surprise, the overwhelming majority decides that all of the photographs in the exhibit should be displayed. The city council must now vote and decide. What would you want them to do? Why?

   a. (if continues to support the ban) But what of the right of free individuals to decide how they will live? The people voted and a majority agreed. Should not the law reflect the wishes of the people? Why or Why not?

   b. (if opposes the ban) But the photographs are obscene. (At this point remind interviewee of values marshaled to justify his/her opposition to the ban.) Despite the vote, do you not think it would be wrong to display the photographs?

[Systematic Manipulation]

6. Let us say the situation is very different. Let us say that we are dealing with a very conservative religious community in the Alabama countryside. There the curator of the little local museum decides to organize an exhibition showing the steps in the evolution from ape to human beings. The community is religious and does not believe in evolution. In fact it is regarded as blasphemy. The town referendum produces a vote where almost everyone

agrees to have the exhibit banned. Do you think it should be banned? Why or Why not?

[Systematic Manipulation]

Foreign Relations Issue: American
Involvement in Bosnia-Herzegovina

This final section of the interview addresses a question of foreign policy. The interview opens with a presentation of the situation in Bosnia-Herzegovina. Interviewees are then asked whether they think the United States should intervene. This is followed by a more detailed inquiry into their assessment of the costs and benefits of involvement in the region. The dilemma and the questions are as follows:

Many times in the past, groups of people who had their own country, their own language, and their own customs have become part of other larger nations. Often this happens when they lose a war. Sometimes a treaty is signed in which a larger nation swallows up a smaller one. Despite the fact that they become part of another country, these peoples often keep their language and customs and continue to live on the same land. They may continue to do this for one hundred years or more.

One example of this is Yugoslavia. Created by other bigger countries, Yugoslavia brought together Croats, Serbs, and Muslims. These are three groups with different customs, religions, and a long history of fighting each other. For a long time, they lived peacefully. Recently, this has changed. Yugoslavia has fallen apart with each group wanting its own country. Things are particularly difficult in one part, Bosnia. People of all three groups have lived together in the same place. Now they are fighting each other to get as much of the land as they can. The results have been terrible. Thousands of ordinary men, women, and children have died and tens of thousands have lost their homes. There are many reports of brutality and torture on all sides. The United States is now trying to decide whether or not it should intervene militarily in the conflict.

Introductory question:

1. What do you think? Would we be better off getting involved and trying to stop the conflict or would we be better off to not get involved and let events take their course?

Why do you say this?

(N.B. At this point the interviewee will mention certain concerns or values. The

meaning of each should be probed with such questions as: What do you mean by this? Why is this important?)

Initial follow-up questions:

1. What does the United States gain from getting involved? What are the benefits?
   (Ask the following about each benefit mentioned.)
   a. What do you mean by _____ ?
   b. Why is _____ desirable?
   (After probing each benefit mentioned, ask the following.)
   c. You have mentioned several benefits. *(List them.)* Which of these is most important? Why?
   d. Which of these is least important? Why?
2. What does the United States stand to lose by getting involved? What are the costs for us?
   (Ask the following about each cost mentioned.)
   a. What do you mean by _____ ?
   b. Why is _____ undesirable?
   (After probing each cost mentioned, ask the following.)
   c. You have mentioned several costs. *(List them.)* Which of these is most important? Why?
   d. Which of these is least important? Why?
3. Given _____ *(most important benefit)_____* and ___ *(most important cost)_____* do you think it is worth getting involved in Bosnia or not? Why?

As in the other sections of the interview, additional concerns were introduced to further explore the interviewee's evaluations. Here, however, this was done in two separate steps. First, explicitly economic considerations were introduced. After the interviewee responded to the initial questions, additional contradictory considerations were introduced at the sequential, linear, and systematic levels. The questions were as follows:

Some people say the United States should not get involved. What must guide our decisions is our national interest—what is good or bad for the United States. Generally this means economic considerations: what will improve the general well-being of the country, perhaps provide more jobs or enable our industries to develop and progress. When the general well-being of the country is not endangered, the United States should not get involved in the affairs of other countries. Bosnia is a little country, one that has almost no economic effect on the United States. Therefore it makes no sense to spend American tax-payers' money and risk American lives.

1. What do you think?
2. Why do you think this?

Follow-up questions:

If Against Intervention:

1. What if the continued conflict in Bosnia did have a major impact on the U.S. economy? In fact, it affected jobs here in ____ so that you might lose your job. Your life will be affected and you will have less—less money to pay house bills, car bills, and so on. Would you want the United States to get in-volved in Bosnia? Why or Why not?

[Sequential Manipulation]

2. What if it didn't affect you directly, but people you care about are affected. Perhaps your parents income is reduced, people in your community suf-fer. Prices go up and incomes go down. After all a country has a responsi-bility to take care of its people. It should protect them. In this case, would you want the United States to do something about Bosnia? Why or why not?

[Linear Manipulation]

3. What if the damage to the economy was severe enough that people began to lose their faith in government. Respect for the rule of law began to dissolve. People began to favor more efficient totalitarian rule, dictatorship, over democracy. Don't you think a government should move to defend itself to save its own principles, principles such as freedom of speech and equality? Why or why not?

[Systematic Manipulation]

(N.B. Be sure to probe the interviewee's understanding of principles mentioned and why she/he values them.)

If Favors Intervention:

1. The decision to intervene, to send troops or other kinds of support, costs money. This could require raising taxes, leaving you with less money. Let's say this is necessary to fund a major commitment by the U.S. government and your life becomes a lot less comfortable. Your take-home pay is reduced enough that making home and car payments is a problem. Do you still think that the United States should intervene? Why or why not?

[Sequential Manipulation]

2. What if the United States decided to engage in a form of military or police

action in Bosnia. You knew if this happened you would be drafted to go. Would you still want the United States to intervene? Why or why not?

[Sequential Manipulation]

3. The decision to intervene could require committing tens of thousands of troops. The Nazis did this in World War II and were still unable to control the country. Such a move could cost the United States an enormous amount of money and affect the well-being of our already weak economy. Lots of people would remain out of work and others would lose their jobs. The country would suffer. If this were to happen, do you think the United States should still intervene? Why or why not?

[Linear Manipulation]

4. What if the damage was so severe that the people began to lose faith in the government. Respect for the rule of law began to dissolve and people began to favor more efficient totalitarian rule, dictatorship, over democracy. Don't you think a government should move to defend itself to save its own principles, such as freedom of speech and equality? Why or why not?

[Systematic Manipulation]

(N.B. Be sure to probe the interviewee's understanding of principles mentioned and why she/he values them.)

Following this discussion of economic dimensions of the foreign policy decision, issues of moral and political principle were explicitly introduced. After the interviewee responded to the initial questions, additional contradictory considerations were introduced at the sequential, linear, and systematic levels. The questions were as follows:

Some people believe that it is appropriate to intervene in the affairs of another country, indeed to go to war, when certain moral and political principles are violated. Examples might be principles such as all individuals are created equal or all people should have the right to freely express themselves and to vote for who will govern them. In Bosnia, it is clear that both principles are badly violated. The conflict is filled with discrimination and the people of none of the groups have any real control over their leadership. In a case such as this the United States should intervene, with the army if necessary.

1. What do you think? Why?

(N.B. Probing the subject's response be sure to examine both military and non-military intervention and probe for differences in evaluation which may be associated with each.)

If Favors Intervention:

1. Remember that what is going on in Bosnia does not affect you personally in any way. It is a little country located 9,000 miles away and has no effect on your life.

   a. Even if what is going on there is wrong, is it really worth spending our money on their problem? Why or why not?

   b. Is it worth risking American lives in an armed intervention? Why or why not?

   [Sequential Manipulation]

2. There may be problems that we would like to fix, but countries should be responsible for themselves. Just because we are big and powerful, we shouldn't be the world's policeman. Even if our intention is to help, we should not interfere in the internal and private business of other countries.

   a. Does it make sense to spend our money on their problem? Why or why not?

   b. Is it worth risking American lives in an armed intervention? Why or why not?

   [Linear Manipulation]

3. Our belief that what is going on in Bosnia is wrong reflects our fundamental values. These values reflect the society in which we have grown up and been educated. Other societies have their own definition of right and wrong that might be quite different than our own. When one country attacks another it often does so because it believes itself to be good and the other country to be evil. This is just another way of one country forcing its values on another, often weaker country.

   a. Aren't we thinking of doing just that in Bosnia? Why or why not?

   [Systematic Manipulation]

If Against Intervention:

1. Remember that what is going on in Bosnia may affect you personally. Everyone sees the news about what is going on in Bosnia. If no one tries to do anything, people may learn that when they have power they can do whatever they like. Someday some group may acquire power here in the United States and try the same thing. You and people like you may be the target.

   a. Thinking about this, don't you think we should be trying to do something in Bosnia? Why or why not?

   [Sequential Manipulation]

2. What is going on in Bosnia is wrong. People are dying. It is the responsibility of countries that have power and money to stop the killing. Countries

that have power also have responsibility and must meet that responsibility. We should do something to stop the fighting in Bosnia.

   a. Thinking about this, don't you think we should be trying to do something in Bosnia? Why or why not?

[Linear Manipulation]

3. We believe that what is going on in Bosnia is wrong. This reflects our ideas of right and wrong. It is the essence of what we are as individuals and as a people. If we fail to act in the world in a way that reflects those ideals, we reduce them to mere words. By not acting in Bosnia, not only do we fail them there, but we also fail ourselves here.

   a. What do you think? Why?

[Systematic Manipulation]

Concluding Comments

I would like to close with a few comments about the actual conduct of the interview. The interview is semistructured. It does not demand rigid adherence to either the order or the substance of the questions in the interview protocol. Remember the aim of the interview is to explore the sense or meaning of the interviewee's evaluations. Consequently, while interviewers are instructed to address all the questions included in the manual, they are also asked to explore the connections that the interviewee makes. The latter often leads to questions that are at a considerable remove from the substantive terrain charted in the interview.

There is an added bonus accrued by following this subject-oriented research strategy. The people being interviewed, regardless of their educational background or level of reasoning, typically enjoy the interview. Many of the interviewees spontaneously made comments after the completion of the interview such as "how interesting it was," "how it was a lot more fun than I expected," or "how it gave me something to think about." This reaction also reflects the fact that interviewers are instructed to always be affirming and supportive of the interviewee's responses. Even when contrary scenarios are introduced, this is done gently and sympathetically. In addition, interviewers attempt to support whatever line of response the interviewee subsequently adopts.

The interviewee's enjoyment of the interview yields a practical, methodological advantage. It insures ongoing interest and cooperation from the interviewee. For those with experience of conducting close-ended, tightly structured interview protocols, the value of this will be clear. Often with surveys such as the National Election Study conducted in the United States, interviewees get quickly frustrated with being forced into limited response choices and being unable to introduce additional considerations. They begin to feel that the interviewer is not really interested in what they think or have to say. The net result is interviewees often lose interest after the first fifteen minutes and respond rather mechanically thereafter. This is almost never a problem with our interviews.

Apart from its advantages, open-ended, semistructured interviews are difficult to conduct. In our experience, there are several difficulties that often emerge. They may prove particularly intractable and disquieting for relatively inexperienced interviewers. This said, any interviewer should keep these in mind while interviewing.

First, the subject-oriented quality of the interview may create a situation where the interviewer loses control of the interview to the interviewee. This happens when the interviewee introduces a quick succession of novel concerns such that the interviewer does not have adequate opportunity to probe the significance of any one of them. While following the interviewee's train of thought, the interviewer must interject periodically and insist on a closer consideration of some of the points made.

Second, the interviewer may find that she cannot complete the interview. Given the practical constraints of time, the willingness to follow the interviewee's lead occasionally does not allow sufficient time to pose all the questions included in the protocol. This is not a problem so long as sufficiently rich data is collected to facilitate a confident interpretation of the underlying structure of the interviewee's evaluations. This said, the interviewer should attempt to cover all the protocol questions.

Third, some interviewees do not respond well to open-ended questions. Some people are shy; others may be intimidated by the interview situation. Individuals who reason in a sequential manner may not be comfortable with talk that is divorced from actually doing things. In any of these cases, the interviewer's interpersonal skills become critical. Two considerations are particularly important. First, one must be supportive of the interviewee. Acknowledge that it can be difficult to talk in such a situation and make it clear that to have such a difficulty is perfectly acceptable and perhaps common. Second, one must be especially sensitive to the interviewee's interests and follow them as they emerge.

Fourth, some interviewees will share much the same social background as the interviewer. As a result, they will address questions in much the same way as the interviewer would. The danger here is that because understanding the interviewee's responses is apparently easy and straightforward, the interviewer may fail to adequately probe their meaning. In such instances, the interviewer must take particular care to probe the responses given.

ANALYSIS OF THE OPEN-ENDED
INTERVIEW DATA

Oriented by structural pragmatic considerations, the coding of the open-ended responses to the interview is a highly interpretative activity. As such, the method used here is even more demanding than that of typical content analyses of open-ended data. In most such analyses, it is presumed that author and reader understand the text being analyzed in basically the same way. Clearly there will be differences. The author or, as in our case, the speaker may express unusual beliefs or values and she may associate them with one another in novel ways. Despite these substantive differences, it is assumed that the basic quality of how she associates beliefs, values, and actions and the formal quality her conception of these objects reflect universal qualities of human reasoning. Consequently, the content analysis focuses on the substance of the text to be analyzed and emphasizes variations or similarities in the content or the theme from one text to another.

In structural pragmatic research such a commonality of meaning cannot be assumed. Instead the analysis of an interview is predicated on the assumption that there may be very little shared understanding between the person interviewed and the person analyzing the interview text. Moreover this may not simply be a matter of the particular substance of what each of them believes or values or of the particular associations each infers. Rather the interviewee and the coder may differ in the quality of the representations they construct and the connections they forge among them. In this vein, the substance of what is said is initially only a point of departure for the interpretative analysis of the underlying quality of the interviewee's reasoning. Through examining a number of the conceptual relationships and definitions an individual offers, an attempt is made to determine the underlying structure of the meaning she typically constructs. This then provides a basis for returning to the substance of what an individual has said and for better understanding its meaning.

In the research reported here, the interpretation of the interviews is oriented by the definition of three types of thinking—sequential, linear, and systematic. Consequently coders must understand the nature of each of these three types very well. This requires considerable training. To provide the requisite theoretical background, coders were required to read the same texts as the interviewers. In several group discussions, there was a focus on issues pertaining to the structural pragmatic analysis of textual materials with particular attention to the distinction among the three types of reasoning. Following this, coders were given a transcript of one section of an interview (personal, domestic, or foreign policy) that, unbeknownst to the coders, had already been coded as linear. They were then asked to go through the interview, make a determination of the nature of the reasoning of the interviewee, and be prepared to defend that judgment by copious reference to the interview itself. This task was then repeated two more times using interviews that had been judged sequential and systematic. This process was then repeated using each of the other two sections of the interview.

The preparation of coders is obviously an extensive and time-consuming exercise. That said, I believe the benefits clearly justify the effort. On one hand, the interpretative coding of interview materials is an inescapably difficult enterprise. Coders are necessarily forced to draw on their own analytical skills to go beyond the substance of what is presented and abstract the formal qualities of the weave of judgments and evaluations that the subject makes. Failure to properly prepare coders will result in mistaken assessments and low reliability between coders. On the other hand, this preparation is not simply a matter of rote learning of proper technique or procedure. To the contrary, the preparation is clearly an educational exercise. Coders are asked to understand a body of theoretical literature and use it to make sense of diverse materials. Students who are learning to code recognize this immediately. The result is typically much more enthusiasm and energy than is displayed by research associates who perform relatively simple, repetitive tasks.

As suggested by the training of the coders, the analysis of interviews depends on a good understanding of the three types of thinking and the kind of evaluation associated with each. A description of these three types of evaluation was presented in considerable detail in chapters 3, 4, and 5. These provide the framework for the interpretation of the interview texts. They are supplemented by coding guides. These provide coders with a relatively brief description of how the different modes of evaluating would be manifest by the specific issues raised in each section of the interview. It should be kept in mind that these coding guides are supplemental. Adequate use of the guides requires a general understanding of the structural pragmatic approach and a good working knowledge of the three types of thinking.

The following are the coding categories that were provided to assist in the in-

terpretation of the personal section of the interview—that is, the section dealing with an evaluation of a significant other and sacrificing to help that person.

Sequential. The focus is on sequences, unfolding series of events, and
the feelings they evoke. These feelings are sensory, concrete, and egocentric. Thus, sequential reasoning may lead to the decision not to steal because this will lead to a sequence of being shot at, being caught, going to
prison, and feeling miserable. Alternatively, it may lead to the choice to
act to save the other because "I love him." This love, however, is later revealed to revolve around the fact that the other does specific pleasurable
things or makes one feel good. When asked about helping if the other is
not pleasant or nice, the latter line of evaluation may lead to a decision
not to steal even if this leads to the other dying. The sequential nature of
the evaluation is also reflected in the repair of a bad sequence. Thus having decided to steal and then having determined stealing is bad because
it leads to some painful end, sequential evaluation may repair the problem by simply returning events to their original position. This might involve suggesting that the stolen drug be returned or that the druggist just
make more of the drug. Evaluations may reflect an empathic confusion
of the other's feelings, the attributes of the event, and one's own feelings
in the event. A focus on the pain or fear of the dying other may consequently lead to a decision to steal. Sequential evaluation may assimilate
the language of higher order evaluations, but these are redefined in similar terms. For example, the issue of fairness may be invoked, but here it
simply means "getting what I want."

Linear. The focus is on specific actors and concrete observable actions
that are evaluated as desirable, good, or correct. This evaluation may involve linking the focal act or actor to another that has already been evaluated. The linkage may be causal or categorical. When causally related, actions are evaluated in terms of their causes or consequences and actors
are evaluated in terms of what they do or have done to them. Thus, the
action of stealing may be deemed good because it saves someone who is
valued or because it is motivated by a good intention. Another person
may be valued because she does good things or because good people like
her. In the case of categorical relationships, actions and actors are evaluated by the category to which they belong. Another person may be
judged to be good because she is a member of a group that is positively
valued. In addition, stealing may be judged negatively because it is something that only a bad person would do. Linear evaluation may also intro-

duce moral considerations expressly or implicitly by invoking concrete standards of how one should specifically behave in the circumstances in question. Here appropriateness is determined by reference to a particular cultural convention, role requirement, or normal practice. Thus, the act of stealing may be negatively valued because it entails breaking the law. Alternatively, it may be positively valued insofar as it conforms to the norm that friends should help one another. The conventions or normal practices called upon in this light are the bases of justification rather than its object. In this context, there may be some concern for fairness or justice, but this is typically equated with doing what is correct. At best, it is framed as an issue of distribution, but it is equated with a conventional procedure for allocating rewards (e.g., an eye for an eye or taking turns).

Systematic. The activity of stealing is seen as one trajectory of activity or one interaction interwoven among several others, including helping another person, placing oneself at risk, and depriving another of her property. At this first level of consideration, actions may have multiple effects and be assessed complexly—that is, as having positive and negative ramifications. These are determined relative to the personal preferences of the people involved and to the social and legal conventions that apply. At a second level, these various dimensions of the interaction are judged by their systemic consequences. Thus, the act of stealing or the failure to steal may be evaluated in terms of its effect on the integrity and coherence of the personality or self-definition of the thief or her beneficiary. Alternatively, the needs of the community, as an organization and regulator of social life, might be invoked. In this context, the theft may be judged by its implications for the functioning of the community as a cultural as well as a social system. The law governing theft may be judged similarly. These pragmatic considerations may be complemented by moral ones that revolve around the relations between systems—either at the same level (individual to individual) or at different levels (individual to community). Here general principles are evoked and then applied deductively to the judgment of exchanges and conventions. For example, a principle of human sociality and mutual obligation between individuals may be invoked. In this context, stealing and the breaking of the law may be judged to be legitimate. Similarly the issue of fairness will be constructed in these terms. Alternatively, some principle of the necessary dependence and subordination of the individual to the community may be asserted, and an act of personal loyalty that involves selflessly helping a loved one may be judged illegitimate.

The next set of categories was provided to help distinguish between sequential, linear, and systematic evaluations of the domestic political issue. The reader will remember the focus here is on the display of Mapplethorpe's controversial photographs in the city museum of a small, relatively conservative city.

Sequential. The focus is on the sequence of unfolding events, the story of Mapplethorpe as told. The sequence presented may evoke feelings as it involves the subject directly in the story, as global events are matched (in sequential fashion) to the subject's own remembered experience, or as the subject empathizes with the observed or imagined feelings of characters in the story (through a confusion of other's feeling, attributes of the event, and one's own response to the event). Thus the exhibition may be negatively valued because it leads to people being upset or hurt. Moreover, this may extend to the fact that their upset may make them angry with the director such that he too is hurt. The effect of the labeling of an event as good or bad is often evident in sequential evaluations as well. Thus, the exhibition may simply be regarded as bad because it involves photos of homosexuality and the topic is just a bad or obscene one. Here there is no sense of why it is bad, it is just bad. The evaluations may also be more straightforwardly egocentric. The exhibition may be negatively valued because the photos evoke personal disgust, or the expression of disapproval is part of a sequence that leads to reward by others. Often one's expression of one's opinion, negative or positive, is defended because one should do as one wants. Comparative judgment of several alternative courses of action is difficult. There is a tendency to remain anchored in a single sequence at a time and evaluate it in terms of the associated feelings. Judgment here will tend not to focus on concerns such as the community or principles of interpersonal relationship. These are little understood or valued. To the degree to which they are brought up, it is merely a matter of repeating oft-heard slogans. For example, the notion of fairness might be raised, but here it is equated with a sequence of events that is rewarding.

Linear. The focus is on the specific actions and actors presented. These are evaluated in terms of their active or categorical links to other actions and actors (which may be remote in space and time), which have already been evaluated. This leads to the determination of whether the actions and actors are desirable or good. Thus the exhibition may be negatively valued because it causes people to act in the manner depicted, which will in turn produce results that they do not want. Similarly it may be positively valued because it "opens up people's minds and gets them to think," something authorities and valued others have declared to be a good thing. Alternatively the exhibition may be judged good because it has been chosen by the director (an expert) or because it is associated with people I like such as artists or homosexuals. Similarly, the exhibition may be negatively evaluated because the action depicted falls into a class of actions, homosexual acts, that are already defined as negative. Claims of correct behavior may also be introduced. These might include the notion that artists have the right to express themselves, that people have the right to choose what they see, that the decision regarding exhibitions is the proper preserve of the museum director, that people ought to be exposed to new things, and so on. Cultural mores, social traditions, moral imperatives, and law all enter in here on an equal footing as conventions regarding correct performance of roles and rituals. These judgments tend to be global and univalent. For example, once the photographs are judged to be bad because they depict a bad act, they may also be judged artistically worthless or aesthetically unattractive. Because they focus on specific action relations, these global judgments may be altered when the interviewer introduces alternative foci (e.g., the effects on other actors or the relation to other cultural norms). Where there is no clear authoritative direction upon which to draw, the ensuing value conflict is often confusing and discomforting. It will often lead to some form of dissonance reduction.

Systematic. The focus is on the various dimensions of the problem in light of the multisided relationships between the director, the artist, the city council, and the public. At the same time, there is a clear recognition of the place and needs of the community as the system that both regulates social exchange and defines social meaning and value. The preferences of the various players and particular social conventions are regarded as first order concerns, ones which have significance, but must be judged in light of second order considerations. For example, the artist's desire to show his photographs or the prevalent cultural norm of freedom of expression will be evaluated in terms of the broader consequences for the integrity and functioning of the artist or the community. When applied to varying circumstances, these overarching values may lead to very different judgments of the same activity enacted in different systemic contexts. Thus, the exhibition of photographs may be deemed appropriate and functional in the context of a multicultural progressive city with a significant homosexual population but unnecessary and destructive in a homogeneous, traditional city. Moral imperatives regarding the relationship between systems may be invoked when judging interpersonal exchanges and social conventions. The problem presented in the interview is particularly difficult because it involves nested systems, that of the individual citizen as a personality and the state as a community of citizens. The systematic thinker will often attempt to allow each system its integrity and to meet its needs. However, this is difficult and will often devolve in a tendency to focus on one level as systemic (and thus the source of meaning and value) and the other as derivative.

The final set of categories was provided to guide the assessment of the section of the interview that dealt with American involvement in Bosnia-Herzegovina. The question here was whether the United States should be involved and why.

Sequential. To the degree to which international events are considered, the focus is on specific isolated concrete sequences of unfolding events presented on television or vividly narrated by others. Such a sequence of events may be judged consequential to the degree to which it is associated with pleasurable or painful sensations or feelings. The ensuing confusion of other-event-self may yield an empathic response. Thus being able to observe an American soldier's joy at hitting a target or a mother's pain at the maiming of her child may evoke the same feeling in the observer. A sequence of events may also evoke feelings if an event evokes the memory of other events embedded in another sequence that was experienced as rewarding or painful. For example, events may be presented as one in which Serbia is bullying the Bosnian Muslims, and this evokes a memory of a sequence in which the subject remembers being bullied. The two sequences may be subjectively fused and the international event sequence may be evaluated accordingly. Evaluations may also be voiced if this expression is associated with pleasurable sequences. For example, if other people reward the subject for condemning the Serbs, then she will do so even if she really does not understand who the Serbs are and the meaning of what they did.

Linear. The focus is on action and actors as discrete units of analysis to be evaluated as good, desirable, or correct. Linear evaluations can readily judge the specific actors (e.g., the United States, Muslims, Croats, and Serbs) and concrete actions (e.g.. the decision to send troops, the bombing of Sarajevo, the burning of houses, the raping of women, etc.) involved in an international incident. Actions and actors such as these are evaluated in three ways. First, by the already evaluated causes and outcomes with which they are associated. Thus intervention may be negatively valued because it will cost money and lives or because other nations will regard us negatively as a result. Second, actions and actors are evaluated by their categorical identification. For example, American intervention may be regarded as a good thing because the United States is a good country and therefore the things that it does are good. Similarly, the Serbs are viewed as part of the group of Russian allies. If this group is negatively valued, the Serbs will be also. Third, actions are evaluated by the degree to which they conform to concrete behavioral norms. For example, American intervention in Bosnia may be negatively valued because it is linked to the norm that one should not meddle in other people's private business. The actions and actors judged in these three ways tend to produce global evaluations of the object considered. This overall evaluation is unidimensional and will be sustained even in the face of specific contrary evidence. This will involve the reinterpretation, denial, or devaluation of the evidence. For example, the Muslims, a good people, may be observed to engage in a bad act (torturing Serbs), but this act may be redefined as a good act (it helped stop Serbian aggression) or its connection to the Muslims reduced (the circumstance forced them to do it).

Systematic. The focus is on interactions, conventions of specific behavior, and cultural values and definitions. Examples would include the mutual aggression of Serbs and Croats, the convention that Europe should look after affairs in their own "backyard," or the value of national sovereignty. On one hand, these are evaluated by examining them in relation to the functioning of political systems. For example, the systematic thinker might evaluate the conflict in Bosnia in terms of the stability of political systems in the region. In this light, the assertion of Serbian power could be judged to have a disintegrating effect on the stability of the area and be judged negatively. Alternatively, American involvement might be evaluated in terms of its consistency with the cultural values of the United States. Thus involvement might be seen as an affirmation of the American way of life and judged positively. On the other hand, interactions and conventions may be judged by the application of general principles of how systems ought to interrelate. Thus, the idea of assassinating the Serbian president might be judged to be an effective military option but ultimately condemned because it does not conform to a principle of international exchange based on free and open negotiation oriented to establishing cooperation.

The procedure for coding was as follows. All interviews were first divided into their three sections: personal, domestic political, and foreign policy. Each section was then coded separately by two coders. Each coder was unaware of the identity of the interviewee or of how the interviewee's performance on the other sections had been judged. Each coder also had no knowledge of the other coder's assessment of the section. Inter-coder reliability was 86 percent. In the 20 cases of disagreement (out of 144 total), the coders met, discussed the cases, and an agreement was reached. The results of the research are presented in the following chapter.

Chapter Seven Results
of the Empirical Research:
Julie, Barbara, and Bill

In this chapter, the results of the empirical research are presented in two parts. In the first part, there is a summary discussion of the results. The reader will note that only the most rudimentary of statistics are reported. Given the clarity of the results, any additional statistical information would simply be redundant. In the second part, an attempt is made to flesh out the numbers provided in the first part. To this end, extensive excerpts of three exemplary interviews, one sequential, one linear, and one systematic, are included. This is done so that the reader may directly examine the nature of the structural similarities across subject matter and the structural differences between individuals who have been identified in the analysis of the interviews. To indicate how this analysis was done, the presentation includes both the text of the interview and the notes made in the analysis of their underlying structure.

SUMMARY STATEMENT OF RESULTS

The aim of the empirical research was to explore two hypotheses. The first was that there is a general structure underlying the way in which an individual evaluates very different kinds of situations. To test this hypothesis, subjects were asked to evaluate three very different situations: one involving a close personal friend, relative, or lover; another involving the display of controversial art in a conservative community; and a third involving American involvement in Bosnia. In the manner described in the preceding chapter, each subject's evaluation of each situation was probed in depth and then analyzed separately. The result was that forty-two, or 88 percent, of the forty-eight subjects evaluated the three different situations in the same manner. When considering this result, it should be kept in mind that this high level of cross-situational consistency is evident across matters about which subjects were likely to have highly variable levels of information and interest.

The claim regarding the structural consistency of subject's evaluations was also supported in a second, albeit more indirect way. The reader will remember that in each section of the interview, alternative scenarios were introduced that were specifically designed to stimulate structurally different considerations. To the degree to which the quality of the individual interviewee's evaluations did not change in response to these manipulations, a single assessment of the structure of the subject's evaluation of the situation becomes possible and assessments of different coders should more readily coincide. This was clearly the case as indicated by the inter-coder reliability of 88 percent. For 124 of the 144 separate texts (the three different parts of the interview for each of the forty-eight subjects), coders came to a single and common judgment of the structure of the individual subject's evaluation despite the attempts that were made to induce the interviewee to consider the question in qualitatively different ways.

The second hypothesis examined was that different individuals may evaluate the same question or situation in structurally different ways. The differences are suggested by the threefold typology of reason and evaluation offered in chapters 3, 4, and 5. In this part of the analysis, all forty-eight subjects were included. Six of the subjects were scored at the same level on only two of the three parts of the interview. For the present purposes, these six were assigned a general score based on their comparable performance on two parts of the interview. Our results indicate that different individuals did evaluate the same issues in qualitatively different ways. Asked to judge the same situations, eleven of the subjects responded in a sequential manner, twenty-seven responded in linear manner, and ten responded in a systematic manner.

In sum, the overall results of the research provide strong support for the twin hypotheses that a given individual may evaluate quite different concerns in a structurally identical manner and that different individuals may evaluate the same concerns in structurally different ways.

SAMPLE INTERVIEWS: JULIE, BARBARA, AND BILL

The foregoing presentation of the results, while strongly confirming, is limited by its abstraction. To provide more substance, the actual text of some of the interviews conducted is presented here. Following common practice, this could have been done by presenting short one- or two-paragraph excerpts from a number of different interviews that illustrate the differences among sequential, linear, and systematic evaluations of the personal, domestic political, and foreign policy issues. This has the advantage of presenting more of the variety of the substance of what is said. I believe, however, that this advantage is more than offset by certain disadvantages. First, in my experience, the meaning of short excerpts is typically ambiguous. Although the substance of the narrative may appear clear, its underlying structure can only be properly assessed in the context of the whole of what an interviewee had to say about a given topic. Frequently a certain set of comments is meaningful only in relation to remarks made much earlier or later in the interview. Second, the reader is presented with a highly truncated version of the data. In the actual coding of interviews, the whole of a given section of the interview (personal, domestic political, or foreign policy) was reviewed and an overall assessment of that section was made. Thus the reader is not presented with data comparable to that evaluated by the coders. Third, the presentation of short excerpts from various interviews does not allow for a clear examination of the continuities of a given individual's reasoning and evaluation across different questions and subject matter. This is a key focus of the current research. For these reasons, I have decided on the less common strategy of presenting most of the text of just three interviews—one sequential, one linear, and one systematic. This demands more of the reader's patience. I believe, however, that the effort will be rewarded by the greater familiarity it offers with both the interviewing and coding phases of the research.

In the following pages, the text of the interviews with three people—Julie, Barbara, and Bill—is presented. Julie was an energetic, outgoing woman. At the time of the interview, she was thirty-two years old and happily married. Julie was well educated. She had graduated from college and had received a masters degree in business administration. She had an executive position in a small company and earned $84,000 per year. Julie's manner of evaluating was scored linear on all three parts of the interview. Barbara had a somewhat similar background to Julie. She had been married, but was now divorced and living with her daughter whom she discusses in the personal section of the interview. At the time of the interview, Barbara was forty-one years old. She was also well educated. She had graduated from college and had spent some time in graduate school before opting for a law degree. She had worked as a lawyer, but dissatisfied, she had left her firm and was working as a chief cook in a restaurant. Barbara's salary in recent years had ranged from $45,000 to 70,000 per year. Barbara's evaluations were judged to be systematic. The third interviewee, Bill, was quite different from the other two. In addition to being male, Bill was much more a member of what might be referred to as the dispossessed. At the time of the interview, Bill was fifty-nine years old. He was single and living with his brother. Bill was relatively uneducated. During his school years, he finished only grammar school. Showing considerable initiative in later life, Bill started a course of high-school-level home study. He continued for two years but in the end did not complete the course. Bill was only occasionally employed. At the time of the interview, he did not have a regular job. Before this, he had worked in the mailroom of a newspaper performing various simple manual tasks. Bill typically earned less than $11,000 per year. Bill's way of evaluating was judged to be sequential.

Rather than presenting each interview in turn, they are organized by topic. First, each interviewee's response to the personal section of the interview is presented. This is followed by their responses to the domestic political section. (To conserve space, the final section of the interview on foreign policy is not presented here but is available on the Internet at http://aris.ss.uci.edu/polpsych/polpsych.html.) This is done to allow the reader to compare the differently structured evaluations of the same subject matter. At the same time, by flipping pages, the reader can follow a single individual's evaluation of the different topics. Throughout, the interview text is presented in the left-hand column and the coding notes and interpretative comments are presented in the right-hand column.

THREE EVALUATIONS OF A PERSONAL ISSUE

Julie's Linear Evaluation

In the interview, Julie focuses on her husband. Her evaluation of him and her consideration of whether to help him bear all the hallmarks of linear thinking. Julie's evaluations focus on behaviors. These are typically considered with reference to a rule of action, a relatively concrete guide of what is the right, good, or best thing to do. These include: be honest (don't lie), give back to the community (act charitably), don't steal, and help one's spouse. She even notes that she generally believes that for each situation there is a clear rule that suggests what is the right thing to do. These rules are guidelines and justifications. They are foundational and are therefore not themselves subject to justification. When asked to justify such a rule, Julie typically reiterates the rule in different words or simply stipulates it is a good, an obligation, or it is just the right thing to do.

Julie's evaluations also tend to generate evaluative consistency or balance. She relies on evaluative anchors. These are actions or outcomes she knows to be good or bad. Behaviors that are causally or categorically linked to these anchors are then evaluated accordingly. The value of the anchor flows to the value of the behavior. Thus she assumes bad behavior will produce negative or undesirable outcomes. This is evident in her analysis of her friend's use of illegal labor and the consequent guilt that ensues. It is also evident in her assumption that a corporation's level of social responsibility is necessarily linked to its financial success. In the latter regard, it is interesting to note that the link between social responsibility and success is evaluative, not causal. When asked for a causal explanation of the linkage, Julie is somewhat confused and flounders.

Julie's responses are clearly not sequential. The reliance on specific rules of action as the key to her evaluations is simply inconsistent with the immediacy of sequential evaluations. Julie even makes clear at one point that rules must be followed even when it is immediately uncomfortable to do so and that self-sacrifice is required. This kind of reasoning goes well beyond the standards of immediate rewards and punishments that guide most sequential evaluation. In addition, Julie frequently offers clear causal analysis of events thereby going well beyond the retracing of sequences characteristic of sequential thought.

Julie's manner of evaluating is also clearly not systematic. The core of the problem is that Julie constructs rules at only one level of conceptualization, that of the concrete guide to behavior. Higher order rules are not constructed. As a result, she is unable to provide justification for the rules she invokes, nor is she able to integrate them relative to one another. There is also no consideration of people or relationships as integrated systems. Thus evaluation is neither relative nor cast in functional terms.

INTRV.: In order to make this particularly concrete, I
would like to talk about someone who's very
close to you, perhaps a family member or a
very close friend.

SUBJ.: Okay.

INTRV.: Who would that be?

SUBJ.: Um, probably my husband.

INTRV.: Okay, what's his name?

SUBJ.: Marty.

INTRV.: What do you like about him?

SUBJ.: Um, I like him because he's very reasonable and he's very thoughtful, where I'm very reactive, he tends to really think things out and provides me with a different perspective on certain situations. And I like him just because his demeanor and personality, and plus the fact that he um also believes in you know the same principles that I do. Therefore, we can do things together and we don't argue about um the fundamentals of life.

> Begins to speak in general personality terms but discussion centers on traits and ultimately sets of behaviors.
>
> Evaluative anchoring: I like him because he likes what I like.

INTRV.: What are some of those principles?

SUBJ.: Well we believe that people should be honest and individually we try to encourage other people to be honest and it sounds really stupid, but we have friends who you know when we talk about doing taxes or hiring help or this and that. Um, they're not that honest.

> Uses the term "principle," suggesting an abstract overarching concept, but in fact is invoking a specific behavioral rule.

INTRV.: Right.

SUBJ.: And they don't think about it. Marty and I will always try to say, well you know we would never do that, and we don't lecture our friends by any means, but we do try to make them take note of their actions. Even though, I mean it's so stupid what people do sometimes, and they just don't think about it. Like, right now we're in the process of figuring out what we're doing for child care. And we've talked to a lot of our friends and one of our friends said, "Well, we intentionally hired an illegal immigrant, because for us that was the easiest and most cost effective way."

> Note that the "concrete principle" of honesty is juxtaposed to a structurally equivalent behavioral rule of "don't lecture friends."

INTRV.: Right.

SUBJ.: And she said, "You know it's a horrible thing

> Doing a bad thing

to say, but that's what we have to live with,"
and I can tell she felt bad about it, but she
went ahead and did it anyway. I don't know
how she justified it, but she justified it because
(1) it was easy enough to do, (2) she didn't
think there was gonna be any negative impact
from it, and (3) it was cost effective. But now
I think it's been just about two years since she
did this, and um now I can tell she had second
thoughts, she has second thoughts about
doing that. And you know it's something that
we wouldn't want to deal with. So, you know.

produces bad
consequences. This
exemplifies the flow of
evaluation from anchor
to that with which it is
associated.

INTRV.: So it's that kind of pragmatic dishonesty?

SUBJ.: Yeah. Yeah, and it just happens all the time.
So um what was the question?

INTRV.: What some of the principles are.

SUBJ.: Oh (laughs) yeah, so honesty is a real big one
for us. We try to hang on to that one, and um
we believe that we have been very fortunate,
one, to be the people that we are and, two, to
have found each other. So we just feel very
lucky about our um situation. And so um he
and I believe that we have things to give back
to the community, whether it be a little
monetary donations or services. And um so
it's like, before I got married, I dated people
who really didn't believe that and it was fine,
but it was hard to always have to explain to
them why I wanted to volunteer for this or
that or whatever, instead of um going to gym
or riding a bike or whatever.

Introduction of another
behavioral convention,
of giving back to the
community.

In discussion of herself
and husband, note overlap
of what is similar and
what is linked by liking.

INTRV.: Why is that important to you and Marty, to
each other?

SUBJ.: Really, I think, I just think that I've been
really fortunate, and um being somebody who
reads the paper and tries to keep up with
current events, um I just think that it's an obligation for me at least to give back, to just do
whatever. And not to, cause I've met saints.
And we don't do that. But we certainly, I've

Request for justifying
cannot be answered.
Just repeats that it is an
obligation or rule.

come to realize because I've been around for a little while now, that we give um far more of our time in resources than the average individual does, and um it's because we want to, it's not because we need anything back um. We don't um seek recognition for that stuff and it's just really important cause um it's weird, when I think about dying or leaving this planet or whatever, one of the things I want to be remembered for is that I tried to improve the situation in the community, and that's it. It's not that I achieved great things, but that I tried and so I sort of keep that as a principle, and it sounds stupid but . . .

Concerned about the impact on self-image. Implicitly that others regard oneself positively.

INTRV.: Okay. So tell me what it is you dislike about him?

SUBJ.: Um, well one of the things I dislike about him is that he um doesn't hesitate to try to fix things around the house, but he doesn't know how to do them very well, and he's not experienced, we've had this house for three years and um like after the earthquake, we had some cracks, I mean nothing major. It didn't bother me. You know, I just didn't look up, it was on the ceiling. And he felt he needed to fix them, and now it looks worse because he put stuff all over it, he didn't sand it down right and he didn't buy the right color paint, so he has a tendency to want to be handy, but then he doesn't take the time out to really find out what it takes to do that job. And so I don't like that part. I try to stop him from doing stuff like that, but he is getting better at doing them. He has ?? And I don't um, he doesn't like to be around a lot of people for a long period of time. Um, and that's just because of the way he was raised. He is from South Dakota and they lived in a remote area over there, and people are very independent over there. And it's not that they're not friendly, it's

Request about dislikes focuses exclusively on specific behaviors. They are defined by the undesirable result they produce.

Given positive view of Marty there is attempt to mitigate criticism by citing improvement. Maintain balanced judgment.

just they would never think of barging in on one another, and it's sort of, it's a very homogenous Norwegian Lutheran type area that he grew up in. And um, and the way I was raised, it was totally opposite. I mean you know people always dropped by, and my parents didn't mind if the house wasn't clean, the people came by, no big deal. As long as there was food, they'd give them, they would, and I mean I didn't care. When we first got married, I didn't care if people would come over sometimes, and do whatever, but Marty needs his peace time. I mean he will go out and do a lot of things, but he needs a few hours in the week where he can just either veg out in front of the TV or do something in the lawn or something. He um really values his peace, but at the same time, sometimes he gets irritated when we have a lot of people over. Whether it be my family or his family or just friends, it exhausts him to have a lot of people over. Instead of enjoying other people's company, sometimes he considers it sort of as work.

INTRV.: Okay. Let's consider a hypothetical situation. Let's say that Marty develops a serious chronic illness. And this is an illness that will stay with him for the rest of his life. . . . If you had the money, but it represented all your savings, all the money you have in the bank, would you give it to him?

SUBJ.: Yes.

INTRV.: Why?

SUBJ.: Because it would cure him, if he was in bad health I think we would try to do everything possible to improve the situation.

INTRV.: Why is that important to you personally?

SUBJ.: Well, one, he doesn't like to be sick. Two, maybe he couldn't take being at home that much, I mean he likes his job, he likes his

Note the simple causal explanation for both Marty's and later her own typical practice. Moreover this provides a mitigation of the criticism. The cause is not Marty. Marty is merely the effect of another cause, his upbringing, and thus is implicitly less responsible for undesirable behavior. Thus balanced value judgment is maintained.

Choice justified in terms of its desirability. It is valued because it is valued career, and um it's one of the priorities of his life is being his health and being able to do what he wants and more than going to work, or recreation or different things. He is invaluable to have anyone else well . . .

INTRV.: What if you didn't have the money that represents all your savings, uh would you be willing to try to steal the drug?

SUBJ.: No.

INTRV.: Why not?

SUBJ.: Why? I wouldn't know how to do that, I mean break into a lab or something, but um no I think we would, of course he wouldn't ask me to steal perhaps. No we wouldn't do that, we'd try to negotiate some other means of acquiring the drug if we didn't have the money. We would figure something else out.

INTRV.: Why don't you think he wouldn't ask you?

SUBJ.: He wouldn't.

INTRV.: To steal the drug?

SUBJ.: Yeah, he just wouldn't have.

INTRV.: Why not?

SUBJ.: Yeah, I really don't think it would be an option for him. Um, cause um and feel guilty, he'd have all this guilt and wouldn't be so happy about it. Um, you know I think we'd come up with better alternatives then stealing.

INTRV.: Like what?

SUBJ.: Um, well we would probably solicit family and friends, yeah. Or we could negotiate some sort of payment schedule or something else.

INTRV.: What if you were in a situation which is perhaps different from the financial situation you have right now. Um, in which it really was not possible to raise the money. Would you still not consider stealing the drug?

SUBJ.: Yeah. Um, maybe like one of us could assist the scientist and provide ?? services in exchange for his drug, or we can market it

by a desired other.

Husband would not request stealing simply because it is bad.

Further, asking to do a bad act would produce bad consequences—guilt and unhappiness. Note this is considered in isolation of the negative effects of extreme illness.

perhaps or something, and um I mean the idea of stealing is it just wouldn't work.

INTRV.: Why is that?

SUBJ.: Um, it's not something that we would want to get involved in, and you know taking some-body else's property whether it, whether it's socially right or wrong, is just not a good thing to do.

A justification in terms of a rule—stealing is bad

INTRV.: What do you mean by socially right or wrong?

SUBJ.: I mean you know social, you can argue that um the scientist should try to accommodate the people who could most benefit from his drug and shouldn't create a situation where the action of stealing is a real option for those individuals who want the drug, so that people could argue that the drug's not doing any good. It's in his laboratory, obviously, so we might as well take it, but it's still his.

INTRV.: Do you agree with that argument that he should be thinking in terms of "he needs this drug"?

SUBJ.: Um, excuse me, I really do believe there's a balance between profitability or you know capitalism and socialism, there is a happy medium which we call democracy where people should think about their social obliga-tions when they are practiced in business. I mean I think businesses that only focus on their economic priorities eventually do fail.

Here again there is an anchoring of values. Businesses that do bad things will end badly. Note that the link is evaluative, not causal. Julie stumbles when she is asked to offer a causal linkage.

INTRV.: Why is that?

SUBJ.: Because I think um I just can't imagine that a business would be able to succeed without thinking about um the social realities of, you know in this country. I think it would have a tremendous effect in the employees of that business, and um I just it's hard for me to picture an organization that doesn't realize it's social obligation just because we have so many problems right now. I mean even when you talk about um big corporations such as IBM, you know oil companies, they do understand about giving back to the community. I mean they understand that it's part of their economic development strategies to give back to the community. To show that they can sponsor March of Dimes or something. So I think it's very important for businesses and individuals running those businesses to think about their social obligations.

INTRV.: And you're saying that if they don't, they'll tend to feel, demoralize it?

SUBJ.: I just can't imagine that they would be able to succeed without instilling that um moral obligation in their employees and in their products, and just in their whole corporate organization. I mean I think, imagine there could be a business that could succeed with um with it's only intent being profit.

Again the notion of good things occur together.

INTRV.: Why is that necessary for success?

SUBJ.: Um, I think it's important for them to realize their social obligation in order to provide products and services that society wants and needs, like I think um that has to be integrated in their entire business plan and the needs of the community. And even they're only I mean I can't think of a product that doesn't provide society with benefits of some sort, but in providing benefits, I think it's important for them to take a larger picture. And it sounds really confusing, but um I think when businesses realize that there's more than just making the profit margin where they actually become most creative and most innovative in the product that they're producing.

Note again the linkage between success and social responsibility is evaluative. Good flows to good. The request for causal link causes difficulty and confusion because the matter is understood satisfactorily in an evaluative fashion.

INTRV.: Okay. So here's the druggist or the scientist who has created this cure. And it's sort of hard to tell what he has in mind. It seems like he's doing it for profit. Um, do you think it's a reasonable justification that you need the drug and he's not willing to meet that social obligation?

SUBJ.: Um, no I don't think that justifies stealing.

INTRV.: Why not?

SUBJ.: I think stealing is stealing, whether it be $1.50 off your taxes or um taking a box of cookies from the supermarket, I mean it's stealing. You want it now. I mean I, you know I . . . it would be pretty hard for me to justify stealing, the constant, just stealing.

Issue of stealing raised again. It is simply a rule that one should not do it. It is a foundational value, which does not itself require justification

INTRV.: Why is that so important?

SUBJ.: Well, it's just not the right thing to do, I mean (laughs) I mean for things that are obviously wrong to do, you know everybody's parents have told them not to steal, which is obviously unacceptable behavior, so to try to justify it by creating a circumstance in which it seems more permissible, I don't think it makes it anymore right.

Rule is validated with reference to authority and tradition.

INTRV.: Okay. Let's assume that if you did steal it, you would never be caught, no one would find out. Would you consider doing it then?

Interviewer attempts to mitigate negative outcomes.

SUBJ.: Um, I don't think so. I get really guilty about stuff. Um, and I just when I do something bad, I mean I just go through a lot of hassle to try and overcompensate for the bad thing that I did, there would be a lot of over compensating. And I don't, I mean you know. I don't wanna steal it.

Reason is there are still other prices to pay, other negative consequences (e.g., guilt).

INTRV.: Well let's assume again that you and Marty are getting along just fine.

SUBJ.: Um hmm.

INTRV.: You are husband and wife after all, you have a certain obligation to one another.

Interviewer introduces alternative behavioral rule.

SUBJ.: Yep.

INTRV.: If this is the only way that you can get the drug, which would completely change his life, get rid of this disease, don't you have that obligation to him? Isn't it worth that sacrifice even if you?

SUBJ.: You know if you put it that way, and if you

This changes frame of

say that's the only way in the whole wide world, which I have a hard time believing that, but if you said it like that, I would consider it, but I probably would have some-body else do it. You know and get it done that way. Um, you know.

reference and subject now would do it. Primitive, virtually sequential mitigation of having somebody else do it.

INTRV.: Why would you have somebody else do it?

SUBJ.: Oh, cause I'm sure if it got to that point, I could get somebody else to do it who cared about us and they wouldn't have any problem living with it, which is fine. I mean I don't know, but it would just be a weird situation.

This response should have been probed further.

INTRV.: (pause) Okay. One could argue that the issue here is really the druggist's selfishness and um the quality of life is more important than property. Stealing is wrong cause we are talking about his property, but that might be a lesser consideration in this case. So it might be possible to justify this without feeling guilty at all. What do you think about that?

Interviewer introduces question of relation between values and what might be conceived as a higher order principle.

SUBJ.: Yeah, I think a lot of people would feel that way. I mean a lot of people feel that about lesser circumstances, where there isn't a life at stake, but improvement of the life of stake, um some of the stuff I've gone through in terms of training and things is um sort of leaning to the point where I do believe there is a right and a wrong for every circumstance and um that's a very hard way of looking at things, because you get disappointed a lot, but um I'm starting to believe that that is the case, like there is only one truth for every second of life, you know. For every second, things only happen one way, there can't be ten versions of one incident. It's just impossible, you know. Um, so having gone through this process where I do believe there is a right and a wrong, it's just hard for me to justify some of the wrong things that people do that we do.

The principle is reconstructed as another opinion—moreover just a way of wavering, of failing to apply a rule in the proper unflinching manner. Thus does not recognize distinction between rules and principles and does not use the latter to evaluate the former.

INTRV.: How do you determine what's wrong and

what's right in a situation? Most people will disagree.

SUBJ.: Yeah, definitely. If it doesn't hurt anybody, they'll say it's okay. Um, well for me what Marty and I usually do is one is how you feel about it. You know, you obviously feel better about doing right things than doing wrong things. Um, no matter who you are whether you're, I think at least, not that I've interviewed many convicts, but I think when people are doing the wrong things, they know it. Whether they acknowledge it that instant, or afterwards or before, they know it. Whether it's doing you know committing a bank robbery or stealing a candy bar, then they know it. I mean you just feel it.

Evaluative anchoring and flow of value from anchor to its associates.

INTRV.: It's kind of like intuition?

SUBJ.: Yeah. I mean no matter who you are um your teacher or your parents or somebody in your life made you realize that it feels good to do the right thing, and it doesn't feel so good to do the wrong thing. Unfortunately, some people don't mind not feeling so good, which is fine, but um you know. It is by intuition. I mean that's one basic way of knowing what's right and wrong, and then . . .

Simple causal explanation

INTRV.: Where do you think this intuition comes from?

SUBJ.: I think a lot of it comes from your childhood teachings. Um, you know if you have somebody in your life like I had um who always said, I mean this is the only thing she ever said, my mother always said, "Don't ever do anything that you don't want somebody to do to you." That was just her motto, whatever it was, that's what she came back with. And so um it's things like that that you learn as a child. Um, that's I think where your intuition and just the foundation of yourself comes from.

Simple linear causal explanation.

Barbara's Systematic Evaluation

Barbara constructs her significant other and her evaluation of how and when to help her in a very different way than Julie. This becomes apparent at the outset. Barbara chooses to focus the discussion on her daughter. She conceives of her daughter not so much with regard to the particular concrete things she does, but rather in terms of the nature of how she thinks and interacts. The focus of consideration thus shifts from specific actions to the connections between actions (or ideas and statements). These connections are in turn evaluated relative to some higher standard. In this regard, Barbara begins to articulate a normative, idealized, and highly abstract notion of a self as a system. It has clear functional requisites, some of which are related to self-maintenance and others which are related to self-realization or self-elaboration. The value of the connections her daughter makes, that is, the meanings she constructs and her manner of engaging others, is judged accordingly.

This kind of evaluation is evident throughout Barbara's consideration of the decision as to whether to give money or steal on her daughter's behalf. At various points, she constructs the problem at two levels: a higher one involving the requisites of the functioning of the self-system and a lower one focused on specific rules of action. She then both interprets and evaluates the lower level concerns relative to those of the higher one. In this way she is able to consider the significance and value of such rules as a mother is obligated to her child and a person should not steal. Similarly, Barbara frequently takes the potentially linear concerns introduced by the interviewer and explicitly suggests that they must be understood relative to some more principled or systemic context in order for their meaning and value to be properly assessed. The two-level quality of Barbara's thought is also evident in her conception of relative value. Speaking of the difference between her daughter and herself, she acknowledges they have different personalities. Consequently, the same people or action may have different significance and value for each of them. At the same time, Barbara invokes a more universalistic conception of any self-system's requirements and from these defines more absolute standards of evaluation.

Barbara's evaluation is clearly not linear. Rather than focusing on particular persons or specific actions, she typically is interested in general interactions, types of meaningful connections, or different kinds of interpersonal interaction. Specific rules of action are not the bases of her judgment but instead are frequently the objects to evaluated. Moreover, value does not flow from one action or actor to another as in the anchored evaluations of linear thinking. In

Barbara's case, value ultimately inheres in the qualities of the self or a type of relationship. Specific behavioral rules or norms are judged accordingly. The unanchored quality of her judgments is also evident in the way in which she readily dissociates issues of preference or of liking another person from the judgment of their weaknesses. Specific instances of what is liked and disliked can thus more readily coexist without any sense of contradiction.

INTRV.: Okay, tell me the name of the most important person in your life?

SUBJ.: Heather.

INTRV.: All right. What is it that you like about Heather?

SUBJ.: She is very . . . She is very warm and personable and creative.

INTRV.: What do you mean by creative? As juxtaposed to someone who's crafty?

SUBJ.: Um, the way she perceives things and creates, she perceives things in a very novel way and has a way of restructuring the facts of reality into something that's insightful and imaginative.

Reference to thinking, to how connections are made and meaning constructed.

INTRV.: She's warm and personable? And you appreciate that. What is it about that that you find important?

SUBJ.: She takes other people's concerns seriously and provides other people with I think a sense of value and comfort that I think is extremely important. I think in that way she contributes ??? to feel good about themselves, secure, happy.

Interactive conception of warmth—a simultaneous conception of the intention and the manner in which it is received.

INTRV.: Restructuring reality in ways that are insightful, explain to me what that is. What is it about it that's appealing?

SUBJ.: I think that most people learn how to see the world from other people, and most people have extremely limited ways of perceiving and expressing what they see in reality, they have very limited vocabulary, limited ways of perceiving things, and a great deal of what

General focus on quality of meaning constructed, on nature of connections made rather than a specific belief or characteristic action.

people do is simply pass around their limited
perceptions, the ones we have all the time. I
think what I value in Heather is that she finds
a new way of perceiving, something that's
different than simply what somebody has
handed to her. The usual clichés don't tend to
simply be spit out by her. I think that she, you
know, she can look at something that a
hundred other people look at and come up
with something that is special and new, and
what that does for me first of all, since she's
my daughter, I know that this will make her
life richer and fuller, because she'll have an
interaction with life that belongs to her. And
then she'll have something to provide to other
people so other people become attracted to
that because you can provide new insights.
People find you interesting and attractive.
And in that way she'll interact with other
people. I think for myself personally when I
think about it is that I like playing with different perceptions. So it is interesting to me as
well, to talk to her about her perceptions. It
gives me insights into who she is as a person.
There's something expansive, something that
is creative because she makes something more
than, more than the ordinary way we do
perceive things and the way we think about
things. And to me interacting with somebody,
why do we, that's why we travel, that's why we
cook interesting things. That's why we like
varied experiences. That's why we like great
literature. It's a perception that if you can take
something from life and connects somewhere
you know emotionally and intellectually with
us, I think if those connections are made, I'll
find life reaffirming.

Value objects are types
of connections, meanings.
All discussed in
generalities with little
concrete reference.

Value is focused on
abstract, general relations:
the connections people
make when they perceive
and act.

Also on the connections
that variously link people
to each other.

INTRV.: So you like her novel approach to some
things, but that doesn't necessarily mean that
everybody likes interesting foods, or every-

body likes to travel. Some people like what is familiar. Some people like to eat the same burrito every night.

SUBJ.: I don't think people choose to be unimaginative. I don't think people are really happy at all that way. I think that small children are trained out of their imaginations from the time they're a year old, and they're looking at something and they're curious about it, somebody tells them to keep their hands to themselves. I mean children are incredibly wonderful, expansive, curious. I mean look at a child drawing a picture, I mean the more freedom they're given, the more things they create. And it's not just novel creations, it's that you bring something to the perception and it's the, other people's perceptions aren't really interesting because they're different than your perceptions. But because they draw something from reality, it's a way of seeing it which usually connects with something else. People can make wonderful metaphors and analogies that connects with something else, because you can always permute somebody's perceptions. That's not interesting by itself, just a difference is not interesting, but something that you know has a new structure, so it's not just different, but it is a difference in a way in which we find interesting and important.

> Focus on self as an abstraction, a potentiality—a system of differences (most latent or potential). Value in the realization of the various elements of the self.

> The value of individuality of perception is in the interactive result. Each individual is elaborated and transformed by the difference in herself introduced by exposure to the difference of the other.

> Difference is not substantive, it is qualitative.

INTRV.: Is there anything that you dislike about Heather?

SUBJ.: Um. Dislike? No. I think she has certain weaknesses to her disadvantage, but they're not things that I dislike about her.

INTRV.: For example?

SUBJ.: Um, when there's a conflict between what she wants and somebody else wants, she often simply tries to please the other person and then gets what she wants on the side, behind

> Reinterprets disapproval and self-consciously disassociates from disliking. Note also that the other person constitutes the standard for evaluation—Heather's needs are the standard.

their back, and I think this is often seen as being manipulative, which it is anyway, and I think that that is to her disadvantage because I think that it's hard for people to trust her when she acts like that. So I think that is disadvantageous to her.

INTRV.: Has she told you that people have perceived her as being manipulative? Or is that something you just observed?

SUBJ.: It's something that I've observed. I've observed her behavior and I've observed, for example, her teachers' reactions to those kinds of things, or her grandparents' reaction.

INTRV.: Does she see that the same way that you do?

SUBJ.: Um, she knows that people have reacted to her the same way. I think she feels that she is doing something more rebellious. I think she thinks she's doing it for reasons for rebellion, okay she rejects what the adults says, she does it anyway. But if you actually observe her behavior, she very much attempts to please, and I think she does strive to please. She does this with, you know, her father. She doesn't want to directly you know, she doesn't want to have any direct conflict. She wants everyone to be happy with her and like her, so she tries to I think make these two goals her own, feeling that she's pleasing somebody that's important. And at the same time, she's very forward when she wants what she wants.

Draws clear line between the meaning of events for her and for her daughter. It is a matter of placing it in different contexts (manipulation or rebellion) and then interpreting differently.

INTRV.: Okay. Let us assume that your daughter was very sick . . . (delivers scenario). Would you give her the money?

Interviewer introduces scenario regarding illness.

SUBJ.: Oh absolutely.

INTRV.: Why?

SUBJ.: I think my relationship with Heather is very like one of unconditional love, and the second is if you're somebody's mother, I think it's as if a certain level of total loyalty that you have to

Defines norm of motherhood and its responsibility. But then

them. And it's as much as it's more for me an emotional connection than an ethical connection, the ethical rule. It's not that I think I should give her the $10,000; instead my relationship with her is that I wouldn't hesitate though to give it to her. I mean there have been a lot of things. I mean I commuted for three years to law school living in Irvine because I thought she should be more near her father. Well that's a very small advantage in her life and a very large disadvantage for me in my life, and I think that was important for me to do. I think that when you have a child, they're very much in your care. To me, the child only really has his mother and father to be devoted to him. And you don't have anybody else that's absolutely necessary yours. And, therefore, to me there's a very large level of loyalty that you want to offer them.

is not satisfied with just asserting conventional norm. Spontaneously moves to justify the norm with reference to the relative dependence of adult and child. (This should, however, be probed further.)

INTRV.: If you didn't have the money, would you steal to get it?

SUBJ.: It depends.

INTRV.: Oh?

SUBJ.: Um, to me it would depend on, would I actually? Do I think it's an ethical violation to steal? Not if I could do it in a way that would harm people very minimally. Would I actually, who would I?

INTRV.: Who are we worried about?

SUBJ.: For example.

INTRV.: Who are we worried about?

SUBJ.: Um, I mean certainly the close family members. The closer people are to you, the more you have to worry about harming them, because if they knew, if they didn't know. There's a loyalty issue to people more close to them. I mean for example like at a job some-place where you know numbers of people have money invested and I can pilfer a little

Considers the interplay of two dimensions: levels of loyalty and amounts of harm done. At the same time, places the consideration of the act of stealing in two contexts: (1) ethical violation and bit from each person and embezzle it, you know always having, putting myself at risk of being caught that's really making very little, putting very little harm on each person that was harmed, it would not be a negative, I think I would do it. If I would actually do it? I mean ethically, it wouldn't bother me, but actually do it? Could I actually bring myself to do it? I don't know, I'm very much a rule-abiding person, so I don't know. I can't hypothetically really put myself in that position.

raises a standard of harm done, (2) her own nature and what she would typically do. However, these latter concerns may be just linear. Further probing required.

INTRV.: Would you consider stealing the drug from the druggist?

SUBJ.: Absolutely not, no. From the pharmacy company? Yeah, I think pharmacy companies rip people off so enormously that if it were a major pharmacy company, I would have no problem with it whatsoever.

INTRV.: It's this druggist who invented the drug. He has it and it's his drug and he wants $10,000 for it that you don't have.

SUBJ.: There's so many other possible solutions that it's hard to see this as the only, I mean it's hard to put yourself in a hypothetical world that doesn't exist. This is the only real, I can analyze it as an ethical question, but is it technically okay? I don't think that people have absolute crossing points. I think a person's well-being is much more important than property rights. So even if it were somebody I didn't know, I think we have to weigh the personal harms to people and I think that overrides the consideration of property rights. So the more extorting the druggist was being, I mean you know if he sweat his whole life, and his whole family depended upon him selling this one vial of the drug, obviously it would be a major harm to him so maybe we'd really have to start

Demands concrete considerations for an evaluation. This does not involve a failure to recognize or understand the general dimension. To the contrary, she does recognize the interviewer's implicit demand for a general analysis but objects to it. Further probing here would have been illuminating.

balancing. But you know if he just invented it, it cost him $.50 to produce, but man to market this stuff. I mean you can charge an incredibly high price and would have no problem.

Ethical standard is relative harm done. Convention of not stealing recast in these terms.

INTRV.: What if you're just weighing your daughter's situation versus stealing this drug and not knowing anything about the druggist's situation, not knowing about his responsibilities to his family or how much time he has invested in developing this drug. All you know is that your daughter's sick, she needs this, and you can't get it.

SUBJ.: I don't know. I have no idea how I'd feel. I have nothing in which to weigh the ethical questions. No I really, I can't evaluate it either intellectually or emotionally.

Again objects here and later against demand for abstract consideration empty of concrete details.

INTRV.: Well it's evaluated ethically. Let's start by saying, actually let's back up a little bit and assume that you are not going to be talked into stealing this drug.

Interviewer should have accepted subject's frame of reference and probed directly to determine why concrete considerations were so critical.

SUBJ.: I don't know, it doesn't really matter. I mean from an ethical position, I can't you're asking me, as an ethical rule can I help somebody because they need to be helped, well it depends what the cost otherwise. I can't evaluate it ethically until I know, unless I know what possible harm it would do. I mean the possible harm it would do. I mean to me, I don't really care. I mean I care very little. I mean if it were death penalty situation, if I had to kill somebody to steal this drug, if I had to kill somebody to get the drug and it would help my daughter but it wouldn't save her life, I couldn't, no. Um, if I had to kill somebody to get the drug to give her to save her life, I don't think I could do that either. I don't think I could play God at that level.

Dealing with issue of interpretation and the difficulty inherent in rule application.

INTRV.: Why not? Just out of curiosity?

SUBJ.: Because I don't think people should have the

Value here is not an act

right to make those kinds of choices and to take one's life to save another. And because I don't think people in general should have that right, I can't take it.

INTRV.: Okay, assume for a second that your daughter can't swim. She's a two year old, she's fallen into this pool. And you can save her, you can get to her, and you can get to her if you jump in on your golf cart. But in order to get to her, you have to drive over somebody.

SUBJ.: Do I think I should be able to do that? No. Do you think I would do it? Yes.

INTRV.: What's the distinction?

SUBJ.: Because it's a totally emotional, irrational behavior. If I saw her drowning, I would do whatever it took to get to her. In the same way, if she were two years, say she was ten years old and somebody seriously molested her in a way that would cause her lifelong damage, could I kill them? Yeah, sure I could. I mean I could think I should do it? If I sat down and calmly, reasonably thought about it, no I wouldn't. Because I don't think you have the right to do it. And I don't think people should, and I wouldn't go out and do it because I don't think people should. And I think to not be law abiding, I mean I know I have those kinds of emotions. I'm an incredible mother bear. I have you know metaphorically ripped people's heads off for doing things that I felt were bad for her. I could see myself doing it in the physical sense, in an emotional state.

INTRV.: So one of those rules is . . .

SUBJ.: In the throes of passion. But that's not actually a rule. I don't think I should. I don't think I should be allowed to.

INTRV.: But you don't think you should be allowed to steal either?

but a kind of choice, a type of consideration.

Again clear distinction between ethical and personal/practical as two somewhat distinct domains or dimensions of consideration. The ethical is a general matter of social relations, the personal is a concrete particular matter of a specific emotional makeup and/or a specific relationship.

SUBJ.: It depends. I mean it depends on the situation, I know that the ethical rule is, I don't think there's an absolute ethical rule that. Let's put it this way, I think there's an ethical rule that it's wrong to steal, but I think the wrong of stealing can be balanced against other wrongs so that, and I don't know that, I mean absolute ethical rules don't particularly interest me. I do think, I think that there should only be rules to the extent that if everybody faces these rules, we don't do things we would otherwise like to do. But I think if by looking at it in a rule-free environment, then I can concoct a rule myself rather than having an absolute rule, you know, laid down by law in some simple fashion. And in that sense, my ethical rule would be that you have to weigh the harms to people. So there's no absolute wrong of stealing. It may be legitimate if the balance of harm is in line, doing the action. . . .

> Here attempts to deal with levels of normative consideration.
>
> Self-consciously constructs a higher order principle in terms of which specific conventions may be evaluated.
>
> The principle of a calculus of relative harm therefore demands the concrete considerations she said she needed to make a judgment earlier in the interview.

INTRV.: Um, and so you can't say given what you know about the situation, you can't say whether or not you'd steal the drug for your daughter? Because you don't know enough about the druggist or . . .

SUBJ.: I wouldn't know how to make that balance.

INTRV.: So let's say that what we know about him is that he's going to make a lot of money off this drug. And it doesn't look like he's going to be at a great loss if he loses a bottle of this drug, but it's still his property, something that he can no longer do, something that he developed, and something that the law protects as he has a right to it. But by his not giving it to you, or working out some kind of deal with you, your daughter is going to suffer. So in that instance, would you steal the drug?

SUBJ.: As a last resort. I mean I would do everything

up to that point. I don't think it's an automatic yes I think it's okay. I don't necessarily think that it's okay if there's any other means. If there are other means that are say less illegal. I think that my general approach would be to see whether I could possibly do it in a means that could bend the rules, fits within the legal structure. If there was no way to do it within the legal structure without having what I see is that enormous wrong, which is my daughter suffering greatly. For the sake of a property right alone, um then I would, yeah.

INTRV.: All right.

SUBJ.: I think what I see is like a threshold, or it's not as if there's just a line where I make up the rules, where I say I'll just weigh the interests of the druggist and my daughter, and if I think my daughter's needs are greater, I'll steal for her no problem. I think that one has to have a respect for the rule, and therefore you can accept a certain imbalance. You can accept some small measures of wrong because you need the rules to keep the system going in an appropriate fashion. And it's only when you see a truly large wrong, some truly large imbalance which you feel makes, becomes ethically wrong to such a degree that you can say I will no longer follow the rule, I will violate the rule because I think there's an ethical reason to do it.

> A new context or dimension of consideration is introduced. Note this is integrated with rather than replaces the prior context.

> Introduces issues of rule following for maintenance of social system as value.

> This concern placed relative to valued principle.

INTRV.: All right. Let's assume that you and Heather aren't as close as you used to be. Your relations are estranged. Maybe you see that she is taking advantage of people in ways that you disapprove of, and her weakness is blossoming into something that you just don't appreciate and you keep your distance because of it. Would you still steal for her? Or would you have the same inclination you would now?

> Interviewer introduces potentially sequential or linear concerns.

SUBJ.: This is what I'm saying. I think that her behavior would have to be very extreme, and I think I would have to believe that she was so totally trashing her life and so disrespectful of her own life that to give her this drug would be ?? If she were using drugs and having unprotected sex and all kinds of things like that, and I just saw her as really throwing her life away. Um, then I think doing major things for her wouldn't be a good thing to do.

INTRV.: Why wouldn't it be a good thing to do?

SUBJ.: Because I think that she needs to either respect her life to some degree or do something to help earn it showing that she has, I mean she has to respect her life to some degree to deserve it.

INTRV.: Respect her life in the sense that you think she should respect her life? Or do you think there's some kind of respect that everybody should have?

SUBJ.: I mean I would have to understand that she was respecting her life, I mean this would have to be very extreme. I think it would take a very extreme behavior on her part, so in the extreme, it would have to be something that would indicate to me that she understood, that she intended to respect her life, rather than just throwing it away. And I think it's different for everybody. I mean I could create scenarios in which she is highly suicidal because she's very depressed, she hates her life and she wants to destroy herself, but even that can show some respect for her life. But I think when somebody is constant, I think people do get to a point where they have become so negative about their lives that they have so cheapened their lives. I think it generally has to do, I think it stems from a whole set of problems and I'm not saying that it's her fault and, therefore, she deserves to be in pain

Response is to reframe concern relative to definition and value of life as self-elaborating system. Earlier life was infused with growth and elaboration. Here we get the complement. A system that is self-destructive is not to be valued.

Is wrestling with the problem that emerges when recognizing the relative meaning and value of life and at the same time wanting some standard for intervening when another is behaving self-destructively. Is thus dealing with systems of meaning and principles of interpersonal exchange.

inside. But I don't think she's going to, I think
that if somebody's going to do something very
major for somebody in a life affirming way, I
think they have to make that connection with   Redefines the nature
something in the person that wants to live and   of and value of giving
cares about their pain. And I think that,   relative to the functioning
because I think otherwise it falls off people   of the recipient
like water on a duck's back. I think people   personality.
that I've seen that are in very severe drug
conditions, for example, have become so
negative about their lives that they can't accept
anything anyway, so giving them something is
sort of a negative gesture. Does that make
sense to you?

INTRV.: If it were just somebody, not Heather, but
somebody you had heard about maybe, but
you knew that this person didn't have any
money at all, and didn't have the resources to
get this drug, would you steal it or would you
consider stealing it? Or would you give them
the money that you had?

SUBJ.: Hmm. That's a hard one. I don't know. I
might. I can see myself possibly doing it. It   Reintroduces principle of
depends I suppose on how, I think there's, it   calculus of relative harm.
sort of depends a little bit on how bad off they
were, how close they were, how destitute that
would leave me.

INTRV.: Why would you consider doing it at all?

SUBJ.: I mean for the same reason, and it might be
on a much larger scale. I've had friends of my
daughter's who are very difficult people,
they've had to live with me for a period of
time because they absolutely didn't get along
with their parents and I felt they might end up   Exemplifies relative worth
on the street. And then I think we all suffer   of certain ends for others
from ?? of having been there. But you know,   (even when they are not
again I thought that way was important. I   valued or even liked
mean I don't really think they had much,   much) justifying sacrifice
anywhere else to go and I thought they were   of own desires, needs, and
much better staying with me than they were   preferences.

anywhere else. I think that, and maybe in that situation, I thought that being around me was good for them and that made me feel good. So there's a certain sense of reward. I think so much of our lives are spent feeling like we can't do anything about it, we have no control over doing anything about the suffering around us, I think a lot of it has to do with the feeling that you can really, I mean it's really hard, $10,000 is not that much money. I mean somehow I can get $10,000. I'm healthy, I'm smart, I've got talents, you know, I can get $10,000 some way or another. And I would be, I mean when I was an attorney, you know I was actually working a whole year and made you know $60 or $70,000 a year, and it's not worth it for living the shitty life you live as an attorney. But if I get to do some major appreciable thing, somebody that I can see, it would be worth slaving for.

INTRV.: Okay. Is that because there's some moral imperative that compels you to do that? Or is it because it feels good.

SUBJ.: We're all imperfect. I mean I think, it's the same thing with Bosnia. Who else is going to go in there and help? You know. I mean somebody should help them. And yet in a world where nobody's bound to help them, who's gonna do it? And I do think sometimes you just need to step in and do it. I mean if you're there and you have some connection, it makes you simply more in a place to do something. And I do think people have a responsibility to people around them to help them out. That's the rule.

> What is impelling is not abstract morality or personal feeling, but the requirements of the system of social life.

INTRV.: Why is that?

SUBJ.: Because I think the world is better off that way. I think that we need each other. If we don't have each other helping us out, we don't survive well as a society. I think we become too cold and heartless, being very bad to people and it's very bad for society. And I think that people should feel that responsibility. Ultimately in the great scheme of things, I think it has.

INTRV.: Have you read the *Communist Manifesto?*

SUBJ.: No.

Atypical move by the interviewer.

INTRV.: He makes the exact opposite argument and says that the closer we become . . .

SUBJ.: Well there you go, who's ethically more ahead?

INTRV.: Well I'm just curious, I'm just curious what you think about this. He makes the argument that as technology advances and we do become more and more dependent on each other, we lose our individuality.

Interviewer introduces alternative conception of social system as base for evaluation.

SUBJ.: Not I.

INTRV.: There was that argument from the beginning, but you're in some sense weakening your views now not letting them realize their own individualities.

SUBJ.: Is this like a Darwinian approach or something? That you need to go out there, Marines? You need to go out there and be tough? Is that it? By not helping anybody, everybody becomes tough enough to survive? I mean you look at children, I mean babies die if they're not held. I think people are like that. I don't think people ever outgrow the need to have other people be there and comfort them, and I think that we depend on our creating relationships and letting people comfort us and who are there for us and who support us. And so we feel an emotional closeness to them. And I think that everybody needs that. And I think that in a world which is increasingly frightening, and in which relationships don't seem very stable for most people, I think that you know if you're one step beyond having a little relationship with

Note the level of abstraction at which this counterargument is conducted. There are rarely specific familiar cases, just a mutually supporting weave of general claims.

somebody, up to the point that you're a
stranger just happening to walk by, I think
you'll do a good thing to recognize a human
who needs someone, to be there for somebody. They need you too. I think it makes us
stronger. I mean you look at people who are
. . . I don't trust people who work independently totally. I think that they tend to be
egomaniacs who tend to be disconnected to
what everybody in the world around them
needs.

Offers a contrary theory
of basic human emotional
interdependence. With-
out probing, however, its
conceptual status is
unclear.

Bill's Sequential Evaluation

The text of the interview with Bill provides a good example of sequential evaluation. His focus is quite concrete and particular. Moreover, these particulars
are understood as they are embedded in specific scenarios. Consequently, when
Bill is asked to discuss a particular person or action, he typically responds by
considering the object as it is embedded in an event and then proceeds to tell
the story in which the event occurs. For example, in his response to a query regarding what he likes about his brother, he initially struggles until he places his
brother in the context of a sequence of events. In typical fashion the events in
this story evoke memories of events in another story. His narrative then continues with this second story. The net result is a somewhat random assemblage
of brief vignettes that abruptly ends at a point bearing little relation to the initial concern addressed.

For Bill, value revolves around what feels good or is enjoyable and what feels
bad or is punishing. As is typical for someone evaluating sequentially, value is
more clearly felt *en vivo* rather than at the remove of relating the story of what
has happened. Thus requests for evaluation typically engender responses that
are more descriptive than evaluative. Values, however, are introduced and they
are generally framed as a matter of feeling and wanting, of reward and punishment, either for himself or for his brother. An exception is when the issue of
stealing is raised. These evoke memories of what happened to Bill personally. In
this instance, his response is more pronounced and quite clear. He remembers
being caught and punished and consequently views stealing in clearly negative
terms. Interestingly, the interviewer's attempt to manipulate Bill's response by
suggesting that the punishment could be removed, that is, Bill could steal without being caught, almost changes his attitude. But the association of punish-

ment with stealing is strong enough in Bill's mind so he does not accept the possibility that no punishment will be associated with the act.

Bill's evaluation of his brother and whether to help him is clearly not linear. Rules of action are rarely in evidence in Bill's considerations. Value is based on feelings, not on acting correctly or incorrectly. These feeling-based evaluations are not justified in terms of norms of good and bad, they are simply described. Consequently, the interviewer's introduction of norms have little effect on Bill's judgment. At one point Bill does indicate a willingness to pay back his brother because his brother has taken care of him. Although the probing of his response is inadequate, it does seem that this "rule" is conceived in terms of the specific scenario of his interaction with his brother. Moreover, it may be only a rhetorical move, a repetition of what has been said to him. When asked why he should want to repay his brother, Bill does not respond with the typically linear claims that it is the correct thing to do or a matter of obligation. Rather he simply indicates that he "never really gave it much thought."

There is also little evidence in Bill's responses of any evaluative anchoring, another hallmark of linear evaluation. In Bill's case, value does not flow from one categorical entity to the next. Instead, statements of value stand largely in isolation from one another. At one point the interviewer introduces a potentially linear connection by suggesting that the pharmacist is a bad person and, by linear implication, may therefore deserve having something bad done to him. Bill does not respond in a linear manner. Consequently, he does not attempt to create any evaluative consistency either by deciding to treat the pharmacist badly or by claiming the pharmacist is not really that bad.

INTRV.: I'd like to talk about something a little different. What I'd like you to do is I'd like you to think of someone who's close to you . . . friend, family member, somebody like that. Who would you like to talk about a little bit?

SUBJ.: Well, my brother.

INTRV.: Okay, and what's your brother's name?

SUBJ.: Stuart.

INTRV.: Okay, we'll talk about Stuart. Um . . . Can you tell me what you like most about Stuart?

SUBJ.: Well, for one thing, he's my brother and um   Fragmentary description.
. . . he's always managed to make a go of it, whatever he did most of the time. And, uh . . . he's really gotten into . . . he's been playing

Santa Claus for like about the last fifteen years. And he is Santa Claus. He gets . . . at Christmas time, he's worked for South Coast Plaza, and Crystal Court, Westminster Mall, places like that. Last year he worked back in Minnesota in Rosedale, the mall back there. The only thing he didn't like about it was that they wouldn't let him change out of his costume in the mall or in where they changed into costume, and so on. He had to wear it outside. And they kept it like 78 degrees inside. You walk outside and here it is 34 below and snowing (laughs). The money was good on it. He'd been working that . . . he loves kids. He gets along great with kids. There's a few kids that argue with him, but most of the time he gets along pretty good with them. He says some of the kids are really a riot because parents will wait in line to get them on his lap, you know, to take a picture, and . . . he had one kid that was still in diapers and the mom says "you go sit on Santa's lap and get your picture" and she put him on Santa's lap and the kid messed up his diaper right there, he was so excited to see him you know. And he said he's had kids that have had ringworm and he's had kids that the mom's . . . His first year at South Coast Plaza, he had parents that were bringing their kids in, they were running a hundred and one, hundred and two temperature. The kids were sick and they were bringing them out to have their picture taken with Santa. They put them on Santa's lap and he puts his hand against their back to hold them, like this. He says you can feel them all congested and everything. You wonder about parents sometimes.

> Thinks in terms of a story, an unfolding sequence of events, rather than in terms of category or categorical evaluation. Therefore leads into a specific concrete story.

> An example of fairly advanced sequential reasoning. An attempt to build a description but ends in a collage of event fragments where an event in one sequence cues a memory of an event in another sequence.

INTRV.: Now . . . it's kind of an interesting thing that your brother plays Santa. Do you think it's a good thing that he does that?

SUBJ.: Oh yeah. He enjoys it. He loves it.

INTRV.: What do you think is good about it?

SUBJ.: That he has so much fun doing it. He enjoys talking to the kids and like, most Santas, they try and . . . like South Coast Plaza last year, they had Santa. And they had kids and, you know, rush them through. Get your picture taken, next kid. And Stuart says you can't do that with the kids. The kids, you have to . . . When they put them on Santa's lap, the kids want to tell Santa what they want and you've got to listen, you've got to talk to them, you know, and try to quiet them. He says, "I found out the last couple years that sometimes it's better if the kid doesn't sit on Santa's lap, if he just stands next to Santa." "Some kids you know are between two and four," he said, "two year olds will have nothing to do with Santa. When you're getting to the age of four, it's fine, it's cool."

INTRV.: Why do you think parents do that if their kids don't want to be with Santa? Why do their parents bring them?

SUBJ.: He says because (whispers) they want a picture to send to the relatives. He says that's what a lot of them want. He says like Rosedale, he said he didn't have any trouble with the kids back there. Most of the kids were real nice, the parents didn't force them into it. He says some of the kids though, it's a riot. They get there and say "I want a combine." And Stuart sitting there thinking "What's a combine?" And it took him awhile before it dawned on him. Most of them have tractors and combines back there and so on. You know it's a farming community type thing. Then he realized what it was, you know.

INTRV.: You know, you also said that one of the things you liked about him was that he's your brother.

Value in terms of feelings.

Question cues an idea which is associated with an event. Following the line of the story, the original point of departure is readily lost.

Does not offer own causal explanation, but repeats his brother's story. Enveloped by the memories of this story, he follows it as it unravels. Note that the story has no categorical relevance to the question posed.

Interviewer request for comparison of brothers

Why is that important? What difference does that make?

SUBJ.: Well, I've never really, you know, made friends with a lot of people. There's guys that I've worked with and everything that you're cordial to but you're not buddy-buddy with them and so on. And . . . I get along with my brother. He chews me out once in awhile and I chew him out, you know. But we get along pretty good for brothers. A lot of brothers don't.

INTRV.: Why do you think you guys get along pretty good?

SUBJ.: I can't really say . . . It's just sort of a mutual bond between us.

INTRV.: Okay, is there anything you don't like about your brother? No? All right, now I'd just like to think about a pretend situation for a moment. Let's say that Stuart gets really sick . . . (interviewer introduces the first scenario) . . . Let's say you had the ten thousand in the bank somewhere, but it was all the money you had, would you give him the money?

SUBJ.: Yeah.

INTRV.: How come?

SUBJ.: Because he's my brother and because it would help him.

INTRV.: Why would you want to do it in the sense that if you give him the money it would help him but all of a sudden you'd be broke again. That would be worth it?

SUBJ.: Yeah.

INTRV.: How come?

SUBJ.: To help him along . . . ? He's been kind of paying the bills on the house and everything for the last couple years, the house payment and everything, while I've been out of work.

INTRV.: Oh, so you're living with him now?

SUBJ.: Yeah.

with other types of people.

Response focuses on his particular experience with his brother and evaluation based on how it feels. (Linear response would focus on convention of special sibling ties.)

Additional probing of meaning needed here.

A value expressed but not probed for meaning.

"He pays and helps me, so I pay." Not articulated as a rule, but might be one. Could also be a matter of confusion of roles in the event, of identifying with the brother and playing out his part. Probing needed here.

INTRV.: Oh, okay. Let's say that . . . how about if you didn't have the money . . . would you be willing to steal the drug? Break into the doctor's office to get the medicine for your brother?

SUBJ.: No.

INTRV.: How come? Why not?

SUBJ.: Because my parents raised me, you know, not to steal. It's wrong. I got busted when I was a young kid because we were . . . Me and two other kids were horsing around one day and we busted into this place and messed it up, you know . . . the juvenile hall line. I learned my lesson real quick.

> Act understood as it is integrated in a story with end that was painful. Hence is part of negatively valued sequence.

INTRV.: Yeah, I must admit when I was a kid I had something similar. You do learn your lesson.

> Move to be supportive of the interviewee.

SUBJ.: Yeah.

INTRV.: Now you said you would be willing to give him the money if you had it. Would you still be willing even if you knew that, okay, I'm not going to have any savings, and I don't have a job now, and so if all of this money is gone, and I'm working day to day and I don't know . . . I could go a week without having a job, and then I'd be flat out of money. Would you still be willing to give him the money?

SUBJ.: Yeah.

INTRV.: It's still important enough to help him? Why do you think it's so important to help him?

SUBJ.: Well, for one thing he's my brother, for another he's been kind of supporting me for the last couple years. He made close to I think it was $12,000 last year playing Santa. Well, a lot of that went to house payments, bills that he paid off that I had, and so on. I figure we'd break about even that way.

> Again invokes standard of obligation between brothers, but earlier probe shows this is more a matter of rhetoric.

INTRV.: So he kind of pays the bills and this would be a way of repaying him.

SUBJ.: Yeah.

> Rule of "he pays so I pay." However not an invoca-

INTRV.: Why should you worry about repaying him?

SUBJ.: I've never really given it much thought, but I figure well, hey, he's supported me and it's only fair if I repay him if I can.

INTRV.: Okay. Let's say that you and Stuart start fighting, don't get along so well for awhile. He says, "Look, I don't like this any more. I'm paying the bills on the house. I want you out." So you move out and sometime passes and then he gets sick. He comes to you and he says, "Look, you know, I'm sick. Would you be willing to give me all your savings for the medicine." Would you be willing to do it then?

SUBJ.: Yeah.

INTRV.: Even though the two of you had been fighting and he threw you out?

SUBJ.: Yeah.

INTRV.: Why would you be willing to do it then?

SUBJ.: We've always fought, ever since we were kids. Most brothers do. But I've got a lot of respect for him and I would figure that it was a really desperate situation and I'd be willing to forget the fighting part and everything.

INTRV.: Okay. You mentioned you wouldn't steal the drug, in part because you learned your lesson when you were a kid. What if you knew that somehow you could steal the drug and never get caught? Would you be willing to do it?

SUBJ.: I'd be tempted but I don't think I'd do it.

INTRV.: How come? You wouldn't get caught, there'd be no price to pay.

SUBJ.: Yeah, but in my mind it would still be wrong.

INTRV.: And why's that?

SUBJ.: It would still be the wrong thing to do. Because it would still be stealing and you may not get caught now, but further down the line you're libel to do something else and get caught.

INTRV.: Okay. But now . . . let's say you can't raise the

---

tion of a general rule of action. It is woven into the particulars of what happens between him and Stuart. Perhaps is repeating what he may have heard. In any case, not regarded as an important concern. Still, more probing needed.

Fighting manipulation fails because it contradicts personal experience and subject does not adopt hypothetical view.

Interviewer removes punishment.

With punishment removed, stealing is now more attractive, but it still is not a chosen option. Problem is being caught and punished still thought of as part of the sequence involving stealing.

money, your brother says, "Bill won't you steal it for me." You explain to him, "No, I won't do that." And then he says, "But look, you're my brother. Brothers are supposed to take care of each other. Why won't you steal it for me?" What would you say?

SUBJ.: Well, in the first place, I don't think he'd ever ask me to steal for him. If he did, I'd just say, "Hey. No way."

INTRV.: All right. Now someone might say the guy, the doctor who invented the drug, he's being real selfish. You know, the drug is supposed to be able to help people and here he is charging a lot of money so that Stuart doesn't have access to it, can't get to it. So he's kind of being bad spirited about the whole thing. Wouldn't it be okay to steal it then?

SUBJ.: No, I don't think so. I'd go to the doctor and I'd say, "Look, why don't you test it . . . give it to my brother, see if it works."

INTRV.: What if the doctor says, "Look. I've done all the testing and I know it works. I don't need to test it anymore. You're just trying to get the drug."

SUBJ.: I would say "Yeah, but if you test it on him . . . or have you tested it in the lab?"

INTRV.: Yeah, they've done that. He's tested it on humans already. That's why he can sell it. So he would say, "No. I've tested it already. I'm sorry about your brother but I've got to earn a living and I want to make more money."

SUBJ.: I would probably try to work something out where I could get money. Put the house up for sale or whatever. Get the money for him.

INTRV.: But what if you did not have a house to sell and there is no way to get another source of money.

SUBJ.: I would . . . I'd just get the money.

INTRV.: Okay.

Invocation of norm of obligation appears to have no effect. Probing required.

Interviewer introduces notion that doctor is a bad person, trying to initiate a value consistency response typical of linear evaluation. Produces no effect.

Tries to resort to alternatives without consideration of probable context. For example, the drug is on the market and therefore has probably already been fully tested, or the druggist will be aware of the interviewee's manipulative attempts to get the drug.

Does not want to risk punishment but wants to help brother. Just thinks of desired end, without considering way to get there. Causal connections just not that meaningful.

THREE EVALUATIONS OF A DOMESTIC
POLITICAL ISSUE

Julie's Linear Evaluation

As in her evaluation of the personal issue, Julie judges the display of Mapplethorpe's art in a manner guided by her arsenal of rules for action. Here the critical rule is the one that calls for the toleration of differences. Depending on the specific question addressed, other rules are also called into play, for example, the rule of deciding collective issues by a democratic vote. Julie also introduces role-specific rules that are a quite common manifestation of linear reasoning. In one case, it applies to public institutions (such as the art museum) and dictates that they should serve the public. In another case, the role of legislators is invoked and their responsibility to make laws.

For Julie, these rules are the foundations of evaluation rather than its object. As a result, there is no spontaneous attempt to justify rules and little justification is provided when directly requested by the interviewer. For example, freedom of speech is not justified; it is simply asserted to be good and associated with the founding of our country. Similarly, rules are not considered relative to one another. Rather one rule at a time is applied. This renders Julie susceptible to significant shifts in judgment depending on the rule applied. On a number of occasions, a new rule of action or bases of judgment is introduced. This then provides a context in which the question is reframed and a different evaluation may follow. This evaluative reframing is particularly evident in her consideration of a popular vote to ban the exhibition of the controversial photographs. A focus on the rule of democratic decision-making leads to a positive judgment of the vote. When the focus shifts to an evaluation of the intolerant and undesirable outcome, she reverses her judgment. Further reversals follow the introduction of the rule of allowing freedom of expression and then the rule of disallowing racist behavior. Throughout, Julie's view of the issue shifts and no overall position integrating the various consequent concerns is constructed.

Julie's judgments also reflect the anchoring characteristic of linear evaluation. At a number of points, she focuses on the already determined value of an outcome and then judges the cause that produces the outcome accordingly. For example, racism is regarded negatively because it produces a bad result, harming people. Similarly, tolerance is regarded positively because it prevents this effect. Her evaluations also go in the other direction. Thus a good causal activity, democratic voting, renders an otherwise unacceptable outcome, banning the photographs, acceptable. The concretely anchored quality of Julie's evaluations are also reflected in her attempt to maintain a consistency in the evaluation of actions or actors who are causally or categorically linked to one another. For example, when an introduction of additional conditions induces Julie to conceal her view that the photographs should be shown, she is confronted with her decision to do something she thinks is wrong (she violates the rule that you express your opinions). In an attempt to maintain her positive self-definition, she diminishes the importance of the issue. Similarly after having changed her opinions on elections from positive to negative, she moves to bolster her new judgment by providing additional negative information about elections (people don't tell you what they mean anyway and it is the legislators' role to make laws, not the public's). Another example is provided by her handling of racist art. The very notion is difficult because it links a positive entity (art) with a negative one (racism). Julie eventually reconstructs the evaluative relation by deciding that racism cannot be artistic and thus there cannot really be racist art.

Julie's evaluation of the showing of the art is clearly not sequential. Her judgments are not made on the basis of specific experience of particular pleasures or pains. Indeed, in response to the interviewer's attempt to introduce this consideration, Julie explicitly distinguishes between her personal reaction and the value of displaying the photographs. The latter depends on its relation to rules of action. This parallels similar moves she made during her consideration of the issues revolving around helping her husband.

Again Julie is clearly not systematic. She does not construct a more abstract or integrative frame of reference within which she can justify rules or place them in relationship to one another. In systematic evaluation, this is typically achieved by considering the systemic concerns of the overarching entity involved. Examples of the latter include the individual as a self-system and the nation or group as a social system. In this context, principles of relations between systems can also be constructed. Julie's evaluations reflect neither kind of systemic construction.

INTRV.: Okay. Would you want the photographs to be displayed or not?

SUBJ.: Um, this art thing is just strange.

INTRV.: Why is that?

SUBJ.: Because you know I've been in situations where I look at something and it looks fine to me and it may not to somebody else. Whenever the ?? it happens. I think it was

Art is strange because the rule she applies is relativistic—in the eye of the beholder. No normal correct when somebody said that art is in the eye of the beholder, because it's just different. Um, visual appreciation is just a different thing. It's not like, well maybe it is like singing to different senses of appreciation depending on your tastes. And I don't know how your taste is developed, but um gosh that's a hard one, cause I have seen some of his stuff and I mean I wouldn't consider it something I would like to look at it a lot, but I mean I can stand it. Um, and I think really that um one of the hardest things to do in life is to be tolerant of people and things that are not so pleasing to you. Um, and so I think exposure to things that aren't Mona Lisas are good because obviously there are people in the world who appreciate the quality of his work. I mean every single piece, that's what makes him who he is. Um, so I would tend to um side with the art director in saying that it's art, it's him, you know this piece is him and so is that piece, but I just, it's not something I could fight for all the way. And I can argue it with somebody and say, I can understand the art director's reasoning, but I can also understand why people don't like to look at it. But then to those people, don't look at it. You know, don't come to this exhibit. Um, don't deprive other people of not seeing what they may enjoy in life.

INTRV.: Do you think that tolerance is important?

SUBJ.: Tolerance is very important.

INTRV.: Why is that?

SUBJ.: Because we are so different from one another. We're one species, but God, tolerance is part I think is one of the most undervalued traits in this country. That if we could teach our kids one thing, that's the one thing I would, I would um try to do, because um I think a lot of the problems that we're having comes from

convention of right and wrong, good and bad, can therefore be applied.

Rule of action outweighs personal feeling.

Definition of self as the specific things one does or produces.

Problem is a practical one of displeasing some. Just avoid the problem by having them not see it. Eliminate the effect.

What "is" (individual differences) is normal and hence "good". Confusion of "is" and "ought."

intolerance. So for art and just for everyday living, tolerance I think is the key and yeah, because intolerance which is . . . can do damage I think.

Tolerance is good because it prevents bad things from happening.

INTRV.: You said earlier that you have become convinced that in a given situation, there's one right thing to do.

SUBJ.: Uh huh.

INTRV.: These people have made a judgment about this, and they're saying it's wrong.

SUBJ.: Uh huh.

INTRV.: Don't they have the right to make that decision?

SUBJ.: Yeah, they certainly do for themselves. You know, everything, they have every right to be offended by a photograph that they don't agree with; however, I think that um they're going over their rights when they try to impose, or when they try to remove the photographs and deprive everyone else of making that judgment or disagreeing with that position.

Distinguishes rule from personal reaction.

INTRV.: So you think everybody should be allowed to make their own individual judgment.

SUBJ.: Um, yes. But only if it doesn't hurt other people, you know physically and emotionally. There is a you know, it's just very different. I mean, your interpretation of something is um good maybe different from others, maybe different from mine, and it's okay as long as we can live with that.

INTRV.: Why is it important to allow for that?

SUBJ.: Well, one, it's very important to be tolerant of differences, because otherwise we argue over the differences, and that I feel is very counterproductive. Two, I think um that our differences um should be valued, and this is corny because all these sessions where they talk about diversity and stuff, and I think people

Value is prevention of bad outcome.

are right when they say that you have to start valuing the differences instead of focusing on them as negatives. Um, cause the fact of the matter is, we are different. We are different genetically, we are different um emotionally, we're different socially, we're different physically, and you know until they come out with something that makes us all homogenous, we're going to remain different and we're gonna get more different, instead of less different, if the cultural trend continues. So I think we need to learn to live with that instead of fighting it.

Again confusion of "is" and "ought," of what is typically or normally the case—the observable fact of difference—with what is good.

INTRV.: So essentially you think tolerance, that freedom is valued because it's just a fact of life?

SUBJ.: Yeah, because the alternative is not much of an alternative. You know if you think about it.

INTRV.: Um, you said you thought exposure to things that are different is a good thing. Why is that?

SUBJ.: Um, one, it gives better understanding to one another, whether it's just individuals who are different, or cultures that are different. Um, and it allows us to get to know one another through our differences, and I think by knowing one another, that's when we can learn to be more tolerant. You know, instead of no I don't want to deal with it and not getting to know what is different, about certain people and individuals, I think the only way that we're gonna learn to live with one another is by getting to know one another. And being aware of the differences. Not loving every single difference and characteristic out there, but just being aware and understanding.

Positive valuation of exposure in terms of chain of positive effects.

INTRV.: Okay, let's say you go to this museum yourself and you see the pictures and decide they're very revolting, there's no art value at all. Would you still want these pictures to be shown?

Introduction of possibly sequential consideration.

SUBJ.: (pause) Um, if I find them revolting, I mean I can live with that. I don't have a desire to um discredit his art, um and I'm certain that there are people out there who appreciate every single photograph he's taken, so I can live with that. You know, I wouldn't act on it. I mean I would probably tell Marty, well, this is strange, and that's it. I mean we've seen strange art before, it's okay.

Subject clearly separates her own reaction to the event from the value of the event. Also allows differing perspectives, different views of the event.

INTRV.: Let's pretend for a moment that you live and work in Cincinnati. What would you tell the committee?

SUBJ.: Um, rather than try to tell them what I told you that I personally may find it um offensive but I don't have any desire to deprive anybody else from seeing it, and that there are others out there who have learned to appreciate it, or do appreciate it for what it is. But I'd be very very diplomatic about it. And you know that comes up around here. I mean there's not very many Democrats around.

INTRV.: Oh really?

SUBJ.: Yeah, and um you know I just some things don't bother me, but other things you know. I just try to be very diplomatic. But I disagree that that's okay. So I wouldn't sign nothing. But I'd you know, like try to get them to understand why.

INTRV.: Would you be worried about the costs? I mean you could lose your job, your security.

SUBJ.: Well yeah, I'd probably assess that, but um you know I don't know. I didn't know you'd come up with that kind of situation. I mean I hope I don't say, I mean I hope I don't get involved in something I really didn't believe in, which would be that art committee.

Mitigation strategy of denying the event could occur.

INTRV.: In other words, trying to shut it down?

SUBJ.: Yeah, I wouldn't do that.

INTRV.: You could just politely refuse to comment on the matter and not give your opinion on it.

SUBJ.: Hmm. (pause) I don't know, I'd have to have to think about it. Yeah, I don't know. I think in the long run, it's probably better to show your opinion um rather than you know not comment.

INTRV.: Why is that?

SUBJ.: Um, and this is ??? Um, I think it's okay to clarify your feelings, cause um one you feel that way for a reason and it's probably a very logical reason. And other people would probably understand it even though they don't agree with it totally. It's good you know to express yourself, you know to get some background to why I feel that way. And when you say "no comment" it sort of leaves the committee the option of interpreting what "no comment" means, and then you know you don't understand it. It doesn't mean, it doesn't give much hint into what you ??

Rule of action: express your feelings because they are good and true. The evident cost associated with this is reduced by mitigation strategy of assuming that committee would "understand."

INTRV.: What about the costs?

SUBJ.: Yeah.

INTRV.: Expressing your honest opinion could prove very costly in this situation as it were.

SUBJ.: Yeah, I don't know. Yeah, I can't imagine getting fired over that kind of situation. Then I don't live in Cincinnati. Um, yeah, I certainly would take reasonable means not to get fired. Um, and when the committee approached me, one of the things I could honestly say is that it just doesn't mean that much to me. I certainly couldn't support them but at the same time, I wouldn't fight for it on the other side either, just cause I really don't feel that strongly about it. I know what's right for me. You know, it's another case when with everything else going on and you have to argue such things like that. It is so trivial.

Problem reframed by real possibility of being fired.

Mitigate negative aspect by emphasizing that it is not important issue.

INTRV.: So do you think, do you think if you started to support the banning of these photographs, would that strike you as particularly important?

SUBJ.: No.

INTRV.: Why not?

SUBJ.: Because I don't think it, I think all the effort that they would have to exert in the fight for the ban could be better utilized somewhere else in the committee, where they're being um voluntary ?? helping their family, making ends meet. You know, in the long run, that art ban is nothing.

> Bolsters choice made by reinforcing how inconsequential the negative outcome is (post-choice dissonance reduction).

INTRV.: Well I guess, what I mean is, let's say they succeed in doing it. And the photographs they considered obscene were removed. Would it bother you enough to do anything about it?

SUBJ.: Um, probably not.

INTRV.: How come?

SUBJ.: I guess that, I just don't think um one way or the other it's worth the resources to expend and um just cause there's so many other things that could be bettered, and you know that would make a difference in somebody's life. But removing the art, I don't think um feeds any more hungry kids or reduces the number of murders or you know some of the very serious problems that we have. So I wouldn't want to partake in the effort to do one thing or the other.

> Issues of principle are not relevant to consideration of the ban. The focus is on substantive outcomes. The ban on art is valued less than other possible effects.

INTRV.: Well let's assume that one way the city tries to deal with this is by bringing in a group of respected art critics and civic leaders to view and evaluate the photographs. And they decide the photographs are really vulgar and have no really artistic value whatsoever, and they suggest that the photographs be removed from the exhibition. What would you suggest? Would you agree that the city should follow their recommendation?

> Interviewer introduces authoritative decision.

SUBJ.: I mean just personally? Hmm, yeah I still

wouldn't agree with it, but it's so hard to go against that kind of public movement because it happens, and it's very I mean I still wouldn't agree with their actions. Um, but I don't know if I would do anything more than disagree with it.

INTRV.: Do you think it's a good way for them to resolve the problem?

SUBJ.: No.

INTRV.: Why not?

SUBJ.: Um, by removing the artwork I think they concede that they cannot tolerate the difference, you know the difference sense of value. Um, it's a sign of intolerance which I just don't think it's healthy. I think I don't know . . . ??

> Invokes rule. Denies authority because it does not behave correctly—does not do what it is supposed to.

INTRV.: Let's say that instead of doing that, the city council decides that this is an issue for the entire community to decide. And they hold a public referendum because it's such a hot local issue.

> Interviewer introduces alternative rule in attempt to reframe issue.

SUBJ.: Um hmm.

INTRV.: Almost everybody comes out to cast a ballot.

SUBJ.: Wow!

INTRV.: To no one's surprise, an overwhelming majority votes to remove these photographs. Um, do you think that that would be a good way to resolve the issue?

SUBJ.: Um, okay you said that almost everybody votes?

INTRV.: Yeah.

SUBJ.: Um, I think in that case, I mean let's call it the democratic process, but um in general I wouldn't think of doing anything by referendum just because nobody votes, and very few people vote, and the outcome of an election I think are inconsistent with the desires of the populations. But if you say that everyone, you know most everybody votes, um I think it

> Moves to create evaluative consistency by devaluing elections as unrepresentative.

would be a good idea to do it that way and
just put the thing to rest.

INTRV.: Why is that the best way of doing it?

SUBJ.: Because it's democratic and you know the
foundation of this country, and um it's okay
to be on the losing side, but it's good for those
of us in the minorities to know what the
majority wants and how much that majority
is. It's hard to argue with um an election that
is all inclusive like that. You know, if it was
just the committee and if it was just the group
of experts, that's one thing. But if you tossed
it out and got 98 percent of the people to vote,
well it's hard to argue with that. You know,
and then those of us who were in the minority
can see we were in the minority.

    *Democratic process
simply stipulated as good.*

    *Bolsters against negative
aspect.*

    *Good process (evaluative
anchor) produces good/
acceptable outcome.*

INTRV.: Do you think that the people of this
community have a legitimate right to decide
issues like this in this way?

SUBJ.: Um, yeah, just because the art museum is a
service to the community and it should try to
cater to the needs and the desires of the
community, and you know like it's a public
institution, so I think it's okay to do it that
way. Use a vote.

    Role related rule of action.

INTRV.: What do you mean when you say it should
cater to the needs and desires?

SUBJ.: Well you know as in other public institutions,
um it should give the public what it wants.
Unfortunately, in this circumstance, the
public didn't want to be exposed to Mapplethorpe's art. You know, that's unfortunate, but
it's hard to argue against an overwhelming
majority. You know, especially when you
know the same people who voted probably
paid, provided the funds. I don't think they're
gonna want their money to be used that way.
What do you do?

    *Rule: people pay for
something hence own it.
It should therefore do
what they want.*

INTRV.: Do you think there's any danger in this kind
of election?

    *Interviewer attempts to
reframe problem with*

SUBJ.: I think there's a lot of danger in public referendums, I mean extreme danger. Um, I wouldn't want anybody's future to be put on any ballot in this state.

> focus on negative outcomes rather than on process.

INTRV.: Why is that?

SUBJ.: Just because of the demographics of those who vote. As you probably know, the voters tend to be more conservative and on the average older than the general population, so I don't, I mean I wouldn't want anything to be, you know, I wouldn't want everything to be decided by a group of older conservative people, I just don't think that would even meet the needs of the population. But you know if there was ever a way to go back and um encourage everybody to participate in the electoral process, I would be interested in putting some measures on the ballot just to find out what people think. Because it's so hard to figure out what people think these days.

> Problem is reframed. Focus on outcomes which are bad (conservative). This is evaluative anchor. In this context, the linked process, democratic process is valued negatively.

INTRV.: Right.

SUBJ.: I mean they don't like doing surveys. They don't, they lie on surveys, and then you try to look at the election results, and it's just, it's hard to make sense of it. To figure out what the average, I guess there's not even an average citizen. What is it that people want? They don't want to tell you. You know I just don't think um ballot measures are the way to go to resolve anything. I mean that's why we elect our legislators, so we don't have to individually vote, so that they can set policies based on why we elected them. And that's the way it's supposed to work, but unfortunately, they don't. They haven't been working that well.

> Bolsters negative view of elections by claim that they are false or do not really reflect opinion.

> Invokes role.

INTRV.: Um, what about the principle of free expression which is part of our constitutional rights? It's kind of a double ??? in this case.

> Interviewer introduces convention or principle (depending on subjective

SUBJ.: Um hmm.

INTRV.: And it allows the community to express itself, but at the cost of individual's freedom.

SUBJ.: Right.

INTRV.: Would that worry you at all?

SUBJ.: Yeah, if it got beyond the city of Cincinnati, it would worry me! But um it, we're talking about a relatively small city and just the quirkiness of that city, I wouldn't lose sleep over it. But um, I think freedom of expression is very important. I mean I think the whole Constitution and the Bill of Rights is very important. Um, and you know that goes back to why I feel so strongly about tolerance. It is, the Bill of Rights was based on tolerance. You know, you can see that the individuals who developed the Bill of Rights understood the value of tolerance and they, I think the reason things are so basic are because they felt that people needed to stick to the basics. Um, so you know believe in the Constitution.

reconstruction).

Mitigates negative effect by reference to small outcome.

Values Bill of Rights because is causally linked to valued anchoring norm of tolerance (or perhaps it is tolerance that is anchored in the Bill of Rights).

INTRV.: What do you mean by the basics?

SUBJ.: Things like freedom of expression. You know, freedom of speech. Those are very basic human rights.

INTRV.: Why is that?

SUBJ.: Um one is that humans have the ability to express themselves. You know, they're born, most individuals at least, um are born with the ability to express themselves. And to speak and to write for that matter. Um, and to censor that, those very human characteristics. Just I don't think it's a very good idea at all.

What is normal becomes basis for norm.

Flounders when trying to justify the rule that one should be free to express oneself.

INTRV.: Why not? What are the consequences to that?

SUBJ.: Well the consequences of that is that we go to a very homogenous society and that wouldn't be very fun at all. And unfortunately that just diverts from the whole consciousness of democracy.

Justification is at same concrete level. Value of rule is in the value of the outcome it produces.

INTRV.: In what sense?

SUBJ.: Well in that the whole appeal of being able to
have a voice in the government, um it's I don't
know, it's ? I was just talking to some folks
about how we sometimes forget that a
government is for the people by the people.
And um because you know politicians and
stuff are just you know sort of a strange breed
these days. Um, and um going back to the
Constitution and the Bill of Rights, I think
the Bill of Rights is our avenue to democracy.
I mean I think that people should be able to   Invokes concrete norm
express themselves to whatever they want and   of proper way to behave.
just say what they want, as long as they're not
physically or emotionally hurting anybody.
And to take that away would be, it would
create a whole different country. It doesn't
make sense does it.

INTRV.: Okay. Last question on this, let's say for a   Interviewer introduces
moment the situation was completely differ-   scenario of Santa Ana.
ent. Let's say the art museum was in Santa
Ana, which is a mixing of whites, African-
Americans, Hispanic Americans, and so on.
And the plan was to have a display of contemporary American art which includes some
famous artists of the day. Surprisingly, they
included some work which was very racist.
Um, racial minorities were shown to be stupid
and ugly. The pictures were clearly degrading.
The community was outraged and demanded
that the pictures be removed or the exhibition
canceled. Would you want the pictures to be
shown?

SUBJ.: Um, I would say I would agree that those   Issue of free expression are
community leaders. Cause I would think that   forgotten entirely as the
those types of pictures do hurt people in most   focus on racism reframes
?? And that it goes beyond the power of art,   the issue.
it's like political statements being made
through the canvas or whatever, the photos. I
can't imagine. You know, I think homosexual

art is one thing, I mean people can appreciate that. I think there are people who appreciate it. But um I can't imagine that there would be any benefit of showing racist art. You know, I think like that oversteps the boundaries of trying to be open to new things and different things.

Racist art judged in a unidimensional manner, of no possible value.

INTRV.: So you don't see any reason to be tolerant of that?

SUBJ.: Racism? No, I don't. I um it's actually, you may not agree with this, but I think it's a classic example of intolerance of an individual who is able to speak freely of racism and to um portray pictures of racism is very intolerant. And to make fun or um you know degrade individuals because of their ?? or their sex, or their sexual preference even is intolerant, because it is hurtful.

Invokes rule of toleration and ignores relation to rule of free speech.

Racism is bad because it causes harm to individuals.

INTRV.: So in a sense, you're saying that it's important to be intolerant of intolerance?

Interviewer states the conundrum.

SUBJ.: There's a line that gets crossed, yeah. That when we're talking about yeah racism, it's just a whole different spectrum of things. You know I don't know what good could come of it.

Racism is bad because it produces nothing good.

INTRV.: It might not be of any good can come of it at all, but wouldn't the artists still have a right to have their works publicly shown?

Interviewer reintroduces issue of rule of freedom of expression.

SUBJ.: Um, maybe in his garage but not in the city of Santa Ana Art Museum. No, it's very damaging, to tolerate intolerance like you said (laughs), it's very damaging.

INTRV.: But in this case, um doesn't the freedom of expression, especially politically expression, even if it's through art, um isn't it just as important to recognize that too?

SUBJ.: Um, no. Yeah, I think if you're, if the community were to tolerate the art of a racist individual, it would send very confusing

Produce bad outcomes.

messages to young people and very confusing.
And um I don't think that's beneficial at all.
And um, you know it goes to right and   Raw assertion that it is
wrong, it's just not right. It's not art to be able   wrong.
to damage somebody's character.

INTRV.: That's what you mean by it going beyond the
power of art?

SUBJ.: Yeah. I mean you know when they, I mean I   Possible reasoning: racism
personally had never seen any racist art but   is bad, art is good, and
um the art depicts um a woman or a African-   hence racist art is not art.
American in a demeaning way, I don't think   Further probing needed.
that's art.

INTRV.: Okay . . . I think that is enough for now

Barbara's Systematic Evaluation

Barbara's considerations of the value of the display of controversial art share
many of the same features as her earlier discussion of her daughter. Her comments are not as well integrated as in the earlier discussion, and she and the interviewer do not seem to be communicating quite as well. I believe that more
than anything else this is due to the fact that the entire interview was done in one
sitting lasting almost three hours, and this section on Mapplethorpe's art was the
last to be addressed. Both the interviewer and interviewee had pushed on for too
long and were tired. The interview should have been cut short and resumed at
some later time. This said, the features of Barbara's thought are still clear.

As in her discussion of her daughter, Barbara focuses on the connections between actions and ideas rather than specific acts. Thus rather than simply evaluating actions with reference to the established value of their outcomes or with
regard to a specific standard of action, Barbara focuses on the meanings that are
constructed and the social norms that are applied. The latter are understood
relative to one another. Because her judgment is thus not anchored in particular concrete acts, Barbara can consider a matter in an abstract way that is free of
any particular concrete reference. These are introduced but usually only in an
illustrative rather than in a defining way. A good example of this level of abstraction is her evaluation of standards or rules of behavior. The concern here is
not any specific standard but standards in general. Some specific cases are introduced, but they exemplify a point that is defined independently of these
cases and their meaning is self-consciously constructed in this context.

In a typically systematic fashion, Barbara creates contexts in which to interpret the meaning and judge the value of certain patterns of behavior or rules of action. A good example of this is her counter to the interviewer's suggestion that gays are not life affirming because they do not act in a way that literally reproduces life. The interviewer's suggestion is linear—gay behavior is defined by its outcome. Barbara responds by explaining that the meaning of procreation is relative to the individual system considered. For heterosexuals it may be an expression of the affirmation of life as they define it, but for gays it may not. Moreover she makes clear that, for her, life is a matter of self-construction and meaning-making, not simply biological existence. The integrity of the self-system emerges as a higher order value here as it did earlier in the discussion of her daughter. It is not elaborated here, nor is it probed by the interviewer because it had been discussed at length earlier, making the separate coding of this section a little more difficult.

To guide her judgment, Barbara constructs two levels of evaluation. At one level, she regularly identifies the concrete values expressed in common practices, social norms, and individual preferences. At a second level, she draws on a sense of the integrity of individual self-systems to judge these values. This yields an inclination to respect differences and freedoms, but at the same time it provides clear indications when these should be curtailed. This two-level mode of evaluation is interestingly illustrated in her consideration of the general value of concrete social ideals and norms of behavior relative to a higher order concern with the integrity of the self. In her view, these concrete social directives interfere with the development of selves by preempting individuals' attempts to experiment and discover the meaning and value which a particular act has for them. This leads to a general suspicion of behavioral norms.

Barbara does not construct the issue of the display of art in linear terms. Rather than being guided by concrete definitions and specific rules of action, she is constantly subjecting these to scrutiny and reevaluation. Again and again, Barbara regards these concrete values as epiphenomenal, considering their meaning in context and occasionally analyzing the manner of their social construction. Moreover, her evaluations are not concretely anchored in the identifiable good of a specific act or person. As a result, there is no evidence of an attempt to maintain value balance.

For Barbara, good need not be associated with good. It can be associated with bad or with something of indeterminate value. This is evident in her early assertion that the prohibition of a display may be bad, but this does not suggest that the initiation of the display is good. It is also evident when considering two frames of reference for evaluating an issue, that of society and that of a mother, she recognizes that two opposite and yet reasonable judgments may be forthcoming. But she makes no move to mitigate what, in linear terms, would be a confusing evaluative contradiction. Armed with specific rules and consistent evaluative categories, linear evaluation provides the needed clear direction for action. In Barbara's case, issues are more multifaceted and complex. The ensuing ambiguity is not only implicitly accommodated, but toward the end, it is explicitly acknowledged as an inevitable element of judgment.

INTRV.: Should the photographs be shown or not?

SUBJ.: Okay. You mean should they not be prevented from being shown? Or do I think it's important that they be shown? I mean I know quite frankly, I mean I don't have any strong feelings, but if there is art, it should be shown. But I think that it should not, that someone should not be prevented from showing it just because there are you know, because of say explicit sexual scenes or images and that offends people. But I think the only legitimate reason not to show something is that it actually causes some harm, and I think in the case of explicit gay scenes, I don't see if there's any social harm in it.

> Value is in terms of effect. The harm done. The meaning of this remains ambiguous until further probed.

INTRV.: But if the public wants to keep them out of the museum?

SUBJ.: No, I don't think that's legitimate.

INTRV.: And why is that?

SUBJ.: Because I think that in the, I think that there is not necessarily any positive social good by showing artwork, but I think that society takes a stand on preventing it. Then I think it delegitimates the existence of gay sexuality. And I think that is a harm and I think to prevent an artist from expressing themselves in a way that doesn't cause any real harm I think lessens the quality of society as a whole. I think we should allow expression that doesn't cause harm.

> General rule, but as elaborated thus far, it may be linear or systematic. Note, however, that good action and bad action are not opposites of one another as is typically the case in linear thinking.

INTRV.: You have a community that has a certain standard. And the community at large wants all its members to live up to that standard.

SUBJ.: But see if the standard . . . a standard is a standard which delegitimates certain things, people that aren't ?? anybody, so I think my general rule would be that I think that's wrong. I think it's wrong to oppose ?? which delegitimate people. In the same sense that you know people may not want to listen to anything to do with racist thought, they want to pretend that it doesn't exist in the same way they want to believe that gay sex doesn't exist, that people don't exist. So they try to hide that and they say, well, that's our standard, our standard is for a family, we don't want to have, you know our standard is heterosexual white, and we don't want to have anything else. But they're delegitimizing a great number of people and that is wrong. And I don't think that society should prevent expression of people that the majority of society don't want to exist or what to delegitimate, want to hide from. I think that's an extremely unhealthy society and for the people that are harmed by it.

> Focuses on social norm as object and attempts to judge it.

> Clearly considering rules at two levels, that of existing norm or convention and that of a general rule in terms of which the former is evaluated.

> Norm evaluated in terms of functional consequences for society.

INTRV.: Somebody might make the argument that there's a group of people who might be harmful, and sure they say that's okay and they say they're happy, but you can also make the argument that, well, they're not ? Can you make the same argument about homosexuals, and yeah they like to do that, but they're harming themselves and they're not really happy, so we as a community shouldn't allow that?

> Interviewer raises problem of determining what is good or harmless.

SUBJ.: I don't think I ?? to say that. I think that in an abusive situation, the only reason that some people might choose to be abused is that they were abused in the first place, it was a wrong.

> Goes beyond substantive claim of what is specifically desirable or harmful to a second order consid-

I think you can look into people's psyche and decide certain things which are very much against somebody's integrity, and I think that's the reason why we have a rule that people can't consent to be killed, and people shouldn't be allowed to commit suicide. Because I think that, without a whole hell of a lot of safeguards, because I think that people can get into modes that are incredibly self-destructive. And I think that we can legitimately say that that is abnormal and undesirable because we as a society are out of a sense of you know, that human beings are by nature life affirming, and if they're not life affirming it's abnormal. If they're enormously self-destructive, then they've probably have been psychologically harmed greatly in the past and this wanting to be harmed is only a symbol a symptom of the harm that was done to them. And I think if people were healthy, they don't want to be harmed. And obviously what's healthy is a problematic issue, what do we consider it. Now certainly people can say well what's natural is heterosexual and that anybody who is homosexual is abnormal and not healthy, but I don't think we have a reason to believe that. I don't believe that. And I think that we cause a lot of harm to people who are born gay by suggesting that that's abnormal. People can't be not gay if they're gay, whereas I think people can become healthy if they've been abused as children.

> eration of the basis for determining whose judgment of harm should be authoritative. Implies that individuals have integrity as a system and hence determine functioning up to the point at which they are self-destructive entities. Then they violate their own integrity and hence lose rights as system.

> Value of life affirmation asserted without elaboration—ambiguous meaning. (Sections of interview judged separately; however, the reader will remember that this value is discussed at length in first section on personal issue.)

INTRV.: Well, you talk about a healthy person being a life-affirming person, and you may think of a life-affirming person as somebody who wants to help the lives around them, but they also want to procreate, they want to perpetuate their species. They want to bear one life to continue.

> Interviewer introduces an ends-oriented, linear definition of affirming life—to want to create life.

SUBJ.: I meant like affirming in terms of their own life.

INTRV.: As it pertains to ?? But at a deeper level might you say that somebody who is not engaging in a sexuality which is perpetuating their species is in some sense?

SUBJ.: No I think that has to do with personal integrity. I don't think that, I mean if you were born gay then it's certainly not life affirming to be you know to be in sexual activity that's procreative because that's heterosexual and that would be very much against your nature.

Rejects concrete ends definition and argues that value and meaning of end is relative to nature of the person.

INTRV.: What if people are born violent?

SUBJ.: I don't think people are born violent. I think you become violent because of the way you were treated. I mean you look at people who are manic depressive. People can be severely violent in a manic period. Well that is very abnormal brain chemistry which we understand is something which is very unhealthy functioning of the brain, it's very self-destructive. And it's something we can help people get out of. We can help them have a life that is, you know, better for them and the people around them. Plus the fact that violence is something that very much harms other people or themselves. So I don't think that if people don't you know.

Issue of an individual's integrity subordinated to broader issue of integrity of all. Consequently, violent individual is discounted because of the violation of others and the truth of the assertion that people are naturally violent is also rejected.

INTRV.: Is there an instance when we shouldn't allow people to live?

SUBJ.: I think there is a point in which, I think the easy line to draw is to say, people can say I don't want to live with artificial means of life support. I don't think you need to go, I don't think people, I don't think it's necessarily positive for people in a society to have to go to every single length to save their life at all costs, even if their life is so diminished at some

General claim of ultimate value (second order value) of affirming life is applied with great consistency across substantively diverse situations rendering them formally identical.

point, and they're so dependent on say life support, without any hope of getting better. I think that that's an easy question, to withdraw life support. Now somebody who is dying in horrible pain, I think first we have to offer people, I mean I think we have a lot of resources for example to offer people so they can really reduce pain. I don't think we explored this thing very much, but I think that if that doesn't work, if people get to the point where given all the social resources that are very positive and allow people to have a life in which they can endure, they end up only with the possibility of a life that they really cannot endure. And I think that if we put in safeguards to allow them some period of time, so they just don't go through some momentary period, a massive depression which they can come out of, you'd be helped out of, so you have some safeguards that will keep people from, in a ?? deciding one end of my life, okay, now I can. I think we'd put some safeguards on it, yes, I think ultimately you have the right to not have a ??

INTRV.: What if it's ?? what if it's not a minimum? What if it's a person who is a great artist, great musician, let's take a great musician, piano player.

SUBJ.: And they're seriously depressed and they don't want to ?? Or they just don't want to live their life without their arms?

INTRV.: Well not that they're seriously depressed, but that is the way they construct their identity as this piano player. And now they have no way of expressing themselves in terms of that identity.

SUBJ.: I think again you have certain safeguards and I think the safeguards are time related.

INTRV.: So you think that we should, as a society, bring them to a point where they can endure their life even though that's not the life that they want? Or you cannot give them . . .

SUBJ.: Well I think that's a little bit . . . I think if they totally lost their sense of identity, I mean it's really their decision, what I'm saying it's a person's decision to make ultimately. And I think that, but I think, the reason we have safeguards is that often people who are facing situations worse than they think they can endure, which look horrible to them, because so many people go through this, you know if you've ever been in a massive depression. But the fact is that a human being tends to, I think by their very nature, tends to want to come out of that if they can, so the safeguards are in place to allow us to be able to reach a point in out life where we do want to have life. But I think ultimately it is the person's individual decision, it has to be because I think we have to preserve some sort of individual integrity or dignity that if you know through some period of time and given some options to improve their life they decide that they cannot endure it. I think they have the right to do that.

> The principle of affirming life used to positively value a decision to terminate life. This is sensible as the meaning of the decision is self-consciously recast in terms of a conception of the individual as a self-directing system.

> In addition, life affirmation is defined not simply in terms of concrete end of living, but with reference to a form of functioning.

INTRV.: The reason I gave you that, let's consider the idea, a little bit about this notion of integrity and manipulating individuals' chemistry. And if you knew somebody who was gay and somebody said I don't want to be or even I'm nor sure about being gay, I'm just sort of exploring that. And you could give him a drug that's going to develop their brain or something, or make them not gay, do you do that? Or what if we decide as a community that that's a behavior that is not normal?

> Interviewer raises issue of community vs. individual determination of value.

SUBJ.: Well we have to, we have decided. I mean there's a tremendous amount of pressure to escape from people.

INTRV.: But it doesn't necessarily mean that they're . . .

SUBJ.: When people are teenagers if we could change their genetics to make them not gay, should we do that? I think a more reasonable question is should we allow them to choose to do it?

Retains notion of value of individual self-direction and redefines concern accordingly.

INTRV.: Well if we identify it when they're infants?

SUBJ.: Um hmm. Your parents have the right to do that? I don't like the idea of genetic manipulation because then I think it reinforces the notion that there are good things and bad things, right things and wrong things. I mean there are a number of examples like that. If we know somebody who's going to be born with you know a shortened thumb, do we create a class of people that are in one image? I think that's a dangerous way to go, more because it reinforces our notion that there's only one that's acceptable. And if we start trying to manipulate our genetics to get only that one . . . I think it's like plastic surgery. I think it's a bad thing to have widespread plastic surgery because it pressures people into being the norm, what we decide is the ideal or the norm. And I think that's dangerous because I think we gain a tremendous amount from our diversity, from the fact that we act differently. You know, there are some that are very excitable and some of us that are very calm. I think that's good. I think that's good because having a mix of people is better for everybody. I mean there's a trade-off; I mean think of the parents' dilemma. If you had a kid that you knew was going to be born gay, if you could change that, would you? I think most parents would say yes, because they don't want their child to go through the stigma of discrimination and pain, but from a social viewpoint, it's very dangerous.

General consideration of specific assertions of right and wrong. These are denigrated as undermining possibilities for self-creation.

Introduction of diversity as value. To disambiguate meaning requires probing. (The reader will remember this was discussed in terms of the self system in the personal section. The coder did not have access to this.)

Constructs second frame of reference which yields different evaluation. Does not integrate the two frames, but recognizes contradiction without trying to mitigate it as a linear would.

INTRV.: Let's go back to the arts. What if it were racist

art. Take it out of Cincinnati and put it in Santa Ana. Now the curator, director wants to have an exhibit where minorities are portrayed as stupid and ignorant, and it's very degrading to certain groups. And there's an outcry in the community that these things shouldn't be shown. They should be taken out of there and ??

> Interviewer introduces shift in context where display demeans rather than expresses the depicted population.

SUBJ.: Well, I think they have a legitimate standing. This is something which exacerbates the degradation of those people and ultimately causes a lot of harm, because the fact that these people are racist puts people in a vulnerable position, a very harmful position to begin with, and then you create something to show the public which harms them even more, which makes them feel even worse. I think it's a different issue if you have an art exhibit which discusses racism, and the subject of it, for example, pictures of the Holocaust. They do have a lot of Jews in the community and they feel uncomfortable having them there, but then there are a lot of other Jews who think no, this is a real issue and the real harm is the fact that nobody believes it's happening. The harm is pretending that it doesn't exist. The same thing, if the exhibit is showing the treatment of blacks and the public, there was a lot of public awareness coming out of it and it says to people this really exists, this is really a bad thing. Now it's going to make everybody feel sort of uncomfortable, but if it ultimately doesn't, it's sort of a social, I think that if it's not something that's really harmful to somebody, I think it should be allowed. Now in this case, the case of the Holocaust, not to show it sort of delegitimates people who were harmed in the Holocaust. Like we're saying we don't want to see it, we don't want to have

> First invokes a general concern that the integrity of individuals or categories of individuals not be compromised.

> Then begins interpretive application of the general concern to the assessment of particular cases of displays that revolve around the degradation of others. The problem is to determine the different meaning and consequence of the same action when done in different contexts.

anything to do with it. There was an exhibit that was supposed to be shown in Washington, D.C., and there was a casket, it was an AIDS, did you hear about this? It was an AIDS exhibit. The Senate said, "no, we don't show caskets." That's bullshit. They don't want to have anything that uncomfortable because it's going to disturb a lot of people, because a lot of people are going to have to realize that AIDS is a real problem. You know, they can't hide from it anymore, it's gory, it's nasty, it makes us feel bad. Why does it make us feel bad? Because we have to admit that there's a real problem with this. It doesn't denigrate people with AIDS, what it's really trying to say is this is a real problem.

Interpreting the meaningful connections that others are making.

INTRV.: Here you've got an artist that is expressing himself through this medium that we don't necessarily know, we can't make a blanket statement and say blacks are or Hispanics are. But here's a guy who's produced this art and wants an opportunity to show it.

SUBJ.: But I mean, well, you said there was a huge outcry by a group of people saying that they felt very denigrated by this.

INTRV.: We'll make the argument that it's for the sake of art, it's art.

SUBJ.: It's art. Well, I don't think there's anything sacrosanct about art. And I don't think that just because of it the art should be shown. I think the question is, is it something that we as a society value being expressed?

Actively interprets meaning and value of art.

INTRV.: Well, it's a medium of expression so to take that part of expression away, now you're not just picking on art as a medium, but you're picking on expression itself.

SUBJ.: Hmm. You're saying that we don't want certain, I think it's legitimate for society to say we don't want certain things expressed in certain frames, in certain ways. I think, for

Value of freedom of expression is defined relative to a higher order concern with integrity of

example, racist speech can be controlled because it really generates and regenerates and exacerbates and plays on a lot of hatred that harms other people. and I think we have the right as a society to say we don't want that. In the same way a family has a right to tell its kids not to use certain words or certain terms or certain attitudes or certain voice levels in the house. Okay, that's legitimate. I think it's legitimate for society to do it, as long as it's an attempted control, a reasonable legitimate attempt to control the harm done to people. Now in a situation where you've got an art exhibit that shows blacks in denigrated positions, and it actually does and it actually is going to harm somebody where there's a lot of people who feel very much denigrated, I think society should say we don't want our public shown that, we don't want to use our museum to show it. And I think it's legitimate to restrict it.

persons. N.B. throughout, the harmful outcome is in part the meaning created, that is how people are defined and valued.

Concern is integrity of individuals and hence must insure social intervention is carefully considered.

INTRV.: What if Cincinnati says this art exhibit is going to give people the wrong idea, it's going to tell people that weak persons are like that, it's going to confuse some people.

SUBJ.: Who's making the decision?

INTRV.: The same community that made it ??

SUBJ.: Okay.

INTRV.: The community at large that has to put its stamp of approval on this art exhibit. So it's one community that says you can't do this, and they're wrong. And another community in southern California that says you can't do this, and you're saying that they're right?

Interviewer tries to introduce a concrete linear contradiction between allowing exhibit in one city and not in another.

SUBJ.: Okay, you've got the gay exhibit and the racist exhibit, and I'm saying one you can't restrict and one you can?

INTRV.: Right.

SUBJ.: Okay. I mean the reason, what was the difference?

INTRV.: Yeah.

SUBJ.: The difference is in one case, there really isn't, I mean in one case by not showing it, you're delegitimating somebody. In this case, we are harming by not showing it. By restricting it, the only thing, I mean I think unless there's something else you're not telling me, the only thing you've said is that it denigrates most people and the only thing we're doing by restricting it is to say to the artist we don't want you to express it here. So you're restricting art. So what I'm saying is I don't think that art is a value, I don't think we need to say that we always want to have artistic expression, that it is valuable. I think we have to measure it in terms of the actual harm done to society. And I think in the first case, you know, the community would say it was harmful, but why? It's just because of their own prejudices. It's not something, I mean the ultimate, in a sense that there was more harm by restricting it than it was by showing it.

> Denies suggested contradiction because she is applying the same principle to two different contexts. The two different substantive decisions, to allow and to disallow, thus mean the same thing.

> Note the abstract and general nature of the discussion throughout.

INTRV.: And that's your assessment?

SUBJ.: That's my assessment, my personal assessment. I think one of the other differences is, let's say the heterosexual community says this denigrates us as heterosexuals, but I'm sorry, the heterosexuals are so oppressive, I mean they are the group that has all the power and all the respect. So I don't think we as a society worry so much about denigrating the, you know, the dominant respected group that has all the power to begin with. I think what you need to have is safeguards, serious safeguards, and I think it is all off balance, but I think the reason that this is a little bit more serious is that this is a group of people who doesn't have the respect, doesn't have the power, who's been denigrated and is vulnerable.

> Differentiates two cases, Cincinnati heterosexual complaint and Santa Ana's Hispanic complaint, in terms of the context of each group, their place relative to other groups.

INTRV.: Well do you have a concern, in the Santa Ana situation, do you have a concern that if you restrict this art exhibit, you send a message that, if you say something that . . .

SUBJ.: Sure . . . that you don't like . . .

INTRV.: The extreme of things, then you're going to get slammed for you know, it's going to discourage expression.

SUBJ.: What we really have to be concerned about is first of all, artistic, freedom of artistic expression has to do with being able to be critical in expressing what's happening in society. And I think we always have to safeguard its freedom, not any particular work of art, but the freedom to have legitimate expression and criticism. Basically, I think it's the expression of ideas and criticisms of society, I think that's what free speech is all about. But we also have to realize that you know we live in a society which has certain power imbalances, and that there are certain individuals and groups of people who are going to be harmed because they have no power. You know, the classic case of that is abused women. Now we make fun of abused women all the time, in various ways. And I don't think . . . that's something that is very difficult for society to safeguard against. We have to recognize when we tromp on the less powerful and that includes blacks, gays, children, and all kinds of other people that can't really stand up and defend themselves. Now part of the function of art is to take nonmainstream views and to bring them up and say hey this is it. But if you have an exhibit that shows the denigration of blacks, essentially what you have is you have an additional weapon. It's not really an interesting expression that criticizes or illuminates society, it's really a weapon in the

Art is an activity self-consciously defined and valued in terms of a societal function it is supposed to serve—to offer critique and thereby maintain diversity. (The value of this function should have been probed more.)

Begins to place a number of different evaluative and analytical concerns in relation to one another. Introduces power as a structural or contextual variable that interacts with evaluative considerations of free expression and preventing harm.

hands of the people who are oppressing in the first place. So I think as a society, we need to have, we need to be honest with ourselves about what really is going on and not just be socially blind to say oh this is art, we have to let it fly. Now the problem of restricting art is it's going to want to crush things that criticize them and make them look bad. And that's where we have to be honest about our discussions. You know, people are coming out and saying gays are bad. We have to think about it. We have to think who are they, why are they? Are they legitimate? And I'm saying they're legitimate because what the hell, they were born that way. I mean they can't help it. It's a choice they made somewhere in their life. Or because we as a society decided that our sexuality is private and free and it doesn't harm anybody else so don't invade that boundary of privacy, but I think we have to be honest about what our discussions are about. You know, to make those judgment calls, and they're always going to be judgment calls. And I think that if we try to set an absolute rule about oh we can just do any kind of artistic expression we want as long as we you know, as long as some court somewhere decides it's not attracting interests, which I think masks the whole problem in the first place, when people can say we have to have all speech free at any cost are not facing the realities of what's really happening.

Focus is on the social dynamics of how meaning and value are constructed.

Focus shifts from judgment to the conditions, process, and quality of judgment. This leads to a concern for flexibility of context dependent application of rules in a world where situations are complex.

Bill's Sequential Evaluation

Bill's consideration of the display of homoerotic art has many of the same clearly sequential features as his response to the issue of helping his brother. Here as there, value is a matter of feelings, his own or the observed responses of others. In this vein, he judges the pictures to be bad because they will ruin kids and he positively values "knowing in your mind that you are right" because it feels good. Similarly, when discussing pornography, he notes how he has talked to some people who claimed not to react at all and he has observed others who were clearly upset and shrank away.

For the most part, Bill's assessment of value is embedded in the unfolding of events. Value is not justified, but rather it is merely described as it emerges in an unfolding story fragment. This sequential quality of Bill's evaluations is evident in his response to requests for justification and explanation. Typically he answers such requests with a story. Often the story begins with the particular event raised in the question and just continues from there. For example, when asked why he would exclude the controversial pictures from the exhibit, Bill says that he would place them in a separate room and have a guard outside to warn people. This embeddedness of value in specific context also means that valued sequences will stand independently of one another. Lacking any evaluative anchoring, judgments are not connected to one another as in linear thought. Thus, Bill can quite comfortably claim that in his opinion the display of art is clearly wrong but at the same time suggest that that the opposing opinion is *not* incorrect.

This issue of the art display is particularly interesting in the analysis of sequential evaluation because it raises a problem with which the interviewee typically has no direct contact. Consequently, it does not allow the interviewee to rely on her specific concrete experience. Instead the problem demands more abstract, linguistically mediated considerations. To construct the unfolding stories in which she frames meaning, the interviewee must rely on events and connections between events as they are cast in language. She is thus thrust quite squarely into the zone of proximal development discussed in chapter 2. Depending on the interviewee, this greater demand may yield disinterest, confusion, and withdrawal. Otherwise it may stimulate the most socially oriented and thus the most sophisticated reasoning of which she is capable. In this latter case, the individual may use the stories she has heard to determine where events are going and to judge how they will feel. Similarly she may use verbal labels for feelings that are at least partially disconnected from experienced or observed reactions and thus achieve a somewhat greater generality in her judgments. Bill clearly responds in this manner. For example, guided by the accounts he has heard, Bill judges the display of photographs to be bad because children will see them and in the long run they will be negatively affected. Such a consideration is clearly beyond the reporting of the particulars of anything Bill has directly experienced. It is even suggestive of straightforwardly causal linear reasoning. The sequential quality of the thinking, however, becomes apparent when probed. When asked to explain the causal connection he had drawn, that is, to explain how the present viewing of homoerotic art will affect the child in the future, Bill cannot do so. He cannot go beyond the steps in the story as he remembers them being told. He responds by saying he has no idea and that he has "never gone into it with anybody." This lacuna is not, however, a problem for Bill because he is recounting a story heard just as he reports sequences of events which he has observed to unfold. The order of their unfolding is the tissue that holds them together, not causal linkages.

This reliance on language also allows Bill to consider matters that are not the typical concrete, experientially grounded events of sequential consideration. An example would be his consideration of the value of his opinion and how it is important to maintain one's point of view. These concerns are again more typically linear. The sequential quality of Bill's use of these concerns, however, becomes apparent when he is asked why it is more important to express one's opinion than safeguard one's job. In his response, Bill says: "Because in your own mind you are doing what you think is right. It's more of a moral judgment on your part than anything else. You're not criticizing them (those who advocate the display), you're not saying it's wrong to show them or anything, but you're saying that in your opinion it shouldn't be shown." He thus reiterates his view that the display of the art is wrong. But the expression of this view is not understood to significantly contradict an opposed view or to imply that the act is wrong. In characteristically sequential fashion, the activity, having an opinion, is embedded in an event in which it is a matter of actually speaking in a manner that feels good. So constituted, stating the opinion has no necessary connection or implication beyond the specific act of its expression.

Despite some of his more sophisticated considerations here, Bill's evaluation is not linear. There is little real use of rules of action as standards for evaluation. Occasionally, when confronted with a rule, Bill acknowledges its force, but this is more a recognition of the sequence of events that unfolds. In Bill's considerations, rules are not constructed apart from specific events as external standards for judgment, which then confer value. For example, in the interview, the interviewer implicitly introduces a rule by stating that a vote was held and the community democratically decided in favor of displaying the pictures. In response, Bill did not refer to this as proper procedure and justify what was done or its outcome in these terms. Rather, he simply acknowledged that this can happen and that the art would then be displayed. When reminded of his negative judgment of the display, it is clear that Bill's view has not changed in anyway. The apparent use of the rule has had no impact on his judgment. Responding sequentially, Bill simply continues on with the story line saying what he would do and what they would do. More generally, lacking the frame of reference afforded by rules, Bill generally does not justify the judgments he makes. As already noted, he merely describes them in context. When justifications are directly requested, he responds by simply reasserting his claim, perhaps describing anew what is the case, or by using the request as a point of departure for an extension of the story a few more steps. Bill's judgments also reflect none of the evaluative anchoring and maintaining of evaluative consistency that is characteristic of linear thought. In this vein, the use of proper procedure does not validate the outcome. Similarly Bill's view that the display is very wrong does not lead to a negative judgment of either those who advocate it (e.g., the authorities or his boss). In both instances, Bill displays none of the sense of evaluative contradiction that linear evaluation would typically produce.

INTRV.: Do you think these photographs should be displayed or not?

SUBJ.: No, I don't.

INTRV.: How come?

SUBJ.: Well, because for one thing it's a regular art museum, parents are going to be bringing their kids in, the kids don't need to see this type of thing. They see enough violence and everything on TV. And they've been raising a big stink here lately on this bit on the Internet with these people are contacting kids over the Internet and a lot of the kids are running away from home, and so on. And I think it's wrong. I think really that the sexual attitude that the country now is more liberal than it was. More easygoing. And they accept the homosexuality, same sex type marriages and stuff like that. And this is fine. But when you start bringing kids into it, no.

Request for justification of value initially produces a loose collage where the overlap is the "bad things that are happening to kids," and this begins to trail off into other bad things. Overlap is linguistic label of "bad for kids."

INTRV.: Okay, why not?

SUBJ.: Because, to me, the kids don't deserve to see this. The parents don't need to see this.

Justification reduced to mere reassertion of claim that it should not be seen.

INTRV.: Why not?

SUBJ.: In a way this is obscene. You're bringing

Obscene is bad, it is tied

maybe a ten- or twelve-year-old kid into a photograph like that and it's going to ruin the kid for the rest of his life. The kid may not realize at the time that they're doing anything wrong but later on in life it's going to affect him.

to bad sequence ending in a child being ruined. Likely mere repetition of rhetoric surrounding this issue.

INTRV.: How do you think it will affect him?

SUBJ.: I have no idea . . . I've never really gone into it with anybody, but I've talked to people who've . . . I talked to a cop that was on a raid to a child pornography ring up here in L.A. and he's a veteran of twenty years and he said it turned his stomach to see some of these pictures.

Simply learns story line, no causal analysis. Concrete value of others' observed reaction.

INTRV.: Okay. Let's say you go to the museum; you're going to go check it out. And you see the pictures, and it's kind of a surprise because, I don't know whether it's the colors or the black-and-white pictures, but you're surprised and you see that they're kind of beautiful in a way. Sometimes, you know when you look at clouds in the sky you can see people in the clouds, sometimes if you see photographs, it's a photograph of a row of books or something, but it looks like something else. You go and his pictures look like that and you're kind of surprised and they're real pretty. Do you still think they should be thrown out of the exhibit?

SUBJ.: I would say yes.

INTRV.: Why would you want that to happen?

SUBJ.: I would say either take them out of this part of the exhibit and put them separately and have a guard where they're at explaining that this is considered obscene art and so on in a separate wing of the museum or something.

Request for justification or explanation just yields story of what he would do.

INTRV.: Let's say we do that. How would that help?

SUBJ.: I think if they did that then they would basically keep the kids away from it and allow parents to go to see it out of curiosity.

INTRV.: Do you think that would be a bad thing? Maybe what we should do . . . The trouble is we don't want the parents to see it either, so maybe we shouldn't have the . . .

SUBJ.: If I was the director of the museum, I wouldn't put them up there at all. I would say he has other pictures that are considered obscene, homosexual and so on, and they're part of the exhibit but I'm not going to put them up because I'm against that kind of thing.

> Obscene is just a label, it is bad. No real evaluative rationale. In explanation to a public, "I won't do it because I just don't like it."

INTRV.: Okay. Let's pretend that you move to Cincinnati. You live there now, and you get a job in the mailroom of the paper there, kind of like the one you had at the Daily Pilot, and your boss tells you . . . And then she says, 'What do you think? Do you think those pictures should be shelved?' Would you tell her?

SUBJ.: Yeah.

INTRV.: Why?

SUBJ.: I'd tell her plain and simply, I'd say I don't think they should be shown. That's my opinion I'd say you can't go against somebody's opinion of something. I'd say if you're going to do that then you take it to the Supreme Court and you go into the Supreme Court and you try to get a judgment against them or whatever.

> Story sequence told rather than reason given. No attempt at argument or persuasion, just assert view. In invoking law and rule, he reconstructs them as a story to be enacted.

INTRV.: Okay, what if she says, "Look, if that's the way you feel, I think it's really wrong and I don't want to work with you. I won't fire you because you might take me to court, but there's no way I'm going to promote you. No way you're going to get a better job."

SUBJ.: I'd just tell her plain and simple, that's fine.

INTRV.: Why would you tell her?

SUBJ.: I'd just tell her that's my opinion. I'm going to stick by my convictions.

INTRV.: Why would you want to do that?

SUBJ.: Well, it's the right of everybody, if they've got a conviction against a certain thing that they should stand by it.

Linear, concrete rule apparently invoked.

INTRV.: Do you think it's worth it even if it will get in the way of you getting in a better job and more money?

SUBJ.: Yeah.

INTRV.: Why is that more important than you getting a better job?

Uses rhetoric of morality, but judgment remains embedded in event and therefore has no necessary link to anything external. Here it is just saying what you think without apparent evaluative implication.

SUBJ.: Because in your own mind you are doing what you think is right. It's more of a moral judgment on your part than anything else. You're not criticizing them, you're not saying that in your opinion it shouldn't be shown.

INTRV.: And now you know that you said that you know in your own mind you're right? Why is that important—that you know in your own mind you're right?

SUBJ.: Well, it makes you feel better . . .

Evaluation based on feeling good. Additional probing needed here.

INTRV.: Okay. Let's say that what the city does is they say, "Okay, we realize there's a controversy here. What we're going to do is we're going to bring in some art experts and some leaders of the community to look at the photographs and see what they think." And so they might bring in priests, politicians, and some art experts. They look at the photographs and they say, "Look. These really are art and although what's being photographed is a problem, the photographs should be shown." And so you hear this. What do you think? Would you say, well, okay, maybe the photographs should be shown? Or would you still think no?

Interviewer introduces authoritative judgment to encourage linear consideration.

SUBJ.: I would think if you get enough politicians, enough priests and stuff in there, that they agree it's art, then fine. It can be shown. But I'd still be kind of against it.

In these four exchanges, the intrv. and subj. are talking at cross purposes. The intrv. is asking for a categorical evaluation to the art. The subj. is evaluating the art

INTRV.: How come?

SUBJ.: Because it would still be considered obscene.

INTRV.: Yeah, because it is homosexual, it is child sexuality, too. But if they say it's okay, why would you still be against it?

SUBJ.: Because it would be my opinion that it was wrong to be shown to the public. I have talked to people that they have gone through nudist magazines. And they think nothing of it. And other people, they see them on news stands and you know, and they shrink away like it's going to jump up and bite them.

INTRV.: So now, do you think then these experts and stuff are wrong? Because they think it's okay?

SUBJ.: No, I think in their opinion it is considered art. Then I'd have to take a second look at it and try to see it in depth as they might have seen it.

INTRV.: Okay, let's say you go again and take a look. And it's no question to you. You see that there's kids involved in sexual acts with men and stuff like that. What would you decide?

SUBJ.: I would decide that it was wrong unless, if you go in as a . . . if you took a real long look at it from different angles and so on and decided it was considered art.

INTRV.: Okay. Let's say the city council decides we're going to have a town referendum, we're going to all vote and decide if this stuff is going to be shown. And they have a vote, and even though the town is conservative, most people in the town vote to have the stuff shown. Do you still think it should not be shown?

SUBJ.: Well, if they voted to have it shown, then I would have to go along with them.

INTRV.: How come?

SUBJ.: I'd say, "Okay look, you guys voted 49 to 18 or whatever to have it shown. Fine. Go ahead. Show it."

INTRV.: Why allow it even if it's bad stuff?

variously depending on the different scenarios in which it is embedded.

Consideration consists of recall of observed sequences and the feelings associated with them.

Value is embedded in specific scenario of someone-doing-something which has feelings embedded in it. Attempt here is to account for difference in opinion in terms of variation in the way a person goes about seeing something.

Interviewer introduces consideration of procedure that may invoke either linear or systematic considerations.

Accepts procedure, but not as rule, but as the way things happen. Thus, responds to request for

SUBJ.: Even if it's bad stuff. But it's your kids that are going to be affected by it in the long run. So then I would say, "You've got to stop and think what the kids are going to think of this if they see it. Is this a good thing or is this a bad thing? Does this actually happen?" And the parents are going to have to sit there with their kids and explain to them that artists do this and they do not think it's bad and yet other people do. There are different opinions and so on.

justification with description of what happens.
Again no justification in terms of value of rule. No value consistency by saying it's okay. Just begins with bad result and continues story of it will be bad for kids, what he would say and what they would have to do.

INTRV.: But one of the concerns is . . . I can understand what you're saying with, look it's their kids, they need to decide, but we know the photographs are obscene and we know that they're probably going to have a bad effect on their kids later on. So don't we, in a way . . . shouldn't we ban the photographs anyway? Not show them anyway?

SUBJ.: In my opinion, yes. But it's like anything. The kids, once they start getting to a certain age, they're going to start getting curious about the different sexes and so on, and what goes on and they're going to learn the hard way if they don't learn from their parents. You know, sneak a *Playboy* magazine or something, you know . . .

Restates opinion, but continues with a story of what typically happens.

INTRV.: Okay.

SUBJ.: I mean, kids will be kids . . .

INTRV.: Okay. I think we have one more part, one and a half. How are you doing? Do you want to stretch for a minute or are you doing okay?

SUBJ.: I'm fine.

INTRV.: Do you find this interesting at all?

SUBJ.: Yeah.

INTRV.: Good.

Concluding Comment

The results of the empirical research on the structure of people's evaluation of social and political events have been presented in this chapter. The summary results indicated very strong support for the twin claims that a given individual will evaluate quite different issues in the same way and that different people will evaluate the same issue in structurally quite different ways. This summary statement of results was supplemented by the transcript of three interviews—one sequential, one linear, and one systematic. For the most part these interviews were typical, both for the quality of the evaluations evidenced and as an indication of the mistakes occasionally made in the course of conducting this kind of interview. When reviewing the coding notes, the reader should keep in mind that although the analysis of the interviews is guided by the coding categories described in the chapter on methodology, this analysis ultimately depends on a good working understanding of the underlying structure of the types of reasoning and evaluation described in chapters 3, 4, and 5.

Chapter Eight Overview
and Concluding Remarks

In chapter 1 I presented several examples of people's responses to the challenges posed by the circumstances of their lives. One was quite general and involved the difficulties many people who live in advanced industrial societies have adjusting to the demands of modern (or postmodern) life in the late twentieth century. The other examples were much more specific. They included the difficulty Chad natives had comprehending the medical advice of a Peace Corps worker, the trouble Appalachian miners had adopting the political strategies taught by a political activist, and the difficulty many undergraduates have in understanding the theoretical or philosophical positions that are presented to them in the classroom. The point of this discussion was not to offer a close or complete analysis of these situations. Rather the intent was to present several suggestive examples that arguably illustrate a similar underlying dynamic, one that involves the inability of many individuals to adapt to certain conditions of social life.

This failure to adapt and the attendant consequences for personal and emotional well-being is often regarded as atypical and thus as the preserve of clinical psychology. Viewed from this perspective, problems of social adaptation are understood in terms of the abnormal characteristics of the particular individuals involved. My purpose in the opening chapter was to recast the problem of adaptation as a more ordinary aspect of social life, one that is profitably considered in the more general terms of social psychology, sociology, and political science. In this context, the question is reframed as one that explores the inability of normal or typical individuals to adjust to the social demands placed upon them, even when the cost of failing to do so can be quite high. The question is of interest on two levels. At a more concrete level, it speaks to phenomena that are ubiquitous. Despite this fact, instances of failing to learn and adapt are typically relegated to the margins of most mainstream social and political theory. There they are understood as failures of socialization or rational consideration, failures that are usually viewed as atypical, inconsequential, or only temporary. This points to the second and more central level of concern, that of social scientific theory. At this level, the issue becomes one of determining why it is that phenomena of this kind are neither regarded as theoretically important nor are they readily comprehended.

To address this last question, I have argued that failures of adaptation highlight qualities of individuals and their relationship with social structure and culture that challenge foundational assumptions of most contemporary liberal institutional and macrosociological theorizing. On one hand, both kinds of theories assume that one level of social analysis, individual or collective, is produced by and thus can be understood in terms of the other. In the case of liberal institutional theory, there is an assumption that collective phenomena are reducible to individual phenomena (via posited mechanisms of choice, self-expression, and aggregation). In the case of macrosociological theory, there is an assumption that individual phenomena are reducible to collective phenomena (via posited mechanisms of learning, socialization, and social regulation or cultural definition). The problem is that the failure to adapt suggests a basic disjunction between individual and collective phenomena—the organization and the meaning of action constructed by individuals often cannot be reduced to the organization and meaning constructed by a collectivity (or vice versa). On the other hand, most mainstream liberal and sociological theory assumes that people reason in basically the same way. Depending on the particular theory, this shared reasoning may be characterized as fully rational or it may be viewed as a limited capacity to recognize and represent how objects and people are related to one another. The problem here is that the examples presented in chapter 1 indicated that some people were able to understand the demands placed upon them and adapt as required. Evidently these people were able to reason in qualitatively different ways than their companions and these differences had significant consequences for how these individuals behaved in social situations. In sum, failures of adaptation contradict the underlying sense of much liberal institutional and sociological theory and therefore cannot be readily characterized or explained in these terms.

The foregoing conclusion set the stage for the structural pragmatic position developed in chapter 2. The aim here was to construct a theoretical orientation that incorporated but went beyond the limits of conventional theorizing. Thus structural pragmatic theory was constructed with regard to two related assumptions. First, just as the conjunction of the individual and collective orchestration of social action is central to the dynamic of social life, so the disjunction of those two forces is equally central. Second, not only are their formal similarities in how people reason, but there are also qualitative differences among them. In this vein, it is argued that social meaning and action are dually structured by the subjective determinations of the individuals involved and by the social structural and discursive determinations of the groups within which the social exchange between individuals occurs. It is further argued that the relationship between these two structuring forces constitutes the fundamental dynamic underlying social life. The structured social conditions of individuals' lives are constantly pressuring individuals to develop modes of reasoning that parallel the logic of social construction. At the same time, subjectively structured actions and reactions of the individual participants in social exchange are constantly pressuring social institutions and discourses to develop modes of regulation that match the needs and capacities of the individuals involved. As a result, social life always oscillates between the structural harmonies and developmental tensions produced as each force operates to transform the other according to its own regulations.

Structural pragmatic theory yields a number of corollary claims. One key claim is that the formal quality of an individual's way of thinking depends, in part, on the structure of the social interactions and discourse in which she participates. People's cognition develops in response to the nature of the tasks that daily social exchange sets for them. Insofar as different people participate in differently structured social environments, the quality of their reasoning, the structure of their cognition, should vary. It is precisely this variance that is explored and substantiated in the main body of the book. In chapters 3, 4, and 5, three developmentally related modes of thinking are explored: sequential, linear, and systematic. In each case, there is an attempt to define the characteristic quality of thinking and the structure of cognition (that is, the quality of the objects of thought and of the relationships among them that are constructed). This underlying way of thinking and its associated structure are then examined as they are manifest in the specific understanding and evaluation of social life and politics generated as the individual subject attempts to judge the world around her.

In chapters 6 and 7, an attempt is made to provide empirical support for the claim of qualitative differences in understanding and evaluation asserted in chapters 3, 4, and 5. To this end, two hypotheses were examined. The first is that a given person may evaluate three very different situations in the same structurally determined way. The focus here is not on the specific beliefs or values a person might express, but on the formal qualities of the meaning and justification in terms of which those particular beliefs and values are understood and judged. To explore this hypothesis, individual subjects are interviewed at length about three quite different topics: helping a close friend or lover, the display of controversial art in a city museum, and American involvement in Bosnia. This insures a relatively stringent test of the hypothesis insofar as it may be assumed that a given person's quantity of knowledge and degree of interest will vary considerably from one of these topics to the next.

The second hypothesis is that different people may evaluate the same situations in structurally different ways. This suggests that even when considering the same situation, the quality of both the objects identified and the relationships constructed among them may differ from one individual to the next. Associated with this second hypothesis is the claim that these qualitative or structural differences in judgment are adequately captured by the typology of sequential, linear, and systematic thinking. Following structural pragmatic theory, it was assumed that individual differences in judgment would be related to differences in the structure of the social environment to which those individuals were exposed. To assure a range of thinking styles would be examined in the course of the empirical research, subjects with very different incomes, educational backgrounds, and work environments were chosen. These were used as rough indicators of differences in the structure of subjects' social contexts.

The results of the research provide strong support for the twin hypotheses of underlying structure and individual differences in reasoning. Individual subjects judged the three different situations (personal, domestic political, and international) in the same structurally determined manner in forty-two of the forty-eight cases. Moreover, there was clear indication of structural differences in judgment between subjects in a manner suggested by the threefold typology of sequential, linear, and systematic. Eleven subjects' thinking was scored sequential, twenty-seven were scored linear, and ten were scored systematic. In chapter 7 this numerical data is supplemented by the presentation of interview responses by three subjects, each of whom evidences one of the three types of thinking.

These results not only provide support for the claim of qualitative differences in how individuals reason, they also provide support for the related claim of the frequent disjuncture between individual subjects' structuring of the meaning and direction of action and the collective structuring of the interactive contexts in which those individuals participate. This is evident in the qualitative differences between the cultural meaning of the dilemmas and questions posed (a meaning that is also constructed by the interviewer) on one hand, and the subjective meaning of these stimuli that are constructed by the interviewee on the other. Indeed, it is precisely this qualitative difference that renders the interview responses of people who think in different ways so interesting. That difference is also what necessitates the initial probing of their statements in the interview phase of the research and the subsequent interpretative attempt to reconstruct the subjective meaning of those statements in the analysis phase.

THE EMPIRICAL RESEARCH: RELATED WORK
AND COMMON CRITICISM

The research reported here on structural differences in cognition by no means stands alone. To begin with, there is a small body of work in political psychology that explores political cognition and ideology in these terms. This work is itself part of a larger tradition of research in developmental psychology that follows the lead of such psychologists as James Mark Baldwin (1913), L. S. Vygotsky (1962, 1978) and most influentially Jean Piaget (1971, 1978; Inhelder and Piaget, 1958). Most of this work, especially the work of Piaget and his followers, focuses on structural differences in how people think about the physical world. In the 1960s and 1970s, Lawrence Kohlberg expanded this focus with his research on the development of moral reasoning. His students, especially Elliot Turiel (1983) and Robert Selman (1980), built on his work to explore the development of social reasoning. A later generation of students, such as Robert Kegan (1982, 1994) and Gil Noam (Noam and Fischer, 1996), further extended this effort to include a consideration of issues of ego development and psychopathology.

Earlier Research

Of the research on political cognition, the most immediately relevant is earlier work that I have done on the development of political reasoning (Rosenberg,

1987, 1988a, 1988b; Rosenberg, Ward, and Chilton, 1988). Although the theory orienting this early work is less developed and its empirical focus is somewhat different, it nonetheless provides evidence that is consistent with the conclusions drawn in the present research regarding structural differences in adult political judgment. In the earlier work, I focused only on the quality of the understandings people constructed when thinking about political phenomena. Thus the research centered on an analysis of how individuals conceptualized the nature of political actors (individuals, groups, or states), the forces that motored political events, and the kinds of outcomes that ensued. As in the current work, types of thinking among individuals were identified as sequential, linear, and systematic. Employing both open-ended depth interviews and experimentation, the results of the empirical research provided strong support for the notion that a given individual will reason about very different phenomena in the same structurally determined manner and that different individuals may analyze the same phenomena in structurally different ways.

In addition to providing supportive results, this earlier research complements the present work in two respects. First, the earlier research has a different focus; it considers analysis rather than evaluation. The results are, however, comparable in the two cases. Together they provide strong evidence for the claim of structural differences in thinking as described by the typology of sequential, linear, and systematic. Second, the earlier research was a first empirical effort to validate claims regarding the structural bases of reasoning. Consequently a broader array of methods was employed than in the present research. In both efforts, the structure of thinking is assessed through in-depth, open-ended interviewing in which several quite different topics are addressed. In the earlier work, however, individuals' thinking was also assessed through several experiments. The latter experiments required subjects to utilize available materials in order to discover a solution to a problem. An example is the use of Piaget's famous chemicals experiment (Inhelder and Piaget, 1958). In the experiment, subjects are shown a chemical reaction. They are provided with a set of chemical solutions, some of which combine to create the reaction. Subjects are then asked to experiment with those solutions in an attempt to recreate the observed reaction. The methodological advantage of this experimental technique over an interview is it enables an assessment of types of thinking which is much less dependent on verbal performance. Assessment is based primarily on what people do rather than on what they say. In the earlier research, there was a very strong relationship between an individual's performance on the two experimental tasks and her response to the different interview topics. This effectively counters methodological criticism that suggests that apparent differences in structure of thinking as measured in an interview may merely reflect differences in verbal skills.

Related Research on Political, Social, and Moral Reasoning

Research on political thinking has largely focused on political attitudes or acquired knowledge, exploring their nature through survey research. Relatively little work has explored the structure of political reasoning in the terms suggested here.[1] That said, a few political psychologists influenced by Jean Piaget have conducted research of this kind. Following Piaget's focus on child development, the early work on political cognition examined the development of political thinking in childhood. Good examples of this are Joseph Adelson's studies of the development of the child's conception of politics and the law (Adelson and O'Neil, 1966; Adelson and Beall, 1970) and Connell's quite imaginative work on what he refers to as the child's construction of politics (1971). Later research focused on structural cognitive differences among adults. A good example is Dana Ward's study of the adult children of the subjects studied twenty-five years earlier in Robert Lane's landmark research on political ideology (Ward, 1982; Rosenberg, Ward, and Chilton, 1988). Utilizing Piaget's early distinctions between egocentric and sociocentric thought, Ward found clear structural differences among the ways his subjects reasoned about political phenomena. Beyond this focus on individuals' reasoning, a number of researchers have attempted to extrapolate from the psychological insights afforded by developmental psychology to make sense of the dynamics and direction of development in whole cultures. Interesting examples of this include Radding's analysis (1985) of the development of legal practice in France and England in the eleventh century, Wilson's explanation (1992) of China's failure to develop in the nineteenth century, and Eklundh's consideration (1998) of issues of political education in present day Sweden.[2] Although most of the foregoing work does not use the same definition of structures of thinking employed here, it nonetheless provides varieties of evidence that support the twin hypotheses of cognitive structure and individual differences examined here.[3]

As already noted, the political research on the structure and development of cognition is part of a much larger body of research on cognition conducted by developmental psychologists. Much of this revolves directly around the work of Piaget.[4] Of more immediate interest to us here is the extension of Piaget's theory into the domain of adult reasoning about more social phenomena. The central figure of interest here is Lawrence Kohlberg (1981b, 1984). Building on Piaget's very early work, Kohlberg developed a theory of moral development. He suggested that, in the process of trying to make sense of and resolve the dilemmas of interpersonal and value conflicts of everyday life, individuals pass through an invariant sequence of levels and stages in the development of their moral reasoning. According to Kohlberg, there are three levels of development, preconventional, conventional, and postconventional. Each level is comprised of two stages. Over the course of development, the individual's moral considerations become less immediate, concrete, and egocentric and more principled, abstract, and sociocentric. To study this development, Kohlberg presented his subjects with hypothetical moral dilemmas and then explored their reasoning through open-ended, probing interviews. From Kohlberg's early doctoral work through to the literally hundreds of studies conducted using his approach, the research has provided a mountain of evidence suggesting that individuals have a characteristic way of reasoning about different moral problems and that qualitative differences in moral reasoning may exist between individuals. As such, Kohlberg's research provides evidence that is broadly consistent with my work on political thinking. That said, there are several important distinctions to be made between his work and my own. Their importance becomes apparent when we consider some of the criticism of his work.

Kohlberg's research provides an unusual and highly controversial mix of a cognitive psychological approach, which posits universal standards for judging the adequacy of different forms of thinking and a subject matter, morality and personal values, that is more typically dealt with by social scientists in relativistic terms. As a result, his research has provoked considerable controversy. Of particular interest here is the criticism levied by other developmental psychologists that Kohlberg's conception of moral development is not universal but rather is a conception biased by his own sociopolitical position. In this vein, it has been argued that Kohlberg's conception of morality reflects a male view of people as essentially separate entities. As such, his theory and research is oriented by a substantive emphasis on a morality of rights. Consequently, his work fails to recognize a more feminine morality of care and thus systematically underestimates the moral reasoning of women (e.g., Gilligan, 1972, 1977). In a similar manner, it is argued that Kohlberg's conception of morality is an essentially liberal one. As such his work is oriented by a substantive emphasis on a contractarian conception of morality and rights. Consequently a more conservative emphasis on community and obligations is not recognized, and those who reason on this basis will be viewed as thinking in a less adequate way (e.g.,

Emler et al., 1983; Reicher et al., 1984). In empirical terms, the feminist critique suggests that Kohlberg's method leads to the unwarranted conclusion that women who advocate an ethic of care are reasoning at the stage 3 level, the stage at which respondents often justify their moral claims by referring to norms that dictate how people in a love or familial relationship should take special care of one another. The conservative critique suggests that conservatives who emphasize the importance of maintaining the community will unwarrantedly be assessed to be reasoning at the stage 4 level, the stage at which issues of the importance of law and the existing social order are emphasized.

I reiterate the foregoing criticism of Kohlberg's work both because I agree with it and because it highlights an important distinction between his approach and mine. In my view the feminist and conservative claims of bias in Kohlberg's conception of stages of moral reasoning are both correct and for the same reason. The underlying problem here is that although Kohlberg is ostensibly offering a structuralist analysis of moral reasoning and therefore differentiating among levels of reasoning on solely formal grounds, the reality is that the definition of stages is infused with a number of substantive considerations.[5] With the resulting confusion of form and content in the stage definitions, there is a tendency to underestimate the formal qualities of any example of reasoning that entails substantive moral claims that deviate from those that Kohlberg adopts. My own work differs significantly from Kohlberg's in this regard. I have taken considerable care to define the mode of thinking and consequent formal structure of each type of thinking without reference to particular substantive claims regarding what is true or right. In each case, it is only after this formal structure is articulated that specific aspects of understanding and evaluation are considered. In this manner, I have attempted to avoid the substantive or content-specific kinds of biases often associated with Kohlberg's analysis of moral development.[6]

The issue of the form-content distinction has plagued a good deal of the research that has followed Kohlberg's lead. In that work, there is a recurring tendency to reconstruct his stages of moral development entirely in substantive terms. Typically this is done in the name of efficiency and involves a streamlining of empirical research rather than any self-conscious theoretical revision. Of particular interest here is the work of James Rest. In his early research, Rest attempted to construct a close-ended pencil and paper version of Kohlberg's Moral Judgment Interview (MJI). The result was the Defining Issues Test (DIT) (Rest, 1974). The DIT offered clear practical advantages over the MJI. It was much more easily administered and scored. Given the very broad interest in Kohlberg's theory of moral development, the DIT was immensely popular and was used in hundreds of studies in which stage of development was used as a dependent or, more typically, as an independent variable (for a review, see Rest et al., 1999).

Rest's practically motivated change in method has been challenged. The claim is that his method cannot be theoretically reconciled with Kohlberg's effort to offer a formal structural conception of reasoning. By reducing the study of moral reasoning to preference for particular substantive moral claims, the test necessarily ignores all concerns regarding the structural qualities of the subjective construction of meaning. In this vein, it ignores Kohlberg's key insight, that the specific claims a person recognizes or prefers are rendered meaningful only as they are reconstructed in the context of that individual's effort to make sense of the meaning and value of a particular concrete situation or set of options. Failing to incorporate these concerns in its design, the DIT would fail to differentiate two people who indicate a preference for the same value claims and yet reason about those claims and therefore understand them in qualitatively different ways. The DIT is therefore an inappropriate test of moral reasoning (e.g., Gibbs, 1992).

Until recently, Rest has attempted to counter such a theoretical argument with an empirical defense. The defense is that his method produces assessments of moral stage that correlate reasonably well with the assessments produced using the open-ended interview approach. I accept Rest's empirical claim but interpret it differently. The evidence of a correlation between the two approaches does not, as Rest has suggested, validate his DIT. Instead and more significantly, it delegitimates Kohlberg's moral judgment interview as a tool for assessing the structure of moral reasoning. In my view, the correlation between a largely substantive measure, the DIT, and a purportedly structural one, the MJI, is a simple indication that the latter is content laden. In this regard, Rest's evidence of the validity of the DIT indicts Kohlberg's conception of moral development in much the same way as the criticisms levied by Gilligan and Emler.

The consideration of Rest's work is interesting in a further regard. A review of his current view of moral judgment allows us to reconsider the difference between more structural approaches to cognition and schema theory. In a recent book (Rest et al., 1999), Rest finally comes to the conclusion that the DIT (and its successor, the DIT2) are best understood in terms of schema theory. In this light, he recognizes that the presentation of the individual items of the DIT essentially operate as cues that activate whatever associated preexisting schemas are held by the person being tested. Thus the manner in which a given person ranks a set of items on the test is less a reflection of some supposed structure of reasoning and more an indication of the relative strength, reward value, or accessibility of the schemas cued. In the end, Rest opts for a schema theoretic notion of moral cognition instead of the more structural developmental one initially proposed by Kohlberg.

Schemas vs. Structures

In my view, given the epistemological assumptions inherent in his choice of methods, Rest's preference for schema theory over a more structural developmental theory makes perfect sense. On the level of their substantive aspirations, schema theory and a cognitive developmental theory, especially one tied to structural pragmatics, share much in common. There is a presumption that individuals actively construct their understanding of events and ideas that are presented to them. At the same time, there is a recognition that events and ideas are also socially regulated and defined, and this has an impact on individuals' subjective constructions. In this regard, both schema theory and a more structural developmental theory attempt to offer an essentially social psychological vision of meaning-making and the organization of action. Because of these common concerns, researchers utilizing schema theory or structural developmental theory have often been attracted to each other's work.

Despite these common aims, there are fundamental differences between the two approaches. Schema theory defines meaning, both personal and social, in substantive terms. Schemas, whether they are subjective constructions or artifacts of a culture, are defined in terms of their content. Consequently, schemas are differentiated in terms of what they are schemas of. Piagetian cognitive developmental theory and structural pragmatics define meaning in more formal structural terms. Therefore structures (be they subjectively or intersubjectively constructed) are differentiated not with respect to the specifics of what is done with what objects, but with regard to the quality of relationships constructed and the nature of the objects thereby related.[7]

There are a number of implications that follow from this key distinction between schema theory and a more structural pragmatic conception. One example is the different ways theorists of each kind may view the theory of the other. Constrained to defining the qualities of subjective construction with regard to its content, the schema theorist lacks the conceptual resources to incorporate the formal structural distinctions posited by the structural pragmatist. Often this results in a reconstruction of structural distinctions in purely substantive terms. In this case, schemas and structures are essentially equated. Practically speaking this is what Rest did. Others who have also conducted quite interesting research have also had difficulty maintaining a schema-structure distinction and often abandon the more cumbersome structural work in favor of schema theory. In the process, claims of general qualities of an individual's thought that are sustained across subject matter are withdrawn and the theoretical interest in structural differences in cognition is diminished. Alternatively, the qualitative distinctions between structures posited by structural developmental theory are translated into schema theory as quantitative differences. Occasionally this is supplemented by some ill-defined conception of integration or abstraction. A good example is the early attempt by Streufert and his colleagues to translate the stage distinctions demonstrated by Piaget into a more accessible theoretical form and more easily replicated empirical method (e.g., Streufert and Driver, 1967; Streufert and Streufert, 1978). The resulting concept and measure of cognitive complexity has been recently resurrected in a more restricted form in the influential work of Tetlock (1984, 1988) and Suedfeld (1985) in the 1980s.

From the structural pragmatic perspective, the distinction between structures and schemas is sustained and the relationship between them is clear. As I have suggested, structures are viewed as formal and general, and schemas are viewed as substantive and specific. The nature of the two is further understood in terms of their relationship. Structures are generative; they produce the formal relationship and identifications that create a range of possibilities. Specific schemas and, more important, the specific ways schemas are used are particular realizations of these structurally delimited possibilities. In this sense, schemas are recognized to be the immediate mediators of thought in specific situations, but at the same time they are understood to be the manifest outcomes of a general mode of thinking. The various schemas an individual deploys therefore have a formal structure and modes of use that reflect the formal qualities of that individual's way of thinking. This suggests that individuals who think in structurally different ways are likely to develop different kinds of schemas and use them differently. The discussion of the nature of sequential, linear, and systematic thinking and the differences between them may be reinterpreted in this light—that is, as different types of schema construction and use.

In conclusion, there is a great deal of research that supports the psychological claims that follow from a structural pragmatic view of cognition. As discussed in the preceding paragraphs, a number of studies of political thinking as well as related work on cognitive development and moral reasoning have explored the twin claims that thinking is structured and that this may vary across individuals. I could add to this other research, much of it done by Kohlberg's students, which has found comparable results when exploring the nature of social reasoning.[8] When reviewing this research, however, it is important to keep in mind that this work does not derive from a structural pragmatic conception. As a result, the concepts orienting the work are different from the ones advanced here and the evidence provided is not fully comparable to my own.

One important difference, the degree to which the conception of thinking is structural, has been mentioned in the preceding discussion of the moral reasoning research. This difference suggests that my work should be less susceptible to certain of the criticisms frequently levied against Kohlberg. Other differences should also be noted. Following Piaget, most of the work I have cited focuses on psychological considerations. Consequently, structures of cognition and their development tend to be viewed primarily in terms of the individual. In the later work there is a greater recognition of social influences, but they are still seen as external factors.[9] In my structural pragmatic work, an attempt has been made to explicate how the social and psychological construction of meaning interpenetrate. One implication of this is that how a person will operate in a given circumstance, that is, how she will actually think, is not only a function of her subjective construction, but also the social structure of the interactive or discursive situation. Unlike classic cognitive developmental theory, this opens the possibility that as the structure of a person's situation varies, so may the quality of that person's thinking. Another important difference between the research cited and my own revolves around conceptions of the result of the development from one form of thinking to another. Those following in the cognitive developmental tradition suggest that when an individual's thinking develops, old as well as new understandings are structured accordingly. Considering the effects of emotion and affect, I have argued that some early learning may continue to structure an individual's understandings in a manner consistent with the earlier form of reasoning in use when that learning first occurred.

Addressing Criticism
of the Empirical Research

A number of criticisms have been made regarding the approach I have adopted here. I have dealt with them more fully elsewhere (Rosenberg, 1988b), and I will discuss them only briefly here. The key point to be kept in mind is that the specific criticisms reflect a particular understanding of social and political phenomena. They make sense only in that context. For the most part, the criticisms emanate from one or the other of the two mainstream perspectives, macrosociological and liberal institutional, which were discussed in chapters 1 and 2. I will discuss criticisms of each kind in turn.

Viewed from a sociological perspective, the difficulty of the research presented here revolves around the claim that an individual will think about very different situations in the same way. Adopting this perspective, a potential critic takes a social learning view of knowledge and understanding. In this context, it is assumed that what an individual knows and cares about is a function of the particular experiences they have. Mediated by learning, differences in exposure should produce differences in understanding and evaluation. This assumption is directly addressed by the design of my research and contradicted by its results. Subjects were asked to evaluate three very different situations, one involving a close friend or lover, one involving an exhibition of controversial art, and one involving American intervention in a foreign country. By the standards of a sociologically oriented learning theory, it is highly probable that a given individual would have very different degrees of exposure to situations of these three kinds. Consequently, her level of knowledge and interest would vary significantly from topic to topic. The results of the research clearly indicate that despite this variation in factors deemed significant from a learning theory point of view, the quality of an individual's reasoning remained the same when addressing these three very different topics.

Confronted by these results, more sociologically minded critics have attempted to explain the results away in a variety of ways. The most common move is to suggest that the interview responses analyzed in chapters 6 and 7 do not reveal the underlying structure of an individual's thought but rather reflect something more epiphenomenal, such as vocabulary or language ability. This would explain consistency across topic; people have a style of talking that is evident across the subjects they address. I have several responses to this suggestion. First, the conduct and analysis of interviews explicitly attempts to go beyond what someone is saying to an exploration of their understanding of what they have said. Second, the earlier research I conducted indicated a strong relationship between the structure of a person's verbal responses to an open-ended interview and the structure of her largely nonverbal attempts to manipulate objects in order to solve a practical problem (Rosenberg, 1988b). This result suggests that it is not simply vocabulary or verbal skills that are being assessed. Third, by appealing to something like verbal ability, the critic is essentially undermining her own position. To introduce a notion of verbal ability is to claim that apart from learning specific skills, individuals learn general ones. As revealed in the research, such skills clearly reflect a general capacity that is quite independent of any particular exposure to the specific interview topic considered. The critic who opts for this explanation is moving in the direction of a structural pragmatic psychology in which individual capacities are quite general and thus are not subject to the regulations or definitions inherent in any specific social interaction in which that individual may be engaged. Needless to say the implied subjectivism and the consequent recognition of the resistance of privately constructed meaning to social determinations are not very consistent with the sociological vision prompting this alternative account of the data.

Viewed from a liberal institutional perspective, evidence that an individual's thinking fails to vary across different tasks is not problematic. With the assumption of a universal rationality, this invariance is assumed. The real difficulty lies with the fact that individuals differ from one another so dramatically when dealing with the same tasks. For a liberal economist or a liberal democrat, there is the troubling evidence that many of the participants in the study, particularly those who reasoned in a sequential or linear manner, do not evidence the rationality typically assumed in their theorizing. For economists who accept a more limited concept of rationality (such as that advocated by Simon, 1986) or social and political psychologists who accept that cognition is typically flawed (e.g., the work on heuristics, cognitive consistency, attribution errors, etc.), the work is also troubling. The problem here is that not all people appear to reason in the same bounded or limited way. Moreover, only those people who were thinking in a linear fashion evidence the kind of bounded rationality or cognitive miserliness expected.

Liberal social scientists tend to account for individual differences by considering factors external to general cognitive capacity. For example, recourse is often made to variation in motivation, relevant substantive knowledge, or specific training in order to explain apparent differences in how people think. If insufficiently motivated, an individual will not make full use of her cognitive abilities when addressing a task. If the individual lacks sufficient information, it may be impossible to make rational sense of a problem or situation. Finally, if an individual has been specifically trained to handle a particular kind of task, she may evidence a greater capacity than most in those situations where that training is directly applicable.

These attempts at an alternative explanation may be readily countered. First, the interview topics and situation are such that we may assume that individuals who think differently may nonetheless have comparable knowledge and interest. The section of the interview on whether to help a significant other person was designed to pose a topic on which people may be assumed to have comparable information. Typically we all have extensive exposure to a close friend or loved one and comparable experience of helping and not being helped. Individual differences in thinking about the problem probably cannot reasonably be explained by claims of differences in relevant information. As for motivation, the interview situation is itself compelling. The interviewee is a volunteer who finds herself confronted with an interviewer in a face-to-face interaction. The social demands present in such a situation combined with the tailoring of the questioning to the interests of the individual interviewee insure that all interviewees are similarly well motivated to think about and respond to the questions posed.

There is also the possible objection that differences in specific training may produce individual differences in response to an interview topic. For example, a person who has been trained in facilitating cooperation on the job is likely to handle questions about helping and obligation in a much more sophisticated fashion than a person who has not had this exposure. Differences of this kind could account for the distinctive ways in which different individuals might reason about the particular sections of the interview. Two points may be made in response to this line of argument. First, in a well-conducted interview, the interviewer's probes should enable her to go beyond the merely skilled responses to the interviewee so as to reveal the interviewee's understanding of the meaning of the learned skills she is reenacting. Second, even if differences in specific training and consequent skill might explain why two people would judge the same phenomenon in qualitatively different ways, such a strategy would necessarily falter when dealing with evidence of qualitative differences that are sustained across different topics or problems the two people encounter. In the case of the interviews, such an explanatory strategy could hardly account for evidence that two interviewees show comparable differences in the quality of their thinking regardless of whether they are talking about a personal matter, a domestic social issue, or an international conflict. It certainly seems unlikely that comparable differences in specific training the two individuals received would be found across such different matters.

A related concern that might be raised here is the possible impact of a general background variable. A good example would be education. The implication here is that education enhances cognitive abilities in a general way. Consequently, individuals with different educational backgrounds might differ from one another in the way they addressed a number of different interview topics or experimental tasks. Broadly speaking, I am quite sympathetic to considerations of this kind. Translated into structural pragmatic terms, the claim might be stated in the following manner. At successive levels of education, there are differences not only in the substance of what is taught but in the structure of the interactions and discourses in which students are asked to participate. Under favorable conditions (like the kind outlined in chapter 2), this may have a transforming effect on the quality of students' thinking. There is cognitive development. Consequently, two people who have had significantly different levels of education are likely to have developed qualitatively different ways of thinking. This would be manifest across a variety of different types of circumstances they are asked to analyze or evaluate.

Whereas concerns for contextual factors like educational exposure are readily incorporated into a structural pragmatic frame of reference, it is important to recognize that these concerns are thereby somewhat reconstituted. Typically analysts who invoke considerations of level of education to differentiate individuals offer little specific discussion of either (1) what is significantly different about the different levels of education or (2) what is the exact nature of the differences in cognition that those different levels of education produce. From a structural pragmatic perspective, these characterizations are essential. To provide insight or assist in prediction, the underlying structure of both the context in question and the modes of cognition it requires or sustains must be specified. In the case of education, this requires looking beyond the substance of what is taught in the classroom to the structure of the interactions that occur between teachers, between teachers and students, and among students themselves. Once this is established, this structure of exchange must be analyzed in terms of the cognitive demands it places on the individuals involved. Next the qualities of the cognitive structures that are fostered or obstructed by the social conditions in question must be specified. Finally, a structural pragmatic analysis must offer some consideration of how the structure of social interaction might be affected by the individuals involved. Here the focus would be on the de-structuring and restructuring potential of individual participants who are oriented by structurally different ways of thinking.[10]

From a structural pragmatic point of view, it is clear that casual reference to education level (distinguished by the number of years in school) and its result (creating individuals who are more "sophisticated" or "knowledgeable") is simply inadequate. The inappropriateness of this use of such demographic categories is evident in empirical research. In the study presented in chapters 6 and 7, subjects' level of education was assessed in typical fashion—high school education or less, some college education, or some postgraduate education. The results suggest that there was some relationship between educational level and types of thinking. None of the subjects who had some college or postgraduate education evidenced any sequential thinking. That said, education measured in this way was a very poor predictor of type of thinking. Almost half of those who had some postgraduate education did not think in a systematic way and a number of the people with less than high school education did think in a linear manner. The complexities of measuring educational experience and determining its effect on modes of thinking are highlighted by other research. In my own work, I found that students in the same year at the same university with the same major did not all reason in the same way. In fact, approximately half reasoned systematically and half reasoned in a linear fashion (Rosenberg, 1988b). Comparable results were reported by Deanna Kuhn and her colleagues in their study of Harvard undergraduates (Kuhn et al., 1977).

TOLERANCE, DELIBERATION,
AND DEMOCRATIC THEORY:
DIRECTIONS FOR FUTURE RESEARCH

The research presented here has a number of implications for social and political inquiry and may be extended in a variety of interesting ways. To begin, let us consider these matters in terms of the largely psychological focus of the concepts defined in chapters 3, 4, and 5 and the empirical research discussed in chapters 6 and 7. The theory and research presented in these chapters imply that any attempt to explore individuals' attitudes, beliefs, or ideologies must be based on a prior determination of the structure of their thinking. The subjective meaning and value of the various claims those individuals make or the actions they engage in can only be understood in this light. Thus it is quite clear that a specific statement of belief, such as "The United States is a democracy" or "God exists," means very different things when uttered by someone who is thinking in a systematic, linear, or sequential manner. Similarly, a specific statement of value, such as "It is important that people have the right to self-expression" or "Tolerance is a virtue," will be understood quite differently depending on the quality of the thinking of the individual making the evaluation.

Let us be clear. These differences in the structure of meaning and value are not only a matter of the niceties of verbal self-expression. Insofar as meanings and values are constructed differently, they will both be affected by different kinds of factors and produce different kinds of subsequent claims and behaviors. Consequently, the analysis of the structural qualities of thinking is necessarily central to most examinations of the individuals' social and political behavior and to the study of the conditions under which that behavior may be sustained or changed. To illustrate, let us briefly consider the value of tolerance and how it is understood within a linear and then a systematic frame of reference. In both instances, we will consider how the value of tolerance orients behavior and under what conditions the value is likely to be rejected.

Conceived in linear terms, tolerance is understood as a guide to behavior. It consists of prescriptions to allow and respect other people's beliefs and actions even when they differ from one's own. It also requires that members of groups other than one's own be treated with similar allowances and respect. Understood in a linear fashion, these prescriptions typically consist of concrete guidelines for how specifically to behave toward a particular category of other people in a particular type of context. Thus, a church sermon on civil rights may discuss racism against African-Americans and focus on the greater difficulty they have in getting employment. Oriented by the specifics of this example, someone reasoning in a linear fashion may come to understand tolerance to mean that as an employer, she should give African-Americans equal access to employment. She may act accordingly. This concrete understanding of the value may not, however, necessarily generalize to other categories of persons or behaviors. Thus, it may not have any consequence for how she chooses her friends or whether she should give homosexuals the same opportunity for employment.

Given the confusion of categorical and evaluative judgments characteristic of linear thought, there is a natural tendency to devalue and therefore disrespect, suppress, and even destroy individuals and groups who display behaviors or beliefs that are significantly different from those of one's own group. In this regard, the norm of tolerance does not resonate with the understandings and values typically constructed in the course of linear thinking. It will be valued only insofar as it is advocated either by an accepted authority (e.g., a parent, teacher, priest, or national leader) or by people who are positively valued (e.g., friends, lovers, people of high status, etc.). In this context, the individual comes to value specific tolerant behaviors or attitudes. So constituted, the linear norm of tolerance is a frail one. It is limited in application and readily abandoned if either valued others or authority figures advocate the beliefs or actions that are intolerant.[11]

Tolerance is understood and valued in quite different terms when reconstructed within a systematic frame of reference. It is meaningful in terms of its position relative to other values (e.g., freedom, equality, etc.) and thus as an element of an ideology or in terms of its function in the larger social system. Alternatively, it may be understood in terms of some higher order principle (e.g., one of cooperation oriented to maintaining the systemic integrity of the actors involved). In either case, the meaning of tolerance is defined without reference to specific behaviors or particular individuals or groups. Rather it is defined in more general and abstract terms. As a result, an individual who reasons systematically does not learn specific tolerant behaviors, but instead deduces the appropriate prescriptive implications of a value of tolerance for different kinds of interactions or situations. Consequently, the systematically conceived norm of tolerance will be applied far more generally than its linear counterpart. It is also more likely to be influenced by reasoned argument focusing on questions of moral principle and collective needs and much less likely to be influenced by any particular claims regardless of who makes them.

In systematic thinking, the value of tolerance is judged in primarily functional or principled terms. Here a system not only constitutes a context of interpretation, it is also establishes a basis for evaluation. The maintenance of an existing system, be it the personality system of an individual or the social system of a group, becomes a higher order standard for judging specific interactions or prescriptive norms. Insofar as the norm or interaction in question contributes to the integrity and coherence of the system, it will be ascribed functional value. Unlike in the linear case, the evaluation of tolerance will therefore tend to be made without consideration of the preferences of legitimate authorities or positively valued others. In this case, the value is not only likely to be more generally applied, it will also be more stable. That said, the norm of tolerance may be rejected on functional or principled grounds. Insofar as particular acts of tolerance threaten the integrity of a system or violate higher order principles such as cooperation, then toleration will be rejected in favor of intolerance. Lacking such a conceptual foundation, many liberals who value tolerance in linear terms may find the question of whether to tolerate such intolerant groups as the American Klu Klux Klan or Austria's Freedom Party confusing and irresolvable. There is the apparent contradiction of being intolerant of intolerance. Liberals who think in systematic terms do have the conceptual resources, such as the ability to consider higher order concerns of social integration and respect for the integrity of systems, to reach a justifiable resolution.

As indicated by the foregoing example of tolerance, structural pragmatic considerations of the underlying structure of cognition have broad implications for the study of individuals' thought and behavior. By delimiting the formal quality of the meaning and value of what the individual considers, the structure of thinking influences a penumbra of related phenomena. On one hand, it helps determine the nature of the effect that a given attitude or behavior may have in shaping the other attitudes the individual may hold or the other behaviors she may enact. On the other hand, it helps determine the kinds of factors that may cause that attitude or behavior to be evoked, sustained, or changed. This suggests one direction for future research: to apply the conception of structures of thinking and the methods of research presented here to additional types of social and political behavior. One example is provided by the preceding discussion of the nature and consequences of the different ways in which the value of tolerance is constructed by individuals who think in qualitatively different ways. This line of inquiry is currently being developed in the work of Chris Hanks (1998). Another exemplary application is offered in the research of Joe Braunwarth (1997, 1999). He applied the distinction between linear and systematic thinking to consider the different ways in which individuals process television news.

Apart from this attempt to consider the ramifications of structures of thinking for various aspects of individuals' social and political behavior, a structural pragmatic consideration of the limitations of the research presented in chapters 6 and 7 suggests another more social psychological line of inquiry. According to structural pragmatic theory, the interaction between individuals is dually structured. It is an uncertain result of subjective structuration on one hand and social or intersubjective structuration on the other. Viewed in this light, it is evident that the research presented in the book bracketed out any consideration of the intersubjective dimension of the interview. This is true in two senses. First, the analysis focused on the interviewee's responses. In so doing, no consideration was given to the interaction between the interviewee and the interviewer, nor was any analysis conducted of the structural or formal qualities of their discourse. Second, the research was designed to observe structural differences in individual performance when the structure of the social context was held constant. Thus while the particular subject matter being discussed in the course of the interview did vary, the conditions under which it was discussed did not. Throughout all the interviews, the social structuring of the exchange remained the same. In all cases it consisted of a meeting between two strangers, each of whom played a prescribed role (that of either interviewer or interviewee).

This suggests a second direction for future research: to examine the impact of differently structured conditions of social interaction on the quality of the discourse produced and the thinking of individuals involved. For example, in the laboratory, one could create a number of small groups, each of which is assigned the task of solving a particular problem or coming to a common judgment of a particular situation. Several different strategies could then be followed in order to assess the impact of social structure. One possibility would be to use the experimental instructions given to subjects to create differently structured groups. To give a crude example, one half of the groups might be structured hierarchically and the other half might be structured in a more egalitarian fashion. Then an attempt may be made to assess the nature of the discourse that ensues and the quality of thinking evidenced by the individual members. An interesting, if complicating, addition would be to have each of these groups meet on a second occasion in order to address another task. On this second occasion, however, the guidelines presented to the participants would be changed so as to alter the social structuring of their interaction. For example, those groups that were initially structured as hierarchies for their first meeting might be restructured in an egalitarian way for the second meeting. The qualities of the discourse of the group and the structure of the individual members' ways of thinking could then be compared across the two sessions. This kind of experimental research might be complemented by field studies comparing institutions (or even societies) where differences in the structuring of interaction or discourse varied in ways that might be predicted to have significant cognitive consequences.

In a complementary fashion, other research might explore the impact of cognition on the structure of social interaction. Research of this kind might also study how individuals interact in a small group situation. Given the interest in the social impact of individuals' thinking styles, the groups might be formed to ensure that the members of any one group all think in the same way. Thus one third of the groups would consist of individuals who think in a sequential way; one third would consist of individuals who think in a linear way; and the last third would consist of individuals who think in a systematic way. Using instructions to the individual subjects, all groups could be structured in the same way. Again as a crude example, the instructions could require open and egalitarian interaction among the group members. An attempt could then be made to examine the qualities of the discourse and the social interaction that actually emerge in the differently constituted groups.

I have spoken of these trajectories of structural pragmatic research in expressly social psychological terms and suggested research designs involving experimental manipulations in a laboratory. This should not lead the reader to underestimate the broader and expressly political implications of this proposed work. For example, the proposed research may readily be cast in terms of democratic theory and practice. The suggested research on the impact of the structure of social exchange on cognition is directly relevant to the debate between participatory and elitist theories of democracy. Following Schumpeter (1942), elitist conceptions of desirable democratic practice are justified on the basis of two claims: (1) that average individuals are incapable of reasoning at the level required by liberally conceived democracy, and (2) that there is little to be done about this. Following Pateman (1970) and Barber (1984), participatory conceptions of democratic practice counter this elitist position by arguing that although most individuals may not currently exhibit the knowledge, skill, or interest required of ideal citizens of a democracy, this is simply because the distribution of power in their environment is such that they are not provided the opportunity to develop what is required. If power relations were altered and people were given the opportunity to participate, their interests would change and they would readily acquire the knowledge and skills necessary for effective citizenship.

This debate is readily reconstructed in structural pragmatic terms. In this context, the elitist position might be characterized as involving the following set of claims. First, democratic participation requires a principled evaluation of laws and norms and a systemic understanding of the function that rules serve both for the polity and for individual citizens. In other words, democracy requires that its citizens think systematically. Second, only a few people think in this way. Most think about social and political issues in a linear fashion. For this majority, laws and norms constitute the basis rather than the object of evaluation and are understood in terms of specific applications and effects rather than in terms of general principles and system functioning. Most people are thus incapable of meeting the requisites of democratic citizenship. Their power and responsibilities should therefore be diminished accordingly. Contrary to structural pragmatic theory, this elitist formulation denies or marginalizes the impact of social structure on political cognition. In terms of the research on small groups proposed earlier, the elitist position suggests that variation in the social structure of the groups will not have any significant impact on the formal quality of the discourse that emerges or on the structure of the thinking of the individuals involved.

In a manner consistent with the conclusions of structural pragmatic theory, the claims of the participatory democrats highlight the effect of social conditions. Despite this shared concern, the participatory democrats remain part of a liberal tradition of political theorizing and therefore typically do not incorporate structural considerations of the kind invoked in structural pragmatic theory. Rather, they offer a decidedly nonstructural consideration of distributions of power and a largely substantive characterization of related decision-making opportunities.[12] Similarly there is a nonstructural assessment of the psychological consequences of these social and political conditions for the individuals involved. Thus the effects of being rendered relatively powerless are to obstruct relevant skill development and to foster a lack of interest in political matters.[13]

In my view, the argument posed by those advocating participatory democracy may be profitably reconstructed in more structural pragmatic terms. The resulting argument would be that the inadequacies evidenced by average citizens may have a structural cognitive basis and this in turn may be the result of the structural conditions of their everyday life. Insofar as these circumstances of everyday life do not present individuals with tasks that require systematic thought and do not provide the social supports that are conducive to its development, those individuals will not be able to meet the demands of full democratic citizenship. If, however, the structure of social organization is changed appropriately, thinking may develop and the citizen skills required may be learned. Some of these changes may be expressly political (e.g., opening up political decision-making to localized community based negotiation), others may be more apparently social (e.g., equalizing the relationship between husband and wife and opening up the terms of the marriage to ongoing negotiation between the two parties). In either case, the hypothesis would now be that appropriate changes in the structuring of social interaction would affect the formal qualities of both the discourse of the groups and the subjective constructions of the individuals involved. The result would produce both discourse and citizenship that is more consistent with the requisites of democratic theory.

It should be clear that this structural pragmatic reconstruction implies a politically significant deviation from the position taken by the participatory democrats. Assuming no structural cognitive basis of citizen inadequacy, the participatory democrats suppose that if laws and formal institutions are changed in a way that provides individuals with power and opportunity, those individuals will naturally be able and interested in filling their roles as citizens. Recognizing that the limits of individuals' skills and interest may reflect the underlying structure of their thought, structural pragmatic theory suggests the problem of fostering democratic citizenship is more complex. Simply providing people who think in a linear fashion with the opportunity to participate in a systematically structured social environment guarantees nothing. On one hand, these people may not understand the social context as it is presented and may simply reconstruct social norms and demands in a manner consistent with their own way of thinking. On the other hand, they may recognize the greater complexity of the new situation but be confused or frightened by it. In this case, they may simply withdraw and thus become marginalized. Alternatively, they may aggressively move to restructure the situation in a more comprehensible way. For example, presented with an institutionally structured opportunity to engage one another in an egalitarian, constructively critical, and rule-transforming fashion, people may respond to the perceived ambiguities and complexities of such a situation by effectively reorganizing in a more hierarchical, authoritarian, and rule-following manner. The long history of failed efforts to institute democratic politics may, in part, be reconsidered in this light.

Structural pragmatic theory thus suggests that the expectations of the participatory democrats are unrealistic. Indeed, the theory implies that the mere presentation of the opportunity to interact in a more structurally advanced way is probably unlikely to foster any structural development in the manner in which the affected individuals understand their circumstance and orient their behavior. The development of subjectivity requires more than socially provided opportunities to judge and act. It also requires the provision of institutions that offer individuals the instruction and guidance they need to help them recognize the inappropriateness of their existing ways of understanding politics and to suggest alternative, more adequate ways of doing so. At the same time, these institutions must provide the social support these people need to feel secure enough to abandon those old understandings and to experiment with the new ones. In this vein, structural pragmatic theory suggests a view of democracy that is expressly pedagogical. The relevant model is not that of the free market, but that of student-centered education.

To conclude, my attempt here has been to take a further step toward constructing a truly integrative social psychology, one that incorporates not only sociology and psychology, but the study of politics as well. Much has been revealed about the "not so common sense" constructed by people who think in qualitatively different ways, but it is clear that a great deal remains to be done. Although general claims have been made regarding the nature of the different types of thinking, there is a need to explore the implications of these differences for how people will respond to and engage one another in a variety of specific social and political situations. For example, in a marriage, how do people who think in different ways understand their circumstance and how does this affect how they will actually interact? In the context of the nation-state, how do people who think in different ways conceptualize their national identity or their role as citizens and how does this affect subsequent political action? Perhaps even more critical, there is a need to extend the arguments of chapter 2 and to study the interplay between cognition on one hand and the conditions of social interaction on the other. This effort must begin with an attempt to clearly identify the structure of social institutions and discourses. Only when the different forms of these social structures are elaborated as well as the forms of cognitive structures can the dynamic interaction between these two levels of structuration be effectively explored. Then it will be possible to address such questions as: What kinds of political institutions facilitate or inhibit the development of a competent and engaged democratic citizenry? Or, alternatively, how are various types of political institutions effectively deconstructed and reorganized by populations who think in different ways? In my view, questions like these define the trajectory that structural pragmatic inquiry must follow. They are also core concerns of both social and political psychology.

Notes

CHAPTER 1. POSTMODERNITY, NOT LEARNING,
AND THE NOT SO COMMON SENSE

1. This has led some to note the addictive qualities of this mode of escape and to regard such addiction as a signature disorder of the twentieth century.

2. This is not to suggest that the problem of postmodernity is merely one of adaptation, of individuals learning to submissively accommodate to an existing order. As becomes clearer in the analysis of the dynamics of change in chapter 2, psychological adaptation carries with it the potential for transforming the social order to which it accommodates.

3. For a contemporary statement of the assumptions of neoclassical political economy, see Riker, 1995. For my analysis of the liberal roots of neoclassical political economy and the inadequacies of this approach, see Rosenberg, 1995.

4. The classic statement of this of course is Thomas Hobbes' *Leviathan* (1958).

5. This reasoning was clearly apparent in the policy advice offered by American economists to the newly democratizing nations of Eastern Europe in the early 1990s.

6. Reference here is the tradition of Edmund Burke and Jonathan Swift.

7. This is articulated in England through the literary expression of such early-nineteenth-century figures as Keats, Shelley, and Wordsworth. The work of the historian Thomas Carlyle is also quite important.

8. The discussion here of sociology and the sociological perspective is juxta-

posed to that of the liberal perspective. It is differentiated by its rejection of the methodological individualism of the latter. The distinction drawn here may be confusing for some readers because liberally oriented, methodologically individualist scholars also study social phenomena. The distinction here does not revolve around what is specifically studied but rather by the underlying orientation that dictates how the phenomena in question will be conceived, studied, and explicated.

9. Durkheim, 1982.

10. See the last part of Althusser's essay "Ideology and Ideological State Apparatuses" in his book *Lenin and Philosophy, and Other Essays.*

11. For a recent discussion of the cognitive assumptions implicit in sociological perspectives, see DiMaggio, 1997. Although his analysis is insightful, it is limited by his choice of cognitive psychology: schema theory. The cognitive psychology most consistent with a cultural sociology of the kind DiMaggio prefers, scheme theory is too limited for my dual purposes of recognizing the structural bases of cognition and for challenging the traditional sociological conception of the individual-society relationship.

12. For an influential summary of this schema approach by two leading proponents of this view, see Fiske and Taylor, 1991.

13. This argument was also made in earlier work, e.g., Rosenberg, 1988, 1991.

14. The present focus is psychological. It is important to keep in mind, however, that this variation in the structuring of meaning is not only a psychological or subjective phenomenon. Either as a matter of intersubjective or collective production, meaning is also structured socially or culturally. As suggested earlier, this cannot be reduced to the activity of individuals and analyzed in those terms. Rather this social structuration has its own distinctive nature. Even if some of the substantive elements of the culture are to be found in the particular claims individuals make, the form or meaning of these cultural artifacts may be structurally different from that which is subjectively constructed by individual members of the group. Just as the form or quality of subjective reasoning may vary, so may the form or quality of the cultural definition and social organization. Indeed, this claim is implicit in our earlier analysis of the transition from traditional to modern society. The forms of society were distinguished not with regard to particular substantive dictates or regulatory demands. Rather they were differentiated as two qualitatively different modes of organizing and defining social life. It is precisely because modernity does not simply involve a new stipulation of specific facts, values, and behaviors, but constitutes a new form of social integration, that the transition has proved so difficult for those individuals involved. They are not required to learn new particular requisites to replace old ones. Instead they must adapt to a basic restructuring of social interaction and discourse.

15. For differing views of rationality that follow this tradition, see the first chapter of Riker and Ordeshook (1973) and Simon (1985).

CHAPTER 2. A STRUCTURAL PRAGMATIC SOCIAL PSYCHOLOGY

1. In earlier work, I have referred to my approach as structural developmental. I think this has been more misleading than helpful. Whereas development is a concern, it is a deriv-

ative one. More basic is the pragmatic view of meaning as operational or as a matter of use and the theoretical reconstruction of this pragmatism from a structuralist perspective. This then provides the basis upon which such issues as the social psychology of meaning and the dynamics of development are considered.

2. For example, see Peirce (1923), James (1909, 1947), Mead (1924–25, 1929), and Dewey (1916, 1930). Recent reconsideration of pragmatism has chosen to emphasize Mead's seminal work on this creative moment. For exemplary discussions of this, see Giddens (1984), Habermas (1984), and Joas (1993).

3. See Dewey (1896)

4. For examples of such a pragmatist conception of language, see Austin (1962), Grice (1968), and Searle (1971).

5. This dynamic relationship between rules of interaction (viewed substantively) and the paritcular ways in which people actually interact is nicely developed by Anthony Giddens in his analysis of the constitution of society (1984).

6. This relationship between the conditions of interaction and the production of subjectivity is interestingly developed by Mead (1924–25) and later elaborated by Berger and Luckmann (1967).

7. For example, see de Saussure, *Course in General Linguistics* (1959); Lévi-Strauss, *Totemism* (1963), *The Savage Mind* (1966); Merleau-Ponty, *The Structure of Behavior* (1963). For more general discussions of structuralism, see Ehrmann (1970) and Piaget (1970)

8. The concepts of system and structure are often readily confused. A good example of such a confusion is evident in William Runciman's essay, "What Is Structuralism?" (1969). For my own earlier discussion of this see, *Reason, Ideology, and Politics* (1988).

9. The example provided simplifies matters. The problems a person addresses are not "given." Rather the mode of structuration determines the kinds of issues that will emerge as problems or appropriate objects of consideration. Thus categorization and linear causality are kinds of problems that emerge as central for the mode of thinking described here.

10. See the final essay in Lévi-Strauss, *The Savage Mind* (1966).

11. Giddens appears to argue along similar lines in his discussion of structuration (1984). There he emphasizes the recursive relationship between social structures as virtual and the specific way in which they are realized in interaction. His view differs in that it is more substantive and particularistic. Giddens thus fails to adequately address the determining and defining power of structures. The net result is an atomistic analysis that in the end offers little conceptual advance beyond the work by Mead upon which Giddens draws.

12. For examples of classic statements of this development, see Inhelder and Piaget (1958). For applications in the arenas of social and moral reasoning, see Kohlberg (1971, 1984), Furth (1980), Selman (1980), Damon and Hart (1988), and Dupont (1994).

13. See Lyotard's final chapter on postmodernism (1984) and Foucault's theoretical essays in *Power/Knowledge*.

14. For an interesting discussion of the cognitive affective dimensions of this confrontation with the demands of the environment, see Kegan (1994).

15. For a discussion of this, see Vygotsky (1978) and Wertsch (1991).

16. It should be emphasized that the socialization process here is different than that typically considered by sociologists and psychologists. In its more usual conception, socialization consists of the transmission of specific content, that is, particular beliefs, preferences, or behaviors, and involves learning. Here, socialization consists of the transmission of an underlying mode of coordinating action and constructing meaning and involves structural transformation.

17. An issue that arises here is the effect of varying distributions of individuals who think differently. For example, what proportion of individuals who are unable to recognize social dictates is sufficient to undermine a social structure. Clearly if all operate in this manner, the social structure will not be realized. But what if only one-third or one-half operate in this adequate manner, but the remainder reason and act in an appropriate way? Will the social structure be sustained and if so in what way? These are important issues that deserve further consideration.

18. Examples of this include the Catholic view of transgression and the reincorporating role of confession and absolution. The latter constitutes an institution constructed upon the premise that, by virtue of their lack of discipline or understanding, many adherents will regularly violate the designated rules of social exchange. Confession becomes a way of both allowing their violation and forcing a recognition, if inadequate or incomplete, of the authority of the rule that has been broken. Another example is provided by the cultural direction offered in the Jewish Passover service. An explicit exercise in socialization, the service recognizes the variation in the people to be socialized through the differentiation of the kinds of children to whom the significance of the ceremony must be explained. Of particular interest is the discussion of the wise child and the simple one and the different ways in which each one must be incorporated into the collective activity.

CHAPTER 3. LINEAR THINKING

1. This is not to suggest that appearance is simply determined by the objective characteristics of the phenomena observed. Rather it is an interaction between these characteristics and the qualities of perception itself.

2. Whereas Smelsund presumes this to be characteristic of all cognition, I am suggesting it is primarily an attribute of linear thought. In systematic thought, double negatives of the kind discussed here are readily comprehended and utilized to make sense of events. In a different direction, sequential reasoning leads to a more primitive understanding of absence than the one discussed here. In this case, the failure of something to occur is regarded, along with its accompanying frustrations, less as an absence and more as the replacement of one event by another. In the latter regard, the new conditions often overwhelm the expectations created by the memory of the old. Even when they do not, this leads to mere expression of the associated frustration or relief and not to any redefinition.

3. For a well-regarded review of this research, see Fiske and Taylor (1991).

4. Even in an ostensibly secular culture such as the United States, people often speak of outcomes as the effect of divine or fateful intervention. Of course, in other cultures and times, this clearly permeates more of the official culture. The early medieval Italian ac-

counts of war provide interesting examples. Typically, the focus here is on the actions of leaders, one deciding to place his army on the hill, the other countering by pulling back behind a river. But in the midst of the account there is regular reference to the specific interventions of God, e.g., causing one army to fight well or creating inclement weather to advantage one of the forces. The divine and human actions exist on the same plane.

5. In the language of cognitive complexity theory (e.g., Streufert and Streufert, 1978; Tetlock, 1984), the category of the stranger is relatively simple and the category of Sarah is relatively complex. The key point here is that simple or complex, both categories are linear.

6. This process of social identification has been interestingly examined in the social psychological literature on groups (e.g., Tajfel, 1982; Hogg and Abrams, 1988). In this literature, social categorization is viewed as an inherent attribute of social cognition. It is assumed that all individuals make sense of themselves and other people by locating them in social categories. Largely a matter of cultural definitions, each category consists of a set of generally concrete, specific attributes. Once internalized, these categories serve as cognitive tools that orient the individual's understanding of and response to the environment. While much of social categorization theory is quite consistent with the definition of linear categorization and identification, it should be kept in mind that the theory does not provide an appropriate account of the social constructions of either sequential or systematic thought.

7. Of course this attention to the implications of the objective conditions that differentiate self and other perception must be tempered by a consideration of the effect of culture. This is of greatest relevance when the culture provides explicit direction for the explanation of behavior that runs counter to what is suggested here.

8. This relation between language and social control is perhaps an unusually obvious example of the power/knowledge nexus that Michel Foucault (1979, 1980) regards to be central to the construction of all meaning. Our analysis here suggests that this may only be applicable in social contexts largely populated by people who think in a linear fashion. Except in the extreme (and theoretically less interesting) cases of direct monitoring of action, those people who reason sequentially will be relatively unaffected by the discourse because they tend not to think through language. Similarly, those who reason systematically will be less directly affected because they are more aware of the construction of meaning and are more self-consciously active in the interpretative reconstruction of the thematic content with which they are presented.

9. In contemporary society, rules of action are often defined in general rather than specific terms. These rules speak less to what to do in a given case than to the essential quality of interpersonal relationships and how that might generally be maintained. For example, the concern might be the integrity of individuals as participants in a relationship and the commensurate need for justice in adjudicating their differences. This rather abstract imperative cannot be understood directly in a linear fashion. Rather it will be assimilated in linear terms and thus translated into a specific direction for action: e.g., when same two people want to do the same thing, let them take turns, or when two people want the thing, divide it in half.

10. This is not to say that in certain subcultural contexts these other activities may not be defined as political and therefore subjectively represented as such.

11. This account of linear evaluation as a three-step process is a descriptive strategy. The steps are not so discrete or so separate from one another in time.

12. As in other cases of illustrative social psychological research, the evidence of derogation provided by Lerner and others is used to make general claims regarding human cognition and judgment (Lerner, 1970). The argument I am advancing suggests that the claim applies to people who are reasoning in a linear fashion and not to those who reason either sequentially or systematically.

13. For research on the evaluation of friends and enemies, see Jervis (1976), Rosenberg and Wolfsfeld (1977), White (1986).

14. See, e.g., Tajfel (1970, 1978), Brewer (1979), Hogg and Abrams (1988).

15. This is not to say that moral claims cannot be criticized in linear terms. This would, however, not be a matter of considering the ethical value of the claim by placing it within some system of moral values. Rather it would consist of invoking one moral claim, simply asserting its primacy, and then using it to contradict and deny another moral claim. Usually criticism of this kind reflects exposure to specific cultural or social direction that explicitly suggests the line adopted.

CHAPTER 4. SYSTEMATIC THINKING

1. This is not to suggest either that there are always regularities in the action or that principles can always be satisfactorily applied. In either case, reasoning will not yield understanding but rather can only conclude by regarding the circumstances to be intrinsically chaotic or incomprehensible or by questioning the adequacy of either the observations or principles upon which the reasoning is based.

2. Here we have the structural basis for the understanding embodied in classic definitions of the scientific method. Demands for controlled experimentation on one hand and interobserver reliability on the other follow directly from the understanding of observation constructed here.

3. There are various ways these may be characterized. For example, Jean Piaget, in his analysis of formal operational thought, suggests four forms of association that together constitute a closed system. They are identity, negation, reciprocity, and correlation. This so-called INRC group is discussed in some length in Inhelder and Piaget (1958). I find his presentation of these four forms persuasive but disagree that the systems are necessarily closed and therefore that this list is necessarily complete.

4. Reasoning in this manner, individuals would not evidence the limitations in correlational reasoning reported by Smelsund (1963). In contrast, those subjects who reason in a linear manner would perform in the flawed manner described in Smelsund's research.

5. This capacity to abstract reflects the power of systematic thought; it also reflects one of its weaknesses. In this construction of the production line, there is no place for the independent nature of workers as entities unto themselves, that is, as defined independently of the workplace. Insofar as they are, in part, self-directing and self-constructing, they as individuals will contribute to their participation in any work relationship and hence delimit what that work relationship may or may not be. Failure to consider this at the same time as considering the systemic interrelationship among work relationships can only

yield a partial and ultimately distorting view of both the current and potential functioning of the production line.

6. While the focus here is on the individual and the community, this is not to imply that an interpersonal relationship or small group may not also be conceived as a system. When these alternative foci are adopted, the ensuing analysis suggests that they are the organizing and defining forces behind whatever social integration or intersubjective meaning is observed.

7. There may be a systematic recognition of the cultural significance of group identification or its implications for a politics of identity. This, however, is conceived in the context of considerations of communities as systems that organize and thereby define individuals in relation to each other. Juxtaposed to an understanding of the individual as a self-constituting system, this illustrates a characteristic dualism of systematic social thought.

8. Much of the current debate between students of political culture and neoclassical political economists can be understood in these terms.

9. Reference here is to sociological work that follows in the tradition of Talcott Parsons or Robert Merton. It is clearly evident in the enormous research literature on socialization that followed in the 1950s and continued through the 1980s. Much of the approach to social identity that has captured the American sociological imagination in the 1990s can also be understood as an expression of this perspective. What are excluded are more specifically structuralist and poststructuralist sociologies. Whereas they also deny the conceptual integrity or theoretical significance of the individual considered in her own terms, their conception of society is not systematic. These sociologies integrate an understanding of the organizing force behind systems and the quality of the outcome in a way beyond the structural capacities of systematic thought. They are better understood as an expression of another higher order form of reasoning.

10. Note that the relationship between the two classes is not direct—one does not lead to the other as in linear thought. Rather, a higher order or overarching consideration mediates the connection between the two.

11. For a good discussion of this case in particular and the problem more generally, see C. Kinnvall's (1995) analysis of cultural learning. Also of relevance here is Pye (1992).

12. Linear thought certainly does allow for extension beyond the known. This is evident in imagination. This linear imagination is, however, limited to building on the specifics of what is known, displacing it to some extraordinary context and refashioning it through imaginary division or combination. Typically the result of this effort remains within the realm of fantasy. Occasionally it offers a model that is introduced as a direction for practical action. This is quite different than constructing a system, deducing real connections heretofore not known, and then making hypothetical claims regarding their true existence.

13. The agenda-setting effect of mass media presentations is reduced by other factors as well. For example, systematic reasoning also leads to an assessment of the intentions and understandings that combine to determine the focus and bias of the newscast itself. In this regard, the focal issue is also placed in a larger context of other concerns thereby diminishing the relative salience of the focal issue and bringing to light the otherwise absent ones.

14. The focus here is political, but of course the structure of nonpolitical conflict is the same. Thus the construction of conflict will be the same whether it is between Hutus and Tutsis or a husband and wife.

15. This self-conscious conception of individuals as fragmentary and derivative does not imply that individuals have no qualities. Clearly they act and react, have beliefs and pursue interests. The point is that these acts, beliefs, and interests that distinguish and orient the individual are themselves social products. For example, if we view neoclassical political economy as an exercise in systematic reasoning, we see that individuals are regarded rather abstractly as agent/decision-makers. However, environments are understood to orchestrate their choices by defining the interactive context (and thus determining what consequences will follow from which choice is made) in which the individual makes her choices.

16. For our purposes here, it makes little difference whether the agents being considered in the analysis are limited to nation-states or include additional players, such as international organizations or business corporations. The key is that all these players are self-constituting agents who define their own purposes that are then played out in a setting of mutual constraint and possibility. While clearly very important, the setting is a creation of the individual players who are themselves not constituted or reconstituted by virtue of their participation in that setting.

17. It is often the case that clinicians view an abusive relationship in these terms. Thus it is presumed even if an abused person is removed from such a relationship she will tend to enter other similar relationships later on. This is because the initial relationship was cooperative and did reflect aspects of her personality organization. That organization is likely to project her into new abusive relationships even if the present one is terminated. In this light, therapy is understood only to begin with the removal of the individual from the abusive relationship. The therapeutic focus is then on the reorganization of her personality so as to render it incompatible with any future abusive interaction.

18. An important point to keep in mind here is that these prior assumptions not only vary with self-conscious constructions of the cases to which they are applied. The assumptions made will also vary with cultural context insofar as that context offers differing characterization of the qualities of human nature.

19. The assumption that there are general principles of social life combined with the recognition of how these principles are variously manifest in the specific settings underlies the logic of much contemporary comparative politics. The justification for this inquiry is that if you compare societies, you may discover dynamics that are common to them all, thus distinguishing what are the essential principles of political life.

20. The recognition of the provisional quality of value judgments does not undermine their force. In this regard, the judgment is regarded as the best available and an appropriate guide to action.

21. In a well-argued critique, Roberto Unger (1975) claims this independence of conception of the good and the just constitutes a central antimony of liberal thought. I agree, but develop the argument differently and ultimately cast the net more broadly. Whereas Unger refers to the general qualities of the structure of liberal theorizing, I have attempted to examine the mode of thinking that engenders such a structure. As a result,

liberalism becomes one possible result, one that is realized under certain sociohistorical circumstances. The essential structure of liberal thinking may, however, have other, distinctly nonliberal, manifestations.

22. This capacity to go beyond what is conventional and to construct the hypothetical as a basis of critique provides the structural underpinnings of the postconventional moral reasoning described by Lawrence Kohlberg (1981a).

23. The argument regarding the nature of the relationship between the ideal implicit in systematic evaluation and the specific evaluations it generates runs parallel to the analysis of communicative action offered by Jürgen Habermas (1979, 1984). More specifically, it roughly parallels his conception of the quality of the ideal inherent in speech and its potentially critical and transformative relationship to the actual practice of speech. Here, however, the ideal inheres in the subjective constructions of systematic thought and bears a potentially critical and transformative relationship to the actual practice of thinking. One key point of difference in the two conceptions is that Habermas suggests that the whole of the progress of the development of communicative activity can be understood in these terms. In my view, this transformative impact occurs only within the framework of systematic thinking itself. It does not account for the development to the point of thinking systematically or for the transformation beyond systematic thought.

CHAPTER 5. SEQUENTIAL THINKING

1. There are of course notable exceptions. Some researchers are willing to accept the burden of actually making direct and extended contact with their interviewees. The results are illuminating. Excellent examples are offered by Robert Lane's landmark study in New England (1962) and the later work of Jennifer Hochschild (1981) and Kristen Monroe (1996). Studies such as these are, unfortunately, rare.

2. A classic example along these lines is Phillip Converse's seminal attempt to analyze people's reasoning (Converse, 1964). For my discussion of the limits of survey research, see my chap. 2 in *Reason, Ideology, and Politics* (1988).

3. Whereas the structural pragmatic view presented here contradicts the classic liberal vision, it should not be construed to suggest that rights and opportunities of those who think in a sequential (or for that matter, linear) fashion should be limited. To the contrary, the theory emphasizes the need to provide individuals with the power and opportunity to consider, make choices, and act. Indeed, the failure to develop that leads to adults thinking in a sequential or a linear fashion is understood to be largely a result of the restrictive social contexts in which they live.

4. A caveat regarding the use of learning theory should be noted. This theory presumes all learning is the same. In the context of the argument being made here, the characterization of stimulus situations, their impact as reinforcements, and their effect on subsequent behavior is most consistent with assimilation of environmental effects through sequential reasoning. Thus while correct, these learning theories offer only a partial account of the mechanisms of learning—an account that misses essential elements of learning that occurs through linear or systematic reasoning.

5. This example is offered with some caution as little can be said with certainty regarding

the subjective meaning of customs of a civilization now long dead. It nonetheless serves the purpose of illustration by indicating how such matters might be understood from a sequential perspective. Of note, the example is also interesting as an indication of the possible cultural consequences of subjective modes of reasoning.

6. Although not cast in structural pragmatic terms, John Cash's interesting discussion of personality and its resistance to self-conscious change may readily be considered from this perspective. See Cash, 1996.

7. It is likely that over time such imaginings are often limited by specific training. Thus when offering accounts of sequences that involve remote or fantastic individuals, the child may be exposed to negative rewards for false report. One by one, she will thus learn to differentiate certain figures such as the president and not include them in the sequences she recounts or attempts to reenact.

8. Interestingly, the severity of the offense is typically judged relative to the outcome rather than with regard to the intention. Thus the accidental breaking of the vase is more serious than an intentional breaking of the glass. This relative disregard for intentionality is another result of the relative lack of causal thinking characteristic of sequential thought.

9. This said, it should be kept in mind that social penetration of an individual's environment is limited and therefore there will be crosscutting influences that will produce recurring, localized, and varying deviation.

10. For example, see Ioanna Dimitracopoulou's discussion of the empathic responses of young children observed during her study of the development of conversational competence (1990).

11. This imitative learning does not imply a taking of the perspective of the other. Rather one is projected into the situation and the distinctive qualities of the other and their particular perspective are lost in the process. Thus one sees and feels the events from one's own perspective. These events are attended and learned because of the identification with the other that leads to a projection of one's affective responses into the situation.

CHAPTER 6. EPISTEMOLOGY, METHODOLOGY, AND RESEARCH DESIGN

1. For the classic study of this, see Converse, 1964.

2. See La Piere, 1934; Wicker, 1969.

3. See, e.g., Converse, 1964; Fishbein and Ajzen, 1975; Ajzen and Fishbein, 1980. In this context, it is worth mentioning the recent work on cognitive complexity. This does seem to constitute research on differences in the quality of thinking. This was the explicit aim of the early research (e.g., Struefert and Struefert, 1978). The more recent work, however, has abandoned the notion of enduring individual differences in complexity. Instead and in a manner more consistent with the general orientation of social psychology, variations in complexity are understood as a function of circumstance or personal intention. Again variation in cognitive functioning is understood as a direct effect of factors external to cognition itself (e.g., Tetlock, 1984, 1988).

4. For more of my view on these points see, Rosenberg, 1988a, chap. 2.

5. A partial exception here is the work on heuristics following on the research of Kahneman, Slovic, and Tversky, 1982.

6. This said, there has been some attention to individual differences at the very periphery of the work on attribution. Examples include Rotter's work on locus of control (1966; Strickland, 1988) and other work on pessimistic attributional styles (e.g., Peterson and Seligman, 1984) and on the impact of depression of attribution of responsibility for negative outcomes (e.g., Sweeny, Anderson, and Bailey, 1986; Peterson, Seligman, and Valliant, 1988). Two points should be made here. First, the work represents a very small fraction of the research on attribution. In this regard, it is also worth noting that in the conclusion of their influential text, *Social Cognition,* Fiske and Taylor (1991) sketch gaps in the research and directions for further research. The exploration of individual differences receives no mention there. Second and more revealing, differences are accounted for in terms of personality, not in terms of inherent differences in cognition itself. This is another example of something external to cognition having an impact on cognitive functioning.

7. See. e.g., Tversky and Kahneman, 1974; Kahneman, Slovic, and Tversky, 1982; and Quattrone and Tversky, 1988. Lacking any overarching theoretical conception of thinking, problems emerge in the heuristics research that are typical of more atomistic approaches. The core limitation is that there is no theoretical basis for category formation. As a result, there is no basis for inferring what new types of heuristics one might seek to discover. One is simply left to intuition or fortuitous circumstance in the effort to discover new aspects of cognition. In addition, there is no basis for determining when all or even most of the types have been explored. As a result, one is left with the prospect of an endlessly expanding laundry list of types of heuristic processing. Finally, there is little basis for differentiating types of heuristics. Empirically generated, they are grouped in a manner that appears sensible. In this latter regard, the researchers are basically left to the same shortcuts they describe—in this case the representativeness heuristic. It is also worth noting that like the attribution research it seeks to supersede, the work on heuristics also presumes that all individuals cognize in basically the same way. Thus virtually no attention is paid to individual differences.

CHAPTER 8. OVERVIEW AND CONCLUDING REMARKS

1. For my review of the research on political attitudes and belief systems, see Rosenberg, 1988a, 2001.

2. Also of immediate interest here is the work on thinking about democracy by Janusz Reykowski (1994). In his research, Reykowski asked subjects in Poland to choose among a set of alternatives to determine what was central or irrelevant to the definition of democracy. Although Reykowski relied on a Q-sort methodology and was not guided by developmental theory, his results indicate that subjects did define democracy in several distinct ways, ways that do seem to correspond to the different structures of thinking I have described (Reykowksi, personal communication, 1996).

3. Richard Merelman's study (1971) of the development of adolescent political thinking is often mentioned in conjunction with this other developmental psychological research. Merelman presents results that contradict Piaget's theory of cognitive development as it might be applied in political research. As I have noted elsewhere (e.g., Rosenberg,

1988b), I believe the issue here is Merelman's interpretation of Piaget. In the course of a rather imaginative attempt to integrate Piaget and Freud (Merelman, 1968), he offers an interpretation of Piaget's theory that strips it of most its structural developmental dimensions. In this light, I believe the evidence that Merelman's research produces constitutes more a disconfirmation of his use of Piaget's theory rather than of Piaget's theory itself.

4. Piaget's ideas dominated both European and American child psychology in the 1960s and 1970s. More recently, it has been subject to a broad range of criticism and consequent revision. For my explication and critique of Piaget's work, see Rosenberg, 1988b, chap. 3. My own earlier work may be regarded as part of this revisionist effort to construct a neo-Piagetian perspective.

5. The confusion of form and content is also reflected in certain inherently untenable stances Kohlberg takes. Influenced by Piaget's structuralism, Kohlberg argues that there are general qualities to an individual's moral reasoning regardless of the substance of the moral dilemma or issues being considered. At the same time, in his later work, he argues that structure of reasoning is domain specific. The structure of an individual's moral reasoning is not necessarily related to the structure of her reasoning about the physical world, and neither is necessarily related to the structure of her reasoning about social phenomena. I regard this claim of structure within but not across substantive domains as untenable for a variety of reasons. Most important, the claim of structure across issues within a domain suggests that structure is independent of content, while the claim of differences in structure across substantively differentiated domains suggests that structure is dependent on content. Of secondary concern, there is the inherent difficulty of offering any persuasive differentiation in terms that might be relevant to cognitive processing among domains defined only by their content. Consider the difficulty of sustaining any coherent and potentially relevant distinction among three such content domains: social life, politics, and morality.

6. My work also deviates from Kohlberg's insofar as I am more sensitive to both psychological and social context factors that affect reasoning. Given my discussion of personality in chapter 2, it should be clear that I maintain that the structure of an individual's reasoning may be influenced by substantive aspects of the topic or situation that she is addressing. If either of these resonates with emotionally laden early experience, other more primitive forms of reasoning may be manifest. Given my discussion of the duality of structuration, it should also be clear that the structure of the discourse or interactive situation may affect the quality of the individual's participation, especially in a way that may produce less developed ways of reasoning.

7. The issues raised here regarding psychologists who seriously address cognitive developmental theory without sufficient regard to the implications of the form-content distinction also apply to psychologists who are oriented by a focus on narratives and discourses. Borrowing from a range of discourse theories, I believe these psychologists have also approached cognitive developmental theory without sufficient regard to the centrality and implication of structuralist considerations (e.g., Day and Tappan, 1996; Wertsch, 1991).

8. For some interesting examples of work on adolescent and adult social reasoning, see Youniss, 1978; Furth, 1980; Selman, 1980; Turiel, 1983; Kegan, 1982, 1994.

9. Kohlberg himself moved in this direction in his later work on moral atmospheres and their effect on the development of moral reasoning. Unfortunately, he was, I believe, too ill at this point to develop his ideas sufficiently.

10. An example of such a sociocognitive analysis of the demands that social contexts place on individuals is offered, albeit in a somewhat cursory fashion, in the discussion of the crisis of modernity in chapter 1. For an example that applies a structural pragmatics directly to the analysis of educational environments, see Sellick, 2000.

11. This understanding of the specificity of learned tolerance is quite consistent with the results of the research on tolerance conducted by John Sullivan and George Marcus (1982). They found that while American's attitudes toward people of African descent had definitely improved over the preceding fifteen or twenty years, the general level of tolerance had not. They were simply intolerant to other groups not specifically targeted by civil rights instruction.

12. Here I exclude the work of the deliberative democrats, such as Warren (1996), who are oriented by the more structural considerations of Jürgen Habermas (1996).

13. This reliance on assumed lack of motivation by theorists to explain of why individuals do not think about politics adequately is paralleled by the explanations of democratically minded public opinion researchers confronted with evidence of apparent incoherence among people's attitudes toward various public policy questions. For the classic statement of this, see Converse, 1964.

Bibliography

Abelson, R. P., E. Aronson, W. J. McGuire, T. M. Newcomb, M. J. Rosenberg, and P. H. Tannenbaum, eds. 1968. *The Theory of Cognitive Consistency: A Sourcebook.* Chicago: Rand McNally.

Adelson, J., and R. O'Neil. 1966. "The Growth of Political Ideas in Adolescence: The Sense of Community." *Journal of Personality and Social Psychology* 4:295–306.

Adelson, J., and L. Beall. 1970. "Adolescent Perspectives on Law and Government." *Law and Society Review* 2:495–504.

Allport, G. W. 1954. *The Nature of Prejudice.* Cambridge: Addison-Wesley.

Almond, G. A., and S. Verba. 1963. *The Civic Culture: Political Attitudes and Democracy in Five Nations.* Princeton: Princeton University Press.

Althusser, L. 1971. *Lenin and Philosophy, and Other Essays.* New York: Monthly Review Press.

Anderson, B. R. 1991. *Imagined Communities: Reflections on the Origin and Spread of Nationalism.* London: Verso.

Aronson, E. 1958. "Some Attempts to Measure Tolerance for Dissonance." *United States Air Force Wright Air Development Center Technical Report,* 458–92.

Austin, J. L. 1962. *How to Do Things with Words.* Cambridge: Harvard University Press.

Baldwin, J. M. 1913. *Social and Ethical Interpretations in Mental Development.* London: Macmillan.

Bandura, A. 1973. *Aggression: A Social Learning Analysis.* Englewood Cliffs, N.J.: Prentice-Hall.

Bandura, A., and R. H. Walters. 1963. *Social Learning and Personality Development.* New York, Holt, Rinehart and Winston.

Barber, B. 1984. *Strong Democracy: Participatory Democracy for a New Age.* Berkeley: University of California Press.

Bartlett, F. C. 1932. *Remembering: A Study in Experimental and Social Psychology.* New York: Cambridge University Press.

Bem, D. J. 1967. "Self-Perception: An Alternative Interpretation of Cognitive Dissonance Phenomena." *Psychological Bulletin* 74(3):183–200.

———. 1970. *Beliefs, Attitudes, and Human Affairs.* Belmont, Calif., Brooks/Cole.

Bishop, G., R. W. Oldendick, and A. J. Tuchfarber. 1984. "Interest in Political Campaigns: The Influence of Question Order and Electoral Context." *Political Behavior* 6(2):159–69.

Borgida, E. N., and R. E. Nisbett. 1977. "The Differential Impact of Abstract vs. Concrete Information on Decisions." *Journal of Applied Social Psychology* 7(3):258–71.

Braunwarth, J. 1996. "Cognitive Reasoning and the Representation of Reality: The Role of the Television News." Paper delivered at the annual meeting of the International Society of Political Psychology, Vancouver.

Brewer, M. B. 1979. "In-Group Bias in the Minimal Intergroup Situation: A Cognitive-Motivational Analysis." *Psychological Bulletin* 86(2):307–24.

Brewer, M. B., and R. M. Kramer. 1985. "The Psychology of Intergroup Attitudes and Behavior." *Annual Review of Psychology* 36:219–43.

Bruner, J. S. 1957. "On Perceptual Readiness." *Psychological Review* 64:123–52.

———. 1958. "A Psychologist's Viewpoint: Review of B. Inhelder and J. Piaget, *The Growth of Logical Thinking.*" *British Journal of Psychology* 50:363–70.

Bruner, J. S., and L. Postman. 1948. "Symbolic Value as an Organizing Factor in Perception." *Journal of Abnormal and Social Psychology* 48:17–24.

Buzan, B. 1991. *People, States, and Fear: An Agenda for International Security Studies in the Post-Cold War Era.* Boulder, Colo.: L. Rienner.

Campbell, A., E. Converse, E. Miller, and D. E. Stokes. 1960. *The American Voter.* New York: John Wiley.

Cantor, N. M., and W. Mischel. 1977. "Traits as Prototypes: Effects on Recognition Memory." *Journal of Personality and Social Psychology* 35(1):38–48.

Cash, J. D. 1996. *Identity, Ideology and Conflict: The Structuration of Politics in Northern Ireland.* New York: Cambridge University Press.

Chapman, L. J., and Jean P. Chapman. 1969. "Illusory Correlation as an Obstacle to the Use of Valid Psychodiagnostic Signs." *Journal of Abnormal Psychology* 74(3):271–80.

Chilton, S. 1988. *Defining Political Development.* Boulder, Colo.: L. Rienner.

Connell, R. W. 1971. *The Child's Construction of Politics.* Melbourne: Melbourne University Press.

Converse, P. E. 1964. "The Nature of Belief Systems in Mass Publics." In *Ideology and Discontent,* ed. D. Apter. New York: Free Press.

Cooper, J. Z., P. M. Zanna, and P. A. Taves. 1978. "Arousal as a Necessary Condition for Attitude Change Following Induced Compliance." *Journal of Personality and Social Psychology* 36(10):1101–6.

Dahl, R. A. 1956. *A Preface to Democratic Theory.* Chicago: University of Chicago Press.

Damon, W., and D. Hart. 1988. *Self-Understanding in Childhood and Adolescence.* Cambridge: Cambridge University Press.

Day, J. M., and MarK B. Tappan. 1996. "The Narrative Approach to Moral Development: From the Epistemic Subject to Dialogical Selves. *Human Development* 39:67–82.

Dewey, J. 1896. "The Reflex Arc Concept in Psychology." *Psychological Review* 3:357–70.

———. 1916. *Democracy and Education: An Introduction to the Philosophy of Education.* New York: Macmillan.

DiMaggio, P. 1997. "Culture and Cognition." *Annual Review of Sociology.* 23:263–87.

Dimitracopoulou, I. 1990. *Conversational Competence and Social Development.* Cambridge: Cambridge University Press.

Doctorow, E. L. 2000. *City of God.* New York: Random House.

Doise, W. M. 1986. *Levels of Explanation in Social Psychology.* Cambridge: Cambridge University Press.

Doise, W. M., G. Mugny, and A. Perret-Clermont. 1975. "Social Interaction and the Development of Cognitive Operations." *European Journal of Social Psychology* 5(3):367–83.

Dollard, J. M., and N. E. Miller. 1950. *Personality and Psychotherapy: An Analysis in Terms of Learning, Thinking, and Culture.* New York: McGraw-Hill.

Dostoyevsky, F. 1992. *The Brothers Karamazov.* New York: Alfred A. Knopf.

Dovidio, J. F., N. Evans, and R. B. Tyler. 1986. "Racial Stereotypes: The Contents of Their Cognitive Representations." *Journal of Experimental Social Psychology* 22(1):22–37.

Dupont, H. 1994. *Emotional Development, Theory and Applications: A Neo-Piagetian Perspective.* Westport, Conn.: Praeger.

Durkheim, E. 1982. *The Rules of Sociological Method and Selected Texts on Sociology and Its Method.* London: Macmillan.

Easton, D., and J. Dennis. 1969. *Children in the Political System: Origins of Political Legitimacy.* New York, McGraw-Hill.

Eckstein, H. 1968. *Authority Relations and Governmental Performance: A Theoretical Framework.* Princeton: Princeton University Press.

———. 1996. *Lessons for the "Third Wave" from the First: An Essay on Democratization.* Irvine: University of California, Irvine, School of Social Sciences.

Ehrmann, J. 1970. *Structuralism.* Garden City, N.Y.: Anchor Books.

Emler, N. R., S. Malone, and B. Malone. 1983. "The Relationship between Moral Reasoning and Political Orientation." *Journal of Personality and Social Psychology* 45(5):1073–80.

Festinger, L. 1957. *A Theory of Cognitive Dissonance.* Stanford: Stanford University Press.

Fiske, S. T., and S. E. Taylor. 1991. *Social Cognition.* New York, McGraw-Hill.

Fletcher, G. J. O, and C. Ward. 1988. "Attribution Theory and Processes: A Cross-Cultural Perspective." In *The Cross-Cultural Challenge to Social Psychology.* ed. M. H. Bond. Newbury Park, Calif.: Sage Publications, 230–44.

Foucault, M. 1979. *Discipline and Punish: The Birth of the Prison.* New York: Vintage Books.

———. 1980. *Power/Knowledge: Selected Interviews and Other Writings, 1972–1977.* New York: Pantheon Books.

Freud, S. 1930. *Civilization and Its Discontents,* London: Hogarth Press.

———. 1955. *The Interpretation of Dreams.* New York: Basic Books.

Furth, H. G. 1980. *The World of Grown-Ups: Children's Conceptions of Society.* New York: Elsevier North Holland.

Gibbs, J. C. 1992. *Moral Maturity: Measuring the Development of Sociomoral Reflection.* Hillsdale, N.J.: Lawrence Erlbaum.

Giddens, A. 1984. *The Constitution of Society.* Berkeley: University of California Press.

———. 1990. *The Consequences of Modernity.* Stanford: Stanford University Press.

———. 1992. *The Transformation of Intimacy: Sexuality, Love, and Eroticism in Modern Societies.* Cambridge, Eng.: Polity Press.

Gilligan, C. 1982. *In a Different Voice: Psychological Theory and Women's Development.* Cambridge: Harvard University Press.

Gray, J. 1992. *Men Are from Mars, Women Are from Venus: A Practical Guide for Improving Communication and Getting What You Want in Your Relationships.* New York: HarperCollins.

Gray, L. N. G., I. Wanda, M. H. Von Broembsen, M. J. Sullivan. 1982. "Group Differentiation: Temporal Effects of Reinforcement." *Social Psychology Quarterly* 45(1):44–49.

Greenstein, F. I. 1965. *Children and Politics.* New Haven: Yale University Press.

Habermas, J. 1979. *Communication and the Evolution of Society.* Boston: Beacon Press.

———. (1981, 1984). *The Theory of Communicative Action.* Boston: Beacon Press.

———. 1987. *The Philosophical Discourse of Modernity: Twelve Lectures.* Cambridge: MIT Press.

———. 1996. *Between Facts and Norms: Contributions to a Discourse Theory of Law and Democracy.* Cambridge: MIT Press.

Hamilton, D. L., and T. K. Trolier. 1986. Stereotypes and Stereotyping: An Overview of the Cognitive Approach. In *Prejudice, Discrimination, and Racism,* ed. J. Dovidio and S. Gaertner. Orlando, Fl.: Academic Press, 127–63.

Hanks, C. 1998. "The Psychology of Principled Tolerance." Paper delivered at the annual meeting of the International Society of Political Psychology, Montreal.

Harris, T. A. 1967. *I'm OK—You're OK.* New York: Harper and Row.

Hass, E. 1990. *When Knowledge Is Power.* Berkeley: University of California, Press.

Heider, F. 1958. *The Psychology of Interpersonal Relations.* Hillsdale, N.J.: Lawrence Erlbaum.

Hess, R. D., and D. Easton. 1960. "The Child's Changing Image of the President." *Public Opinion Quarterly* 24(4):632–44.

Hobbes, T. 1958. *Leviathan.* Oxford: Clarendon Press.

Hogg, M. A., and D. Abrams. 1988. *Social Identifications: A Social Psychology of Intergroup Relations and Group Processes.* London: Routledge.

Ichilov, O., ed. 1990. *Political Socialization, Citizenship Education, and Democracy.* New York: Teachers College Press.

Inglehart, R. 1990. *Culture Shift in Advanced Industrial Society.* Princeton: Princeton University Press.

Inhelder, B., and J. Piaget. 1958. *The Growth of Logical Thinking from Childhood to Adolescence: An Essay on the Construction of Formal Operational Structures.* New York: Basic Books.

Iyengar, S. K., and D. R. Kinder. 1987. *News That Matters: Television and American Opinion.* Chicago: University of Chicago Press.

James, W. 1909. *Pragmatism, a New Name for Some Old Ways of Thinking: Popular Lectures on Philosophy.* New York: Longmans, Green.

———. 1947. *Essays in Radical Empiricism [and] a Pluralistic Universe.* New York: Longmans, Green.

Jameson, F. 1991. *Postmodernism, or, the Cultural Logic of Late Capitalism.* Durham: Duke University Press.

Jennings, M. K., and R. Niemi. 1974. *The Political Character of Adolescence: The Influence of Families and Schools.* Princeton: Princeton University Press.

Jervis, R. 1976. *Perception and Misperception in International Politics.* Princeton: Princeton University Press.

Joas, H. 1993. *Pragmatism and Social Theory.* Chicago: University of Chicago Press.

Kahneman, D., and A. Tversky. 1972. "Subjective Probability: A Judgment of Representativeness." *Cognitive Psychology* 3(3):430–54.

———. 1973. "On the Psychology of Prediction." *Psychological Review* 80(4):237–51.

Kazantzakis, N. 1956. *Freedom or Death.* New York: Simon and Schuster.

Kegan, R. 1982. *The Evolving Self: Problem and Process in Human Development.* Cambridge: Harvard University Press.

———. 1994. *In Over Our Heads: The Mental Demands of Modern Life.* Cambridge: Harvard University Press.

Kelley, H. H. 1973. "The Processes of Causal Attribution." *American Psychologist* 28(2):107–28.

Keohane, R. O., and J. S. Nye. 1977. *Power and Interdependence: World Politics in Transition.* Boston: Little, Brown.

Kinnvall, C. 1995. *Cultural Diffusion and Political Learning: The Democratization of China.* Lund, Sweden: Lund Political Studies.

Kohlberg, L. 1981a. *The Meaning and Measurement of Moral Development.* Worcester, Mass.: Clark University Press.

———. 1981b. *The Philosophy of Moral Development: Moral Stages and the Idea of Justice.* San Francisco: Harper and Row.

———. 1984. *The Psychology of Moral Development: The Nature and Validity of Moral Stages.* San Francisco: Harper and Row.

Krizanc, J. 1989. *Tamara: A Play.* Toronto: Stoddart.

Kuhn, D., J. Langer, L. Kohlberg, and N. Haan. 1977. "The Development of Formal Operations in Logical and Moral Development." *Genetic Psychology Monographs* 95:97–188.

Lane, R. E. 1962. *Political Ideology: Why the American Common Man Believes What He Does.* New York: Free Press.

———. 1972. *Political Man.* New York: Free Press.

Leaf, W. A., D. Kanouse, J. M. Jones, and R. P. Abelson. 1968. "Balance, Character Expression, and the Justice Principle: An Analysis of Sentence Evaluations." *Proceedings of the Annual Convention of the American Psychological Association* 3:423–24.

Lerner, M. J. 1970. "The Desire for Justice and Reactons to Victims." In *Altruism and Helping Behavior,* ed. J. Macauley and L. Berkowitz. New York: Academic Press.

Lévi-Strauss, C. 1963. *Totemism.* Boston: Beacon Press.

———. 1966. *The Savage Mind.* Chicago: University of Chicago Press.

Linville, P., W. Gregory, and P. Salovey. 1989. "Perceived Distributions of the Characteristics of In-Group and Out-Group Members: Empirical Evidence and a Computer Simulation." *Journal of Personality and Social Psychology* 57(2):165–88.

Loevinger, J. 1976. *Ego Development: Conceptions and Theories.* San Francisco: Jossey-Bass.

Lyotard, J. F. 1984. *The Postmodern Condition: A Report on Knowledge.* Minneapolis: University of Minnesota Press.

Mamet, D. 1976. *American Buffalo: A Play.* New York: Grove Press.

Marx, K. 1970. *The German Ideology.* New York: International Publishers.

McArthur, L. 1972. "The How and What of Why: Some Determinants and Consequences of Causal Attribution." *Journal of Personality and Social Psychology* 22(2):171–93.

Mead, G. H. (1924–25). "The Genesis of Self and Social Control." *International Journal of Ethics* 35:251–77.

———. 1934. *Mind, Self and Society from the Standpoint of a Social Behaviorist.* Chicago: University of Chicago Press.

Medin, D. L., and E. E. Smith. 1981. "Strategies and Classification Learning." *Journal of Experimental Psychology: Human Learning and Memory* 7(4):241–53.

Merelman, R. M. 1969. "The Development of Political Ideology: A Framework for the Analysis of Political Socialization." *American Political Science Review* 63:750–67.

———. 1971. "The Development of Policy Thinking in Adolescence." *American Political Science Review* 65:1033–47.

Merleau-Ponty, M. 1963. *The Structure of Behavior.* Boston: Beacon Press.

Monroe, K. 1996. *The Heart of Altruism.* Princeton: Princeton University Press.

Moser, P. K. 1989. *Knowledge and Evidence.* New York: Cambridge University Press.

Mueller, J. E. 1973. *War, Presidents and Public Opinion.* New York: Wiley.

Mugny, G., W. Doise, and A. Perret-Clermont. 1975–76. "Sociocognitive Conflict and Cognitive Progress." *Bulletin de Psychologie* 29(4–7):199–204.

Nicolopoulou, A., and J. Weintraub. 1998. Individual and Collective Representations in Social Context: A Modest Contribution to Resuming the Interrupted Project of a Sociocultural Developmental Psychology. *Human Development* 41: 215–35.

Nisbett, R. E., C. Caputo, P. Legant, and J. Marecek. 1973. "Behavior as Seen by the Actor and as Seen by the Observer." *Journal of Personality and Social Psychology* 27(2):154–64.

Noam, G., and K. W. Fischer, eds. 1996. *Development and Vulnerability in Close Relationships.* Mahwah, N.J.: Lawrence Erlbaum.

Parsons, T. 1964. *Social Structure and Personality.* New York: Free Press.

Pateman, C. 1970. *Participation and Democratic Theory.* Cambridge: Cambridge University Press.

Pavlov, I. P. 1927. *Conditioned Reflexes: An Investigation of the Physiological Activity of the Cerebral Cortex.* London: Oxford University Press.

Peterson, C. S., and E. Martin. 1984. "Causal Explanations as a Risk Factor for Depression: Theory and Evidence." *Psychological Review* 91(3):347–74.

Peterson, C. S., E. P. Martin, and George E. Vaillant. 1994. "Pessimistic Explanatory Style Is a Risk Factor for Physical Illness: A Thirty-five-Year Longitudinal Study." Pages 235–46 in *Psychosocial Processes and Health: A Reader,* ed. J. W. Steptoe. Cambridge: Cambridge University Press.

Piaget, J. 1970a. *Genetic Epistemology*. New York: Columbia University Press.

———. 1970b. *Structuralism*. New York: Basic Books.

———. 1971. *Biology and Knowledge*. Chicago: University of Chicago.

———. 1978. *The Development of Thought: Equilibration of Cognitive Structures*. New York: Basic Books.

Peirce, C. S. 1923. *Chance, Love and Logic*. New York: Harcourt, Brace.

Putnam, R. D. 1993. *Making Democracy Work: Civic Traditions in Modern Italy*. Princeton: Princeton University Press.

Pye, L. W. 1991. "Political Culture Revisited." *Political Psychology* 12(3):487–508.

———. 1992. *The Spirit of Chinese Politics*, rev. ed. Cambridge: Harvard University Press.

Quattrone, G. A., and A. Tversky. 1984. "Causal versus Diagnostic Contingencies: On Self-Deception and on the Voter's Illusion." *Journal of Personality and Social Psychology* 46(2): 237–48.

———. 1988. "Contrasting Rational and Psychological Analyses of Political Choice." *American Political Science Review* 82(3):719–36.

Radding, C. 1985. *A World Made by Men*. Madison: University of Wisconsin Press.

Regan, D. T., and J. Totten. 1975. "Empathy and Attribution: Turning Observers into Actors." *Journal of Personality and Social Psychology* 32(5):850–56.

Reicher, S. E., and N. Emler. 1984. "Moral Orientation as a Cue to Political Identity." *Political Psychology* 5(4):543–51.

Rest, J. 1974. "Judging the Important Isses in Moral Dilemmas: An Objective Measure of Development." *Developmental Psychology* 10(4):491–501.

Rest, J., D. Narvaez, M. Bebeau, and S. Thoma. 1999. *Postconventional Moral Thinking: A Neo-Kohlbergian Approach*. Mahwah, N.J.: Lawrence Erlbaum.

Reykowksi, J. 1994. "Popular Concept of Democracy and Perception of the Socio-Political Situation." Paper presented at the Twentiety-seventh World Congress of the International Political Science Association, Berlin.

Riesman, D. 1950. *The Lonely Crowd: A Study of the Changing American Character*. New Haven: Yale University Press.

Riker, W. H. 1995. "The Political Psychology of Rational Choice." *Political Psychology* 16(1): 23–44.

Riker, W. H., and P. Ordeshook. 1973. *An Introduction to Positive Political Theory*. Englewood Cliffs, N.J.: Prentice-Hall.

Rosenberg, S. W. 1987. "Reason and Ideology: Interpreting People's Understanding of American Politics," *Polity* 20:114–44.

———. 1991. "Habermas, Piaget and Social Theory: Subjectivity, Intersubjectivity and Social Action." Paper presented at the annual meeting of the American Political Science Association, San Francisco.

———. 1988a. *Reason, Ideology, and Politics*. Princeton: Princeton University Press.

———. 1988b. "The Structure of Political Thinking." *American Journal of Political Science*, 32:539–66.

———. 1995. "Against Neoclassical Political Economy: A Political Psychological Critique." *Political Psychology* 16(1):99–136.

———. 2001. "Opinion Formation," In *The Encyclopedia of the Social and Behavioral Sciences,* ed. N. Smelser and P. Baltes. Oxford: Elsevier.

Rosenberg, S. W., S. Kahn, and T. Tran. 1991. "Creating a Political Image: Shaping Appearance and Manipulating the Vote." *Political Behavior* 13(4).

Rosenberg, S. W., D. Ward, and S. Chilton. 1988. *Political Reasoning and Cognition: A Piagetian View.* Durham, N.C.: Duke University Press.

Rosenberg, S. W., and G. Wolfsfeld. 1977. "International Conflict and the Problem of Attribution." *Journal of Conflict Resolution* 21(1):75–103.

Ross, L., T. Amabile, and J. L. Steinmetz. 1977. "Social Roles, Social Control, and Biases in Social-Perception Processes." *Journal of Personality and Social Psychology* 35(7):485–94.

Ross, L., and R. E. Nisbett. 1991. *The Person and the Situation: Perspectives of Social Psychology.* New York: McGraw-Hill.

Rotter, J. B. 1966. "Generalized Expectancies for Internal versus External Control of Reinforcement." *Psychological Monographs: General and Applied* 80(1):1–28.

Runciman, W. 1969. "What Is Structuralism?" *British Journal of Sociology* 20:253–65.

Saussure, F. de. 1959. *Course in General Linguistics.* New York: Philosophical Library.

Schneider, A., and H. Ingram. 1992. "The Social Construction of Target Populations: Implications for Politics and Policy." *American Political Science Review* 87(2):334–47.

Schumpeter, J. A. 1942. *Capitalism, Socialism, and Democracy.* New York: Harper and Row.

Searle, J. R., ed. 1971. *The Philosophy of Language.* London: Oxford University Press.

Selman, R. L. 1977. "A Structural-Developmental Model of Social Cognition: Implications for Intervention Research." *Counseling Psychologist* 6(4):3–6.

———. 1980. *The Growth of Interpersonal Understanding: Developmental and Clinical Analyses.* New York: Academic Press.

Sigel, R. S., and M. B. Hoskin. 1981. *The Political Involvement of Adolescents.* New Brunswick, N.J.: Rutgers University Press.

Simon, H. A. *Human Nature in Politics: The Dialogue of Psychology with Political Science* 79:293–304.

Skinner, B. F. 1953. *Science and Human Behavior.* New York: Macmillan.

Smelsund, J. 1963. "The Concept of Correlation in Adults." *Scandnavian Journal of Psychology* 4:165–73.

Snyder, M., and W. B. Swann. 1978. "Hypothesis-Testing Processes in Social Interaction." *Journal of Personality and Social Psychology* 36(11):1202–12.

Streufert, S., and M. J. Driver. 1967. "Impression Formation as a Measure of the Complexity of Conceptual Structure." *Educational and Psychological Measurement* 27(4, pt. 2): 1025–39.

Streufert, S., and S. C. Streufert. 1978. *Behavior in the Complex Environment.* Washington, D.C.: V. H. Winston and Sons.

Styron, W. 1979. *Sophie's Choice.* New York: Random House.

Suedfeld, P. 1985. "APA Presidential Address: The Relation of Integrative Complexity to Historical, Professional and Personal Factors." *Journal of Personality and Social Psychology* 49(6):1643–51.

Sullivan, J., and G. Marcus. 1982. *Political Tolerance and American Democracy.* Chicago: University of Chicago Press.

Sweeney, P. D., K. Anderson, and S. Bailey. 1986. "Attributional Style in Depression: A Meta-Analytic Review." *Journal of Personality and Social Psychology* 50(5):974–91.

Tajfel, H. 1978. *Differentiation between Social Groups: Studies in the Social Psychology of Intergroup Relations.* New York: Academic Press.

———. 1982. "Social Psychology of Intergroup Relations." *Annual Review of Psychology* 33:1–39.

Taylor, S. E., and S. T. Fiske. 1975. "Point of View and Perceptions of Causality." *Journal of Personality and Social Psychology* 32(3):439–45.

———. 1978. "Salience, Attention and Attribution: Top of the Head Phenomena." In *Advances in Experimental Social Psychology,* vol. 2, ed. L. Berkowitz. New York: Academic Press.

Taylor, S. E., S. T. Fiske, N. L. Etcoff, and A. J. Ruderman. 1978. "Categorical and Contextual Bases of Person Memory and Stereotyping." *Journal of Personality and Social Psychology* 36(7):778–93.

Tetlock, P. E. 1984. "Cognitive Style and Political Belief Systems in the British House of Commons." *Journal of Personality and Social Psychology* 46(2):365–75.

———. 1988. "Monitoring the Integrative Complexity of American and Soviet Policy Rhetoric: What Can Be Learned?" *Journal of Social Issues* 44(2):101–31.

Tetlock, P. E., and P. Suedfeld. 1988. "Integrative Complexity Coding of Verbal Behaviour." In *Analysing Everyday Explanation: A Casebook of Methods,* ed., C. Antaki. London: Sage Publications.

Turiel, E. 1983. *The Development of Social Knowledge.* New York: Cambridge University Press.

Tversky, A., and D. Kahneman. 1973. *Judgment under Uncertainty: Heuristics and Biases.* Eugene: Oregon Research Institute.

Unger, R. M. 1975. *Knowledge and Politics.* New York: Free Press.

Vaughan, G. M., H. Tajfel, and J. Williams. 1981. "Bias in Reward Allocation in an Intergroup and an Interpersonal Context." *Social Psychology Quarterly* 44(1):37–42.

Vygotsky, L. S. 1962. *Thought and Language.* New York: Wiley.

———. 1978. *Mind in Society: The Development of Higher Psychological Processes.* Cambridge: Harvard University Press.

Wallerstein, I. M. 1979. *The Capitalist World-Economy.* Cambridge: Cambridge University Press.

Ward, D. 1982. "Genetic Epistemology and the Structure of Political Belief Systems: An Introduction to Piaget for Political Scientists." Paper presented at the annual meeting of the American Political Science Association, Denver.

Warren, M. 1996. "Deliberative Democracy and Authority." *American Political Science Review* 90(1):46–60.

Welsh, I. 1993. *Trainspotting.* London: Secker and Warburg.

Wertsch, J. V. 1991. *Voices of the Mind: A Sociocultural Approach to Mediated Action.* Cambridge: Harvard University Press.

Wicker, A. W. 1969. "Attitudes versus Actions: The Relationship of Verbal and Overt Behavioral Responses to Attitude Objects." *Journal of Social Issues* 25(4):41–78.

Wilson, R. W. 1992. *Compliance Ideologies: Rethinking Political Culture.* New York: Cambridge University Press.

Wyer, R. S. S., K. Thomas, S. E. Gordon, and J. Hartwick. 1982. "Effects of Processing Objectives on the Recall of Prose Material." *Journal of Personality and Social Psychology* 43(4): 674–88.

Youniss, J. 1978. "Dialectical Theory and Piaget on Social Knowledge." *Human Development* 21:234–47.

Index